THE
OLD TESTAMENT

Text and Context

THE
OLD TESTAMENT

Text and Context

Victor H. Matthews
James C. Moyer

© 1997 by Hendrickson Publishers, Inc.
P. O. Box 3473
Peabody, Massachusetts 01961–3473
All rights reserved
Printed in the United States of America

ISBN 1–56563–168–4

First Printing—August 1997

Library of Congress Cataloging-in-Publication Data

Matthews, Victor Harold.
     The Old Testament: text and context   /   Victor H. Matthews, James C. Moyer
Includes bibliographical references and indexes.
     ISBN 1–56563–168–4 (cloth)
     1. Bible. O.T.—Criticism, interpretation, etc.   2. Bible. O.T.—History of Biblical
events.   I. Moyer, James C.   II. Title.
BS1171.2.m287 1997
221.6′1—dc21   97-2428
                                                                                     CIP

The ivory openwork plaque on the cover depicts a seated lion wearing an Egyptian
pectoral and sun-disc. Excavated in the Assyrian capital at Nimrud in northern Iraq.
Phoenician, ca. 800–700 BCE. Photo courtesy of the British Museum. Used with
permission.

TABLE OF CONTENTS

CHAPTER 6: CONCLUDING REMARKS   **278**

1

INTRODUCTION

THE PURPOSE OF THIS BOOK

This book is written for the beginning student. It introduces the literature, history, and social context of the Old Testament/Hebrew Bible and is designed not only to keep the student's interest, but to also say something about why studying this ancient material is relevant, and why it is essential that it be studied today. No writings have had as profound an influence on Western culture as those compiled in the Bible. Our value system, our reaction to injustice, our basic sense of appropriate behavior as well as much of our own literature is still modeled in large part on these writings. Those who ignore them miss the opportunity to come to grips with who we are as a people. The Bible, therefore, cannot simply be dismissed as "ancient" and thus irrelevant. It remains an intregral part of our modern culture.

The Bible's general impact on modern society is reason enough for any educated person to study it. But for many the Bible is their sacred literature and the God of the Bible is their own God. This religious significance makes the study of the Bible especially important to them.

To assist the student we have used a style of writing and a basic design in each chapter that will make this textbook as interactive as possible. In addition to relating ancient stories, explaining methodologies, and providing a sense of historical context, we have included information boxes that will provide biblical and extrabiblical quotations. This material is designed to shed light on our understanding of other biblical or ancient Near Eastern texts or modern life and literature.

One of the principal keys to learning any material is to understand how material relates. What we mean by this is that a single fact may be important in and of itself. It becomes infinitely more valuable, however, when it is seen as a part of the whole picture of the narrative. For instance, we know from the Bible's many references that David worked as a shepherd while he was a boy. That creates one picture in our mind, but it does not give us the larger picture of David the warrior, David the king, and David the champion of Yahweh. At the same time, however, David the shepherd protected his flock from danger just as David the warrior struggled to win battles to make his people safe. David the shepherd managed his animals to ensure they would increase and provide a good livelihood for his family; David the king administered the affairs of state in such a way as to build up the economy and bring a greater measure of prosperity to his country. And finally, David the shepherd, alone with his flock, examined God's creation and built a foundation of faith (see Psalm 23) which helped form his policies when he established Yahweh as the God of Israel and brought the ark of the covenant to Jerusalem.

Making connections such as these helps increase the basic familiarity with the stories. At the same time they open up the mind to possibilities of actual situations, choices being made, and relationships being built. If the characters remain only characters in a story, they will never have any reality for the reader. The characters in the Bible are too often idealized as a body of saints and sinners, but not real people. Once the student realizes that many of the episodes involve normal human activities from that time period, then the characters and their social setting can be explored more fully. This approach to the biblical accounts differs from that found in devotional or religious contexts. At the same time, what we are doing in this textbook is essential for understanding the Bible on any level. Our goal is to assist the student to understand the ancient meaning in its context. This will benefit all types of Bible students.

It is also clear to us that a textbook which does not follow a logical order will not be widely used by teachers or students. Many textbooks attempt to create a sense of literary chronology which radically rearranges the biblical material. For instance, it is well accepted by scholars that much of the Genesis material was composed or compiled during the monarchic and postexilic periods of Israelite history. Taking this as a given, many introductions begin their discussion with the monarchy and only discuss the creation and flood epics and the ancestral narratives as they relate to and are reflections of the monarchic or postexilic periods. This can be extremely confusing to students. We believe a better way is to present the material in the order of the books as they are arranged in most Bibles, starting with Genesis and running through much of 2 Kings. The only exception to this will be when dealing with the prophets whose **canonical** order has little relation to their chronological order (divided as they are into "major" and "minor" prophets).

Because we are both historians, we will place a great deal of emphasis on the historical narrative presented in the biblical text. We will also attempt to recreate, where possible, the social setting of basic institutions (marriage, clientage, business practices). Obviously, caution will have to be taken not to impose a solution or a rigid assessment of these narratives since there is always new data surfacing from archaeological and social-scientific research.

To provide a measure of continuity within the book, we will emphasize four basic concepts: **covenant**, **universalism**, **wisdom**, and **remnant**. These concepts provide general themes for much of biblical narrative, plot, and dialogue. Here is a brief sketch of each:

Covenant: A covenant is a contractual arrangement between two parties. In the biblical text it is used for: (1) The promise of "land and children" made to Abraham by Yahweh in exchange for Abraham's sole allegiance and obedience to Yahweh. This is a *conditional* covenant that requires both sides to fulfill all of the stipulations of the agreement. There are periodic *renewals* of this covenant as the people or their leaders believe a fresh start is necessary.

(2) The basis of the **Law (Torah)** originated in the Abrahamic covenant. It is expanded upon in the **Decalogue** (Ten Commandments), which was given to Moses. Subsequent legal codes reflect the growing complexity of the nation, but they retain the covenant as their central principle.

(3) The "everlasting covenant" is made between King David and Yahweh. According to this agreement, Yahweh promises that there will always be a king of the "line of David" ruling in Jerusalem. It is a *nonconditional* covenant, which means that no matter how bad a particular descendant of David may be, that does not terminate the agreement. Eventually, after the monarchy ends (587 BCE) this covenant is transformed into a *messianic expectation,* which assumes that Yahweh will provide a **Messiah** figure who will restore the nation to its former independence and glory.

Universalism: This term is used in the sense of the power and concern of Yahweh extending over the entire creation. In their attempt to portray Yahweh as supreme among the gods, the biblical writers periodically inject this element into narratives. It generally involves the use of a non-Israelite character, who, because of knowledge of what Yahweh has done for the Israelites (crossing the Red Sea, etc.) or because of a personal experience (cure from disease, etc.), makes a statement of faith that Yahweh is the most powerful or the only true god. Eventually, this will be expanded to an exclusive belief in Yahweh as the only true god, but this monotheistic belief will not take its full form until late (post 400 BCE) in Israelite history.

Wisdom: While there is a specific section of the Bible that is recognized as Wisdom literature (Job, Proverbs, Ecclesiastes), the theme of Wisdom is found throughout the biblical text. It embodies both common sense and basic social values in antiquity. Ultimately, all wisdom comes from God. The Wisdom theme includes such ideas as: (1) wise behavior: no action taken hastily or without thinking; (2) wise speech: no word spoken that may injure someone else; (3) wise person: one who walks in the "way/path" of **Yahweh**; one who recognizes that wisdom may be acquired from persons of all ages, genders, and occupations.

Remnant: Because the people were unable to keep the covenant, recognize the universal character of Yahweh, or act wisely, Yahweh periodically punished them. The **theodicy** (an explanation for God's actions) that the prophets used to explain why the nation was conquered by non-Yahweh worshiping peoples included the idea that God felt constrained under the covenant to provide a warning. It was assumed that the righteous (always a minority or remnant) would heed this warning, take appropriate action to come back into compliance with the covenant, and, after the punishment had occurred, become the people—a righteous **remnant**—who would restore the nation.

HOW TO USE THIS BOOK

The intent of this book is to provide an objective presentation of the materials found in the Old Testament/Hebrew Bible. No denominational viewpoint will be espoused, and as many different theories and interpretations on the text will be presented as possible. The translation of the Bible that we have used is the New Revised Standard Version (NRSV). We have chosen it because of its literal translation of the Hebrew and Aramaic text and because of its use of inclusive language. A number of features in this volume are designed to aid the student in dealing most effectively with the material. These include:

Insets. These boxes provide a variety of information for the student. They may have a translation of an ancient text which parallels the biblical narrative. There may be a chart outlining the structure of a biblical passage, or there may be examples of a particular issue addressed in the biblical text. In every case, the box will be referred to and attention drawn to it for specific purposes by the authors.

Maps. The maps included in nearly every chapter are designed to provide a visual and spatial sense of direction, distance, and topography for the student.

Glossary. Throughout the text technical terms associated with biblical studies have been set in bold. They are usually defined in the text at that point, but a complete glossary of these technical terms is also found at the end of the volume.

Study Questions. We have provided study questions at the end of each chapter. These are intended to promote class discussion or to reiterate major points in the chapter.

Indexes. At the end of the volume the following information is indexed separately: subjects, personal and place names, and scripture citations. These will help the student more easily find particular topics in the text.

Certain abbreviations and conventions will be used by the authors in this textbook. These include:

Old Testament/Hebrew Bible. Since the material found in scripture belongs to more than one religious tradition, we have chosen to use this longer title (abbreviated OT/HB) throughout the volume. It also identifies that portion of scripture which has been recognized by Jews and Protestants as their canon. The expanded canon of the Septuagint and the Catholic Bible, which includes the Apocrypha or Deutero-canonical books, will be described and referred to, but not outlined in detail here.

BCE *and* CE. These abbreviations stand for "before the Common Era" and "Common Era." They correspond precisely to BC and AD dates, but they are more religiously neutral designations than "before Christ" and "in the year of our Lord (anno Domini)."

ANET. James Pritchard, *Ancient Near Eastern Texts Relating to the Old Testament,* 3d ed. with supplement. Princeton, N.J.: Princeton University Press, 1969.

OTPar. Victor H. Matthews and Don C. Benjamin, *Old Testament Parallels: Laws and Stories from the Ancient Near East.* Mahwah, N.J.: Paulist Press, 1991 (2d ed. to appear in 1997).

A GUIDE TO ADDITIONAL SOURCES FOR BIBLICAL STUDY

Multivolume Dictionary. The best multivolume dictionary currently on the market is *The Anchor Bible Dictionary* (abbreviated *ABD*) in six volumes (Doubleday, 1992). It has the most balanced and complete treatment of textual, theological, and archaeological data. Although the price for six volumes may be somewhat prohibitive, it far surpasses any other multivolume resource available. It is also available on CD-ROM. It should be noted, however, that the *Interpreter's Dictionary of the Bible* (4 vols.; Abingdon, 1962; plus supplement, 1976) does contain some articles not found in *ABD* and, although dated, is still a valuable resource. Most student questions can be answered by using either of these dictionaries. Bibliographies at the end of most articles will be especially helpful to students writing papers.

One-volume Bible Dictionary. The single most important resource for students other than the Bible is a one-volume Bible dictionary. This aid is affordable for personal collections, and it allows for quick reference to all the persons, places, and major concepts of the Bible. There are four one-volume Bible dictionaries on the market which can be recommended. The *Harper's Bible Dictionary* (ed. Paul J. Achtemeier; rev. ed; HarperSanFrancisco, 1996) is the best Bible dictionary currently available. The *New Bible Dictionary* (rev. ed.; Tyndale, 1993), the *Holman Bible Dictionary* (Holman, 1991), and the *Eerdmans Bible Dictionary* (Eerdmans, 1987) are more conservative in orientation. The *New Bible Dictionary* has recently been updated, but not all of the articles have been rewritten. *The Holman Bible Dictionary* is also available on computer disk. A somewhat different volume is the *Mercer Dictionary of the Bible* (Mercer, 1990). It is designed as a textbook and therefore does not have as many minor articles as other dictionaries. Still it is highly recommended.

Multivolume Commentary. Since the 1950s this category has been dominated by the twelve-volume *Interpreter's Bible* (Abingdon, 1952). This was the first real attempt to provide a scholarly treatment of the biblical text for ministers. Now an updated, thoroughly revised edition is being released, called the *New Interpreter's Bible.*

One-volume Bible Commentary. The *New Jerome Biblical Commentary* (Prentice Hall, 1990) is the best of this genre on the market. Produced by Roman Catholic clerical and lay scholars, it provides an amazing depth of theological, textual, and archaeological discussion. Two pairs of volumes—the *Harper's Bible Commentary* (Harper & Row, 1988) and *Harper's Bible Dictionary*, and the *Mercer Commentary on the Bible* (Mercer, 1994) and the *Mercer Dictionary of the Bible*—if used in conjunction with each other, provide similar coverage. A more specialized volume, *The Women's Bible Commentary* (Westminster/John Knox, 1992), provides a feminist perspective on the text.

Bible Handbook. This is a much abused category of biblical resources. It has been dominated in the past by such works as *Halley's Bible Handbook* (Zondervan, 1959). Unfortunately, this book has not been updated and is badly out-of-date. We would not recommend any of the volumes in this general category, simply because they tend to be abbreviated versions of one-volume commentaries, are superficial, and in many cases are apologetic or rigidly fundamentalist in their treatment of the Bible. Instead, we would suggest the purchase of a volume dealing with the social world of the Bible. Victor H. Matthews, *Manners and Customs in the Bible* (rev. ed.; Hendrickson, 1991), provides historical summaries of each of the biblical periods from the time of Abraham through the New Testament. Among the topics discussed are marriage customs, clothing styles, diet, economic life, warfare, architecture, and burial customs. A similar volume in this genre is J. A. Thompson, *IVP Handbook of*

Life in Bible Times (InterVarsity, 1987). Also useful are two new books which attempt to define biblical concepts, B. Malina and J. Pilch, *Biblical Social Values and their Meanings* (Hendrickson, 1993), or biblical terminology, D. Bergant, *The Collegeville Concise Glossary of Biblical Terms* (Liturgical Press, 1994).

Bible Atlas. One of the least understood aspects of biblical studies is the spatial and environmental character of Palestine and the ancient Mediterranean world. Bible atlases can fill this void; they come in all price ranges and are available in electronic form. For instance, *Hammond's Atlas of the Bible Lands* (Hammond, Inc., 1990) is an inexpensive but serviceable atlas. Slightly more expensive, but also in paperback, is the *Oxford Bible Atlas* (3d ed.; Oxford, 1985). The model for most modern reference atlases is Y. Aharoni, M. Avi-Yonah and A. Rainey, *The Macmillan Bible Atlas* (3d ed.; Macmillan, 1993). Several new atlases have recently appeared, and some, like *The Harper Atlas of the Bible* (Harper & Row, 1987), C. Rasmussen, *Zondervan NIV Atlas of the Bible* (Zondervan, 1989), and B. Beitzel, *The Moody Atlas of Bible Lands* (Moody, 1985), have spectacular color pictures and excellent discussions of geography. However, they are all fairly expensive, and this expense must be weighed against the need to purchase other resources. Bible dictionaries and commentaries do deal at least somewhat with biblical geography and usually contain a set of color maps.

Study Bible. Recently several new study Bibles have come on the market. These are a useful resource, especially for studying a particular book in the Bible, because the notes on each page provide quick insights and philological and historical data. We recommend either *The HarperCollins Study Bible* (NRSV; HarperCollins, 1993), *The Catholic Study Bible* (NAB; Oxford, 1990) or the *Oxford Study Bible* (REB; Oxford, 1992).

Bible Abstracts. Since a student will not always have access to scholarly publications, one way to keep up is to regularly check *New Testament Abstracts* and *Old Testament Abstracts*. These quarterly publications of the Catholic Biblical Association provide brief summaries of hundreds of articles and books published each year.

Biblical Journals. While a student's interests may vary, four popular journals currently available by subscription, will be useful to all. They are *Biblical Archaeologist, Biblical Archaeology Review, Bible Review,* and *The Bible Today.* The first two deal primarily with developments in archaeology while the last two are concerned with current developments and controversies in biblical studies. They are an inexpensive way to stay up on modern theological discussions and archaeological discoveries.

More technical discussion of biblical issues can be found in *Interpretation,* the *Journal of Biblical Literature,* the *Catholic Biblical Quarterly,* and *Biblical Theology Bulletin.*

Archaeology and Ancient Texts. For those students who wish to know more about archaeological methods and the results of excavations in biblical lands over the last century, we would recommend the following: A. Mazar, *Archaeology of the Land of the Bible* (Doubleday, 1990) and W. E. Rast, *Through the Ages in Palestinian Archaeology* (Trinity, 1992). While there are a number of other volumes available, these two affordable studies provide good, readable coverage. For a more comprehensive reference work, consult the multivolume *Oxford Encyclopedia of Archaeology in the Near East* (Oxford, 1997). Since this textbook contains excerpts from many ancient Near Eastern texts, some students may wish to examine collections of the texts in translation. We recommend J. Pritchard, *Ancient Near Eastern Texts Relating to the Old Testament* (3d ed. with Supplement; Princeton, 1969), which also comes in an abridged paperback edition, and V. H. Matthews and D. C. Benjamin, *Old Testament Parallels: Laws and Stories from the Ancient Near East* (Paulist, 1991), which contains more colloquial translations.

HOW TO EVALUATE BIBLE TRANSLATIONS

It is essential that the student find a translation that will encourage reading and study. Many good translations are available, and no single one is superior for every purpose. The questions and explanations below can be used to evaluate Bible translations.

Has the Best "Text" Been Used to Make this Translation? We do not possess the original manuscripts of any biblical writer. In fact, we only rarely have the original manuscript for any ancient text. The exceptions are inscriptions that have been carved in stone or clay tablets. So what we have for the Bible are many copies of those originals made by hand by scribes and monks over many centuries. Like other human copies they are not always identical. Each manuscript differs here and there from the next one. Today we have hundreds, even thousands, of manuscripts in many languages available to help us reconstruct the original text. That reconstruction is called *textual criticism* (or analysis, if criticism holds too many negative connotations), and the goal is to reconstruct as accurately as possible all of the words of the Bible. Scholars have to use the many different manuscripts to determine what might be the most likely original words. So no single manuscript always has the best readings. The best text to use for translation is therefore an *eclectic* text. This means each variant in the ancient manuscripts has been evaluated separately to determine its proximity to the original.

It is obvious that all of us are greatly indebted to those scholars who labor diligently over many ancient texts and variant readings to reconstruct as accurately as possible all of the words of the Bible. Their work is never final because of the subjective nature of any reconstruction of the text, which does not exist in its entirety in any single manuscript. It should also be clear that older translations, such as the King James Version (KJV), are not based on a text that benefits from all of the new manuscripts discovered in the nearly 400 years since it was completed in 1611.

To decide whether a translation is based on the best text, check the introductory preface for specific statements. Does it say that this is an eclectic text, or that each variant in the ancient manuscripts has been evaluated separately? Check key passages. Almost all modern translations indicate the questionable nature of certain passages. Determine whether they have been omitted entirely, put in the footnotes or margins, put in the text, or set in brackets. The preferred approach is to put questionable words or passages in footnotes or to omit them.

How Accurate Is the Translation? Have the latest *philological* and *linguistic* insights been used? Is there a fidelity to the original? Here the average student has no way of checking since he or she seldom knows Greek or Hebrew. Two general questions will test the accuracy of a translation.

Is it up-to-date? Check the copyright date. In general the newer the translation the more likely it is up-to-date. Try to determine if the translation is a revision of an earlier translation or a reprinting of an earlier translation. There are several reprints with new names. Do not take the date of printing at face value.

Has a team of scholars representing a cross-section of religious groups made the translation? No single individual can stay current with of the vast amount of new scholarship that is necessary to make the best translation. Team translations are always preferable. Generally the greater the diversity of the team the better the translation.

Is the Translation Readable? Check the introductory preface to see if stylistic experts have been used in addition to Greek and Hebrew experts. Check some test passages. Readability differs from one person to another, but some translations, in an effort to be comprehensive or "amplified," are not very readable. Likewise, rigidly literal translations are often too hard to read for some students. There are three methods of translation: (1) the concordant method or word-for-word translation tends to be the least readable; (2) the free paraphrase tends to be the most readable; (3) the equivalence method is based on the closest equivalents in two languages, and tends to avoid awkward literalness on the one hand and inaccuracies on the other hand.

How Is the Translation Intended to be Used?   Is the translation for church or synagogue use? If so, then it should be more formal and dignified. Paraphrased translations use more colloquial and slang expressions, which would not be appropriate for formal religious use. Is the translation for private reading (especially for those who seldom read the Bible or for those who frequently do and are looking for some new expression or insight)? Here is where the colloquial or slang expression of a paraphrased translation is more appropriate. Is it readable and intelligible to the average person?

Is the translation intended for study purposes? If so, then the translation should preserve the ambiguity of the original and the distance between the ancient and modern world. A careful student wants to know what the text said and draw out the relevance on his or her own. In general, the paraphrases and idiomatic translations are least satisfactory for careful study.

What Kind of Information Is in the Annotations and Notes?   Check to see if the annotations are slanted to a particular religious approach. Are the notes helpful or distracting? Since the average person tends to accept the notes on the same level as the biblical text itself, we recommend a Bible with as few notes as possible for the beginning student. Nevertheless, consumers are demanding Bibles specifically targeted for women, men, athletes, young people, etc. "Study Bibles" are thus popular, but they must be used cautiously.

What Is the General Format Like?   Is the text easily readable? Are there illustrations, and do you need them? Are there paragraph divisions? Divisions did not appear in the original text. Are there paragraph headings? Remember these are also not in the original text. How are the verses laid out? Is poetry put in a different format?

Is Inclusive Language Used?   Inclusive language attempts to avoid sexist language and to include both women and men where it is clear that both genders are being addressed (e.g., he or she, humankind, people). Some translations are rightfully gender-inclusive, but go further and make God female. In this textbook we have tried to include women wherever the text does not specify males, but we have not strayed from the original languages in our discussion. We have not treated God as male or female, although there are biblical images of God that are female (Isa 42:14) and male (Hos 11:1–7).

No translation is best for every purpose. Since there are about 450 different versions now available, each individual has to decide for himself or herself. Hopefully, each person will take the time to use the above tests in conjunction with the kind of use he or she will make of the Bible. Fortunately most of the Bibles translated in the last thirty to forty years are far superior to those made earlier. For instance, despite its literary beauty and long-standing use in the church, we cannot recommend the King James Version because it contains archaic language and reflects out-of-date scholarship (published in 1611). It is simply necessary to realize that some translations are much better than others. We recommend:

> Revised Standard Version (RSV)
> New Revised Standard Version (NRSV)
> New International Version (NIV)
> New American Bible (NAB)
> *TANAKH:* A New Translation of the Holy Scriptures according to the Traditional Hebrew Text (NJPS)
> Revised English Bible (REB)
> New Jerusalem Bible (NJB)
> Contemporary English Version (CEV)

ARCHAEOLOGY AND THE BIBLE

The ability of archaeology to enhance our understanding of the Bible and its world affords it a special status for many. In particular, archaeology enhances our understanding of the written text with physical evidence. Over the last century archaeology has revolutionized the study of the text of the Bible. We turn next to show how archaeology helps us to understand the world of the Bible.

Archaeological evidence provides the best information on life in ancient times. When careful methods are applied to the excavation of ancient city and village sites, information slowly emerges from the ground that can aid our understanding of the people of the past. These methods include:

Systematic Recording of Finds. Photographic and written records are made of each level within the dig, special finds are noted and drawn to scale, and a clear sense of the location and dimensions of the excavation is maintained with the use of surveying equipment. All of this record keeping is necessary because once the levels of a site have been excavated they cannot be reexcavated. Although the work of recording is slow and costly, archaeology would be nothing but treasure hunting without it.

Careful Attention to Digging Methods. Much of what comes out of the ground is grimy, broken, or corroded. Thus it takes care and experience to recognize a coin, a particular style of pottery, or an inscription on a wall. Field supervisors spend a great deal of their time training the volunteer workers how to use tools, how to excavate properly, and how to identify artifacts.

Artifactual Material Is Shared with a Wide Range of Experts. In order to gain the most information and to draw a more complete conclusion on life in the biblical period than the archaeologists can obtain alone, what comes out of the ground must be made public. For instance, the carbonized remains found in storage jars and on the floors of excavated threshing floors, when examined by teams of microbiologists, botanists, and paleobotanists, can lead to the discovery of the diet of ancient humans. Their general level of health can be surmised, and the sophistication of their methods of agriculture and animal husbandry can be at least partially ascertained.

From Nimrod; woman looking from window.
Courtesy of the British Museum.

Results of Each Year's Excavation Must Be Published. This includes the site plans, the photographs and drawings of the artifacts, quantified data of the scientific team, and the reconstructive analysis of the site director. Publication enables other archaeologists to better interpret their own finds from other sites.

Advantages and Limitations of Archaeology

We can summarize the advantages of archaeology as follows:

It adds new evidence to help reconstruct the biblical world (i.e. inscriptions, objects from daily life).

It helps us visualize objects mentioned in the Bible.

It helps illuminate some (difficult) sections of the Bible.

It makes biblical people come alive as real people who used tools, weapons, etc.

It creates interest, excitement, and enthusiasm by making new discoveries.

It supplements written records (written records tend to depict upper classes; archaeological discoveries tend to add the artifacts of the lower classes as well).

We can summarize the limitations of archaeology as follows:

The evidence (physical remains) is fragmentary.

The evidence is mute or silent. It needs to be interpreted, and that interpretation is subjective.

It deals with physical remains but not the abstract. (Therefore it cannot prove or disprove theological statements such as "There is [not] a God.")

It is an issue of scholarly debate, but literary evidence (the Bible) often takes priority over archaeological evidence.

Archaeological techniques are constantly improving. Older excavations usually have limitations and should be used with care.

Advantages and Limitations of Archaeology for Understanding the Bible

To expect archaeological discoveries to conclusively "prove the truth of the Bible" is unreasonable. The findings of archaeologists are only mute evidence of life in the ancient past. In other words, to say, as John Garstang did earlier in this century, that a particular wall found in the excavations at Jericho was the one that fell to the trumpet blasts of Joshua, without examining all of the surrounding evidence (pottery, building styles, depth within the **tell**), is unfair to the student and to the biblical text as well. Improved methods of excavation later proved Garstang to be incorrect even in his identification of the stratigraphic level of Joshua's Jericho, and this mistake led to controversy and a misunderstanding of the proper role of archaeological research in relation to the study of the Bible.

Finds must first be accepted for what they are in the context of the tell (the artificial mound created by accumulated occupation levels) as a whole. The sites of ancient Canaanite cities are layered, with each level representing a different phase in the history of the city. Since objects found lower in the tell can generally be assumed to be older than those found closer to the surface, a chronology of the various levels or strata can be developed.

Some confusion of the strata does occur due to earthquake activity and the digging of pits and foundations by later inhabitants. To overcome this obstacle and establish a relative chronology for each city site, archaeologists examine pottery types and other artifacts from each layer. The findings are then compared with finds from the same levels in several similar sites. **Carbon-14** dating, as well as other scientific methods, also aids in the process.

Due to the limitations of time and money, archaeologists seldom uncover an entire mound. They carefully map out squares for excavation or dig exploratory shafts in those portions of the mound that surveys have shown to contain the most important structures (temples, palaces, gates) or the most representative objects of interest.

The most recently developed archaeological techniques do try to obtain a broader perspective on the entire mound, but it is unlikely that every shovel full of dirt will be turned or every object uncovered. Magnifying the difficulties of obtaining a complete picture of how a site was occupied is the fact that many sites were excavated before the development of modern methods. This means that a great deal of valuable information has been lost forever. Archaeology is a destructive process (each level must be recorded and then removed to get to the level below it), and what has been removed can never be replaced. As a result, we learn, but we can not learn all there is to know about life in these ancient cities through archaeology. Thus, responsible archaeologists today intentionally leave some portions of the mound untouched for later generations and their more advanced excavation methods.

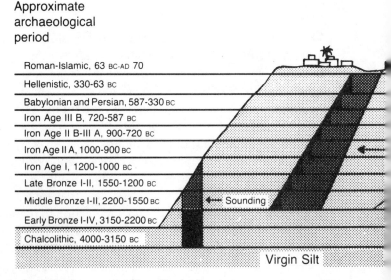

Approximate
archaeological
period

| Roman-Islamic, 63 BC-AD 70 |
| Hellenistic, 330-63 BC |
| Babylonian and Persian, 587-330 BC |
| Iron Age III B, 720-587 BC |
| Iron Age II B-III A, 900-720 BC |
| Iron Age II A, 1000-900 BC |
| Iron Age I, 1200-1000 BC |
| Late Bronze I-II, 1550-1200 BC |
| Middle Bronze I-II, 2200-1550 BC |
| Early Bronze I-IV, 3150-2200 BC |
| Chalcolithic, 4000-3150 BC |

Sounding

Virgin Silt

Cross-section of tell. Used courtesy of InterVarsity Press.

Mound or tell of ancient Bethshan in the background
with the remains of Scythopolis, a NT city in the foreground.
Photo L. Devries.

Chronological
Periods of
Biblical History

For convenience' sake, the various periods of biblical history have been divided into chronological periods (see chart on page 17). This can be somewhat misleading in the earliest

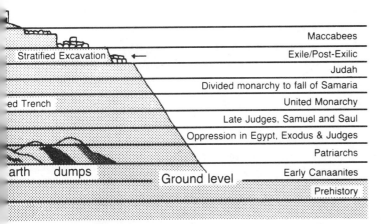

	Approximate biblical period
	Maccabees
Stratified Excavation	Exile/Post-Exilic
	Judah
	Divided monarchy to fall of Samaria
ed Trench	United Monarchy
	Late Judges, Samuel and Saul
	Oppression in Egypt, Exodus & Judges
	Patriarchs
arth dumps — Ground level	Early Canaanites
	Prehistory

periods since there is no extrabiblical evidence for the existence of the characters described in the Bible prior to the monarchy (ca. tenth century BCE). Archaeology, however, has provided us with chronological divisions based on technology levels and these will be used to identify these uncertain periods of Israelite history.

Written in wedge-shaped writing called cuneiform, the Babylonian Chronicle records Nebuchadnezzar's victory over Jerusalem in 567 BCE.
Courtesy of the British Museum.

The earliest historical period associated with the Israelites is the *Middle Bronze Age* (ca. 2000–1550 BCE). This is so-named because bronze (an alloy of copper and tin) was the chief metal used in making tools, utensils, and implements. It is also delimited by styles and techniques of firing pottery. Tradition places the ancestral narratives in this period, but there are no existing extrabiblical written materials which mention Abraham, Isaac, or Jacob by name. Texts written in the **cuneiform** (wedge-shaped) script from Mari, Nuzi, and Alalakh in Mesopotamia and the El Amarna and **execration** texts from Egypt (see geography section below for these sites) have helped to illuminate the world described in these narratives, but, like all archaeological artifacts, they cannot prove the historicity of these characters.

The *Late Bronze Age* (ca. 1550–1200 BCE) is generally associated with the periods of the exodus, conquest, and settlement in Israelite history. Archaeological evidence can be used to note population shifts, the establishment of new settlements, and the

CHART OF HISTORICAL PERIODS

ARCHAEOLOGICAL PERIODS	EGYPT	ISRAEL	MESOPOTAMIA
Paleolithic (Old Stone Age) prior to 10,000 BCE			
Mesolithic (Middle Stone Age) 10,000–8000 BCE			
Neolithic (New Stone Age) 8000–4000 BCE			
Chalcolithic (Bronze-Stone Age) 4000–3100 BCE			
Early Bronze (or Early Canaanite Age) 3100–2000 BCE	Early Dynastic 3000–2700 BCE Dynasties I–II		Early Dynastic Period 2900–2350 BCE
	Old Kingdom 2700–2200 BCE Dynasties III–VI		Akkadian Period 2350–2100 BCE
	First Intermediate 2200–2040 BCE Dynasties (VII–X)		Ur III Period 2100–2000 BCE
Middle Bronze (Middle Canaanite) 2000–1550 BCE	Middle Kingdom 2040–1640 Dynasties XI–XIV	Patriarchal Period	Early Old Babylonian 2000–1800 BCE
			Old Babylonian Period 1800–1600 BCE Hammurabi Age 1792–1750 BCE
	Second Intermediate 1640–1550 BCE Dynasties XV–XVII Hyksos Period	Joseph's Descent	
Late Bronze (Late Canaanite) 1550–1200 BCE	New Kingdom 1550–1070 BCE Dynasties XVIII–XX Amama Age	Oppression	Middle Babylonian 1600–1000 BCE
		Exodus Conquest	
Iron Age I (Early Israelite) 1200–900 BCE	Late Period 1070–332 BCE Dynasties XXI–XXXI	Period of the Judges United Monarchy	Assyrian Period 1000–626 BCE
Iron Age II (Middle & Late Israelite) 900–600 BCE		Divided Monarchy Fall of Samaria	
			Neo-Babylonian Period 626–539 BCE
Iron Age III 600–300 BCE Babylonian Period 587–539 BCE Persian Period 539–332 BCE		Fall of Jerusalem Exilic Period Post-Exilic Period	Persian Period 539–332 BCE
Hellenistic Period 332–64 BCE			Greek Period 332–200 BCE
Roman Period 64 BCE–324 CE		New Testament Period	
Byzantine Period 324–640 CE			

destruction of existing towns and villages. Nevertheless, the only piece of extrabiblical evidence during this period that points to the existence of the Israelites is the Merneptah Stele from Egypt, which mentions Israel as a people conquered by the pharaoh. The exact nature of this text is not certain.

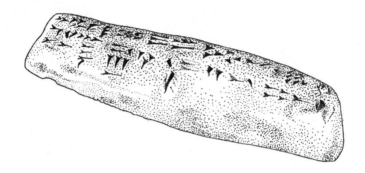

First recorded alphabet from Ugarit (thirty characters) on clay tablet,
ca. fourteenth cent. BCE.

The introduction of new peoples and new technologies into Canaan brought the advent of the *Iron Age* (1200–332 BCE). *Iron I* (1200–900 BCE) is associated with the early monarchy in Israel. The first inscriptional evidence mentioning biblical characters comes from this period (Mesha Stele from Moab, House of David Stele from Dan, Assyrian Annals).

During *Iron II* (900–600 BCE) Israel divided into two nations: Judah in the south with its capital at *Jerusalem,* and Israel in the north with its eventual capital at *Samaria.* This was the time of considerable contact with other nations, and as a result archaeology reveals the construction and fortification of many walled cities (Hazor, Megiddo, Gezer, Jerusalem; see map for these sites), and the presence of trade goods from all over the Mediterranean world (pottery, jewelry, metals, incense). There is also a much larger number of inscriptions mentioning biblical characters and events. Some of these, like the annals of the Assyrian kings (Sargon II, Sennacherib) and King Nebuchadnezzar of Babylon, reflect the dangers presented by empire-building superpowers. A few Israelite inscriptions, such as the Arad ostraca and the Lachish letters, afford a glimpse of Israelite writing style and the concerns of individuals in these troubled times.

The final historical period we will consider in this volume is the postexilic era. During this time, the surviving nation of Judah was reestablished under Persian rule (540–332 BCE). The temple in Jerusalem was rebuilt. Relations with the Persian government can be seen in the minting of coins and in written materials such as the Cyrus Cylinder.

This era ended with the conquests of Alexander the Great of Macedonia and the initiation of the Hellenistic period (332–63 BCE). The blending of cultures that resulted from the infusion of Greek philosophy, religion, art, and literature into the Near East transformed that region and led Judaism to further define itself within a broader cultural context.

The Taylor Prism mentions the Assyrian ruler Sennacherib's victory over the Israelite king Hezekiah (ca. 701 BCE). Courtesy of the British Museum.

A brief period of Jewish independence does occur during the Hasmonean period (168–63 BCE). The Maccabean revolt, sparked by the repressive decrees of Antiochus IV, had driven the Seleucid Greek rulers out of Palestine; the Jews were able to rule themselves for several generations. Eventually, the corruption of their kings and the fighting among the various religious factions made them easy prey for Pompey and the Romans in 63 BCE.

Roman rule invigorated Palestine's economy and saw the construction of monumental buildings, roads, and water systems. The New Testament and the works of the Jewish historian Flavius Josephus contain a wealth of information on the social world of the Jews under the Romans during the first century CE. These documents describe the various factions (Sadducees, Pharisees, Essenes, and Zealots) that existed at that time as well as the currents of discontent among the people. The basis for their anger was the imposition of Roman custom and law as well as the tyrannical and economy-draining policies of the Herods. The desire of the Jews to be free of foreign rule and to worship as they pleased led to numerous uprisings. In response the Romans in 70 CE destroyed Jerusalem and the temple, which had been built by Herod. This, plus the expulsion of most of the Jews from Palestine following the Bar Kochba Revolt (135 CE), was the final step in pushing the Jews into a religion of the book—one not tied to temple, priesthood, or land.

STUDY QUESTIONS

1. Describe the methods used to excavate sites in the biblical regions.

2. List and explain the advantages and limitations of archaeology for understanding the Bible.

3. List the five chronological periods covering the time of the Old Testament/Hebrew Bible.

4. Define: artifact, tell, carbon 14, ostraca, stele.

ORAL TRADITION AND THE DEVELOPMENT OF THE CANON

In the beginning was the spoken word. The biblical stories as we read them today began as orally transmitted episodes, told by elders, parents, and itinerant story-tellers. The nearly universal illiteracy among the earliest people of the ancient Near East made oral transmission of information, history, and poetry necessary. Although the ancient cultures of Egypt and Mesopotamia invented writing systems as early as 3500 BCE, they were very difficult to learn. These ancient languages were written syllabically. This means that every sound is represented by a different symbol, as many as nine hundred in some cases. As a result, only trained scribes, who had devoted many years to study, knew how to read and write. Elite members of society employed scribes to write for them. But in everyday situations, they relied upon spoken communication, not written.

This remained true until an alphabetic system of writing was invented around 1600 BCE by the people of Ugarit, a seaport city at the extreme northern edge of Syria's Mediterranean coastline and fifty miles east of the island of Cyprus. Because merchants found it inconvenient and expensive to employ scribes to maintain their business records, a simplified script, using only thirty cuneiform signs was developed. This easy-to-learn system allowed anyone, with a minimum amount of study, to prepare documents and examine those of customers and suppliers. It also contributed to the development of cursive, alphabetic scripts throughout Syro-Palestine and eventually to a rise in the general literacy level.

Governments and religious institutions used the oral tradition for their own purposes as these stories were edited for publication. The result was court histories, religious literature and drama, and a large body of folk stories woven into narrative form. The written biblical narrative originated in the wave of nationalism created by the establishment of the monarchy after 1000 BCE. The body of literature grew, but not all of it became a part of the "official" version of events. Volumes of histories, like the "Book of Jashar" (Josh 10:13b), presumably provided detailed accounts of battles and leaders, but only such elusive references exist. Once the establishment realized that a single "voice" was necessary to standardize the people's understanding and knowledge of events, editors were employed to shape the narratives.

This editorial process continued throughout the period prior to about 200 BCE. By that time a large number of books had been identified as belonging to a **canon** (i.e., sacred scripture) by the Jewish community. For instance, the Prologue to the apocryphal/deuterocanonical (see below) book of Sirach mentions the "Law and the Prophets." Although these books still existed in various versions, the basic form of the **Hebrew canon** had taken shape. The Hebrew canon contains the following divisions:

Law: Pentateuch (Genesis–Deuteronomy) or Torah

Prophets: Former (Joshua–2 Kings) and Latter (Isaiah–Malachi)

Writings (Esther–Song of Solomon)

Additional books were composed during the Second Temple period that did not make their way into the Hebrew Bible canon. These volumes, largely written in Greek and known as the **deuterocanonical** books or the **Apocrypha**, include histories such as 1–2 Maccabees, as well as continuations of some of the canonical books (Additions to Esther [Esther]; Bel and the Dragon [Daniel]). Although these books were not included in the final order and composition of the Hebrew canon, they are important for understanding the history and traditions of the Second Temple period; that is, the period of early Judaism leading up to the birth of Christianity. Many modern scholars maintain that the decision to exclude them from the canon was determined at a conference at Jamnia in 90–100 CE. Here, it is presumed, a group of Jewish scholars argued over versions and volumes and eventually set the canon in its present form. Their intent was to standardize the text for use by Jews wherever they were scattered after the destruction of Jerusalem in 70 CE.

At approximately the same time that the apocryphal books were being written, the first translation of the Hebrew text was produced in Greek. This project, initiated by the Jewish community in Alexandria, Egypt, was necessitated by the decline of

Hebrew as a spoken language, especially in the settlements of the Diaspora. Jews wished to read and study their holy texts in the language they used everyday. The translation which they produced is known as the **Septuagint** (abbr. LXX).

Any translation, ancient or modern, will have its problems due to cultural and linguistic difficulties. There are simply some words, phrases, and colloquialisms that do not translate from one language to another. The translators of the Septuagint, likewise, had to make judgment calls and in some cases interpret the meaning of the passage. An example of this may be found in the dilemma over the word "love." Hebrew has several words for love, *ahabh*, *khesed*, and *hashaq*, which are used in a variety of contexts, from human love to the love expressed in God's covenant with the people of Israel. Greek also has three: *eros*, *agape*, and *philia*. Being able to match the correct linguistic equivalent is the task and the trial of the translator.

The Canon of the Old Testament/Hebrew Bible with the Abbreviation of Each Book
(Included in Jewish, Protestant, Roman Catholic, and Eastern Orthodox Canons)

Pentateuch, Law, or Torah
  Genesis (Gen)
  Exodus (Exod)
  Leviticus (Lev)
  Numbers (Num)
  Deuteronomy (Deut)

Wisdom, Liturgy, and Songs
  Job (Job)
  Psalms (singular, Ps; plural Pss)
  Proverbs (Prov)
  Ecclesiastes or Qoheleth
    (Eccl or Qoh)
  Song of Solomon (Song Sol),
    or Song of Songs, or
    Canticles (Cant)

Historical books
Deuteronomic Histories
  Joshua (Josh)
  Judges (Judg)
  1 Samuel (1 Sam)
  2 Samuel (2 Sam)
  1 Kings (1 Kgs)
  2 Kings (2 Kgs)
Postexilic Histories
  1 Chronicles (1 Chron)
  2 Chronicles (2 Chron)
  Ezra (Ezra)
  Nehemiah (Neh)
Popular Histories
  Ruth (Ruth)
  Daniel (Dan)
  Esther (Esth)

Prophets
Major Prophets
  Isaiah (Isa)
  Jeremiah (Jer)
  Ezekiel (Ezek)
Minor Prophets or The Twelve
  Hosea (Hos)
  Joel (Joel)
  Amos (Amos)
  Obadiah (Obad)
  Jonah (Jonah)
  Micah (Mic)
  Nahum (Nah)
  Habakkuk (Hab)
  Zephaniah (Zeph)
  Haggai (Hag)
  Zechariah (Zech)
  Malachi (Mal)

The Apocrypha or Deuterocanonical Books with the Abbreviations of Each Book
(Included in Roman Catholic and Eastern Orthodox Canons)*

Historical and Moralistic Tales
Tobit (Tob)
Judith (Jud)
1 Maccabees (1 Macc)
2 Maccabees (2 Macc)
3 Maccabees (3 Macc)*
4 Maccabees (4 Macc)*

Wisdom and Liturgy
Wisdom of Solomon (Wis)
Sirach or Ecclesiasticus or
   Wisdom of Jesus the Son of Sirach
   or Wisdom of Joshua ben Sira (Sir)
Psalm 151 (Ps 151)*

Expansions of the OT/HB
1 Esdras or 3 Esdras (1 Esdr)*
2 Esdras, 4 Esdras, or 4 Ezra, 5 Ezra,
   and 6 Ezra (2 Esdr or 4 Ezra, 5 Ezra,
   and 6 Ezra)*
Baruch (Bar)
Letter of Jeremiah or Epistle of
   Jeremiah (Let Jer)
Additions to Esther (Add Esth)
Prayer of Azariah and Song of the
   Three Jews (Pr Azar)
Susanna (Sus)
Bel and the Dragon (Bel)
Prayer of Manasseh (Pr Man)*

*With the exception of 4 Maccabees, books marked with an asterisk are found only in certain Eastern Orthodox canons and are not considered canonical in Roman Catholicism. 4 Maccabees has never been canonized in any tradition but it is included in some Eastern Orthodox Bibles. 1 Esdras, 2 Esdras, and Prayer of Manasseh are included as an appendix in Roman Catholic Bibles.

Old Testament/ Hebrew Bible Canon

The Septuagint was only the first of the biblical translations. It was followed by many others, including the Christian Latin translation, the **Vulgate**. This work was commissioned by the Roman emperor Constantine after his Edict of Milan (315 CE) had declared that all Roman citizens were to convert to Christianity. A leading scholar of the time, Jerome, translated both the Old and New Testaments and included the books of the Apocrypha in this new Bible. Jerome's Vulgate became the standard and official Bible of the Roman Catholic Church throughout the Middle Ages. No alteration or translation of its text was allowed on pain of death. This did not change until the leaders of the Protestant Reformation (Martin Luther, Thomas Cranmer, John Calvin) translated the Bible into their own national languages. Luther changed the canon once again in his translation by excluding the Apocrypha, so that the Protestant canon of thirty-nine books is different from the Catholic canon, which contains forty-six books.

In England, as part of the general wave of translations being produced, James I commissioned a group of thirty scholars to create a standard, authorized version for use in his kingdom. The resultant so-called King James Version, along with the works of Shakespeare, are the chief contributors to the development of modern English.

Modern translations of the Bible have continued and in recent years have become a source of theological contention for denominations. The discovery of the **Dead Sea Scrolls** in caves near the settlement of **Qumran** created an explosion of new scholarship and new translations. These scrolls, which date to 100 BCE–70 CE, contain most of the books of the Hebrew canon in versions older than any other manuscript available to us. They predate the Jamnia conference (90–100 CE) and are 1,000 years older than the **codices** (book manuscripts) of the Hebrew text copied in the Middle Ages. While they do demonstrate that several versions of the biblical books existed prior to the final setting of the canon, they have not revealed any major contradictions or provided materials that would require a radical rethinking of the biblical message.

The Hebrew text as it existed in the time of the Qumran community did not contain vowel signs or punctuation. When it ceased to be a living language, difficulties over pronunciation and translation arose. These problems were dealt with by a group of Jewish scholars known as the Masoretes. They developed a system of counting the number of letters in each manuscript and then, when making a new copy, counting them once again to be sure nothing had been added or deleted. They also invented a system of vowel and punctuation marks, placed above and below the now sacred letters, to aid in reading the text. Their task prevented further changes in the text which had appeared due to errors by copyists over the centuries. Among the copyist errors that they were able to prevent by their system were: **dittography**—accidently writing the same word twice; **haplography**—accidentally deleting a word or a phrase; scribal **glosses**—marginal notes or explanations which were later incorporated into the text itself.

The biblical text as we have it today is a product of writers, editors, and copyists. Its revelatory character is based on the belief system of its own day and must be understood within that social and historical context. Applications of the biblical material to later periods and cultures come most easily from the wisdom and poetic materials. Genealogies, histories, and political propaganda have more interest to historians than to theologians.

Cautions about Ancient Literature

1. The most crucial question about ancient literature, including the Bible, is *not* whether it should be interpreted literally or figuratively but *how* one interprets figuratively and literally. Even those who claim to take the text literally do not really do so in every case:

    (a) Isa 55:12—mountains singing and trees clapping their hands—is obviously considered figurative language.

    (b) 2 Chron 16:9, "The eyes of the Lord run to and fro throughout the whole earth," is clearly an **anthropomorphism** (describing God with human characteristics).

2. What does the author intend to say in light of his or her cultural background and time period? Only by answering this question can we hope to understand the biblical writer. *Example*: in Gen 16:1–4, Abram impregnates Hagar, his wife's slave, in order to produce a son. Why does he do this to get a son?

    (a) A son carried on the family name and was the inheritor of property. This helps explain why there are so many genealogies in the Bible.

    (b) A son could take care of his elderly parents (a form of social security).

    (c) Sons were needed in war and for the work of farming and herding.

3. The Bible is not the product of a scientific age and therefore it should not be pressed to make scientific statements or to be a scientific textbook.

4. Numbers or statistics are not necessarily used with a scientific or statistical precision. *Examples*: Moses' life is divided into three periods of forty years. Joseph and Joshua both die at age one hundred and ten, and they both have connections with Egypt, where one hundred and ten is the ideal age.

5. Ancient literature was not written like most modern Western literature. There is rarely any author listed and copyrights did not exist. Most of the earliest works are the product of oral tradition, and are thus the property of the community, not of a particular person.

6. One must determine the type of literature one is reading before trying to interpret it. Worshipful and hymnic literature (e.g., Ps 84:1–2) has a much different purpose than adventurous, "heroic" literature (e.g., Judg 4:12–22).

7. For nearly all of ancient literature, we do not have the author's original version. Thus we are dependent on whatever hand copies have survived. Of course, hand copies may have errors made in the process of copying. Numbers are especially hard to transcribe accurately. *Example*: 1 Sam 13:1 reads, "Saul was ? (or one) year old when he began to reign and he reigned for ? years over Israel." Probably a number has dropped out in both cases.

8. We are too far removed in time to expect to clear up every problem or discrepancy. Therefore, we should honestly admit problems and work to resolve them with any new evidence that becomes available.

MODERN METHODS IN STUDYING THE BIBLE

Today students and scholars rely upon a variety of methods to study the Bible. This is due to the fact that ancient documents, like the Bible, are subject to uninformed interpretation, based on modern misconceptions or biases. Devotional or doctrinal interpretations may also slant the meaning of the text or harmonize stories to eliminate inconsistencies or contradictions. The inset dealing with "Cautions about Ancient Literature" attempts to describe and deal with some of these issues.

As we will explain below, a scientific or analytical examination of the biblical text attempts to establish the original meaning and purpose of the narrative. We will briefly examine several of these scientific methods. Each will be referred to as "criticism." This should not be understood as a negative term, but one used to describe analysis and study.

Textual Criticism. Not a single **autograph** (original manuscript) of any biblical writer survives today. So it is necessary to study those ancient manuscripts of the biblical text which have survived. Because these ancient manuscripts have all been copied by hand, they vary. Therefore, careful comparisons must be made between scrolls, codices, and fragments in all of the original biblical languages: Hebrew, Greek, and Aramaic, and early translations of the Bible in Syriac, Latin, and other languages. Through these comparisons scholars reconstruct the original words of the text to the best of their ability. Text critics also do comparative work with other languages from the ancient Near East such as Akkadian, Phoenician, Ugaritic, Hittite, Egyptian, and Canaanite dialects like Moabite and Edomite. In some cases this has made it possible to translate Hebrew words that had previously been considered a misspelling or were just unknown.

Historical Criticism. This method attempts to determine the historical context out of which the text grew and eventually took its shape. Items of importance to the historical critic are original audience, the intent of the writer in addressing specific historical events, and the influence of the place and time (context) in which a document was written. Archaeological data, textual clues on dating the text (e.g., Isa 6:1 or Jer 1:1–3), and extrabiblical evidence are utilized. Historical critics concern themselves with matters of (1) authorship, (2) date of composition, (3) literary genre, (4) style of writing, and (5) vocabulary.

Source Criticism. Since none of the biblical material still exists in its original manuscripts and none has been proven to be written by any single individual, the determination of authorship or source has become a separate category all its own. Much of modern scholarship is based on the work of the nineteenth century German scholar Julius Wellhausen. He developed what came to be known as the **documentary hypothesis**, a theory which originally divided the **Pentateuch**

(Genesis through Deuteronomy) into historical periods and ascribed authorship to groups of editors. His suggestion of four sources known as J, E, D, and P has been expanded by later scholars to deal with the entire Hebrew Bible.

The first compilation and editing of the biblical narratives took place during the early monarchic period (ca. 1000–900 BCE) during the reigns of David and Solomon. Wellhausen identified this source/editor as **J** which stood for *Jahweh* (the German spelling of **Yahweh**), the most commonly used name for God in this portion of the text. His **J-source** included most of Genesis and is considered the oldest story told by the Israelites about themselves. Because this source was compiled during the early monarchy, Jerusalem and the claim to the "Promised Land" are very prominent in these stories. It is also "rougher" than later stories, allowing the ancestors to display human errors and uncertainties. For instance, Abraham lies to and cheats the pharaoh in Genesis 12, telling him that Sarah is his sister rather than his wife.

The second source identified by Wellhausen is called the **E-source**. Dating it to the period of the divided monarchy (about 850–750 BCE), he saw this as a development of the political changes caused by the division of Israel. This material was blended with the J-source, adding a greater emphasis on northern sites like Shechem, and using the Hebrew word **Elohim** for "God." There is also a greater emphasis in this source on the use of angelic messengers rather than direct communication with God.

The **D-source** is the third hypothetical source. Composed of the material from Deuteronomy (technically chs. 12–26, but generally referred to as all of Deuteronomy), it is a retelling of the history of Sinai and the wilderness, and a renewal of the covenantal relationship with Yahweh. It has been identified primarily by vocabulary and the use of a "black-and-white" morality. Because it is history composed in hindsight (written and edited after the end of the monarchy in 587 BCE), it is able to look back at the mistakes made by kings and other leaders, highlight them, and then explain the consequences based on a failure to uphold the covenant. For example, the term "Jeroboam's sin," referring to the policies of an Israelite king who promoted the use of worship centers other than Jerusalem, is used as the basis for determining whether a king is "good" or "bad."

The fourth source and the final attempt at editing the biblical narrative is the **P-source**. Wellhausen dates it to the postexilic period (after 500 BCE) when the monarchy had been eliminated and the priestly community led the returned exiles in Jerusalem. This source is identified by its interest in priestly matters: liturgy, genealogy, ritual, and sacrifice. Because it is the last editing job, it puts a final stamp on the contents of the stories and the sequence of events. One example of the P-source is the creation story in Gen 1:1–2:4a, which is more of an outline than a narrative.

While Wellhausen's hypothesis is no longer accepted in its original form, it was the method against which all others were tested. The conspicuous editing of some narratives, especially in terms of the elimination or shortening of stories (i.e., chronicles of the kings), can be seen by any careful reader. The shades of authorial enhancement or agenda, however, are not always that obvious, and many interpretations are possible. The student should also note that source criticism is sometimes called literary criticism. But the latter term we reserve for the following method of analysis.

Literary Criticism. The literary critic is concerned with the biblical text as a piece of literature. Using the tools of language study, philology, and lexicography, the literary critic analyzes the words of the text in terms of syntax, grammar, and vocabulary. The use of parallelism, metaphor, and other stylistic devices are commented on as well as the choice of words or phrases. Genres, such as poetry and wisdom literature, are determined and categorized. This then aids in the interpretation of a text because literary classification of a story as myth, allegory, history, etc. informs the interpreter as to how to approach a given text.

Narrative Criticism. Through a close reading, this method identifies formal and conventional structures of the narrative, determines plot, develops characterization, distinguishes point of view, exposes language play, and relates it all to some overarching theme. New Testament narrative criticism has tended to note the mechanics or artistry of literary construction, but has also remained committed to historical criticism's desire to determine the author's "intention" and the text's "original" readership. Hebrew Bible studies have gone further in the direction of a purely literary approach.

Form Criticism. The form critic is primarily concerned with the shape of the text. This means that an attempt is made to determine the original form of each portion of the narrative and the reason it was eventually set in its final form. Comparison is often made between different versions of the same episode or narrative item. For example, the wording of the Ten Commandments in Exod 20:1–17 differs from the set of laws listed in Exod 34:17–26. The form critic attempts to determine the "tradition history" and the social background of the text by examining structure, vocabulary, and style.

Redaction Criticism. Because the text shows signs of editing, the redaction critic attempts to identify where such edits occur—the "rough edges" of combined narratives, the presence of anachronisms, and references to outside sources. This method examines the intentions of the editors or redactors who compiled the biblical texts out of earlier source materials. For example, the redaction critic would be interested in the editorial insertions (e.g., Hos 14:9) or asides addressed to the reader (e.g., 2 Kgs 17:7–41). Redaction critics are also interested in the arrangement of the text (see the placement of oracles in Isaiah 1–5 prior to the prophet's call narrative in Isa 6) since placement or evidence or reorganization can be significant for interpretation.

Canonical Criticism. Canonical critics are less interested in the process of textual development and more interested in the final form of the text within the larger context of the canon. Primary here is the perspective of the text as "sacred" or "canonical" and the process of asking questions about the ways in which the text is used to address the faith concerns of the communities that use it. The books of the Bible are also addressed as part of an overall story, not just as individual texts, and no single passage may then be taken in isolation as the basis for study.

Social-Scientific Criticism. With the advent of the social sciences in the late nineteenth century, it has become increasingly clear that the biblical text can be understood only within the context of its social world. Thus social science critics utilize methods developed by psychologists, anthropologists, and sociologists to recreate the biblical world and to gain insights into the reasoning behind such things as ritual, shame as a social control device, and legal procedure. One example would be the use of labeling theory in examining the names in a passage. "Leper" is a label which leads to exclusion from society while "king" or "prophet" are generally honorable titles.

Feminist Criticism. The feminist movement, as it developed in the latter half of this century, made it evident that patriarchal interpretation of the biblical text was no longer socially acceptable, nor was it correct in terms of the world of the biblical writers. Feminist critics attempt to show the intrinsic importance of women in the ancient world and the influence they had in shaping its culture as well as the biblical narrative. For instance, the wives of the ancestors in Genesis are named and become more than shadowy companions. They take on the strong narrative roles given to them by the authors when chauvinistic biases are removed. Feminist critics are also interested in showing the limits of the biblical text in terms of theology, due to its overwhelming gender bias.

Reader Response Criticism. This method assumes that the communication process, as evidenced in the received text, can be described in terms of the basic relationships between sender, message, and receiver. Concentration is placed on the interaction between the text and its receiver(s). The basic assumption is that every text presupposes a specific reader, whether this is a concrete person or only a hypothetical receiver. This reader influences the way in which the text is structured and framed, and the author of the text assumes that the reader has the ability required to decode and understand what is written.

Rhetorical Criticism.   This method first began with an interest in the study of the stylistics of Hebrew prose and poetry. It has evolved into a method that focuses on close readings of singular texts, which are often studied in isolation. Of particular interest are those literary or poetic devices that are clearly rhetorical in form and usage such as repetition, parallelism, analogy, and inclusio. Recent discussion has moved to expand its scope beyond stylistics, in order to probe the persuasive power of texts to influence action or practice. Thus the texts can no longer be viewed as isolated objects of study. Rather, they are placed back within their historical context in order to see how cultural preconceptions inevitably influence the writers and the readers. The aim is to describe the ideology that is embedded in the text in order to see how its very construction has preconditioned experience for both the writer and the reader.

Tradition Criticism.   This method inquires about the community or group responsible for the shaping and transmission of a particular text. A second area of importance is the particular geographical location with which a tradition was associated. There is also a concern for certain dynamics that are present in the origin and reformulation of a tradition, including sociological, political, or cultic influences. Tradition criticism also emphasizes searching for the way particular themes of the OT/HB came to be formulated and the role they continued to play as they were brought into different contexts.

Each of these methodologies has value to students of the Bible. While it is not our intent to force students into one of these molds, it is important that students understand each approach and how it helps us understand the Bible better.

STUDY QUESTIONS

1. Define canon and give examples of canonical books other than those in the Bible.

2. Using the glossary, define the terms deuterocanonical and apocryphal and point out which religious groups use each of these terms.

3. Explain each of the methods scholars use to study the Bible. How do they differ from the devotional study used by many religious people? Are the methods mutually exclusive or complementary? Justify your answer.

4. What is the documentary hypothesis? List and describe the four sources it suggests stand behind the Pentateuch.

5. Define: autograph, Septuagint, Vulgate, anthropomorphism.

The Authorship of the Pentateuch

As a way of helping the reader discover the complexity of biblical criticism and the difficulties that can arise from a careful reading of the text, we offer this exercise as an opportunity for students to discuss some of the issues that they will encounter as they read the biblical stories.

From ancient times, it was commonly theorized that Moses had written the first five books of the Bible (the "Pentateuch"). There are several places in the Pentateuch where we read about Moses' writing laws, memorials, or travel records (Exod 17:14; 24:4; Num 33:2), and many people concluded from this that Moses wrote all five books.

One of the tasks of biblical criticism has been to analyze this assumption and see if it is convincing. The following questions will enable you to practice a bit of biblical criticism and to develop your own answers. Note that there is not necessarily any "right or wrong" answer to these questions, but be prepared to explain and defend your answers.

1. Examine Gen 4:26, which refers to the time of Adam's grandson; Gen 15:7, which refers to the divine name used in the time of Abraham; and Exod 6:2–3, which speaks of the time of Moses. When was the name of **Yahweh** (LORD) first used? (Clue: English Bibles often translate Yahweh with "LORD" and Elohim with "God.")

2. In the story of Noah and the great flood, God told Noah to construct the ark and to load into the ark the living creatures of the earth. Examine Gen 6:18–20 and 7:1–3, and answer the following question: How many of each species of animal and bird was Noah told to take into the ark? What might you conclude from this?

3. The story of Joseph tells of a young man who was mistreated and sold as a slave by his jealous brothers. The brothers sold Joseph to the Midianites in Gen 37:28. Now read Gen 37:28–36 carefully and answer the following question: To whom did the Midianites sell Joseph?

4. Read Gen 36:31. What clue do you find in this verse to help you date the writing of that passage?

5. Read Num 12:3. Who most likely wrote this verse? (a) Moses; (b) someone who thought highly of Moses; (c) someone who disliked Moses; or (d) someone who did not know Moses.

6. Read Deut 34:1–12. From your study of the passage, which of the following is the most likely date for the writing of this text? (a) During Moses' career as an Israelite leader; (b) during the period of mourning following Moses' death; (c) shortly after the mourning for Moses' death was completed; or (d) a time considerably later than any of the above.

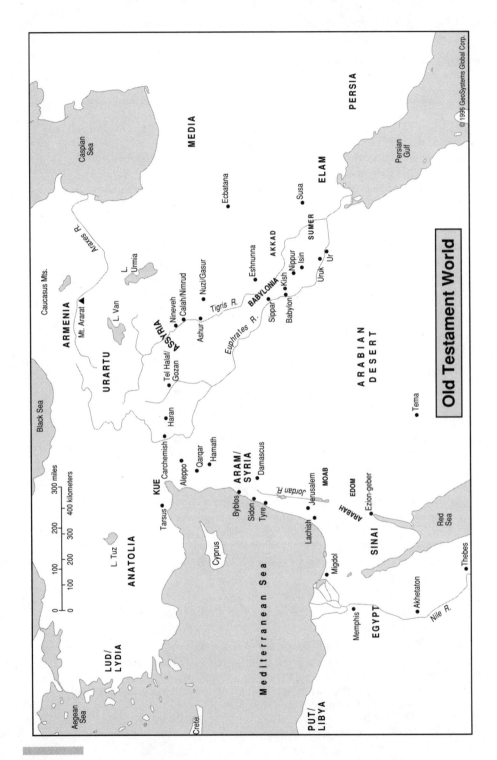

Old Testament World

GEOGRAPHY AND CLIMATE OF THE ANCIENT NEAR EAST

The ancient Near East is divided into three primary geographic areas: Mesopotamia, Egypt, and Syro-Palestine. Adjacent to these regions are Anatolia (modern Turkey), Persia (modern Iran), Arabia (modern Saudi Arabia), and the island of Cyprus. They also figure in the history and the development of human cultures during this period, but are less important than the others.

Mesopotamia   The region of ancient Mesopotamia, which today comprises the area of Iraq and portions of Syria and Turkey, was dominated by the twin river system of the Tigris and Euphrates. These rivers, fed by the melting snows in the mountains of eastern Anatolia, flow southward into the Persian gulf. Because of the unpredictable amount of snow available in any one year, it was impossible to determine flood levels. This, combined with the flat surface of much of southern Mesopotamia, led to periodic, devastating floods which covered miles on either side of the rivers and even washed over whole cities. This may be the origin of the flood epics that appear in some of the earliest literature from ancient Mesopotamia.

The southernmost reaches of the Tigris and Euphrates system form a marshy region that was the home of the earliest human settlements in this area and still serves as the dwelling place for the "marsh Arabs" of Iraq. The rivers are widely separated as they traverse the hilly region of the southern Caucasus mountains, but at one point in their southern march, near the site of ancient Babylon, they are only a few miles apart.

The land the Tigris and Euphrates travel through is arid, and it is their waters that make life possible here. Initially, the marshy area in the south provided inhabitants fish and wild game as well as protection from outsiders. As the population grew, however, settlements moved northward and by 4000 BCE several **city-states** had developed in what will later become known as Sumer. This region comprised the land from the narrow confluence of the rivers south to the Persian Gulf. Cities like Ur, Nippur, Kish, Uruk, and Lagash were founded here, and they shaped their culture around life drawn from the rivers. Irrigation canals allowed them to extend their plots of farm land, create a surplus for trade, and expand their populations. The elements of their cultures, including writing systems, political organization, and religion will be discussed in the chapter on the history of these regions.

In this section, we will examine the other geographic areas of Mesopotamia. The region north of Sumer eventually developed another major population center, Babylonia. This section of the country came to dominate all of Mesopotamia during the period from 2000 to 1000 BCE. It borrowed many of the cultural advancements developed in Sumer, but its basic existence was still dominated by the dependence on managing the waters taken from the Tigris and Euphrates. Because rainfall is minimal throughout this region, irrigation is the only means of growing crops.

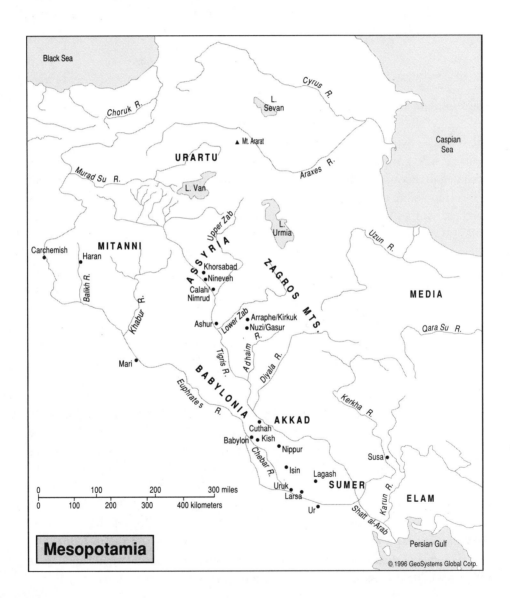

The third major region of Mesopotamia lies in the northern reaches of the Tigris and is known as Assyria. Here, from their capital at Nineveh, emerged some of the most savage and warlike people of the ancient world. Because of their northern position, they had a harsher climate, with greater temperature extremes, a shorter growing season, and more mountainous terrain. When they began to push out of their own area about 1000 BCE, the Assyrians quickly took control over the more temperate regions to the south and eventually extended their empire as far as Egypt. They were the first to control all of the regions of the ancient Near East and the first people to have to cope with the environmental as well as social demands of each of its geographic areas.

Egypt   Egypt is also dominated by a river system, the Nile. Nearly all of Egypt's culture and history developed within the Nile river valley since it is otherwise arid wastes and desert. The Nile flows north from the mountains of Kenya to the Mediterranean where it forms a fan-shaped estuary much like that near New Orleans on the Mississippi River. It is broken periodically in its flow by cataracts (rapids and waterfalls) which prevent easy passage to its source. Thus travel routes, guiding merchants carrying frankincense from Arabia and other exotic products, followed the Nile, but these travelers did not always voyage upon it.

Due to its more isolated position, cut off from the west by the Sahara, from the south by the Nilotic cataracts, and from the east by the Red Sea and the desert of the Sinai peninsula, Egypt developed much of its culture independently. There was contact with other peoples early in Egyptian history, but the Egyptians always considered their culture superior to all others and became quite **xenophobic** (fearful of foreigners) in their attitudes.

Unlike the unpredictable character of the Tigris and Euphrates Rivers, the Nile had an established cycle of flooding, which brought new layers of rich soil to the irrigated fields of the Egyptians. By building canals and dikes, farmers were able to reinvigorate their fields each year, making Egypt the breadbasket of the ancient world (see Gen 12:10 and 41:53–57).

The climate in this region is dry, having only small annual rainfall amounts. Temperatures are hot nearly year round, although they do moderate in the evening, and in the desert it can become quite cold. Egyptian culture, throughout its history, has been attuned to the rise and fall of the Nile and has acclimated itself, through clothing and architectural styles, to the extremes in temperature.

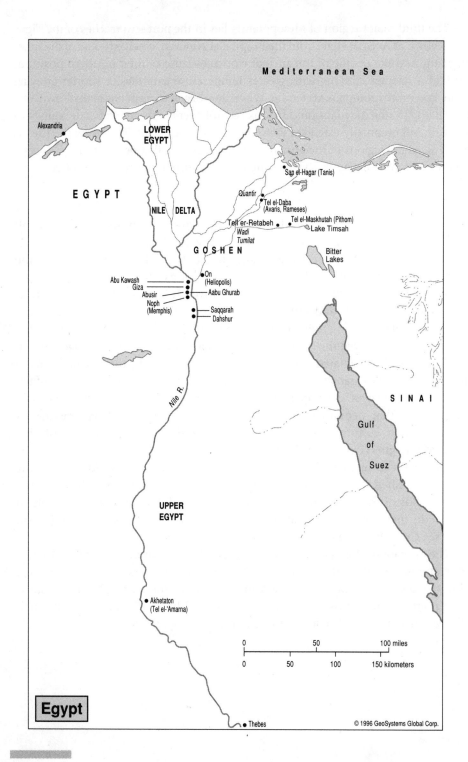

Egypt

© 1996 GeoSystems Global Corp.

Syro-Palestine No one can really understand the Bible without studying the geography and climate of Syro-Palestine. The events of the Bible happened in the spacial realm—mostly a small area—but this region contains a tremendous geographical and climatic diversity. Ideally we should charter a jet and take a trip to the Middle East to see and experience this for ourselves. Better yet, we could take a whole year to live and study abroad. Since these options are not always available, we will settle for a brief description based on the authors' experiences.

The areas to the north and east of Palestine include most of the traditional enemies and allies of ancient Israel. Immediately north is the region of Phoenicia (modern Lebanon), which dominated the trade on the Mediterranean Sea from approximately 1100 BCE until their absorption into the Persian empire after 540 BCE. Its climate is tempered by the sea breezes off the Mediterranean, but the mountain range that runs north–south through the country enjoys abundant rainfall (850–930 mm/year), supporting cedar forests in antiquity. The area has chilling temperatures during the winter months. The principal cities of Tyre and Sidon were the only deep-water ports along the coast, and this gave them the opportunity to take advantage of this. In fact, they are the second people in this area to control trade. From 1600 to 1200 BCE, the northern Syrian seaport city of Ugarit served the merchants who traveled throughout the Mediterranean. But it was conquered in 1200, and its expertise was inherited by the Phoenicians.

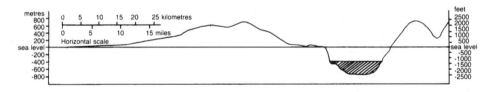

Cross-section of Holy Land. Design adapted with
permission from InterVarsity Press.

Syria, or Aram, comprised the land between northern Mesopotamia and Phoenicia. Its capital city of Damascus was a station stop for caravans as far back as 2500 BCE, and it served as the chief rival to the kingdoms of Israel and Judah during the biblical monarchic period. This city, located on the only perennial river, the Barada, in an otherwise arid region, created an oasis with enough irrigated land to support a large population. A land of mountains, plains, and deserts, Syria was able to maintain itself through trade and agriculture. Its temperature ranges are quite extreme due to the variations in elevation. In Damascus, it is hot and dry much of the year, but a few miles north, in the mountains, winter can have bitingly cold temperatures. Because of its strategic location on the trade routes, it was generally dominated by one of the Mesopotamian empires.

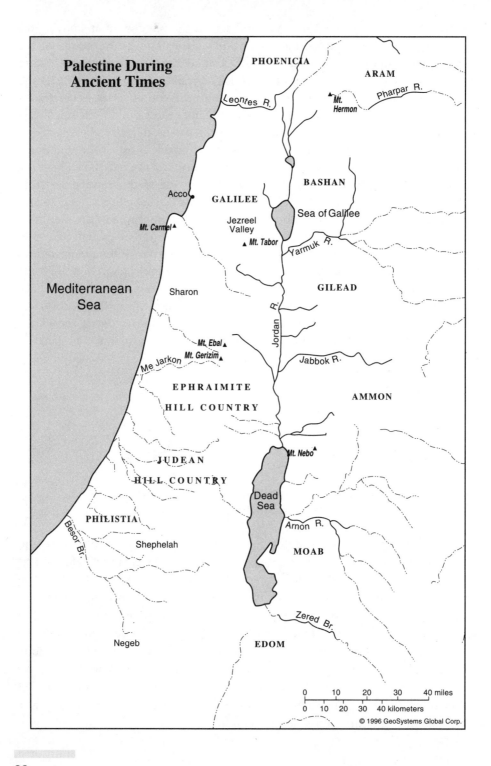

**Palestine During
Ancient Times**

PHOENICIA

ARAM

Leontes R.

Pharpar R.

▲ Mt.
Hermon

BASHAN

Acco

GALILEE

Sea of Galilee

Jezreel
Valley

Mt. Carmel ▲

▲ Mt. Tabor

Yarmuk R.

Mediterranean
Sea

Sharon

GILEAD

Jordan R.

Mt. Ebal ▲
Me Jarkon   Mt. Gerizim ▲

Jabbok R.

EPHRAIMITE

HILL COUNTRY

AMMON

JUDEAN

Mt. Nebo ▲

HILL COUNTRY

Dead
Sea

PHILISTIA

Arnon R.

Shephelah

MOAB

Besor Br.

Zered Br.

Negeb

EDOM

| 0 | 10 | 20 | 30 | 40 miles |
| 0 | 10 | 20 | 30 | 40 kilometers |

© 1996 GeoSystems Global Corp.

Turning south to Palestine, we begin with one December day, while we were living in Jerusalem, having bundled up in our heaviest overcoat. It was damp and blustery; the wind was whipping the cold through us, chilling us to the bone. We left Jerusalem, went twenty miles in about thirty-five to forty minutes, and came to the Dead Sea. There the temperature was in the balmy seventies, and we were soon swimming in the Dead Sea. How could this be? Though Jerusalem is only about twenty miles from the Dead Sea, it sits almost 2,700 feet above sea level while the Dead Sea is about 1,300 feet below sea level. The result is a 4,000-foot drop that results in a temperature change of about forty degrees. This kind of diversity is one reason for studying the climate and geography of Israel. Another significant reason is the fact that Israel has always been a centrally located land bridge between the two ancient super powers: ancient Egypt to the south (in Africa), and ancient Mesopotamia to the north. Travel between the two was not usually done on the Mediterranean Sea, nor was it done through the desert. Instead people traveled on land fairly close to the coast. This meant that ancient Israel served as a land bridge between the two superpowers. Its central location gave it a significance and prominence far exceeding the size of the country or its political power. Furthermore, it was impossible for ancient Israel to isolate itself completely from the superpowers. Consequently, throughout much of its history Israel was dominated by either Egypt or Mesopotamia.

What was the size of Israel? The best estimates suggest a total land area of approximately 8,000 square miles. This is slightly less than one of the small New England states like Vermont or New Hampshire. From a northern extremity to a southern extremity, such as Dan to Beersheba (Judg 20:1; 1 Sam 3:20), the distance was about one hundred forty-five miles. An average east–west distance would be from the coast to Jerusalem (around thirty miles) and from Jerusalem to the northern tip of the Dead Sea (about twenty miles); thus the east–west dimensions total about fifty miles. A helpful way to understand the geography and climate of the country is to think of the country as divided into four north–south strips of land:

Coastal Plain. Starting on the west is the coastal plain, which is characterized as a flat, low land with sand dunes right on the coast. A little further inland there were in ancient times fertile areas as well as forested or marshy areas. Lacking natural harbors, the ancient Israelites never really developed into a seafaring state, unlike their Phoenician neighbors.

The coastal plain includes three very fertile plains: Acre, Sharon, and Philistia. The Plain of Acre stretched to the north from Mount Carmel about twenty-five miles and extended inland anywhere from five to eight miles. It never figures prominently as a significant geographical feature during biblical times. Probably it was controlled much of the time by Phoenicia. To the south of Carmel for about fifty miles lay the Plain of Sharon. It extended inland about ten miles. Because it was generally a marshy wasteland in biblical times, it did not figure as a prominent region either. Still further to the south was the Plain of Philistia, named after the Philistines, another of Israel's neighbors. It was one of the most fertile areas in the country. The Philistines conquered and controlled it until the days of David.

Through this coastal plain stretched an international route or highway called the *Via Maris*. It ran a few miles inland from the sea, and near the northern part of the Plain of Sharon it cut inland through a mountain pass in the Carmel range. Armies and traders usually did not continue further north because the Carmel range of hills extend to within one hundred fifty yards of the sea. That narrow pass was not safe to travel through since it would make the traveler an easy prey for enemies or bandits. So Megiddo became especially prominent because it guarded the mountain pass through which the Via Maris extended.

The climate in the coastal plain is extremely hot in the summer. During the day the temperatures range around one hundred degrees. A sea breeze at night makes the temperature tolerable. Most modern inhabitants of Israel live in Tel Aviv, which is in this coastal plain. They have balconies on their apartments so they can enjoy the night breezes. In the winter the temperatures go down into the forties and fifties, though there is no frost because of the moderating influence of the Mediterranean Sea. This allows all kinds of citrus fruits to be grown in the coastal plain, including the famous Jaffa orange, as well as grapefruits, lemons, limes, and avocados. A large portion of the coast has inviting sandy beaches where many Israelis head on weekends.

Central Hill Country. The second north–south strip is called the central hill country. As one moves from the coastal plain up to this hilly region there is a transitional region called, in Hebrew, the Shephelah. This Shephelah region is characterized by gently rolling hills as one goes further and further inland toward the east and up into the central hill country. The hills are really just low, ranging slopes. They extend up to 3,300 feet high in the area around Hebron, but they certainly are not high enough to be called mountains.

The central hill country was the chief center of ancient Israel's population in antiquity. This is because these hills were heavily wooded in antiquity, and were the easiest region for ancient Israel to capture without the advanced weaponry of the Canaanites. The area can be conveniently divided into three sections: in the north was Galilee, in the center was Samaria, and in the south was Judah. The most important geographical feature in Galilee was the Valley of Jezreel. This was an important and fertile region. The city of Megiddo was located here and gained its importance because it guarded a mountain pass along the international highway, the Via Maris. In the center were the hills of Samaria. The most famous hills here were Mount Ebal and Mount Gerizim. To the south were the hills of Judah. In the most southern sections of Judah was a desert.

A limited amount of grain could be grown in the central hill country, but agricultural work was difficult. The hillsides had to be terraced. Fig and olive trees were common. The grazing of goats and sheep was also more typical here than in the coastal plain.

During the summer the climate is hot and dry with temperatures around ninety degrees. At night it is breezy and comfortable, at least most of the time. Because of the wind that comes up in the evening, it can get chilly at night. During the winter this is a difficult place to live. The temperatures are in the thirties and forties, and it is rainy, damp, and blustery. There is even some frost, though the average temperature does not often go below thirty-two degrees and snow is uncommon.

Jordan River Valley. The third north–south strip is the Jordan River Valley. This is a gigantic rift or geological fault starting in the north in Syria and extending southward all the way into Africa. Much of it is below sea level. Lake Hulah in the north was two hundred thirty feet above sea level. However, in the twentieth century it has been drained and so it does not appear on modern maps. Only ten miles to the south is the Sea of Galilee, which is seven hundred feet below sea level. The Jordan River flows out of the Sea of Galilee and empties into the Dead Sea. The Jordan River covers a distance of only about seventy miles, but it travels such a circuitous route that the actual banks of the Jordan River cover close to two hundred miles. The Dead Sea is well known as the lowest water surface on earth. It is about 1,300 feet below sea level, with the lowest depth of the sea at the northern end somewhere around 2,600 feet below sea level. It is so warm in this region that no outlet is needed. The water evaporates and the salt content is so high that nothing can live in the Dead Sea. Around Jericho, just north of the Dead Sea, the average annual rainfall is only two inches per year. Furthermore, the Jordan River cuts such a deep path into the soil that it is not very valuable for irrigation purposes. In biblical times, it was too difficult to raise the water level to the surrounding land to use for irrigation. The result was that little land was tilled in this region except around Jericho where there was a spring that allowed for the growing of citrus fruits and vegetables. During the summer the hot and dry temperature averages around one hundred degrees. At night the temperature cools down to the sixties. In winter the high temperature is in the seventies and swimming in the Dead Sea is always a possibility. As with the coastal plain there is no frost in winter.

Transjordan Plateau. The fourth north–south area is the Transjordan Plateau. The climate is similar to the central hill country, but the terrain is flat ranging from about 2,000 feet high in the north to about 5,000 feet high in the extreme south. The region is fairly fertile but there is not enough rain in much of the area to produce extensive crops. Again, as in the central hill country, sheep and goats are common livestock. This north–south strip is divided by four streams. They are the

Yarmuk, the Jabbok, the Arnon, and the Zered. Each flows to the west and together they divide the transjordan plateau into five areas: to the north of the Yarmuk was the land of Bashan; between the Yarmuk and Jabbok was Gilead; between the Jabbok and the Arnon Rivers was the kingdom of Ammon; south of the Arnon was Moab; and finally south of Zered was Edom. The Ammonites, Moabites, and Edomites were neighbors of ancient Israel.

Exceptions to the Rule. It is important to understand that there is a dry season in the summer that extends from much of May into most of September. So for four to five months each year one can plan each day without ever having to worry about rain. There is also a rainy season that is concentrated between December and March. Of course, the total rainfall varies dramatically from around two inches in the desert regions to over forty-five inches in parts of Galilee.

CONCLUSIONS

It is now time to draw some conclusions about what we have learned. First, it is obvious that ancient Israel was primarily agricultural and pastoral. The majority of the people throughout biblical history earned their living from agriculture and/or from animal husbandry. Second, the hills and valleys made transportation difficult from one region to another. Therefore the regions developed in their own distinctive ways and attempted to preserve those distinctions. Third, the hills and valleys kept people isolated from each other and prevented political unification. When we read the book of Judges, for example, it is obvious why the tribes could not get together and unify. They were basically people with regional differences who did not easily mingle with each other or join together as political entities.

STUDY QUESTIONS

1. What are the most important geographical features of Mesopotamia and Egypt and how do they affect those countries?

2. Why is it valuable to study the climate and geography of ancient Israel?

3. Describe the four regions of Israel with respect to climate, geography, and location.

4. Define: city-state, xenophobic, Via Maris.

2

THE PREMONARCHIC PERIOD

THE BOOK OF GENESIS

We have chosen to begin our survey of the Old Testament/Hebrew Bible with Genesis because we find students respond best to a linear approach based upon the Bible itself. Since Genesis purports to describe the beginnings of the universe, it is a natural beginning for us as well. The material in the book of Genesis was not compiled and edited until the latter part of the monarchy or the early Persian period (ca. 500 BCE). Genesis describes the political and religious foundations of the nation of Israel rather than offering a scientific picture of the origins of the earth and the human race. Where **anachronisms** (terms or events in the text that do not fit the time period being described) occur in this description, we will point them out and try to explain them.

Primeval History: Like many of the nations and cultures of the ancient Near East,
Genesis 1–11   the Israelites formulated their own history of the "beginning
                         time." The Israelites had two main goals in their primeval epics:
(1) to portray their god as sovereign, without challenge, and **transcendent** over creation; (2) to present a pattern of relationship with their god that eventually led to the covenant with Abraham in Genesis 12 and the establishment of the Israelite people in the exodus event. These goals were accomplished through a series of **etiologies** (stories explaining origin and causation) and **genealogies** (family histories).

The Israelites shared much of the world view of ancient Mesopotamia. Much of the material contained in the primeval epics in Genesis is borrowed from other ancient Near Eastern cultures. This is what makes the study of nonbiblical epics so valuable. By making comparisons and by seeing the general religious and literary environment of the ancient Near East, it is possible to understand better how the Israelites perceived their world.

Peace panel from Ur (twenty-fifth century BCE), the purported home of the famous ancestor Abraham. Courtesy of the British Museum.

What is particularly interesting about the Israelite use of foreign epic material is the ability of the Israelites to transform the religious dramas and the epic motifs and structures of the ancient Near East into a distinctive model that was uniquely their own. The exact time period in which this process began is unknown. Most likely it started about 900 BCE as part of the efforts of the monarchy to solidify its power more fully and to demonstrate a longstanding claim to the land of Palestine. The structuring of some of this material into **liturgical** drama (patterned sequences in worship or ritual; see p. 48 on Gen 1:1–2:4a) and the material's descriptions of monotheistic religion suggest a strong priestly influence. The union of political and priestly elements in the primeval epics may be the result of a partnership between palace and temple that was designed to create a sense of "roots" for the nation. It could also reflect a later reworking of the stories shortly after the exile (ca. 500 BCE).

Perhaps the best way to demonstrate the use of ancient Near Eastern material in biblical epic is by comparison. Later we will sketch the close ties between Mesopotamian creation epics and those in Genesis. Both are products of a literary and cultural climate shared; the points where they diverge indicate distinct theological perspectives.

In the chart below, the differences between the polytheistic system of ancient Mesopotamia and the Israelite monotheistic system portrayed in Genesis 1–4 and 6–9 can be clearly seen. In ancient Mesopotamia and Egypt, the gods were personifications of the forces of nature. They represented the wind, the storm, the sea, and the forces of fertility, all of which both harassed and benefited the human communities. Like the forces of nature, they at times appeared to be at odds with each other. Rain is needed for crops, but too much rain becomes a flood that carries away people, houses, animals, and crops. The sun can ripen grain or burn it to nothing. The sea provides a bounty, but it also erodes the land, becomes a raging monster when driven by the winds, and can take a voyager's life all too easily.

Polytheism Compared to Monotheism	
Polytheism	**Monotheism**
many gods	one God
immanent gods	transcendent God
capricious gods	consistent God
amoral gods	moral God
cosmic combat between gods	absence of divine challengers to the one God
different gods associated with each human political entity	a universal God operating outside human political entities
gods dependent on humans	God independent of humans

Because these mighty forces could not easily be addressed or visualized, they were portrayed as nearly human and given **anthropomorphic** qualities. They spoke, walked, and made love just like humans. The epics characterized them with human emotions and failings, such as jealousy, anger, and ambition.

The composers of the creation and flood epics of ancient Mesopotamia used these human characteristics and combined them with the imagery of the tensions that they observed in nature to create their descriptions of primeval events. The resulting narratives described primordial history in terms of cosmic combat for supremacy among the gods. Thus when Apsu, the primordial god of watery chaos, decided to destroy all of the younger gods in order to restore the "peacefulness" of original chaos, Ea, the god of the channeled (ordered) waters, assassinates his father and becomes the ruler of the gods. In this way political change takes place (one god kills another), and order symbolically triumphs over chaos.

This drama illustrates both how early farmers managed their water resources with irrigation canals and how such resources figured in the politics of that day. It was believed that each of the gods was the patron of one of the ancient city-states of Mesopotamia. When the city-states went to war against each other, the gods also fought. The winning city-state would not only loot the towns and villages of the loser, but they would also collect the images of the losing gods and hold them hostage in the temple of their victorious patron god. Ea's defeat of Apsu thus represents a political change of fortunes.

Tiamat, the opponent of Marduk in the *Enuma Elish*
creation epic, in monstrous form.

A transfer of political power is also the basis for the second stage of the *Enuma Elish* creation epic. The version used by scholars dates to the Old Babylonian period (2000–1500 BCE) and is obviously intended as both religious and political propaganda. Babylon and its chief god, Marduk, gain supremacy through a cosmic battle and an ordering of the world. Again, the principal danger to the order of existence and the gods is a primordial deity—Tiamat, the female counterpart to Apsu. With the help of an army of dragons, she prepares to seize control and take revenge for the murder of her consort Apsu. To meet this threat, the gods turn to a new champion, Marduk, the god of storms and patron of Babylon. Ea's withdrawal from this struggle and his replacement by Marduk serve as a political statement of change in regimes from southern to central Mesopotamia.

Marduk meets Tiamat in single combat, and with the aid of the winds that he commands he kills her. Her army of dragons and rebellious gods is rounded up and her lover Kingu is executed. From the blood and bodies of the slain will come the creation of the earth. Tiamat's body is cut in half, with the upper portion becoming the heavens and the lower becoming the earth. Her blood becomes the oceans, rivers, and streams. The gods are each given tasks to perform in this newly created universe, but the real work is assigned to humans, who are created from the blood of the slain rebel Kingu. It will be their job to manage the resources of the earth and pay homage to the gods through prayer and sacrifice.

The epic concludes with the construction of a massive stepped pyramid in Babylon, known as the *Esagila* temple. This structure, probably the model for the story of the tower of Babel in Gen 11:1–9, provided the symbol of power for Marduk and Babylon, marking them as the chief powers in Mesopotamia. The political aspect of the epic is emphasized by the ascent of Marduk to the position of "king" of the gods and the placement of Babylon and the dynasty of the human king Hammurabi at the center of a Mesopotamian empire.

Genesis Creation Accounts. The Genesis accounts of the creation utilize some of this Mesopotamian material as well as other epics composed in ancient Egypt. However, they contain unique reorientations of the material that make them distinctively Israelite. The first of these accounts, Gen 1:1–2:4a, is composed in the form of an outline. Only the bare minimum of information needed to provide sequence and order in the story of the creation of the universe is given. This matches what would be expected in a literary **framework story**, a device common in biblical narrative. A framework story is a narrative that has an outline that can be used to provide structure for other narratives. It offers a sort of fill-in-the-blank form that can be utilized for different stories. The inset on the liturgical framework of Gen 1:1–2:4a presents the elements of the creation framework. If we can assume that the role of creation stories in other ancient traditions has relevance, the creation story may have served as the outline for a religious drama performed as part of the new year's celebration. It could also have functioned as a set of steps in a liturgy or sacrificial ritual designed to celebrate the Sabbath, the day of rest established to commemorate Yahweh's creative act.

Gilgamesh, the Mesopotamian hero of the Akkadian *Epic of Gilgamesh*.

The Liturgical Framework of Gen 1:1–2:4a

1. Creation by the word ("And God said, 'let there be . . . ' ")
2. Certification ("God saw that it was good")
3. Manipulation of the newly-created item
4. Naming
5. Transition ("And there was evening and there was morning, the ___ day")

There are some similarities between the version of creation in Gen 1:1–2:4a and that found in the Egyptian "Memphite Creation Story." For instance, a sense of majesty and complete control over creation is shared by the Memphite version and the account in Gen 1:1–2:4a. In both epics creation takes place by means of the word. This contrasts with the picture of the creation of humankind through the manipulation of the substance of the creation in Gen 2:7 (dust) and in Marduk's creation of humans in the *Enuma Elish* from the blood of a rebellious god.

The creation story found in Gen 2:4b–24 is more of a narrative with a story line, emotion, crisis, and instructive qualities. In this account, the single human is created first, rather than in a pair at the end of creation as in Gen 1:26–27. The purpose of the human is not made clear in this story until a second human is formed as a "partner" to the first (Gen 2:18–22). Together they are given charge of the garden of Eden and its inhabitants. The story then concerns itself with the etiology of why humans are no longer living in the garden and why death came into the world. The expulsion of Adam and Eve from the garden marks one of many turning points in the human story, in this case from an existence of deathless leisure to a world of work, pain, and personal striving.

In both Genesis stories, only one deity is named, although Gen 1:26 mentions the **Divine Assembly:** God says, "Let us make humankind" (NRSV); and in Gen 3:22: "See, man has become like one of us." Like other ancient Near Eastern cultures, the Israelites projected into the divine realm their own use of an assembly of advisors who assisted royal decision making. The use of the plural pronoun here therefore reflects a heavenly court over which Yahweh presides (see also 1 Kgs 22:19–23).

The biblical account assumes no cosmic battle with other gods. Yahweh is completely transcendent over the creation, untouched by the power of nature. However, the use of the word *tehom* for the "void" may be a reference to Tiamat of the Babylonian epic. If this is the case, then it is a clear attempt to **demythologize** the story by turning a divine being into an unpersonified state of nature. The only interaction in the Genesis narrative is between Yahweh and the humans, and there is no sense that they have any power to contravene the creator's intentions.

Genesis Flood Accounts. Other elements of difference between the Genesis accounts and those from Mesopotamia are more evident in the flood epics. The various ancient Near Eastern accounts of the flood, including those in Genesis, provide many close parallels with each other. They all follow the same basic sequence of events: (1) a decision is made to destroy all life on earth with a flood; (2) a god warns a human and instructs him to build an ark, or boat, that will allow the survival of a portion of the human and animal life; (3) the flood waters are unleashed on the earth and all life outside the ark is exterminated; (4) the ark comes to rest on a mountaintop and a series of birds are sent out to determine when the waters have receded; (5) a sacrifice is made after the ark is emptied; (6) a sign is placed in the heavens marking the end of the flood. Where differences occur between the stories, they are based in large part on the contrast between polytheism and monotheism (see the inset above). The comparisons and contrasts listed below attempt to show that Noah, unlike Utnapishtim in the Gilgamesh epic, is never left to his own resources during the flood. His survival is due to God's intervention. Utnapishtim's survival reflects the triumph of humanity over the destructiveness of nature.

(1) The decision to destroy all life on earth is made by the assembly of the gods in the Gilgamesh and Atrahasis epics. In the Gilgamesh epic no reason is given for the flood. In the Atrahasis epic the flood is designed to eliminate a noisy nuisance without any concern for a moral judgment.

(2) When Utnapishtim is warned by the god Ea in the Gilgamesh epic, it seems almost accidental that he is on the other side of the wall when Ea speaks. The god thereby maintains a degree of deniability by not seeking out Utnapishtim. He apparently picks a spot at random in which to speak a warning.

(3) It takes the collective efforts of all the gods in both the Gilgamesh and Atrahasis epics to bring the flood into being. Each god contributes his or her particular attribute of power. In the Gilgamesh epic, Utnapishtim is forced to lock himself within the ark only after it has begun to rain. In Genesis, Yahweh closed the ark for Noah before it began to rain, showing divine concern that is lacking in the Gilgamesh epic.

(4) During the height of the storm in the Mesopotamian epics, the gods cower like frightened dogs behind a wall or scream in terror. Only when the powers that have been unleashed by the gods subside do the flood waters begin to recede. The arks of the Mesopotamian heroes come to rest without the guidance or help of the gods. The Mesopotamian gods neither can nor desire to help the survivors of the flood.

(5) Once they exit the ark Utnapishtim and Noah both build altars. Noah's altar is designed to give thanks, but Utnapishtim's altar simply forms the basis for reviving the old symbiotic relationship between humans and the gods. Utnapishtim's sacrifice basically serves as a bribe to secure the hope that no further calamity will occur.

The Mesopotamian gods respond to Utnapishtim's offering "like flies" who have been starved, rushing to the sacrifice to feed. Ironically, they apparently had overlooked their own dependence on the sacrifices of humankind to maintain themselves.

(6) In the epic of Gilgamesh, Ishtar places her necklace in the heavens once the flood sequence is completed. Ishtar's necklace serves as a memorial of the flood, but unlike Yahweh's rainbow in Genesis, Ishtar's necklace does not function as a guarantee that floods will not devastate human society again. Utnapishtim and his wife are taken away to the Eden-like land of Dilmun where they become immortals. In contrast, Noah is faced with the task of rebuilding human culture. He is given the same command to "be fruitful and multiply" (Gen 9:1) that had been given to humankind (Gen 1:28) in the first version of creation.

The similarities between the stories suggests that literary borrowing may have occurred between the Israelites and Mesopotamian culture. Since the Gilgamesh and Atrahasis epics predate the composition of the Genesis account, it is most likely that they served as the model for the Noah story. It is possible that the Mesopotamian epics and the Genesis account are all based on an earlier version, but there is no proof of its existence. In any case, once the Israelites had reshaped their story, it took on the elements of their own understanding of Yahweh, the transcendent creator God, who deals justly with the creation.

This latter attribute will become a favorite theme throughout the Bible. In the flood story it is assumed that Yahweh is just and therefore by definition cannot destroy righteous humans without first warning them of the approaching doom. Thus Noah, the only righteous man of his time, is warned of the flood, is given the chance to take action, and survives as a remnant of earth's population. His family benefits from his righteousness based on the legal principle of **corporate identity:** because the head of the household is the legal representative for the entire family, what he does can bring reward or punishment on them all. This legal idea dominated much of Israelite thought and history until the time of Jeremiah and Ezekiel (sixth century BCE) when the crisis of the destruction of Jerusalem and the exile transformed Israel's understanding of redemption and individual responsibility.

Ancestral Narratives: Genesis 12–50   The primeval history concludes with a section listing the genealogies following the flood and a few etiological stories explaining the dispersal of the earth's peoples (tower of Babel, Gen 11:1–9). After the primeval history, a quasi-historical narrative begins. Genesis 12–50 describes several generations of a family founded by a couple named Abram and Sarai. During the course of the story God changed the names of this couple to Abraham (meaning in Hebrew "father of a multitude") and

Sarah ("princess") to signify that God had chosen them to be the ancestors of the great nation of people that would later be known as Israel. The story is set first in Mesopotamia, in the ancient city of Ur of the Chaldees. The use of "Chaldees" is an **anachronism** because "Chaldees" is an ethnic term that applies to a people who dominated Mesopotamia from 600 BCE until 540 BCE. This gives us a clue as to when this material might have been edited into its final form. Certainly, some of it may date back to the second millennium BCE, but in many cases the events and places of the story are more important to the political history of the Israelite monarchy or even the exilic period (after 600 BCE) than to the time ascribed to the ancestors (about 1800–1600 BCE).

Abrahamic Covenant

- God promises Abraham land and children
- Sign of the covenant:
  Circumcision serves as a physical sign of covenant membership and as a sacrifice
  Abraham promises God obedience and worship

The principle theme throughout the ancestral narratives is the establishment of the **covenant** and the trials associated with determining who would become the heir of that covenantal promise. A **motif**, a repeated story line, appears in which the potential or the "proper" heir is endangered. This is accomplished by the **barren wife** theme, and the search-for-the-heir theme. Each of the primary ancestral wives is barren for long periods of time (Sarah for ninety years, Rebekah for twenty years, Rachel for an unspecified period). The difficulty of overcoming a wife's inability to produce an heir is combined with numerous attempts on the part of the ancestors to create and identify the heir for themselves. Abraham does this three times before Yahweh provides a son to the elderly couple. Isaac chooses the wrong twin son as his heir, and Rebekah and Yahweh have to join forces to straighten out the problem. Jacob, who has twelve sons, eventually has to acknowledge as his heir one of the youngest, Joseph. In each case, the tension created by the "search for the heir" leads to a climax when the heir is identified (or born). The movement of the narrative toward this climax underscores the heir's importance.

Another of the curiosities of the ancestral narratives is the limited details in the stories. The historicity of the characters cannot be established with any certainty, and the storyteller does not seem to be concerned with fleshing out the details of social life in a way that would provide a more comprehensive picture of the times being portrayed. For instance, Abraham is called from Haran to Canaan by Yahweh, but there is no mention of the events of the journey. In one verse he and his household

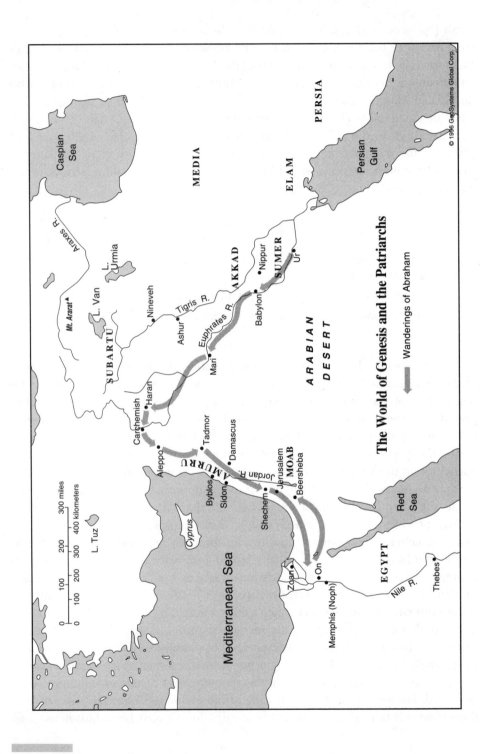

The World of Genesis and the Patriarchs

➡ Wanderings of Abraham

are in Mesopotamia and in the next they are in Canaan, near the city of Shechem. Such a monumental trek surely generated an epic tale, but for reasons known only to the editor of this text, it is not included here. Speculation is possible, of course. For some features of Abraham's journey, a fairly full picture can be drawn based on our knowledge of the movements of peoples during the second millennium BCE and the practical needs of travelers in that time period.

Route of Travel.   After leaving Haran, which was located near the headwaters of the Euphrates River, the most likely route traveled by Abraham's household was the international trade route that curved southwest from the northern Euphrates region to Tadmor (Palmyra). From Tadmor the route continued on to Damascus and Hazor, passed through the Jezreel valley to Megiddo, headed southward through Canaan, and stopped in Egypt. This well-traveled road was used by merchant caravans, messengers from various governments, and pastoral nomadic groups. Pastoral nomads probably used the highway more as a marker than an actual route of travel. They would have allowed their flocks and herds to graze along the way; they would not, as stateless persons, have wanted frequent contact with persons or groups outside their own company. One such group is known in ancient texts as **khabiru** (in Mesopotamia; ʿapiru in Egypt).

Since the biblical text does not explicitly mention any of the probable stops along the route, one can only surmise brief stops for supplies, perhaps bartered in exchange for a surplus lamb or goat. The only indication of one of these stops may be the mention of Eliezer of Damascus in Gen 15:2–3. He is described as Abraham's heir, a "slave born in my house." Adoption of a servant as an heir is certainly not unknown in the ancient Near East. What may be important here is that the young(?) man may have been picked up by Abraham during a stop in Damascus, just as Hagar, the Egyptian slave woman, was apparently added to the group during its stay in Egypt.

Retribalization.   Preparations for Abraham's departure from Haran include only the statement: "Abram took his wife Sarai, and his brother's son Lot, and all the possessions that they had gathered, and the persons whom they had acquired in Haran; and they set forth to go to the land of Canaan" (Gen 12:5a).

A household group is described here: a head of household, his wife and heir, their servants, and their baggage. This is the bare minimum of detail needed by the audience. Surely this household group realized that a journey of several hundred miles was about to be undertaken through sometimes hostile regions. Some provision had to have been made to protect the family and provide for its needs along the way.

Later in the narrative we are told that Abraham had flocks and herds. These animals would have served as a form of "capital on the hoof," a combination of ready food supply and portable bank account. We are not told whether Abraham had any previous experience handling animals. But most persons of that time and place surely would have had some familiarity with them, and his servants would have functioned as herdsmen.

How does a person hitherto associated only with village living make the transition to life as a pastoral nomad? One possible way of answering this is by referring to the process of adaptation known as **retribalization**. This phenomenum, noted among Middle Eastern peoples in modern times, involves the movement back and forth between sedentary village life and seminomadic pastoralism. The transition away from sedentary life sometimes occurs because of economic exigency (such as a business failure), a war, too much political pressure from the local or national government, or a famine or epidemic that requires a move away from the village. A return to the village may be the result of a disaster that decimates the herd, growing economic prosperity that allows for the purchase of property, or the influence of government agencies to control the movement of herdsmen.

In Genesis, Abraham is portrayed as a villager who becomes a pastoral nomad. The description of Abraham's transition to pastoral nomadism was not intended to represent a shift in permanent occupation. The intent of the narrative is to picture him as an immigrant who, for the purposes of the journey and until he can acquire a holding in the new land, must maintain flocks and herds as his livelihood (see the map for major sites associated with the ancestral narratives).

Immigrant Psychology.   This change of social condition would have brought with it a change in social attitude as well. Abraham, on the death of his father Terah, had assumed the role of head of the household. The responsibilities and powers of village life differed from those in the tents of a nomadic group. There would have been elders in the village to consult, friends and neighbors with whom to socialize and share concerns. From the moment his household left Haran, Abraham was faced with the opportunities and the dangers of being a "stranger in a strange land."

The traveling company associated with Abraham would have had to rely upon each other completely. They could not have expected to receive more than simple hospitality from strangers, and quite often they could anticipate being treated as undesirables. They would have immediately been recognized as strangers by their manner of dress, their speech, and their general appearance. Because they were not citizens of the places that they visited, they would not have been protected by local laws. Their unfamiliarity with local custom could have drawn them into hostile encounters.

They would not have been welcomed in every village or city. When a famine struck Canaan (Gen 12:10), Abraham's household was forced to leave and seek food and perhaps employment in Egypt. Even when they had gained a certain measure of respect, such as Lot's right to sit (doing business) in the gate area at Sodom, their status as resident aliens (Hebrew *ger*) sometimes was used against them by the local population (see Gen 19:9). Abraham was called "a prince among us" by the elders of Hebron (Gen 23:6), but they took advantage of him when he bargained with them for a burial place for his wife.

The result was the development of defense mechanisms designed to either camouflage or protect the members of the group. For example, Abraham demonstrated diplomatic abilities in his encounters with the pharaoh of Egypt and Abimelech of Gerar. He was willing to deceive both of these kings, lying about his marital status and accepting their proffered bride price for his wife and sister Sarai. In addition, Abraham performed a series of acts designed to lay claim to the land of Canaan. His first official act upon entering Canaan was to build an altar near Shechem (Gen 12:7). He repeated this ritual performance east of Bethel (Gen 12:8), near Hebron (Gen 13:18), and on Moriah (Gen 22:9). His planting of a tamarisk tree at Beersheba had a similar ritual function (Gen 21:33). Each of these places (if the tradition that equates Moriah with Jerusalem is correct) became a major cultic or historical site in later Israelite history. Abraham's association with these places, rather than the many others his group visited, shows the selective editing process once again.

Abraham's two final steps in laying claim to the land suggest Abraham's (or the editor's) intentions to obtain legal title to this area. In the first, Abraham makes a covenant with Abimelech of Gerar that substantiates the pastoralist's right to dig and use wells in that region (Gen 21:25–34). The narrative also includes the statement that Abraham "sojourned many days in the land of the Philistines" (Gen 21:34). While the term "Philistine" is anachronistic, because "Philistines" were not present until after 1200 BCE, one of the elements of the text indicates that gaining access to water rights allowed a nomadic group to settle for a time (compare Isaac's similar experience in Gen 26:12–22).

The second episode that functions as a legal claim to the land is found in the story of the cave of Machpelah (Gen 23). Abraham, who has apparently dwelled with his household near the settlement of Hebron for a fairly long period, follows the proper legal protocol when attempting to purchase a burial cave for his family. He speaks first to the elders, asks for their help as witnesses and intermediaries, and then negotiates with the owner of the cave. In the process, he is charged an exorbitant price and forced to accept adjoining property that he originally did not request. The editor's intent may be to demonstrate how the Israelites first gained legal title to the Promised Land, but the elements of the narrative expose once again the reality of immigrant life—strangers are most often at the mercy of the local inhabitants.

Trickster Themes.   The tenuous position in which the ancestors found themselves required inventive responses. Each ancestor figure functions as a trickster, a character who takes advantage of the weaknesses or even the strengths of their antagonists.

One of the most important trickster stories is the **wife-sister motif** found twice in the Abraham/Sarah cycle (Gen 12:10–20 and Gen 20) and once again in the Isaac narrative (Gen 26:1–11). This **framework story** includes the following elements: (a) instruction to lie about the wife's status to save the life of the husband; (b) payment of the bride price by a local ruler; (c) Yahweh's infliction of the local ruler; (d) recrimination and return of the wife. The story functions as a contest between Yahweh and the local deities (i.e., pharoah), demonstrating who is the most powerful (compare the story of the ten plagues in Exod 7–12). As such, it provides both enrichment for the ancestral household and comic relief as the weak defeat the strong. Finally, it fits into the search-for-the-heir theme in which the wife (and thus the potential heir), in danger, is rescued by Yahweh.

The Jacob cycle is a continuous series of trickster stories in which Jacob successively tricks his brother Esau (Gen 25:29–34), his father Isaac (Gen 27:5–29), and his uncle/father-in-law Laban (Gen 30:35–43). Jacob, like most trickster figures, is tricked in turn by Laban (Gen 29:22–28) and by Yahweh's angel (Gen 32:24–31). Many of the intricate maneuvers in these episodes revolve around the search-for-the-heir theme, attempting to ascertain first who will receive the blessing of the covenant and then showing how Jacob eventually achieved the status to take up his role as heir of the covenant (which in this case involves household and possessions).

The narrator helps the audience see who the rightful heir will be by employing **disqualification stories**, narratives that portray the other candidate(s) as unworthy. For additional examples of this literary form see the anti-Saul stories in Judg 19; 1 Sam 10:17–27; 13:1–15:35.

In the Joseph cycle of stories (Gen 37; 39–50), the extraordinary abilities of one of Jacob's sons provide the backdrop to another contest with pharaoh. Joseph sinks to slave status and then rises to a position of great power and authority. His life functions as a microcosm for the past and future history of the Israelites during the monarchy and exilic period. They saw themselves as rising from slavery to new heights. Joseph's abilities to interpret dreams merely provides him with the edge needed to trick the pharaoh and his own brothers and is the basis for the move to Egypt. His rise to prominence, despite the fact that he is not the oldest son of Jacob, is the political model for David to become king, despite his being the youngest son of Jesse.

In spite of the sketchy character of much of the ancestral narratives, they provide a basis for inferences about the social world that is the setting for the episodes. This is not to say that the ancestors are historical characters. Even composite creations must follow established social patterns to maintain a modicum of reality in the stories. Certain actions would have to be taken to make the journey from Haran possible. Certain attitudes, including suspicion and near paranoia, would be generated by both the immigrant group and the people of the lands the group visited. By reading the text in the light of the elements of retribalization and immigrant psychology, we can uncover some of the text's ancient context.

STUDY QUESTIONS

1. Discuss the literary and religious connections between Mesopotamia's creation and flood stories and those in the Bible.

2. Describe the terms of the covenant with Abraham and the way in which the wife-sister strategy endangered it in the narrative.

3. Define "trickster" and point out how Jacob and Laban fit the definition using specific examples from the text.

4. Define: anachronism, transcendent, etiological, genealogies, liturgical, framework story, divine assembly, demythologize, symbiotic relationship, corporate identity, covenant, retribalization, disqualification stories, anthropomorphic.

THE EXODUS-SETTLEMENT PERIOD

Historical
Background

The second major historical era described in the biblical text is the period of the exodus-settlement. This period includes the escape from Egypt, the wilderness wanderings, the conquest, and the era of the judges. There is a great diversity of lifestyle described in the biblical text, based on the transition from pastoral nomadic wandering after the flight from Egypt to a sedentary existence in the village culture of Palestine. Refugee groups were forced to adjust to new patterns of living and accommodate themselves to life within Canaan. Lacking the strength to capture walled cities, the people who would eventually become the Israelites settled primarily in the hill country of central Palestine.

Establishing a clear historical setting for this period is not easy. The biblical account in 1 Kgs 6:1 places the exodus in the fifteenth century BCE. The strength of the Egyptian presence in Canaan during this period and other chronological difficulties make this date problematic.

Biblical Date of the Exodus

In the four hundred eightieth year after the Israelites came out of the land of Egypt, in the fourth year of Solomon's reign over Israel . . . he began to build the house of the Lord (1 Kgs 6:1).

Extrabiblical sources for a clear date for the exodus-settlement period are very scarce. The evidence of archaeology is also incomplete and in some cases contradictory. Egyptian sources do not mention the exodus, although there is evidence of the use of forced labor gangs to construct the Egyptian storehouse cities of Pithom and Pi-Ramses in the time of Seti I and Ramses II (ca. 1300–1250 BCE). This fits the description of the Israelite slaves who built these cities or others of similar name recorded in Exod 1:11.

The settlement of so-called *ʿapiru* tribes in the delta region of Egypt is also mentioned in Egyptian texts. The name *ʿapiru* or *khabiru* appears to be a generic term for stateless persons or tribal groups who lived on the fringes of the settled areas of the ancient Near East. They sometimes served as surplus labor or as mercenaries, but they appear as brigands and raiders in texts from several different historical periods (from 2000 to 1200 BCE) and in several different areas. While there is no direct linguistic connection between *khabiru* and Hebrew, the description of a people without roots who live on the fringes of society and who sometimes infiltrate the poorly defended areas does fit the biblical description of the Israelites.

Tomb painting from Beni Hasan, the Aamu Group.

The only documentary evidence from Egypt of Israel as a people is found in a victory stele of Pharaoh Merneptah dated to ca. 1208 BCE. This inscription lists the regions and cities that the pharaoh conquered during an expedition into Palestine. In the only line in the inscription that mentions a specific people, it states that Israel was laid waste. The language of the inscription is typical of many other similar victory announcements, and the inclusion of Israel may reflect knowledge of their existence, but not necessarily contact with them. The pharaoh may just be boasting that he has subdued all of the peoples in the area. Still, it is the first known extrabiblical mention of the name Israel and the best available evidence of this people's existence in the thirteenth century BCE. Additional discussion of this period and the conquest narrative will appear later in this chapter when we deal with the book of Joshua.

The Figure of Moses
Moses dominates the Exodus narrative and ultimately becomes a prototypical Israelite leader and prophetic figure. His life story is divided into three periods of exactly forty years each and begins with a "miraculous survival" story, a form often used in the ancient world to signify that an individual is a significant person. For instance, there are great similarities between Moses' birth story and those of Sargon of Akkad, a great ruler of ancient Mesopotamia (ca. 2500 BCE), and Jesus in the New Testament (Matt 2). In each case the child survives a potential death threat, is raised in a foreign land or foster household, and eventually becomes an influential leader of his people.

The career for which Moses has been spared premature death begins during his second forty-year period. He had been forced to flee Egypt after killing an Egyptian taskmaster and had joined the company of a pastoral nomadic tribe living in Midian (Sinai and eastern Arabia). Moses had married one of the daughters of Jethro and it appeared that he would spend the remainder of his life in obscurity. However, that tranquil existence ended with a **theophany** on Mount Sinai (exact location unknown, traditional site is in the southern part of the Sinai peninsula). Moses was "called" to lead his people out of Egypt (Exod 3–4). This "call narrative" provided a model for the call narratives in the later prophetic tradition. Prophetic call narratives follow this pattern: (1) the appearance to a human of a divine being; (2) the demur or excuse made by the person called to serve; (3) an empowering event that puts aside all such excuses; and (4) a charge for mission that provides explicit instructions.

Moses is accompanied by his brother Aaron in this mission, which ultimately becomes a contest with the pharaoh, who was considered to be a god in Egypt. Thus the struggle for supremacy in this story is actually a contest between gods: Yahweh and pharaoh. The "plague sequence," which forms the body of this contest, is simply designed to demonstrate that Yahweh, the God of creation, is superior to the forces of nature. All but the last plague contains elements of environmental disaster (polluted river, plagues of insects, diseased animals, hail, and darkness), and in every case the pharaoh is unable to deal effectively with the challenge.

Perhaps the most important element in this **framework story** is Moses' ability to predict a plague, have it occur on cue, and then predict the end of the plague and have this occur on cue as well. The question might be asked, Why are there ten plagues? The repetition may simply be didactic or have some connection with the Ten Commandments, which form a significant part of a later portion of the Moses narrative.

Plague Sequence Pattern

- Moses and Aaron ask the pharaoh to allow the Israelites to worship for three days in the desert.
- When the pharaoh refuses, Moses predicts a plague.
- Pharaoh, unable to stop the plague, asks Moses to intercede and promises to allow them to go.
- Moses prays and Yahweh ends the plague.
- Yahweh "hardens pharaoh's heart" and the Israelites are not allowed to leave.
- Moses once again approaches pharaoh.

The most important of the plagues is the last one, the death of the firstborn son. This final plague, which convinces the pharaoh to actually allow the Israelites to depart, has a much more important ritual purpose. The sequence of actions described in Exod 12 form the basis for later reenactments of the Passover and become the single most important ritual in the Israelite religious calendar.

Route of the Exodus After departing from their villages in Egypt, the Israelites travel south (Exod 12:37). This was done to avoid the Egyptian military posts along the more direct "Way of the Philistines," which ran along the coast. (The name of this road in the narrative is anachronistic, because the Philistines did not settle in Canaan until after 1200 BCE.) The Israelites are guided by a pillar of cloud during the day and a pillar of fire at night. These are divine manifestations of Yahweh's power (Exod 13:20–22). During this journey a motif appears that will dominate the story of the Israelite wanderings—the **murmuring motif.** The Israelites grumble about a lack of food or water or about Moses' leadership. This motif is followed, in most examples, by the punishment of the Israelites. In the narrative of the departure from Egypt the murmuring motif serves as a prelude to the Red Sea crossing.

The story of the crossing of the Red Sea (Exod 14) fits into a category of stories involving miraculous events. The ancient Israelites, not living under the influence of a modern scientific worldview, saw no problem in describing the waters of the Red Sea opening up, allowing the Israelites to cross on dry land. This simply served as another example of Yahweh's power as creator. There are many other miracle stories found in the biblical text. They too reflect a belief in the intervention of Yahweh into human affairs and the manifestation of God's power over the elements of nature.

The events described in the biblical narrative of the Red Sea crossing are difficult for the modern student and scholar alike. Scholars attempt to understand this story in essentially two ways: (1) they search for natural explanations, or (2) they investigate the possible symbolic/mythic patterns that provide the context for these events. For example, many scholars point to the words *yam suph* in the Hebrew text and translate them "Reed Sea." This fresh-water marsh existed in the area of Egypt where the Suez Canal now connects the Mediterranean Sea with the Red Sea. It is easier to imagine a group of Israelites escaping through a marsh while the heavy chariots of the pharaoh became bogged down. Other scholars translate this phrase as "Sea of the South," a legendary region where watery chaos threatened to overwhelm the ordered universe. Yahweh's ability to hold these waters in check thus represents God's protective attitude toward the Israelites.

Having escaped Egypt, Moses leads the Israelites through the Sinai wilderness to Mount Sinai. Along the way two important events take place. First, the people's murmuring leads Moses to ask Yahweh for help, and God provides "manna and quail" (Exod 16:1–21). The quail are migratory birds that regularly fly over the Sinai and thus their presence can be explained easily. The "manna," a breadlike substance that melts in the sunlight, is more difficult to identify. Among the suggestions is the excrement of a kind of locust that taps the moisture of desert plant life and leaves an edible residue on the stems. Yahweh's initial provision of food was the occasion for the institution of the first law. They were instructed not to gather manna on the Sabbath (Exod 16:22–30).

The other major event during this trek is the confrontation with the Amalekites (Exod 17:8–16). These people were pastoral nomadic tribes who did not appreciate a new people entering their territory and using up their water and pasture. The conflict between the Amalekites and the Israelites furnished an opportunity to present the **Divine Warrior** theme. The Israelites were not well armed or trained as warriors. Thus in order to defeat the Amalekites, Moses was instructed to raise his arms over his head. As long as he stood in this position the Israelites were victorious, and Yahweh fought for them (Exod 17:14–16).

The Giving of the Law   The events at Mount Sinai center on a renewal of the cove-nant that Yahweh originally made with Abraham and an exten-sion of that agreement to include a more formal "treaty" with the Israelites known as the Decalogue or Ten Commandments. As part of these events, the role of Moses as the supreme leader of the people is highlighted and enhanced. He alone speaks directly with God, and even his brother Aaron, who serves as chief priest for the people, is portrayed as a weak leader when Moses is absent (Exod 32).

The giving of the Ten Commandments is preceded in the text by a statement of purpose in Exod 19:4–6. These verses state the reason for Yahweh's intervention on behalf of the Israelites in Egypt and then set forth the terms upon which the future relationship with the Israelites will be based. This, along with the Shema, "Hear, O Israel: the LORD is our God, the LORD alone" (Deut 6:4), forms the basic creedal statements of Judaism.

Eagles' Wings Catechism (Exod 19:4–6)

[4] You have seen what I did to the Egyptians, and how I bore you on eagles' wings and brought you to myself. [5] Now therefore, if you obey my voice and keep my covenant, you shall be my treasured possession out of all the peoples. Indeed, the whole earth is mine, [6] but you shall be for me a priestly kingdom and a holy nation.

Then, in Exod 20:1–17, the Decalogue is set forth in **apodictic** style. These are "command" laws, which do not require much explanation and do not contain the "If . . . then" sequence more common in "case" law. The Ten Commandments can be divided into two segments:

Communal statutes apply to the conduct of the entire nation. (a) They are to worship only one God. There is to be no other god set "before" Yahweh. This is not a statement of monotheism. It is **henotheism**, the belief in many gods with a greater emphasis placed on a particular one. (b) They are forbidden to construct or worship idols. Idol worship was a common practice in the ancient Near East. To restrict the people from the use of images made them unique and increased the mysterious character of Yahweh. (c) They, like other peoples, were to be cautious in invoking the name of God since that made the deity a party to their oath. (d) The setting aside of a day of rest each week was unique to Israel. Sabbath (seven) was a recognition of Yahweh as creator. (e) The command to "honor your father and mother" ensured that the aged would be taken care of and the wisdom of elders would be respected. Note the equality of genders here.

Personal statutes set the code of conduct for each person. These laws were common in other cultures and were designed to maintain order and protect the rights of property owners.

Law Codes   It should be noted that the remainder of the laws in Exodus, and those found in Numbers, Leviticus, and Deuteronomy, are primarily case laws. In nearly every instance, they are reflections of the legal formulas presented in the Ten Commandments and are the result of judges or individuals asking the question, But what if? about a particular legal phrase. Since they are designed to regulate the life of the people, it was necessary for the law to change as the social situation of the people changed. They could not be governed by laws meant only for nomadic herders when they had become farmers and urban dwellers ruled by a king. For example, the group of laws that relate to caring for the "poor" (including widows, orphans, and resident aliens) can be traced back to the commandments to honor parents, the prohibition against theft, and the injunction against coveting. They each speak to a particular legal situation that required an expansion of the law so that it dealt more directly with current concerns. At the heart of this expansion is an exhortation to remember "where you came from." The period of slavery in Egypt is continually cited as the basis for legal restraint or legal guarantees (Deut 5:15; 15:15; 16:12; 24:18).

Seven Major Bodies of Law

1. **Decalogue:** Exod 20:1–17; Deut 5:6–21
2. **Covenant Code:** Exod 20:18–23:33
3. **Ritual Decalogue:** Exod 34:11–26
4. **Deuteronomic Code:** Deut 12–26
5. **Holiness Code:** Lev 17–26
6. **Priestly Code:** Lev 1–16, 27; Num 1–10
7. **Curses Code:** Deut 27:14–26

There are many similarities between these law codes and those found elsewhere in the ancient Near East. The *Code of Hammurabi* (*CH*; eighteenth century BCE) and the *Middle Assyrian Law Code* (*MAL*; eighth–seventh centuries BCE) contain so many laws that are similar to those in the Bible that it seems quite likely that legal formulas were transmitted between cultures just as other ideas, customs, technologies, and styles were. For instance, both Hammurabi's Code and biblical law contain the principle of **lex talionis**, "an eye for an eye." This is based on the idea of complete reciprocity for loss or injury. Even here, however, the primary difference between ancient Near Eastern and biblical law can be found. The legal codes of the Israelites demanded full equality for all of the people, with no exceptions even for the king. In ancient Babylon, there was a multitiered social system in which citizens did not receive the same punishment as slaves for similar injuries.

Israelite Laws Relating to the Poor

- Debts were to be canceled every seventh year (Deut 15:1–2).
- Loans to the poor should be made without interest (Lev 25:35–37).
- Debt slaves were to be freed after six years of labor (Exod 21:2).
- The edges of fields were not to be harvested so that the poor could glean them (Lev 19:9).
- The poor were entitled to the same legal rights as the rich in the courts (Deut 16:19).

Another difference is found in the apparent harshness of Israelite law. There are many crimes for which capital punishment is prescribed, and in no case is there a loophole that allows the convicted parties to be released or to pay a fine, as is the case in the laws from Mesopotamia. This is due to the concept of purity which is inherent to biblical law. If the society wished to remain pure, it could not take half measures in dealing with criminal behavior because this would eventually contaminate the entire nation. Thus a rebellious son is to be stoned to death (Deut 21:18–21) in order to "purge the evil from your midst."

The inset below illustrates some of the similarities and differences between ancient Near Eastern and biblical law. What is particularly striking in these examples is the more objective character of Mesopotamian law. For instance, there is a sense of poetic justice in requiring the amputation of the hand of a son who strikes his father (*CH* 195). In Israelite law, however, both father and mother are mentioned and the death penalty is imposed to prevent this action from becoming acceptable in their society.

Crime and Punishment in Mesopotamia and Ancient Israel

False Witness:

CH (Code of Hammurabi) 1: If one citizen charges another with murder without the evidence to prove it, then the plaintiff is sentenced to death.

Deut 19:16–19: If a malicious witness comes forward to accuse someone of wrongdoing, then both parties to the dispute shall appear before the LORD, before the priests and the judges who are in office in those days, and the judges shall make a thorough inquiry. If the witness is a false witness, . . . then you shall do to the false witness just as the false witness had meant to do to the other. So you shall purge the evil from your midst.

Adultery:

CH 129: If the wife of one citizen is caught having sexual intercourse with another, then both are sentenced to the ordeal of being tied and thrown into the river; however, if the woman's husband grants her a pardon, then the monarch can pardon her partner.

Deut 22:22: If a man is caught lying with the wife of another man, both of them shall die, the man who lay with the woman as well as the woman. So you shall purge the evil from Israel.

Parent Abuse:

CH 195: If a citizen strikes his father, then the sentence is the amputation of a hand.

Exod 21:15: Whoever strikes father or mother shall be put to death.

Sorcery:

MAL (Middle Assyrian Law Code) 47: If either a man or a woman prepares magical potions or objects and is caught with them in his or her possession, then the sentence, following due process, is death.

Lev 20:27: A man or a woman who is a medium or a wizard shall be put to death; they shall be stoned to death, their blood is upon them.

The **covenant renewal ceremony** found in Exod 24:3–8 completes the picture of the rededication of the people at Mount Sinai. It also provides the model for understanding three other major shifts in the history of the Israelite people. The purpose in Exodus is to reestablish the covenantal relationship with Yahweh's chosen people and set them on a course that will once again bring them to the Promised Land. Moses' orchestration of a communal renewal of the people's vow of obedience to the covenant also expresses the ideology behind the commandment about using God's name. By accepting their position as people of the covenant, they invoke Yahweh as their judge. This will later be the principle upon which God will punish their disobedience as they begin their trek from Sinai to the Promised Land.

Covenant Renewal Ceremony

- Assemble the people.
- Publicly read the law.
- Ask for a recommitment to the law by the people.
- Perform a sacrifice or tie the recommitment to a major religious festival.

The Wilderness Period   Shortly before leaving Mount Sinai, Aaron and his sons were instructed to construct a portable shrine known as the **ark of the covenant**. This was a lidded box that contained the tablets of the Law as well as other sacred objects. It was carried by members of Moses' tribe, the Levites, and it was housed, while the people were encamped, in an elaborate tent. This **tabernacle**, or tent of meeting, was structured so that the ark was placed in a separate part of the tent (the Holy of Holies). The tent was surrounded on all sides by a high screen that formed a rectangular courtyard around the tent. In this courtyard, Aaron and his sons would perform animal sacrifices for the people. This portable shrine and its priests set a precedent and pattern for religious activity in later periods when the temple was constructed in Jerusalem.

With these objects in hand as symbols of God's presence with the people, the trek from Sinai began. Preceding the settlement in the Promised Land was a period of purification and punishment during which the entire older generation of Israelites died in the wilderness. This was a result of their failure to keep the covenantal agreement (they worshiped a golden calf in Exod 32:1–10) and the recurring **murmuring motif,** which included periodic rebellions against Moses' leadership (Num 12:1–3; 16:1–35). All of those who were adults at the time of the departure from Egypt, except for Joshua and Caleb, died during this forty-year period. They were the only ones among the twelve spies sent by Moses into Canaan who reported that the Israelites could successfully take the land (Num 13:25–33). Even Moses and Aaron died before entry into the land because they also failed to obey Yahweh's commands on every occasion (Num 20:2–13).

In addition to the **culling process** that gradually diminished the Israelites' numbers (Num 21:4–9), the wilderness period was also characterized by the emergence of Joshua as a military leader, a role he continued to play in the conquest of Canaan. As the wilderness period came to an end, the Israelites engaged in a series of military encounters in Transjordan that highlight Joshua as the new leader of the people. This is also when Moses dies, an event which takes place on Mount Nebo shortly after Moses is allowed to view the land that he would never enter (Deut 34). Once again the people have been brought to a new stage in their history. Now their task is to conquer and settle the land.

Arguments for an Exodus Event

- The negative depiction of Israel in Egypt is not likely to be a total invention. People seldom tell such stories about themselves unless they have some historical background.

- The detailed description of the events again points to a strong historical tradition for the exodus.

A postscript to this narrative must include the warning that there is no extrabiblical evidence for these stories or any others prior to the monarchy. Moses is never mentioned in contemporary Egyptian records and neither is the exodus itself. Assuming that the exodus did take place, it is possible that only a portion of the Israelites, perhaps only the Levites, were involved. The importance of the Levites within the temple community during the monarchy could then explain the magnification of the role of Moses in this narrative.

The exodus event is extremely important in the theology of the prophets. Many times Yahweh used the exodus as the basis for recriminations against Israelites who did not appreciate what had been done for them (Jer 2:6–8; Hos 11:1–7; Amos 3:1).

STUDY QUESTIONS

1. Discuss the chronological problems for dating the exodus.

2. Discuss the significance of the following: burning bush theophany, plague sequence, Passover, and Red Sea crossing.

3. Discuss the difference between apodictic and casuistic law and give examples of specific case laws that evolved from the Decalogue.

4. Why are the laws of ancient Israel often similar to those of ancient Mesopotamia?

5. Define: *yam suph,* henotheism, lex talionis, ark of the covenant, tabernacle, culling process, framework story.

THE BOOK OF JOSHUA

The book of Joshua portrays the conquest of Canaan in an idealized manner as a series of victories (often miraculously won) by Yahweh, the **Divine Warrior,** and the people of Israel. In these stories, Joshua emerges as a "new Moses," and on many occasions his career parallels that of Moses. This portrayal was necessary to ensure that he would be accepted as the new leader of the people. It also ensured continuity of leadership and commitment to the covenant.

Moses and Joshua Compared

- Yahweh tells Joshua he will be with him "just as I was with Moses . . . " (Josh 1:5; cf. Exod 3:12).

- Both Moses and Joshua send spies into Canaan (Num 13:1–3; Josh 2:1).

- Both Moses and Joshua direct the Israelites to cross a body of water miraculously on dry land (Exod 14; Josh 3:7–17).

- Both Moses and Joshua hold out their hands until military victory is complete (Exod 17:8–12; Josh 8:18–26).

- Moses brings Israel into the covenant and performs a covenant renewal ceremony; Joshua also performs a covenant renewal ceremony (Exod 24:3–11; Deut 29:2–30:20; Josh 24:1–28).

Joshua's task as Moses' successor was not an easy one. He had to shoulder the responsibilities of leadership and conduct a military campaign. The biblical writers portray him as an obedient servant of Yahweh, but there are at least two instances where his personality comes through in the narrative. The first is found when he is surprised by the Israelites' failure to capture Ai (Josh 7:6–15). He discovers that God considers a commander responsible for the actions of his soldiers as well as his own. In the other example, Joshua's ego is inflated by the false claims of the Gibeonites who are trying to save themselves from defeat by the Israelites. Joshua takes an oath that he cannot break and finds himself defending a portion of his sworn enemies because of this personal mistake (Josh 9:3–27).

The Conquest Account   Evidence for the conquest period, as described in the book of Joshua, is problematic. The only discussion of this holy war occurs in the biblical text. Archaeological investigations of the major sites said to have been destroyed by the Israelites have provided mixed results.

Jericho, the first city listed as conquered by the Israelites, has been extensively excavated three times in the twentieth century. Despite some early claims that the remains of Joshua's Jericho had been found, it has generally been determined that there was no major walled city existing on that site in the period between 2000 and 1100 BCE.

Ai has also proven to be a puzzle. Excavations at this site (1965–75) by Joseph Callaway demonstrated that the mound was not a significant population center between 2400 and 1200 BCE. It is possible that it was used as a military outpost by the nearby city of Bethel, which does show evidence of destruction in the thirteenth century, but there was no major settlement of Ai as described in Joshua. The name of Ai, which means "the ruin," may have contributed to its addition to Joshua's list of conquests, but there is no way to prove this.

Excavations at Jericho, the reputed site of Joshua's first victory
in the Israelites' conquest of Canaan. Photo L. DeVries.

Other cities, including Hazor, Lachish, and Tell Beit Mirsim, do have destruction levels that date to the thirteenth century. However, it is unclear whether their destruction is the result of any effort by the Israelites. They could just as easily have been part of the general destruction of the area during Merneptah's expedition, or they could have been the victims of the invading Sea Peoples. This latter group raided much of the Near East around 1200 BCE. They conquered the Hittite kingdom in Anatolia, destroyed the seaport city of Ugarit in northern Syria, and nearly defeated the Egyptians. Portions of their group split off after 1200 BCE to settle in Palestine, and they became known as the Philistines.

With so many conflicting pieces of information, it is best to take a cautious view of the Israelite conquest of Canaan. Several theories have been proposed to explain the disparities between the archaeological evidence and the description of a nearly total victory sweep by the Israelites in Josh 1–12. One possible explanation is that the text in Joshua is not as interested in historical details as it is in making the theological point that the victory was engineered by Yahweh, the **Divine Warrior**. Each battle is won because of the direct intervention of God. For instance, the fall of Jericho is not based on a conventional siege or strategy, but rather on the opening given to the Israelites when Yahweh destroyed the city's walls.

A certain selectivity may also be evident in the conquest account. There is no clear indication of how long the conquest took to complete. Possibly some cities fell to a wave of immigrants while others succumbed to later attacks. The Israelite tribes may have entered Canaan over a fairly long period of time, with each successive wave adding to their numbers and victories. Other migrating groups or even Canaanites (e.g., the Gibeonites in Josh 9:3–15) may have joined forces with the Israelite tribes as they began to settle in the hill country. This could have in turn undermined the authority and strength of the Canaanite culture, already under fire from both the Egyptians and the Sea Peoples, and eventually allowed the Israelites to dominate some areas.

Joshua is said to have destroyed the strategic city of Hazor in his
northern campaign (Josh 11). Photo L. DeVries.

The Israelites assimilated themselves into Canaanite culture after settling initially in the underpopulated areas of the hill country. As they learned the technology and social skills of the Canaanites, they gradually merged with the dominant culture. In time the Israelites came to control larger areas and some cities with only the Philistine city-states in the south central plains of Palestine providing major opposition by the time of King David (ca. 1000 BCE).

The conquest of Canaan is depicted in the book of Joshua as a swift, three-pronged campaign. In chapters 1–12, the Israelites gain almost immediate access to this promised territory because of two things: (1) the obedience of the people to Yahweh's commands and (2) the repeated intervention of the Divine Warrior. Thus the walls of Jericho fall flat because Joshua follows Yahweh's instructions to stage a series of religious processions around the city for a seven-day period (a number commonly associated with Yahweh's creative act in Gen 1). The shout of the Israelites on the seventh day invokes the presence of Yahweh and ensures victory (Josh 6:1–21). Similarly, in the battle against the combined forces of the five Amorite kings (Josh 10), Joshua follows Yahweh's instructions to attack after an all-night march from Gilgal. Because of this unfailing obedience, Yahweh joins the battle, casting hailstones on the enemy to confuse them and then miraculously extending the daylight so that the slaughter could be completed (Josh 10:12–13).

Besides episodes of obedience, the biblical text also reports an example of what happened when the Israelites failed to follow instructions. In Josh 7:2–5, Joshua's forces fail to capture the city of Ai. After praying to Yahweh to determine why they had been defeated, it was revealed that a man had taken loot from the city of Jericho (Josh 7:6–15). This violated the **kherem** command of complete destruction and in essence was a theft from God. The punishment of all the people for the sin of one is an example of **corporate identity.** Lots were cast to identify the culprit, a man named Achan, and then he and his entire family and their animals were stoned to death as an example to all the Israelites (Josh 7:16–26). This use of a technique of psychological warfare ensured strict obedience on the part of the Israelites and demonstrated to the enemy the determination of Israel to capture the land. It also reflects the continued emphasis on the Deuteronomist's theology of total obedience.

Another theme in the conquest narrative in the book of Joshua is **universalism**. In the case of Rahab, the prostitute of Jericho, one interpretation of her actions in helping Joshua's spies escape is that they were based on a genuine conversion to Israel's God. This allows her to save her family's life as well, but that is secondary to the supremacy of the power of Yahweh. Having recognized Yahweh's power, she makes a statement of faith far stronger than anything previously ascribed to an Israelite: "The LORD your God is indeed God in heaven above and on earth below" (Josh 2:9–11). This type of statement, made by a non-Israelite, functions as a recurring theme throughout the biblical text (see inset).

The Universalism Theme

The theme of universalism pervades the biblical text from the book of Joshua through the later prophetic writings of Isaiah and Jonah. As it initially appears, the theme is introduced through a *non-Israelite* character, who performs some task that shows Yahweh's power (Balaam, Num 22–24), or a personally experienced work of power (Naaman, 2 Kgs 5). What makes this so effective as a theme is that these actions or statements often show a greater faith in Yahweh than some of the people of Yahweh demonstrate.

A later usage of the universalism theme attempts to show that it is the job of the chosen people to share their knowledge of Yahweh's power with non-Israelite people. Thus Second Isaiah, in his "Servant Songs," says that once the returning exiles have restored Zion, their mission is to be a "light to the nations" (Isa 49:6). Like a lighthouse, the Israelites are to bring the Gentiles to the light of the Torah. Similarly, in Third Isaiah, the prophet argues against restrictions on those who may worship in the newly rebuilt temple in Jeruslaem. He says that only an acknowledgment of and an adherence to Sabbath worship is required to become a worshiper of Yahweh (Isa 58:13–14).

Perhaps the most powerful of the later universalistic stories is found in Jonah. In this book, set in the period of Assyrian domination (eighth century BCE) but most likely written after the exile, God directs the prophet to preach repentance to the city of Nineveh. This city was greatly hated by the people that Assyria conquered; Nineveh's inhabitants were the target of many imprecations (e.g., see the curses laid on them in the book of Nahum). Thus it is not surprising that Jonah refuses. However, the prophetic commission cannot be resisted, and ultimately Jonah carries out his task and saves the city. This story thereby demonstrates Yahweh's concern for his entire creation, even the most onerous.

Conquest Theories   One of the primary difficulties with the account of the conquest in Josh 1–12 is that there is no supportive physical evidence (either artifactual or textual) supplied by archaeological excavation. Jericho in the twelfth century BCE was apparently only partially occupied. The massive wall systems uncovered by archaeologists have been proven to date to the period around 2200 BCE, long before the time assigned for the conquest period. Similarly, Ai was an abandoned ruin during much of the twelfth century BCE and was only reoccupied when a small village site was established there in the latter part of that century, perhaps by Israelite settlers. It too had once been a large city, but this earlier occupation was also dated to the third millennium BCE.

While there are other sites (Bethel, Lachish, Hazor) that do have evidence of destruction dating to the twelfth century BCE, there is no way to assign these attacks with certainty to the Israelites. It could be possible to ascribe them to the Sea Peoples, the Egyptians, or some other people.

Because of the failure to discover corroborating archaeological evidence that matches the account in the book of Joshua, scholars have attempted to provide alternative theories on the conquest. These theories are based on known historical events and economic pressures during the time associated with the conquest; i.e., the twelfth century BCE.

Infiltration/Migration Theory. According to this theory, a series of migrations took place in which Israelites (or peoples who eventually became identified as Israelites) gradually moved into the region of the central hill country in Canaan. This theory is bolstered by archaeological surveys in the area, which have shown the establishment of over one hundred new village sites (most housing seventy-five to one hundred twenty-five people) during this period of time. There is no conclusive explanation given for why this occurred. It may be the result of the invasion of the Near East by the Sea Peoples after 1200 BCE. Remnants of the Canaanite population may have fled to the hill country when the Sea Peoples attacked or after the Philistine segment of this invading force established itself along the southern coast and in the Shephelah. These indigenous Canaanites would have retained a portion of their previous culture and technology, but the hardships of life in the marginal region of the hill country would have driven them into a lifestyle based more on a subsistence economy. In this situation, the local supply of labor may have been inadequate and they may have welcomed the addition of new people who entered the area. Thus a synthesis of Canaanite and "Israelite" forces would have created a new culture in the hill country. A conquest per se would have never taken place (thus explaining the lack of archaeological data). Instead, the situation as described in the book of Judges, in which the Israelites are "oppressed" by their neighbors, would be the real picture of the early settlement period.

Withdrawal Theory. Taking into account the likelihood of a political vacuum after the invasion of the Sea Peoples and the movement of new peoples into the hill country, this theory adds the factor of economic and social exploitation of the lower classes by the ruling elite in the Canaanite cities. According to this view, the rigid social structure in these cities prevented movement between social classes or political and economic advancement. This caused major discontent among the lower classes. The monumental construction projects, heavy taxes, forced labor, and military service of these Canaanite states further contributed to the climate of discontent. When the Israelite threat appeared, people from the Canaanite peasant classes chose to withdraw their support from their own leaders and joined the Israelites. They were attracted by the egalitarian spirit of the Israelites and the chance to advance themselves among a new people. One example that is pointed to in support of this view is the story of Rahab. As a prostitute, she would be a member of the lower class and thus her willingness to help Joshua's spies is based more on the survival of her family and the likelihood of a better life among the Israelites than on the strength of their god. Her statement of faith in Josh 2:9–11, while typical of the belief that victorious peoples have powerful gods, is designed to ingratiate and explain her actions to the spies.

The actual explanation for the conquest narrative in Joshua may share elements from the ancient narrative and from both modern theories. It is impossible to prove whether or not the exodus occurred, and whether or not ex-slaves actually forced their way into Canaan and eventually established a people known as Israel. It may be that the Joshua account, written down during the later monarchic period, is idealized because its purpose was to bolster public support for the monarchy and the state. The narrative in Judges, which was probably compiled in the period shortly after the establishment of the monarchy and which speaks of the failure of the Israelites to capture portions of the land, may have a different purpose. The book of Judges was a strong argument for the existence of the monarchy, as opposed to the weak, anarchic tribal period that preceded it. By promising strong centralized leadership, David and his successors could use the Judges material to their political advantage.

Settlement in the Hill Country   Whether the taking of Canaan is the result of a "conquest," as is depicted in Joshua 1–12, a mass immigration of new peoples as a result of the invasion of the Sea Peoples after 1200 BCE, or a rejection of the legal and social constraints of the Canaanite urban centers of the plains, the hill country villages formed a new social environment for the settlers. They were faced with new environmental and economic challenges in this marginal region. They were also removed from continuous contact with the urban centers of Canaan. The result was a struggle to survive as a viable economic group and as a political entity separate from the urban centers of the plain.

The economy of the biblical world relied upon the two basic resources of land and progeny (Gen 12:1–8), which it was committed to develop (Gen 1:26–28). Land and progeny distinguished free households from their slaves. The free citizen had land and progeny; the slave did not.

While these villagers were mostly farmers and herders, the Bible seldom explains farming or herding, but simply assumes that the audience understands these jobs so well that no additional details are needed. Farmers are simply portrayed as using the tools and installations necessary for life in the hill country. Plowing, planting, threshing, and winnowing form a part of their everyday life. For instance, the stories of Gideon (Judg 6:11, 36–40) refer to a threshing floor and wine press at Ophrah, but the writers do not describe them because there was a threshing floor to process grain and a wine press to squeeze grapes in or near every village. Herdsmen are said to take their flocks to pasture as needed, but there is no detailed discussion of this process (see Gen 37:12–17 and the allegory of the good shepherd in Ezek 34:11–24).

Oil press. Olive oil was a staple of life in the ancient Mediterranean, a resource for food, fuel, cosmetics, and medicine. Photo A. Kerkeslager.

The range of what each village planted and of the animals they herded was determined by the physical environment of their settlement site. There were many different kinds of local geography with which farmers had to contend. There was desert to the east; highlands to the north and south; slopes and foothills to the west. For instance, the Hebrew villages farthest north of Jerusalem lived on a land marked by outcroppings of limestone and poor soil. Each village, by necessity, adapted its farming techniques to match the potential of its environmental conditions with existing technology. Experimentation undoubtedly took place, and successful farmers would have become the models for others until new technology allowed for differentiation or expansion into previously unworkable regions.

A standard harvest in the hills produced ten to fifteen times the grain which was needed to plant it. Positive changes in the quality of the land, the number of farmers available, and the way in which they worked could increase the standard harvest. But there was always a greater risk of negative changes that could destroy the economy of the village and its households. Fields that produced as little as a tenfold to fifteenfold harvest in good years failed altogether in three years out of ten.

To get the most from the labor available in the village, farmers used a variety of techniques. They managed their time, pooled their resources, and had as many children as possible. Farmers staggered sowing by planting a single crop in several stages over a period of time. Although it would be impossible for them to care for a single large crop at one time, the same number of farmers could handle the comparable size crop one section at a time. Planting in stages also provided some insurance against losing an entire crop when the planting and harvesting rains were off-cycle.

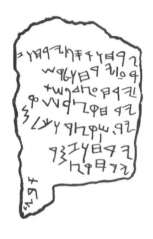

The Gezer Almanac

Two months to pick the olives,

[One] . . . month to sow the barley.

Two months to sow the wheat,

One month to pull the flax.

Two months to harvest the barley,

One month to harvest the wheat . . . and to feast!

Two months to prune the vines,

One month to pick the fruit of summer

(*OTPar*, p. 105).

The Gezer almanac offers a unique glimpse into the ancient agricultural cycle.

Farmers planted a variety of cereals along with tree, vine, fruit, vegetable, and nut crops. The technique had two effects. Like staggering the sowing of a single crop, varying the kinds of crops they planted allowed farmers to spread out their work. Trees and vines do not require attention at the same time as cereals. Planting more than one crop also restricted the damage done by plant disease. Since the disease or drought that affects one crop does not always affect others, planting a variety of crops prevented the loss of an entire harvest. Even when one particular crop failed completely, there was still a chance that others would survive.

The Gezer Almanac preserves an example of a typical farm schedule indicating the kinds of crops planted. Around 1000 BCE, a young farmer at Gezer practiced writing on a piece of soft rectangular limestone about four inches long and four inches wide. The text was an almanac that matched each month with a particular chore. It had the same number of seasonal divisions as the year. Like the agricultural cycle, it arranged the parts of the year in a planting-cultivating-harvesting pattern. The almanac graphically demonstrates the diversified agricultural picture of the hill country. The use of both wheat, which is a slow maturing grain, and barley, which matures quickly in poor or salty soil, provided successive harvests and allowed the work force time to harvest one crop and process it before the next one ripened. Finally, grapes and figs could be harvested at the end of the summer without interfering with major grain harvests. In a region where the labor supply seldom met labor requirements, spacing of major farming events would have been absolutely necessary.

Farmers in the villages in early Israel worked long hours and full weeks. Together they cleared land, terraced fields, planted, cultivated, and harvested crops. Living together in pillared houses made it easier for farmers to pool their labor.

The pillared house was one of the most common types of dwelling found in ancient Israelite villages. Pillared houses excavated so far reveal a variety of different patterns employed to meet space and environmental demands. These houses were designed to meet the same three basic needs: living and working space, space for livestock, and storage space for grain, animal fodder, and products such as wool.

The pillared house was a simple rectangle, divided lengthwise into three areas by a row of roof-supporting pillars on one side and a solid wall on the other. The row of pillars was nearer to one long wall, creating an area about four and one-half feet wide on the narrow side and about ten feet wide on the other. Some houses had an additional room across the back of the basic rectangle, entered through a door off the main section of the house. Wooden beams six to eight inches in diameter were set into notches in the solid outer wall of the house and extended to the pillars and inside wall. They supported a roof which was six feet above the floor. The roof itself was made up of slats coated with a layer of white clay. There was no furniture. People sat cross-legged on the packed clay and stone floor or on a stone ledge along the base of the inside wall of the house. Flat stones were used for stools. Everyone slept on the floor. Several households shared a common outdoor courtyard kitchen. Bread was baked on a pottery bowl inverted over the coals (Hos 7:8).

Hebrew villagers wore a loincloth and a tunic. Everyone also had a cloak that doubled as a blanket. Hence there were no closets in a pillared house. Few villagers regularly bathed or washed their clothes, so there were no rooms for washing or bathing. They relieved themselves in the fields that they farmed (Gen 24:63; 37:15).

Some farmers also herded sheep, goats, and cattle. Herd animals provided milk, meat, wool, and a reserve food supply in case of a bad harvest or incursions from neighboring peoples (Judg 6:4). Herding was often carried out by children to prevent the village from losing needed field labor (1 Sam 16:11).

Farmers often served as trading partners, especially in metals, which were acquired as imports and shaped into tools. They also turned their own pottery, wove linen from flax, and fashioned tools of wood, flint, and bronze. By combining farming with herding, raiding, trading, and manufacturing, farmers distributed their labor more evenly and ensured that they would not face the dry season without producing any food at all.

Pillared house found at Ai, the second major victory for Joshua in his conquest of Canaan. Photo L. DeVries.

Another major strategy that farmers used to improve their labor force was to increase the number of workers by having more children. The major obstacle to this strategy was that the population of the Hebrew villages in the hills during the Iron I period (1200–1000 BCE) suffered a high infant mortality rate. With every woman who carried four pregnancies to term, less than two newborns survived. The attempt to increase the size of the household also meant that there were more mouths to feed. Increasing the number of workers by itself did not create a higher standard of living.

Farming the hills demanded adaptations based on the economic and social reaction of the Hebrews to their new physical and cultural environment. It was farming, more than any other challenge, that created a new people from the Hebrew villagers who settled in Palestine after 1250 BCE. To meet the demands of peak labor periods and to fill the times between with maintenance of facilities (and less intensive work periods such as the grape harvest), both men and women farmed. The lives of these village farmers, while hard, contained both a healthy respect for the environment and an appreciation for its bounty (Judg 21:19). But even with the concerted efforts of everyone, no single village could have coped in every instance with their local environmental constraints or the labor needs in their fields without the help of other villages.

Consequently, villages shared the risk and responsibility of farming a marginal agricultural region by forming tribes. The continued reliance of the villages upon the tribe eventually forged permanent political networks. The village culture of these tribes eventually grew in size and organization to the point that the Hebrews began to compete economically and militarily with their neighbors in the cities to the west. By 1000 BCE, the tightly knit political relationships into which the farmers had been drawn had reached the level necessary for the creation of a state.

STUDY QUESTIONS

1. Point out how the text identifies Joshua as Moses' successor.
2. Discuss the various theories on the conquest.
3. Discuss the significance of Achan's sin and punishment.
4. What is the universalism theme?
5. Define: Divine Warrior, corporate identity, covenant renewal.

THE BOOK OF JUDGES

The book of Judges provides both a literary and historical transition between the exodus-conquest sequence of stories and the beginning of the monarchy. This compilation of episodes portrays the difficulties of life as the Israelites began to settle in Canaan, and it provided a strong argument for why the establishment of the monarchy was necessary. Much of this material was probably drawn from oral tradition (especially "hero" stories) and tapped the memories of all of the tribes. Some of the episodes are fragmentary, but that also probably reflects the fact that oral tradition is not always as perfectly or completely preserved as what is written down.

Literary Analysis The distinctive literary characteristic of the book of Judges is that it is systematically arranged. A three-part division provides

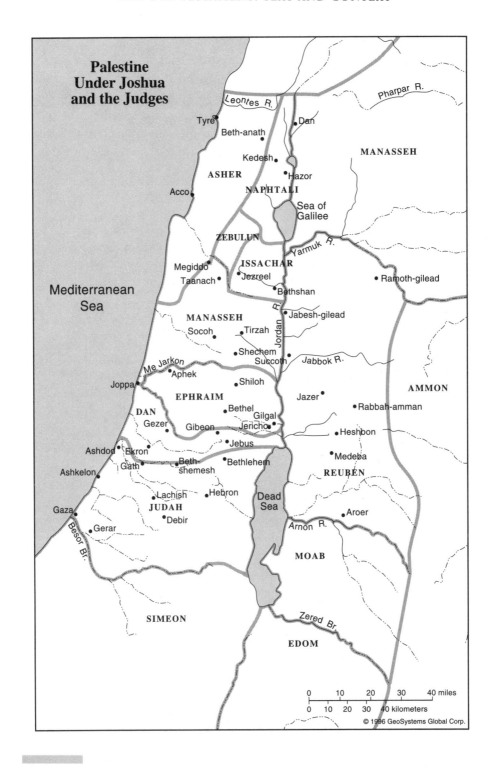

Palestine
Under Joshua
and the Judges

Leontes R.

Pharpar R.

Tyre

Beth-anath

Dan

MANASSEH

Kedesh

Hazor

ASHER

Acco

NAPHTALI

Sea of
Galilee

ZEBULUN

Yarmuk R.

Megiddo

ISSACHAR

Taanach

Jezreel

Mediterranean
Sea

Bethshan

Ramoth-gilead

MANASSEH

Jabesh-gilead

Socoh

Tirzah

Jordan R.

Shechem

Succoth

Jabbok R.

Me Jarkon

Aphek

Shiloh

AMMON

Joppa

EPHRAIM

Jazer

Bethel

Rabbah-amman

DAN

Gilgal

Gezer

Gibeon

Jericho

Heshbon

Jebus

Ashdod

Ekron

Beth-
shemesh

Bethlehem

Medeba

Ashkelon

Gath

REUBEN

Lachish

Hebron

Dead
Sea

Gaza

JUDAH

Debir

Aroer

Gerar

Arnon R.

Besor Br.

MOAB

SIMEON

Zered Br.

EDOM

0   10   20   30   40 miles
0   10   20   30   40 kilometers

© 1996 GeoSystems Global Corp.

(1) an introductory and explanatory narrative, (2) a collection of tales about the judges, and (3) two episodes that accentuate the anarchic character of the time period.

The book of Judges begins with a general introduction, which provides a transition from the orderly period of Joshua's leadership to the chaotic conditions which necessitate the "raising" of judges. What is particularly interesting in these first two chapters is the explanation of why the Israelite tribes were not able to complete their conquest of the Canaanites and other inhabitants of the promised land. One example appears in Judg 1:19, where it states that Yahweh (the Divine Warrior) gave the Israelite tribe of Judah a victory in the hill country, but the Israelites were not able to defeat the people of the plain because they had "iron chariots." This is an unusual admission of failure considering the victories over chariot armies described in Josh 11:6–9 and Judg 4:13–16. However, it provides a more realistic appraisal of the Israelites' ability to conquer occupied territory than the idealized narrative in the first twelve chapters of the book of Joshua. It also emphasizes the differences in material culture between the Israelites and the indigenous inhabitants of Canaan.

The explanatory material, which is representative of the work of the **Deuteronomic historian,** also contains two statements concerning the retention of some of these enemy peoples in Canaan. Yahweh decided to allow them to survive (i.e., God would not drive them out) in order "to test Israel, whether or not they would take care to walk in the way of the LORD as their ancestors did" (Judg 2:22). God used these people "to teach those [Israelites] who had no experience of [war]" how to engage in warfare (Judg 3:2). Rationalizations such as these are often placed in parentheses by modern translators to show that they were not part of the original story. They are only later commentary on the narrative material. It is unlikely that the Israelites during the Judges period would have appreciated the value of having Canaanites as "test administrators" or "military drill instructors," especially while the Israelites were being oppressed by these people. However, the **Deuteronomist** views these events from hindsight and can therefore present them in a manner that will illustrate the point that the people deserved their punishment and only Yahweh could relieve them of their oppressors.

The stories in the middle portion of the book are chaotic, and the world described in the stories is clearly anarchic, but a very conscious effort has been made by the biblical editors to tie these episodes into an apparently chronological narrative. Nevertheless, the stories are not in chronological order and the only element that they share is the disorder of the times. The cycle or framework that is used to tie the stories together gives them a sense of unity, but it is artificial.

The framework used by the biblical editors is quite simple. It follows the following pattern (Judg 2:11–19):

- The people of Israel sin (defined as turning away from Yahweh and worshiping other gods).
- Yahweh becomes angry and allows the Israelites to be oppressed by their neighbors. This is an excellent example of a **theodicy**, an explanation for why God allows bad things to happen. It is also not unique to the Israelites. Such an explanation is expressed in the Stele of Mesha, a stone inscription found in 1868. King Mesha of Moab explains why his people have been oppressed by the Israelites, saying: "Omri, the king of Israel controlled Moab for many years because Chemosh, our chief god, was angry at his people."
- The Israelites repent or at least recognize the source of their present condition, namely, Yahweh's wrath.
- Yahweh responds by "raising up a judge" to deal with the *current, local* crisis. This usually takes the form of military activity, although it is not always organized warfare.
- A period of peace and order (usually in increments of twenty, forty, or eighty years), which coincides with the period of the judge, is almost immediately followed by a return to the sin that had precipitated the original crisis. The cycle resumes.

The final five chapters (Judg 17–21) are distinct because they do not contain any mention of a judge. The stories are filled with the same sorts of anarchic events as in other portions of the book—rape, civil war, and idolatry—but no judge arises to meet the problems described here. While it is tempting to say that these stories were tacked on to the end of the book simply because of their similarity to other Judges material, it is more likely that they provide a final literary transition for the opening of the monarchic period. The theme that "in those days there was no king in Israel; all the people did what was right in their own eyes" (Judg 21:25) is best exemplified in these final chapters. They provide a crowning argument for the establishment of the monarchy and lay the foundation for the anointing of Saul and David as the first kings of Israel.

Analysis of Distinctive Features

One cannot help but appreciate the ability of the authors and editors of the book of Judges to tell stories. While the stories are often descriptions of events that would shock most modern people, they do have entertainment value as well as a clear propagandistic slant. For example, why does Jephthah sacrifice his daughter? Perhaps more important, why does his daughter take control of the situation and insist that he sacrifice her? What is it about this time period or this culture that could produce such a bizarre set of circumstances, especially when human sacrifice seems to have been implicitly forbidden in the episode with Isaac (Gen 22)? The answer appears to be that Jephthah's culture emphasized the need to maintain honor through the keeping of an oath. A desperate general, in need of a victory to retain his position of authority, was willing to bet his future, in the person of his only child, in order to defeat the enemy. He knew it was likely that she or some other member of his household would come out to greet him in celebration of a victory (see 1 Sam 18:6–7). His daughter, recognizing the stakes, sacrificed herself on the altar of her father's ambition, retained her family's honor, and acquired a measure of personal honor in the face of her own death. Of this stuff legends are made.

The modern reader might also ask what value is to be found in the story of the Levite's concubine (Judg 19–20). In this story, an almost perfect parallel to the story of Lot in Sodom in Gen 19, a severely abused woman is sacrificed to save her husband from a mob in the Benjaminite village of Gibeah. When the crowd demands that the Levite be given to them, he unceremoniously thrusts his concubine into the arms of a group of ruffians who rape her to death. The aftermath of this tragedy was a civil war between the tribe of Benjamin, in whose territory the outlaw community of Gibeah was located, and the rest of the Israelite tribes. This is in fact the only time when all the tribes fully cooperate in the book of Judges (chapters 20–21) and the only time that the ark of the covenant is mentioned (Judg 20:27–28)!

Such violent activities hardly encourage the modern reader with a message of hope or inspiration. One interpretation is that they represent a political strategy to mar the reputation of Saul, Israel's first king. Gibeah was his hometown and tying him, even peripherally, to these horrible events could provide an argument for David's takeover of the government and the elimination of a political faction led by Saul's family.

To understand the Judges material it is necessary to understand the intention of the authors of these stories and the editors who compiled them into an extended narrative. Nations are typically the end product of a long period of faction, strife, and disorder—a period still very important in the development of the people into a nation. Tribal Israel was at best a loose confederation of tribes that occasionally cooperated. As the "Song of Deborah" (Judg 5:12–18) and the feud between Jephthah and the Ephraimites (Judg 12:1–6) demonstrate, that cooperation was never universal. Rules of law and allegiance to a covenant that bound the people into a single political unit came later. It might well have been impossible for that union to take place without the chaos of the Judges period as a reminder of the need for order. In this way, a case was made, however propagandistic, for law, order, and the establishment of a government that could ensure stability.

*A Summary
of Judges*
Following the introductory section of the book of Judges, with its explanation of the failure of a total conquest, the narrative of the episodes of various judges begins. Many of the leaders, some of whom are heroic, have distinctive characteristics: Ehud is left-handed; Deborah is the only female judge; Gideon (like Jacob) is a **trickster;** Jephthah is an outcast; and Samson is a **Nazirite**. The stories center around these narrative motifs, using them as signposts for the audience. These motifs heighten the interest of the audience. They make long stories easier to follow because repetition of these motifs throughout the narrative constantly reminds the listeners of what has happened and what will be occurring again.

The motif of Ehud's left-handedness provides the key for his assassination of the king of the Moabites. Ehud secretly brought a specially fabricated weapon, a double-edged dagger, into the palace of Eglon. Since most people are right-handed, the left side would be searched more carefully than the right. Weapons are drawn most effectively across the body and a left-hander wears a weapon on the right side.

Deborah predicts that the Israelite general Barak will be given the victory over Jabin and Sisera of Hazor through the hand of a woman. The role of the woman Jael in killing Sisera is then made the climax of the story. Like other underdog stories, the seemingly weakest member of society triumphs because of the intervention of Yahweh. The twist that produces an unexpected female heroine increases the entertainment value of the story.

Gideon's career is marked by a sequence of crafty tricks: grinding grain in a wine press, asking God to demonstrate his power before Gideon will accept his call to be a judge, and using trickery and surprise to win military victories. He is thus in a long line of trickster figures that includes Abraham, Rebekah, Jacob, and Laban.

Jephthah is forced into a life as a *khabiru*, a stateless person, because his mother was a prostitute. He became the leader of a band of outcasts and became such an effective military commander that his tribe and family asked him to return and save them from the oppression of the Ammonites. His reversal of fortune is a model for the culture of the Israelites under the monarchy, who rose from servitude to sovereignty over neighboring peoples. It also underscores Jephthah's willingness to engage in unorthodox strategies, such as his use of an oath to convince Yahweh to help him obtain a military victory.

Samson's **Nazirite** status was signalled by his long hair. However, his violation of Nazirite regulations (regarding contact with the dead, cutting the hair, and presumably drinking wine) marked him as a rule-breaker. This may indicate that the authors of Judges used Samson as a model for the Israelites during the Judges period. Samson's penchant for violating his Nazirite vow was the basis for his eventual downfall.

The ironic touches in the narratives of these judges entertain, but they also serve as signals to the audience. Whenever a particular physical characteristic (such as long hair) is emphasized, it is a clue that this feature will figure in the resolution of the story.

In addition to the major judges, there are minor figures mentioned in only a few lines. Some, like Shamgar, are similar to Samson in style and strength. In a single verse (Judg 3:31), we are told he kills six hundred Philistines with an oxgoad—a pointed stick used to prod oxen and break up the clods of dirt turned up by the plow. Others, like Tola and Jair, are not tied to any event or accomplishment other than their tribal affiliation, wealth, and large families (Judg 10:1–4). In one instance, a non-judge is given a full chapter (Judg 9). This character is Abimelech, son of the judge Gideon. Abimelech may be the perfect example of a leader in the period of the Judges. He murders sixty-nine of his half-brothers, solicits funds from his mother's clan to hire a mercenary army, and sets himself up as a warlord. Naturally, he comes to a bad end, being slain by a woman who hits him with a millstone during one of his many military exploits. Even in death, his name becomes a part of popular folklore. In 2 Sam 11:20–21, Abimelech's name is cited as the model of the foolish soldier who makes the error of getting too close to the city wall during a battle. In this and in other ways, the Judges material served as a foundation for later Israelite tradition and self-evaluation.

Cultural Analysis   In approaching the study of the book of Judges, it may be most useful to recall a period in American history when lawlessness and disregard for tradition were rampant. In frontier life during the latter half of the nineteenth century, the man with the most firepower and the ability to trick, cajole, or threaten his way through every situation was heralded as a hero or at least an anti-hero. Names like Billy the Kid, Jessie James, and Wild Bill Hickok come to mind, and their excesses and flaunting of the law have become just as legendary as some of the figures described in Judges. They are bigger than life and the exaggerations about their lives and accomplishments furnish a typology for an era rather than a chronicle of its history.

The judges period of Israelite history was a time of new settlements and of the struggle to survive both the social and physical environment. As yet, no evidence has been uncovered that would provide proof of a discernable ethnic difference between the Canaanites and those people who eventually became the Israelites. In fact, many of the "Israelite" villages were probably made up of Canaanites who had fled their former homes to escape the warfare, famine, and disease that plagued the area of Syro-Palestine between 1200 BCE and 1000 BCE. During this time, when the incursions of the Sea Peoples ended Egyptian control over the area, new social groups were founded based on a common need to pool their labor to produce crops and establish new settlements in quieter regions of the country.

The culture that did develop in the hill country was initially based on former Canaanite models, but it eventually took on a character of its own. These pioneers had to be tougher and more resourceful to survive in the more marginal environment that they chose. The pragmatism of village life, directed by elders and idealizing the **egalitarian** virtues of trust and shared responsibility created a distinct people that became the Israelites.

Life in this village culture was dependent on the forces of nature to provide them with the rain in season and to protect them from devastating winds and plagues of locusts. The people worked extremely hard in their fields and when they made sacrifices they did so in thanks to Yahweh and in expectation of continued good fortune and sustained fertility. Their villages were mapped out, not in grids, but according to the function of each villager. A potter, a tanner, and a dye-maker all had their shops (probably attached to their houses). These "specialists" offered simple wares while also working their own farm plots or vineyards.

Village law and the assembly of the people were conducted on the village threshing floor. Threshing floors were the places where grain was processed and distributed, disputes were settled, and the needs of the poor were evaluated and supplied. In this way the village cared for its own and managed its harvest to the benefit and survival of the entire community. Such a shared system worked best on a small scale. This system was employed by the monarchy, but eventually its resources were drained by taxes. Once the monarchy was established, **egalitarianism** weakened and a structured, multi-level social system replaced the simpler village culture.

The material culture of the hill country settlements could be described as subsistence level. Just enough grain was produced to maintain the population and perhaps provide a small surplus that could be used for trade or stored against the inevitable bad years. Population growth could provide a larger work force, but it would also drain, at least temporarily, the food supply. In other words, life was a gamble. For the Israelites to master their new environment and expand beyond the hill country they had to do two things: (1) increase their population, and (2) borrow many of the useful aspects of the material culture of the Canaanite cities of the plains. It was this latter requirement, however, that was the principal danger. When one culture borrows from another **(syncretism)** the temptation is to become "just like" that other culture and allow the distinctive aspects of one's culture to be submerged or lost. The biblical writers continually argue against syncretism, especially with regard to the worship of foreign gods. The stories in the book of Judges suggest that the Israelites were neither true to Yahweh nor to the covenant made at Sinai.

***Analysis of
Point of View***   Benjamin Franklin is said to have remarked during the Continental Congress that "treason is a term invented by the winners to describe the losers." It can also be said that "terrorism is in the eye of the beholder." Many of the figures who are represented as judges are, by modern standards, not models of propriety or good judgment. For example, Ehud murdered Eglon, the king of the Moabites, by pretending to have a secret message for the king and arranging to get him alone so that he could stab him (Judg 3:15–30). If the Moabites had been telling the story, Ehud would have been labeled the worst kind of villain, not a valiant judge who rallied his troops with his courageous action and provided his people with their longest period of peace (eighty years).

Threshing Floors and Gates

Unlike modern cities and towns that have city halls and courthouse buildings, villages and towns in ancient Israel conducted their public business on threshing floors and at gates. The threshing floor was a flat area near a village or villages where the harvested grain was processed using a threshing sled, winnowing forks, and sieves. After processing, the grain was distributed to its owners and a portion was set aside for widows and orphans. The economic importance of this installation caused it to be used eventually for legal matters as well. Thus, Ruth approaches Boaz for help as he lays on the threshing floor (Ruth 3:6–13). It was a legally significant act for her to approach him there.

Walled towns conducted their legal and economic activity at their gate areas. Some retained the memory of the threshing floor by building the city gate upon the site of one of these installations (1 Kgs 22:10). Since towns were more dependent on commerce than agriculture, they chose to conduct business in a high-traffic area. Just as merchants today attempt to locate their store in a place where the high volume of traffic will ensure that many people see them, the merchants of ancient Israel set up shop either within the chambers of the gate or immediately on either side of it. Similarly, trials were held in gateways to ensure public visibility for these legal matters and because of the symbolic value attached to them. Persons who were free to pass back and forth through the city gate were considered citizens and those entering and leaving the temple were considered ritually "clean." Examples of trials in a gateway include Deut 21:18–21; 22:13–19; Ruth 4:1–13.

In Judges 4, Jael plays the trickster in her feigned hospitality for Sisera, the general of the Hazor forces. Ultimately, Jael proves herself to be a strong character and a courageous woman. She avoids what may have constituted a planned rape on Sisera's part. After lulling the general to sleep, she drives a tent peg through his temple. Such behavior is certainly not what one expects of a hostess, but that is exactly the point of many of the episodes in Judges. The world of the characters is turned upside down and no law other than personal honor and personal power exists. Jael defends her honor and that of her Kenite household through the use of deadly force against a man who planned to take over their encampment by force. Although she is not an Israelite, she is proclaimed "blessed" (Judg 5:24) for an action that today might put her in the same company with Lizzie Borden or Mata Hari. It is the perspective of the biblical writer that transforms Jael from a monster into a hero.

Other more famous characters in the book of Judges are Gideon and Samson. Both of these men appear to be great leaders of their people, despite less than noble characteristics. Gideon cheated the Ammonite tribute collectors by secretly grinding his grain in a wine press (Judg 6:11) and repeatedly forced Yahweh to perform miracles to prove that God really intended to provide a military victory over the Midianites (Judg 6:36–40). Samson, supposedly a Nazirite from birth, violated every stipulation of the Nazirite's vow (Num 6:1–12). In fact, the storyteller seems to have taken delight in Samson's excesses and his inflated ego. Most of Samson's exploits center around his dealings with non-Israelite women such as Delilah and are in most cases self-centered. Even his death, while it claimed the lives of thousands of the enemy, centered on his personal revenge for the loss of his eyes (Judg 16:28).

Before it appears that only negative conclusions can be drawn from the Judges narrative, it should be explained that the editors are primarily interested in portraying a world where even God's chosen leaders are far from perfect. They do provide needed aid to the oppressed Israelites—winning a number of battles, staging demonstrations of Yahweh's power as the Divine Warrior, and occasionally setting an example of proper behavior. For example, Gideon musters a huge army of 32,000, but then he is instructed to reduce it through a variety of measures to a ridiculously small three hundred men (Judg 7:2–23). As is the case in the conquest narrative of Joshua, this strategy is designed to present the Israelites as underdogs who could not win a battle on their own (Josh 6:1–22; 10:8–14; 11:6–15). Only Yahweh can give them the victory and they must rely upon Yahweh for their deliverance. The Israelite audience, listening to this story, could nod their heads and agree that a small force, led by God's chosen general and using surprise as their ally, could confuse an enemy and win a victory over the Midianites.

Gideon provides an example of the religious cleanser of his village. He pulls down an altar dedicated to the Canaanite god Baal and in its place erects an altar for Yahweh and makes a sacrifice (Judg 6:25–32). This act then sets the stage for a contest between Yahweh and Baal (reminiscent of the confrontation in Exodus with pharaoh and the contest in 2 Kgs 18 involving Elijah and the four hundred prophets of Baal). Gideon's father calls on the outraged villagers to spare Gideon's life and allow Baal, if he is able, to take revenge on the man who had destroyed his altar. If he could not, then he is no god! The theme of a Canaanite god's inability to defend himself or herself allows the audience to proclaim that there is no god but Yahweh. This theme is found elsewhere in the Bible and thus brings the Judges material into the mainstream of the biblical narrative and its proclamation of Yahweh's power.

An Early Bronze Age altar. Altars played a role in the religion of Israel
as well as in the religions of its neighbors. Photo L. DeVries.

Samson is also an example of the positive nature of the judge. At one point he goes to the Philistine city of Gaza (Judg 16:1–3). He boldly walks through the city gate, without any pretense of hiding his intentions, and visits the house of a local prostitute. The men of the city lay a trap for the Israelite hero, but he foils their plans by leaving before dawn. To instruct them in the power he represents (not implicitly Yahweh's but perhaps the connection can be made here), Samson rips the city gates from their sockets and carries them nearly forty miles to a hill near the city of Hebron. They are left there, a monument to the futility of the Philistines to harness Samson's power. The symbolic value of this action, whether it was intended to be a joke or was a serious attempt to humble the Philistines, is profound. A city's gate represents its power. Deprived of these protective doors, the city was shorn of its strength and open to invasion. This is a striking irony considering how Samson lost his strength when he was shorn of his hair.

Archaeological Analysis   Because this period is not documented except in the Bible, most of what we can learn about life during the Iron Age is based on archaeological remains. Over one hundred thirty sites in which settlements first appeared in the hill country during the Iron Age were excavated or surveyed prior to 1995. The pattern of these new settlements suggests a migration of the population to this previously underpopulated region. In their examination of these village sites, archaeologists try to identify patterns of culture based on pottery types, architectural styles, and technologies. Often a new people entering an area will bring in a distinctive culture, evidenced by burial styles and possessions such as pottery, jewelry, and weapons.

Although it would be helpful if there were startling differences between Israelite and Canaanite material culture, that does not seem to be the case. Housing styles do change somewhat, but primarily this is due to the environment of the hill country where most new settlements were established. Pottery types remain virtually the same, again with the indication that storage jars were modified for use in a slightly different climatic area. Innovations such as terracing of hillsides for farming and the plastering of cisterns to prevent seepage of water into the porous limestone seem to be more a matter of the natural developments of life in the hill country than they do inventions that changed the region.

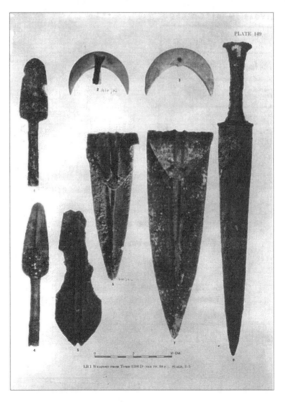

Weapons found at Megiddo from the Late Bronze Age I period.
Courtesy of The Oriental Institute of The University of Chicago.

What has come out of the ground in the last three decades of archaeological investigation is a fuller understanding of the Philistine presence in Canaan. Sites like Gezer and Tell Miqne-Ekron reveal well-established urban cultures. They maintained large-scale industry, especially in the production of olive oil, and established trade contacts in areas from Egypt to Phoenicia. The purported widespread use of iron technology by the Philistines appears to be exaggerated. They possessed a knowledge of iron, but bronze continued to be the principle metal used for the fashioning of weapons, farm implements, and industrial tools. The statement in 1 Sam 13:19 that there was "no smith to be found throughout all the land of Israel" and that the Israelites were forced to rely upon the Philistines to sharpen their farm implements suggests a monopoly on metalworking in general, rather than one on iron technology alone. Intensive specialization of labor would have been less likely to occur in the Israelite villages where most of their efforts had to be directed to farming. They would most likely have produced their own commonware pottery, tanned their own hides, and woven their own cloth for clothing. Blacksmithing is a dedicated profession, not one that can be practiced part-time.

One thing that can be traced are the place names mentioned in the biblical text. The Philistine cities of Ashkelon, Ashdod, Ekron, Gaza, and Gezer, as well as the Canaanite and Phoenician cities of Megiddo, Acco, Sidon, Beth-Shemesh, Jebus (Jerusalem), and Hazor have all been located. All of these sites furnish evidence that they were inhabited during the Iron Age. It is more difficult to authenticate the social and religious practices of this period. Some **cultic sites** (e.g., temples and shrines) have been excavated and cult images have been discovered. Sacrifices from this period are described in documents written in later eras (such as the **Stele of Mesha** of the late ninth century BCE). These kinds of data, however, must be examined with caution. Archaeological finds are especially difficult to interpret because they are only mute objects. Drawing conclusions or parallels based on similar but later social customs may be misleading. As is the case with other poorly documented periods of biblical history, reconstructions of the age of the judges must, for now, remain more tentative than concrete.

STUDY QUESTIONS

Assignment: Read the book of Judges with the following questions in mind. Then answer the questions for yourself and be prepared to discuss them.

1. What is a judge? What would be a good job description if you were going to advertise an opening for a judge? Is the position hereditary? Does the judge administer all of the tribes? On this see Judg 5:12–18 and 12:1–6.

2. What is the cycle of history recounted in this book? Look especially at Judg 2:11–3:4. Try to list the elements in the cycle that are recounted here. Are there any events that are not attributed directly to God or do not fit into the cycle? On this see Judg 1:19.

3. When should this book be dated? See Judg 1:21; 17:6; 18:30–31; 19:10.

4. What kind of society is pictured in this book? Can you think of any parallels to this type of society in the history of your country?

5. Read the story of Ehud (Judg 3:15–30). How do you explain the apparent approval of his deception?

6. Read the Deborah narrative (Judg 4:4–5:31). Why is Jael celebrated as a heroine after apparently violating the law of hospitality?

7. Read the story of Gideon's battle strategy (Judg 7). How does this compare to the strategy in Josh 6?

8. Read the Samson narrative (Judg 13–16). Are his excesses simply typical of epic heroes or do they have a deeper purpose? What is a Nazirite (Num 6)?

9. Read the story of the Levite's concubine (Judg 19–21). How does this compare to Gen 19? Why include a story like this in Judges?

10. What have you learned while reading this book about Israel's religion? Are all of the people monotheistic? Is there a central shrine for the worship of Yahweh? (a) Read Judg 6:7–32 and 8:22–35 in the Gideon narrative. What evidence appears here of proper Yahweh worship? (b) Read the story of Jephthah (Judg 11). How do his actions conflict with previous law and tradition? (c) Read the story of Micah's idol (Judg 17–18). How does this conflict with the laws given at Mount Sinai?

11. Note the type of weapons that are used in the book of Judges and what they are made of during this period. What does this tell you about the material culture of the Hebrews? See Judg 1:19; 3:16, 31; 4:21; 7:16–22; 9:46–55; 15:15; 20:16.

3

THE MONARCHIC PERIOD

THE EARLY MONARCHY

The End of the Judges' Model of Administration

The transition from the anarchic settlement/judges period to the monarchy is found in the career of the last judge, Samuel. The narrative of this monumental figure describes both the best and the worst of the premonarchic age: single-minded direction of the people by God's representative as well as the corruption of power and the diminishing of the people's confidence in nonpolitically-oriented leadership.

Like Moses', Samuel's story begins with a birth narrative. It resembles the barren wife theme found in the ancestral stories: Samuel's mother Hannah is childless when she is first introduced. As we know from previous instances of this theme, children born to barren wives are special and their births are usually announced by an angel or some other agent of God (see Gen 18:9–14 and Judg 13:2–5). In this case Eli, the priest in charge of the ark of the covenant and its shrine at Shiloh, foretells the child's birth (1Sam 1:17).

Eli and his sons Hophni and Phineas serve another role. Their actions as priests at Shiloh open a series of episodes in 1Samuel in which the leaders of the people are shown to be corrupt or undeserving of the authority that they exercise. This provides a basis for the argument for the establishment of the monarchy in 1Sam 8. This is reminiscent of the **disqualification stories** in the Jacob narrative that were designed to eliminate Esau as the heir to the covenant (see Gen 25:29–34; 26:34–35; 27:5–46; 33:12–16).

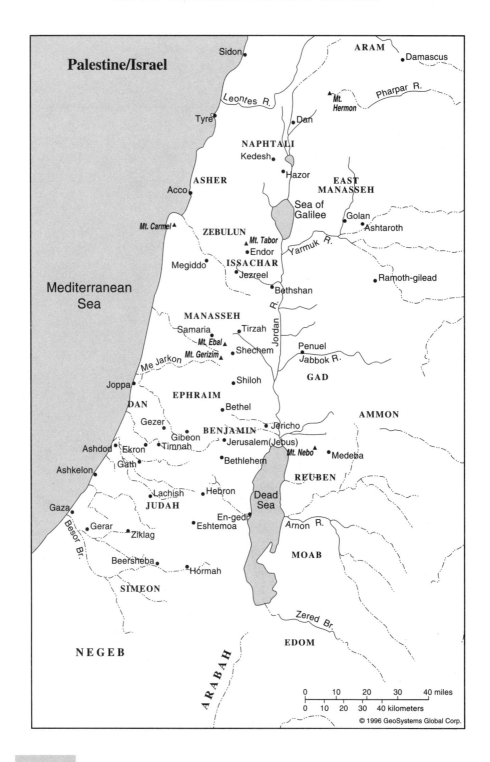

Palestine/Israel

ARAM
Damascus
Sidon
Leontes R.
Pharpar R.
Tyre
Mt. Hermon
Dan
NAPHTALI
Kedesh
Acco
ASHER
Hazor
EAST MANASSEH
Sea of Galilee
Golan
Ashtaroth
Mt. Carmel
ZEBULUN
Mt. Tabor
Yarmuk R.
Endor
Megiddo
ISSACHAR
Jezreel
Bethshan
Ramoth-gilead
Mediterranean Sea
MANASSEH
Samaria
Tirzah
Mt. Ebal
Penuel
Me Jarkon
Mt. Gerizim
Shechem
Jabbok R.
Shiloh
GAD
Joppa
EPHRAIM
Bethel
DAN
AMMON
Gezer
Jericho
Gibeon
BENJAMIN
Ashdod
Ekron
Timnah
Jerusalem (Jebus)
Mt. Nebo
Medeba
Gath
Bethlehem
Ashkelon
REUBEN
Hebron
Dead Sea
Gaza
Lachish
JUDAH
En-gedi
Eshtemoa
Gerar
Ziklag
Arnon R.
Beersheba
Hormah
MOAB
SIMEON
Zered Br.
NEGEB
EDOM
ARABAH
Besor Br.
Jordan R.

0   10   20   30   40 miles
0   10   20   30   40 kilometers
© 1996 GeoSystems Global Corp.

The Samuel narrative includes a number of highlights. One is a dream **theophany** in which the child Samuel is told that he will replace Eli and his sons as leader of the people (1 Sam 3:3–14). The theophany serves as the basis for Samuel's call as a priest and prophet. It also provides him with the authority that he will need later to act as a judge and leader.

Another highlight of the Samuel narrative is a sequence of stories describing the death of Eli and his sons, the capture of the ark by the Philistines, the manifestation of Yahweh's power in bringing a plague on the Philistines, the ark's return to the Israelites, and the provisions made for housing the ark in the absence of an adult member of Aaron's family to officiate before the ark (1 Sam 4–6). The ark represents God's presence and was carried into battle in the Joshua narrative of the conquest. But the story in 1 Samuel shows that Yahweh was not limited to the ark's interior and was not forced to help the Israelites if they failed to obey the covenant and the laws.

A third factor of the Samuel narrative is its description of Samuel's role as circuit judge and priestly figure (1 Sam 7). Samuel, who was not a Levite, replaced the traditional priestly family of Eli as the spiritual leader of the people. He performed sacrifices and served as a prophetic figure. Samuel's acquisition of a priestly office may have been typical of the judges period in which the idea that only Levites could serve as priests was not yet firmly established.

Arguments for and against Establishing a Monarchy

Arguments for a Monarchy

- Every other nation has a king.
- A king provides leadership for national defense.
- A king functions as a diplomatic focus for foreign policy.
- A king is able to institute a national economic policy.
- A king can support the development of the national religion by establishing a central shrine.

Arguments against a Monarchy

- Selection of a human king signifies the rejection of Yahweh as king.
- The advantages cited in the arguments for a monarchy are secured at the expense of losing personal freedom. A king will require taxes, institute a military and civil draft, place restraints on travel and trade, and deprive the people of local religious shrines.
- A king will abuse his power by means of nepotism and other practices.

After assuming his leadership position, Samuel's career as a judge is glossed over very quickly since his primary role in the narrative is to choose a king for the Israelites. When his sons are proven to be corrupt (1 Sam 8:3), the days of the judges and their temporary leadership is finished. The elders of the people call out for a king, and there is no turning back (1 Sam 8:4–5).

At this point, the narrative becomes somewhat complex. Portions of the text are clearly pro-monarchic while other sections, interwoven with the rest, strongly argue against a king (see the inset detailing these positions). First Samuel 8, 10:17–23a, and 12 are all slanted against the monarchy in general and against Saul as the first candidate for that position. But 1 Sam 9:1–10:16 and 10:23–11:15 are unquestionably pro-monarchy and pro-Saul.

At the heart of each position is the issue of who will protect and feed the nation. To this point, it has been Yahweh's role as Divine Warrior to win battles for the Israelites and to feed them when they call upon their God (e.g., by means of manna in the wilderness, Exod 16:4–8). Now the people are advocating replacing Yahweh with a king, who will become responsible for their defense (leading the army) and their food (organizing national resources and promoting trade).

Having these two opposing positions side-by-side suggests that a real struggle existed at the time of the establishment of the monarchy and continued throughout its existence. Some people never reconciled themselves to being ruled by a king. Their position was reinforced during those periods when kings abused their powers or the nation was dominated by outside forces. But because much of the material in the books of Samuel and Kings is based on the court histories of the kings, much of the positive information derived from the court histories is retained in the Samuel-Kings narrative. Perhaps this is not enough to prevent a bad impression of many of the kings, but it is enough to suggest that the monarchy was not as big a disaster for Israel as some of the biblical writers and the prophets would have us believe.

Saul's Reign as Israel's First King   To create the perception that the kings were chosen directly by God, Samuel was instructed to receive the candidate whom God would direct to him and anoint his head with oil (1 Sam 9:15–10:1). While anointing may have had other significance, in this case it symbolized the purification of the person designated as king. (It incidentally shows the importance of olive oil as a staple of the Israelite economy.)

However, Saul's career as king did not begin immediately. Saul was a handsome young man who might have been expected to become a leader someday (1 Sam 9:2). He had demonstrated his ability to be open to God's voice by dancing and prophesying with a group of ecstatic prophets (1 Sam 10:10–13). But the idea of a king was still too radical for many Israelites to accept. The description of the staged event that took place when Saul was appointed by lot as the Israelite king reflects the anti-monarchic portion of the narrative. This initial appointment was not conclusive because Saul did not immediately demonstrate his ability to take command, and Samuel appears to make the appointment with some reluctance (1 Sam 10:17–24).

As a result, Saul does not actually assume the role of king until after a sparkling victory over the Ammonites, described in 1 Sam 11. This victory, which lifted the siege of the city of Jabesh-Gilead, allowed him to claim the loyalty of the people. As a result he was crowned king at Gilgal, the site of the crossing of the Jordan in Joshua's time. Like politicians of every age, Saul recognized the importance of place for his coronation. He knew that being crowned at Gilgal right after winning a military victory would create the impression among the people that he was a "new Joshua" (compare Josh 6 and the statement, "So the LORD was with Joshua; and his fame was in all the land," v. 27).

Looking at Saul's reign as one that set a number of precedents, it is easy to recognize why he eventually came to a bad end. It is difficult to be the "first" anything and being the first king was a particularly difficult job. In fact, Saul was more a chief than a king. He held the loyalty of some but not all of the Israelites. When he called them to war, he did not have a professional army upon which to draw. Instead, many of his "citizen soldiers" were just as likely to find some reason not to come or to leave before the war was over (1 Sam 13:8). He also had to rely too heavily upon **nepotism** (granting office to members of one's own family), especially in the responsibilities that he granted to his son Jonathan. This policy ensures that one knows one's employees and advisers, but it also places on the leader additional burdens produced by personal relationships and kinship ties.

A Kingdom Lost (1 Sam 15:22–23)

[22]And Samuel said,
> "Has the LORD as great delight in burnt offerings and sacrifices,
>> as in obeying the voice of the LORD?
> Surely, to obey is better than sacrifice,
>> and to heed than the fat of rams.
> [23]For rebellion is no less a sin than divination,
>> and stubbornness is like iniquity and idolatry.
> Because you have rejected the word of the LORD,
>> he has also rejected you from being king."

The most difficult problem Saul faced, other than the continuing military crisis of dealing with the Philistines, was Samuel. At issue was "turf" or who had the power to do what. Does the king also function as a priest? Are there restrictions that a priestly or prophetic figure can place on the actions of the king (1 Sam 13:10–14)? Is the king above the law imposed on ordinary citizens (1 Sam 15:10–35)? All of these questions and more are brought out in the series of confrontations between Samuel and Saul. In each case, the king's role as war chief conflicted with the prophet's role as religious official and spokesperson for Yahweh. The conflicts between Samuel and Saul serve as an introduction to the difficulties that later arose for every king in dealing with the leaders of the temple and with the independent representatives of Yahweh (the prophets).

Saul failed to obey the prophet Samuel's instructions to properly wage an all-out war, a *kherem*, against the Amalekites (1 Sam 15:10–35). As the **Deuteronomic historian** explains it, Saul had spared the life of the Amalekite king, Agag, and had taken a portion of the Amalekite herds while destroying all the rest. Yet he greeted Samuel with a claim to have fulfilled Samuel's instructions. Samuel sarcastically confronted the king, "What then is this bleating of sheep in my ears, and the lowing of cattle that I hear?" (1 Sam 15:14). Saul's only response was the excuse that the people had spared them as a sacrifice to God. Samuel had no patience with this and he predicted God's total rejection of Saul's family as future rulers over Israel (1 Sam 15:22–23). Samuel did acknowledge Saul's pleas of repentance, and he agreed at least publicly to support the king before the elders (1 Sam 15:30–31), but the king's violation of the law cost his family the kingdom. The kingship was taken away from Saul's descendants and given to a new claimant, David, who was secretly anointed by Samuel.

The Basis of Saul's Jealousy (1 Sam 18:5–8)

[5]David went out and was successful wherever Saul sent him; as a result, Saul set him over the army. And all the people, even the servants of Saul, approved.

[6]As they were coming home, when David returned from killing the Philistine, the women came out of all the towns of Israel, singing and dancing, to meet King Saul, with tambourines, with songs of joy, and with musical instruments. [7]And the women sang to one another as they made merry,

"Saul has killed his thousands,
and David his ten thousands."

[8]Saul was very angry, for this saying displeased him. He said, "They have ascribed to David ten thousands, and to me they have ascribed thousands; what more can he have but the kingdom?"

What follows is a narrative sympathetic to David which portrays the aging Saul as mentally unstable and incapable of ruling the country. The story of David's rise to power is in fact the story of Saul's demise. It was probably written by members of the royal court of David or Solomon to favor their claims to the throne over those of Saul and his family.

The first major episode in David's rise to power is his anointing by Samuel as the future king of Israel (1 Sam 16:10–13). As was the case for Saul (1 Sam 10:1–8), this was done to designate David as Yahweh's choice for king. It was many years, however, before David could claim the throne.

The Goliath episode (1 Sam 17) provided David with hero status and a royal marriage to Saul's daughter Michal. The description of this event resembles the one-on-one combat scenes in Homer's epic poem *The Iliad*, which is set in approximately the same time period as the early monarchy. Goliath's huge size and armored body stand in contrast to the young, unarmored David (1 Sam 17:4–7). Since the Israelites have often been portrayed as the underdog in battles against their enemies (Exod 17:8–13; Josh 10:5–14; Judg 7), David provides the perfect paradigm for the nation.

The Goliath narrative is problematic because it assumes that Saul did not know David (1 Sam 17:55–58), although in 1 Sam 16:18–23 David had already served as Saul's musician and armor-bearer. Furthermore, 2 Sam 21:19 credits Elhanan with killing Goliath (cf. 1 Chron 20:5). Another question is whether the royal marriage to Michal was granted in exchange for David's victory over Goliath or for a bride price of one hundred Philistine foreskins. In either case it provided David with an official tie to the royal succession and thereby legitimized his later claim to the kingship. It also initiates the "jealousy theme" that dominates his relationship with Saul for the remainder of Saul's life.

Because of Saul's jealousy of David's popularity, David was forced to flee the royal court. He was aided in his escape by Saul's son Jonathan (1 Sam 20) and by Michal, who placed a *terafim* (a household idol) in his bed to deceive anyone who might come to see him (1 Sam 19:11–17).

Over the next several years, David lived like an outlaw (1 Sam 19–31) during which he built a network of support through marriages (Abigail, Ahinoam; 1 Sam 25:39–43), through gifts given to the elders of Judah (1 Sam 30:26), and by gaining the friendship of key individuals. Among these was the priest Abiathar, who was the only survivor of Saul's massacre of the priestly community at Nob (1 Sam 22:9–23). By taking the fugitive priest into his company, David was able to draw another contrast between himself and the king, who did not respect the sanctity of God's priests.

As long as Saul remained king, David refused to take direct action against him. This theme highlights the importance of "the Lord's anointed" and also serves as the foundation for the Davidic **apology** narrative, which is designed to show David's worthiness to rule by portraying him as a sympathetic character. On two occasions (1 Sam 24 and 26) David spares Saul's life because he is "the Lord's anointed." The first of these occurs in a cave near the oasis of Engedi, by the Dead Sea (1 Sam 24:1–7). In this case, David's men urge him to slay the king and thus end the frustrating cycle of hiding and flight that they had suffered. However, David is extremely adamant that no harm should come to the king. He is even remorseful over cutting off a portion of Saul's robe and thus, at least symbolically, depriving the king of a portion of his authority (1 Sam 24:5). This sets a precedent against regicide that would of course be valuable to David when he in turn became king.

During the outlaw period David spent time as a mercenary leader, working for the Philistine Achish of Gath. He was given a headquarters at Ziklag and from there staged raids that gave him military experience and may have contributed to his knowledge of Philistine tactics and iron technology. To prevent anyone from informing the Philistines of his activities, David ordered that no prisoners be taken in his raids against Philistine and Philistine-allied villages. Thus Achish remained pleased with a faithful vassal who supplied him with a large quantity of loot (1 Sam 27:8–12). Although David was acting here as a double-agent, his duping of the Philistines (1 Sam 27:5–12) is typical of the **trickster** figures we have seen in earlier periods of Israelite history (Jacob, Ehud, Samson).

The Use of a Ritual Pit

- *Odyssey* 11.23–29, 34–42: Here Perimedes and Eurylochus held the victims, while I drew my sharp sword from beside my thigh and dug a pit of a cubit's length this way and that, and around it I poured a libation to all the dead, first with honeyed milk, thereafter with sweet wine, and in the third place with water, and I sprinkled thereon white barley meal. . . . But when with vows and prayers I had made supplication to the tribes of the dead, I took the sheep and cut their throats over the pit, and the dark blood ran forth. Then there gathered from out of Erebus the spirits of those that are dead (A.T. Murray, trans. *Homer, The Odyssey* [Loeb Classical Library; Cambridge, Mass.: Harvard University Press, 1975, (1919)], 387–89).

- Hittite KUB 29.4 rev. 4.31–36: When at night on the second day (of the ritual) a star leaps, the offerer comes to the temple and bows to the deity. The two daggers which were made along with the (statue of) the new deity they take, and (with them) dig a pit for the deity in front of the table. They offer one sheep to the deity for *enumassiyya* and slaughter it down in the pit.

- Gilgamesh Epic 12.83–84: Scarcely had he (Nergal) opened a hole in the earth, when the spirit of Enkidu, like a wind-puff, issued forth from the nether world (*ANET*, p. 98).

- 1 Sam 28:7–8: Then Saul said to his servants, "Seek out for me a woman who is a medium (literally: 'owner of a pit'), so that I may go to her and inquire of her." His servants said to him, "There is a medium at Endor." So Saul disguised himself and put on other clothes and went there, he and two men with him. They came to the woman by night. And he said, "Consult a spirit for me, and bring up for me the one whom I name to you."

Saul's reign ended with a disheartening story of an abandoned king who is forced to resort to consulting a witch because God will no longer speak to him. Dressed in disguise, Saul crossed the northern border of his realm to ask the witch of Endor to conjure up the spirit of Samuel so he can ask him whether God will give them a victory in the next day's battle (1 Sam 28:8–14). The witch, like all other mediums and magicians, had been expelled from Saul's kingdom; ironically Saul went to confer with her. She uses a **ritual pit** as the symbolic opening to the underworld. The text does not describe her conjuring methods, but similar stories in Hittite and Babylonian texts and in Homer's *Odyssey* suggest the use of blood or a mixture of bread and honey to attract the spirits of the dead. Saul is disappointed, however, in Samuel's ghostly response. He is told that he and his sons will die in the conflict and the kingdom will pass from his family (1 Sam 28:15–19).

When Saul and his sons are killed in battle against the Philistines at Gilboa (1 Sam 31), a confusing period follows in which the leadership of the people of Israel is divided. David rules in Judah at Hebron and Saul's son Eshbaal (Ishbosheth) nominally rules the northern tribes. But Eshbaal must exericse his rule from the Transjordanian city of Mahanaim, since the Philistines now control the area of northern Palestine (2 Sam 2). There is conflict between David and Eshbaal, but it seems to be primarily border skirmishes.

Joab: Patriot or Opportunist?

One of the questions raised about Joab, David's general and principal adviser, is whether he is an opportunist or a patriot.

- Joab murders Eshbaal's general Abner to satisfy a blood feud. Abner's murder eliminates a potential threat to both himself as general of David's army and to David, and it provides David with a scapegoat to shift public opinion in his favor when Joab is shamed (2 Sam 3:23–39).

- Joab sends his soldier Uriah the Hittite to be killed in the front lines. This was intended to spare David from a charge of adultery, and it put David in debt to Joab (2 Sam 11:14–25).

- Joab sends the wise woman of Tekoa to David to convince him to return Absalom to court. This restores royal favor to a strong claimant to the throne and thus prevents potential unrest if David dies without designating an heir (2 Sam 14).

- Joab kills Absalom. This prevents a recurrence of rebellion, but violates a direct order given by David (2 Sam 18:5–18).

- Joab kills Amasa. This breaks a stalemate of leadership, and allows Joab to put down Sheba's rebellion (2 Sam 20:4–22).

- Joab backs Adonijah to succeed David. This leads Solomon to purge the kingdom of Joab and other leaders when Solomon gains the throne (1 Kgs 2:13–46).

The principal figures in this period were not the kings, but their generals, Abner and Joab. Joab was David's general and Abner was Eshbaal's general. Abner and Joab led the raids, provided advice, and ultimately engineered the unification of the nation under David's rule. Joab was David's first cousin and thus was tied to him by blood as well as service. They made a strong team, although it is sometimes difficult to tell who is the leader of the nation and who is the loyal servant in every episode. The climax of this set of stories occurs when Joab murders Abner. Abner had had a falling out with Eshbaal (2 Sam 3:6–11) and had made overtures to David indicating that he would be willing to give his support to David. Joab did not want a rival and he already had sworn to take revenge on Abner for killing his brother during one of the border clashes. Joab's murder of Abner (significantly in a gate area; 2 Sam 3:27) precipitated a chain reaction in which Eshbaal was murdered by his own advisers (2 Sam 4:1–3). David was forced temporarily to discharge Joab as his military commander (2 Sam 3:31–39). Eshbaal's death left the northern tribes of Israel with no other strong claimant to the throne because only Mephibosheth, the crippled son of Jonathan, remained of the house of Saul (2 Sam 9). The elders of Israel then came to David and asked him to assume the leadership of the nation as a whole (2 Sam 5:1–5).

STUDY QUESTIONS

1. Discuss the pros and cons for the establishment of the monarchy.
2. Describe the mistakes which eventually doom Saul's dynasty.
3. Discuss the statement: David was an excellent politician.
4. Define: theophany, nepotism, *kherem*.

David the King   Upon his coronation as king over a united Israel, David completed a cycle of events that had begun with his anointing by Samuel. To become a true king rather than a war chief like Saul, David took a series of steps to create a national identity for the people. The first of these was to establish a capital city. The criteria for this government center included: (1) a centralized location, (2) strong defenses, (3) political neutrality, (4) accessibility.

Since Jerusalem had never been captured by the Israelites during the settlement period, its political neutrality was intact. No state in the United States can exercise special privileges by claiming that Washington, D.C. is a part of its territory. Likewise, no tribe of Israel could claim Jerusalem as part of its territory. There were no previous Israelite leaders associated with this city. Jerusalem's political neutrality allowed the Davidic dynasty to make a fresh start without concern for the entrenched patterns of local politics that would have existed in an Israelite city. Jerusalem's defenses, which had proven invulnerable to this point, made it an ideal capital. Its location in the central hill country, with easy access to Jericho and the Dead Sea region, also made it a good choice. Its fall to David points up the flaw of cities that depended on water tunnels to supply them during sieges: when the entrance to the water tunnel is found, the city can be captured from within (2 Sam 5:8).

Once settled in Jerusalem David needed to expand it to accommodate its growing population. David therefore initiated a building program to transform the city into a regal display. In this he followed the lead of other kings who used monumental construction, such as massive city walls and great palaces, as a form of political propaganda (2 Sam 5:9–12). He also ordered that the ark of the covenant be brought to the city as a symbol of Yahweh's presence and as a means of identifying Jerusalem as the central cultic site for the nation. David's ego may have been deflated somewhat when one of the men bringing the ark was struck down by God for touching the sacred object (2 Sam 6:6–11). However, he is portrayed in high spirits when the ark was paraded into the city (2 Sam 6:12–15). This event marks the acme of David's power and popularity and signals the demise of the last remnant of Saul's family. When Michal, Saul's daughter, criticizes David for dancing naked before the people, the king relegates her to the silence of the harem (2 Sam 6:20–23). She is never mentioned again.

One part of David's plan to strengthen Jerusalem's prestige as his capital city was to build a temple to house the ark of the covenant. The text offers a variety of reasons why David was not allowed to build the temple. In 2 Sam 7:5–7, Yahweh's prophet Nathan told the king that he would not be allowed to build a temple. The reason given was that God did not desire a house since that would bring his worship into comparison with that of other gods in Canaan. First Kings 5:3 excuses David from building a temple because of the press of military campaigns to protect the nation. First Chronicles 28, despite giving David credit for establishing the priestly bureaucracy to supervise temple worship, says that he could not build the temple because he was "a warrior and had shed blood" (v. 3). There was probably a good deal of negative sentiment among the people, who realized the cost in taxes and labor of such a project and also were uncertain about investing so much power in a single cultic site. In the face of this opposition, David relented.

In place of a temple, David constructed a dynasty. Nathan provides God's blessing, and the roots of a divine-right hereditary monarchy were born. A new covenant was announced in which Yahweh promises that there will always be a king of the line of David ruling in Jerusalem (2 Sam 7:7–17). This is known as the "everlasting covenant." This covenant functioned as a royal insurance policy against assassination. There are only two recorded assassinations of a Davidic ruler in Judah mentioned in the text (Joash, 2 Kgs 12:20; Amon, 2 Kgs 21:23). During the entire four hundred years of Judah's existence as a nation, the everlasting covenant successfully maintained the ideology granting the Davidic dynasty a divine right to rule.

David's Court
History
(2 Sam 10–20)

David is portrayed as leading military campaigns against neighboring kingdoms after he becomes king (2 Sam 6 and 8). But eventually age and the increasing bureaucracy of the monarchy relegated David to the sidelines. Gradually, David became identified with the institution of the monarchy, and thus his personal life became more restricted. For instance, he could no longer lead the army (2 Sam 11:1). If he were killed in battle, this would throw the nation into turmoil, for at that time the idea of hereditary succession was not yet firmly established. Thus David became more of an administrator. This does not seem to have been his strongest talent. Much of the narrative about his life as king is filled with the problems he had while managing the activities of the people and his own family.

For example, David's power relative to other kingdoms is called into question by the actions of the newly installed king of Ammon. When David sends emissaries to officially greet the new king and reaffirm previous treaty agreements, Hanun, the son of Nahash, decides to test David's resolve. He orders that the Israelite messengers be disgraced and sent back to David as a symbolic challenge. The Ammonites shave off half of David's envoys' beards and cut away the lower half of their garments (2 Sam 10:3–5). This insult to their dignity was really a slap in David's face that could only be met with force. David thus has to resolve this crisis by sending Joab and the army into Ammon to defeat them and their Aramean allies (2 Sam 10:6–19).

On the domestic front, David once again finds himself using violence to handle a problem. It begins when he commits adultery with a woman named Bathsheba (2 Sam 11:2–5). To cover up this crime, he arranges for her husband, Uriah the Hittite, to be killed in battle (2 Sam 11:14–21). This lawless act sets the stage for a theme that will dominate relations between kings and prophets throughout the history of the nation. David's adultery is revealed and condemned by the prophet Nathan using a motif known as **the king's call to justice.** It emphasizes that even the king is not above the law and will be called to justice by Yahweh, a justice that will affect his rule and that of his descendants.

The King's Call to Justice Motif

- The king sins.
- The king is confronted by a prophet about his sin.
- The king repents.
- The punishment that should be imposed on the king is instead imposed on the next generation.

Nathan predicts that trouble will be "raised up" against David from within his "own house" and that another man will steal his wives, just as David has stolen Uriah's wife (2 Sam 12:11). After hearing the prophet's denunciation, David admits to Nathan that he has "sinned against the Lord" (2 Sam 12:13). Nathan replies that the punishment for adultery (death) is lifted from David's shoulders, but Bathsheba's child, the physical evidence of David's crime, will die (2 Sam 12:14).

Almost immediately, the problems that Nathan had predicted begin as David's sons jockey for position as his successor. The most disruptive of these maneuvers began with a conflict between David's sons Amnon and Absalom. Each sought to weaken the other's position. The conflict between the two brothers is underscored in the events of 2 Sam 13. Amnon raped Tamar (his half-sister, Absalom's full sister), and in response Absalom arranged the murder of Amnon. He is then forced to spend several years in exile (2 Sam 13:23–39).

Such sordid events had to be set aside when political reality required that Absalom be returned to court. Absalom was the heir to the throne. Joab arranged his return with the assistance of a wise woman (a female elder) from Tekoa (2 Sam 14:1–24). Once again it is possible to see in this episode that Joab is often David's political reality check. It was Joab's murder of Abner that had opened the way for David to become king and it had been Joab who had arranged Uriah's death in battle. Now, when the king seemed powerless in a dangerous situation, Joab took the action necessary to convince David to return Absalom to Jerusalem.

The period of exile had convinced Absalom that he should take the throne, not wait for it to be given to him. He built a following among the younger leaders. This was actually aided by David's own inattention to administrative matters, such as his failure either to hear legal cases or to appoint judges to hear them (2 Sam 15:2–6). Having "stolen the hearts" of the people, Absalom stages a successful coup d'état by having himself proclaimed king in Hebron (David's first seat of power; 2 Sam 15:6–12). The magnitude of Absalom's popular support forces David to retreat from the capital in disgrace (2 Sam 15:13–37). The final element of Nathan's predictions comes true when Absalom publicly has sex with ten of David's concubines (2 Sam 16:20–22).

In this darkest period of his life, David reemerges as the decisive leader who had outwitted Saul and the Philistines (see inset for the specific political moves he makes). Perhaps most important, he leaves a double-agent, Hushai, in Jerusalem to confuse Absalom's counselors (2 Sam 15:32–37). This allows him to buy enough time to reorganize his army and ultimately defeat Absalom in battle (2 Samuel 16–19).

David's Strategy to Regain the Kingdom

After being forced by Absalom's army to flee Jerusalem, David takes a series of steps that will ultimately allow him to reclaim his throne:

- He leaves ten concubines in the palace to maintain his royal presence there (2 Sam 15:15–16).

- He ascertains the loyalty of his Gittite mercenary troops (2 Sam 15:18–22).

- He sends the high priests, Levites, and the ark back into Jerusalem, thereby separating his political fortunes from the establishment of Jerusalem as the religious capital of Israel (2 Sam 15:24–29).

- He sends his adviser Hushai to Absalom as a double-agent to disrupt the counsel of other advisers such as Ahithophel, to delay pursuit of David's forces, and to provide information, through the priests, to David's army (2 Sam 15:32–37).

- He takes steps to prevent Mephibosheth, Saul's grandson, from taking advantage of Absalom's rebellion (2 Sam 16:1–4).

- He does not punish the shaming taunts of Shimei, thus humbling himself and demonstrating his acceptance of Yahweh's judgment (2 Sam 16:5–13).

These internal struggles are symptomatic of newly formed nations that do not yet have an established line of succession. David even had to shame his own tribal elders to publicly welcome him back as king after Absalom's defeat (2 Sam 19:9–12). Considerable effort had to be made to reestablish political ties with potentially dangerous members of his court, like Jonathan's son Mephibosheth (2 Sam 19:24–30), and David was not able completely to satisfy the elders of the northern tribes (2 Sam 19:41–43).

The strains made evident in the nation by this struggle also spawned another revolt, led this time by a northern leader named Sheba. His cry of secession, "We have no portion in David, no share in the son of Jesse! Everyone to your tents, O Israel!" (2 Sam 20:1), was echoed in a later conflict that resulted in a permanent division of the nation.

Sheba's revolt once again required Joab to step in to quell a storm. David relieved Joab of his command after he had disobeyed orders and killed Absalom (2 Sam 18:5–15). But Amasa, the man who replaced Joab, was an ineffective commander. Joab eliminated Amasa, relying on his army to support his callous murder (2 Sam 20:7–13). At the end of the campaign, Joab trapped the rebels in the city of Abel Beth-maacah and negotiated there with a wise woman (a female elder), who spoke for her people and traded Sheba's life for the lives of those of her city (2 Sam 20:14–22). As a result the nation remained intact for another generation.

The Contest for Kingship

Adonijah's Faction:	**Solomon's Faction:**
Joab, Abiathar	Benaiah, Zadok, Nathan, Bathsheba

David's reign ends with an embarrassing story of his physical decline. He fails to have intercourse with his last "wife," Abishag (1 Kgs 1:4), and this signals to his surviving sons that it is time to choose his successor. Factions arose favoring two of David's sons, Adonijah and Solomon. These factions split along the lines of the categories "old men" and "new men." One group consisted of leaders who had served David throughout his career and the other was made up of men who had come to power only after David became king in Jerusalem. The conflict was resolved when Bathsheba and Nathan joined together in convincing David to name Solomon as his heir. Once this was accomplished, Solomon's succession was assured and all Adonijah could do was accept the situation. There was some purging of the administration, when Joab was executed for past crimes (1 Kgs 2:28–34) and Abiathar, the high priest, was exiled. This latter move is particularly important in the history of the priesthood because from this point on the priests are led by the descendants of Abiathar's priestly rival, Zadok (1 Kgs 2:26–27, 35).

Solomon's Reign
(1 Kgs 1–11;
2 Chron 1–9)
The narrative of Solomon's reign is not as complete or developed as the narrative of David's reign. In the account in the book of Kings, much more attention is given to Solomon's administrative activities than to his personal life. This could reflect the author's interest in the evolution of the monarchy into an institution. In former times the monarchy had functioned more as a personal vehicle of power. The version of these events that appears in the book of Chronicles (2 Chron 1–9) is much more concerned with Solomon's construction of the temple in Jerusalem. But this material dates to the period after the exile when the priestly community had replaced the monarchy as the leaders of the people, and thus their interest would be primarily in the temple, not politics.

Two themes dominate Solomon's reign:

The Wisdom Theme. This is designed to portray the king as the source of wisdom and justice for his people. One of David's principal mistakes was his failure to appoint judges and to hear cases (2 Sam 15:1-6). With the story of the two prostitutes (1 Kgs 3:16-28), Solomon's official recorder emphasizes that this king will have the wisdom to dispense justice fairly from the beginning of his reign.

Perhaps an even better demonstration of Solomon's wisdom can be found in his administrative policies. Recognizing that many of his father's problems had been caused by lingering tribal and regional loyalties, Solomon restructured the national administrative districts, **gerrymandering** (redrawing political boundaries) them in such a way that none of the old tribal territories were left intact (1 Kgs 4:7-19). He also initiated a program of public works that improved the transportation system and **infrastructure** (roads, bridges, public buildings), thus promoting a national economy and a greater identification with the state. Fortresses were constructed along the borders and new defensive systems were built at major strategic points like Gezer, Hazor, and Megiddo (1 Kgs 9:15-19) to ensure internal security.

Perhaps most important among Solomon's policies was the transformation of Israel into a nation among the nations. He made an alliance with the Phoenician king Hiram of Tyre. They became trading partners, operating a shipping enterprise that sailed the Mediterranean and the Red Sea and brought wealth and influence to both countries (1 Kgs 10). Solomon's new-found importance is evidenced by his marriage alliances with neighboring states, including a marriage with a daughter of the Egyptian pharaoh (1 Kgs 3:1).

The Temple Theme. Unlike his father, Solomon built a temple to Yahweh in Jerusalem (1 Kgs 5-7). This temple housed the ark of the covenant, although this object is almost never mentioned again after Solomon's time; e.g., see Jer 3:16 and 2 Chron 35:3. The temple became the home of the Israelite priesthood, led by Zadok, which established norms for Israelite religious practice. Solomon's alliance with Hiram was useful in supplying construction materials and the skilled workmen needed to build the temple and its furnishings. This monumental structure, built on Mount Zion, supersedes the ark and even the city of Jerusalem in importance in the traditions of the people.

The temple of Solomon became a symbol for the Davidic monarchy. Its site, like Jerusalem, was on politically neutral ground—the threshing floor of Araunah (2 Chron 3:1). The only event tied to this place was the sacrifice David made there to mark the end of the plague that God had sent to punish the king for taking a census (2 Sam 24:18-25). Suggestion of previous cultic usage was thus eliminated and the priestly community of Yahweh was given exclusive rights to the site. The purchase of the threshing floor (a place associated with dispensing of justice in the village culture) by King David and the building of the temple by King Solomon placed royal sanction on the Yahweh cult.

In his dedication of the completed temple, Solomon followed David's example and initiated sacrifices of various kinds (peace offerings, burnt offerings, cereal offerings), followed by a seven-day feast for all of the people (1 Kgs 8:62–65). This set a precedent for the king to officiate at sacrifices and initiate worship services. But it was left to the priests to conduct these religious activities.

Despite the wealth and national spirit created by Solomon, the biblical writers ultimately chose to focus on his failure to obey the covenant with Yahweh and thus blamed Solomon for the political division of the kingdom (1 Kgs 11:1–13). They pointed to the **cosmopolitan** (culturally diverse) influence of the international builders of the temple as well as the many foreign wives Solomon brought to the capital. They emphasized that the influences of other cultures and the worship of other gods caused the Israelites to lose sight of the God who had made the kingdom possible. **Syncretism**, the borrowing of cultural ideas, thus became the great sin of the Israelite people and a principal theme in the writing of their history by the Deuteronomic historian.

Once again, the motif of calling the king to justice appears in the narrative, and Solomon is confronted with his **apostasy** by Yahweh (1 Kgs 11:11–13). He is told that the kingdom will be torn away from his descendants, but Yahweh will allow them to retain control over Judah and Jerusalem. Then the prophet Ahijah anounces the divine recognition of a new political figure, a former public-works official named Jeroboam. The stage is set for the division of the kingdom that will occur after Solomon's death (1 Kgs 11:29–40).

The story of the early monarchic period sets precedents for later rulers. Two paths to leadership emerge. In the southern kingdom of Judah, the everlasting covenant was employed to ensure the continuation of David's dynasty. In the northern kingdom of Israel, the pattern of succession was often based on the intervention of prophetic figures and the assassination of rulers by rebel leaders.

The establishment of the monarchy marked a centralization of both political and religious leadership. The priesthood quickly became linked with the monarchy, and in order to keep their positions of power and privilege, they often served the interests of the king rather than of God. In the later monarchic period this resulted in the emergence of prophets who serve as the loyal opposition to palace and temple.

STUDY QUESTIONS

1. Discuss the theme of calling the king to justice in the story of David's adultery with Bathsheba.

2. Discuss the role played by Joab in David's court.

3. Point out the actions taken by Solomon to transform Israel into a nation-state.

4. Define: syncretism, apostasy, concubine.

THE DIVIDED MONARCHY

***Division within
the Kingdom*** After the death of Solomon, his son Rehoboam assumed the throne of Israel. There is no problem of succession mentioned in the text, and therefore the idea of hereditary monarchy seems to have become well established by this time. However, Rehoboam inherited a kingdom that was discontented with Davidic rule, and he faced the demands of the elders of the northern tribes, who requested that he allow more local autonomy in the various regions of the nation. Rehoboam attempted to intimidate these elders at a conference held at Shechem and only managed to infuriate them (1 Kgs 12:1–15). As a result the kingdom divided along a line just south of Bethel. The elders of the northern tribes denounced their former monarch and his dynasty with the words: "What share do we have in David? . . . To your tents, O Israel!" (1 Kgs 12:16). This same rallying cry had been used during Sheba's revolt in David's time (2 Sam 20:1), but this time there was no Joab to put down the rebellion.

Within this new political structure, Jeroboam emerged as the king of the northern kingdom of Israel with his capital at Tirzah. He had been appointed to serve by the prophet Ahijah (1 Kgs 11:26–40) and was hailed by the elders as king. Rehoboam continued to rule the southern kingdom of Judah from Jerusalem. This weakened both areas and their future problems are reflected in the almost immediate invasion of Judah by the Egyptian pharaoh Shishak, who looted its cities and took a ransom from the treasury of the Jerusalem temple (1 Kgs 14:25–26).

In order to establish an identity for his new kingdom and his dynasty, Jeroboam issued a series of decrees, which later became known as **Jeroboam's sin** in the biblical narrative. His actions were shrewd political moves, but the biblical writers, through the perspective of the **Deuteronomist** (which is a southern kingdom voice), brand them as the worst kind of heresy. After this point in the text, all kings are judged based on whether or not they continued to support Jeroboam's policies.

Jeroboam's Sin (1 Kgs 12:28–33)

- Jeroboam created a shrine at each end of his kingdom, one at Dan and one at Bethel, to serve as alternatives to Jerusalem.
- He placed golden calves in each shrine as substitutes for the ark and as symbols of the god "who brought us out of the land of Egypt."
- He used high places *(bamot)* for worship in the local areas.
- He appointed non-Levitical priests to replace the Levites, who were tied politically to the Jerusalem temple.
- He changed the religious calendar.

Because of his "sin," Jeroboam's house (royal dynasty) was condemned by the prophet Ahijah (1 Kgs 14:6–16; another example of calling the king to justice). No other specific claimant is designated by the prophet to take the throne. Thus succession by assassination becomes the rule in the northern kingdom. There were regular revolts, usually staged by military leaders, which resulted in a change of leadership. For example, a military commander named Zimri assassinated King Elah and crowned himself king (1 Kgs 16:8–14). However, Zimri held the throne for only seven days before he was assassinated by another military leader, Omri (1 Kgs 16:15–20). Subsequently, Zimri's name became synonymous with "traitor" in Israelite tradition, and men like him had to face the charge of sedition when they attempted to take control of the nation (2 Kgs 9:30–33). These political coups disrupted Israel's government and left it open to exploitation by larger nations. It is not surprising therefore that the northern kingdom was conquered and its people were carried off into exile well over a century before similar events took place in the southern kingdom of Judah.

Kings and Prophets in the Divided Kingdom   The division of the Israelite nation could not have come at a worse time. David's kingdom had been able to develop in large part because the Syro-Palestinian region had gained political independence from Egypt after the invasion of the Sea Peoples. From 1200 BCE to 800 BCE, a large number of small states like Israel formed (e.g., Philistia, Phoenicia, and Syria). They struggled among themselves, as is evidenced by the conflicts between Israel and Syria (1 Kgs 20:1–35; 22:29–40; 2 Kgs 12:17–18; 13:22–25). The diplomatic and military endeavors of these small states were based on their own policies and were not dictated to them by outside forces.

This all changed in the period after ca. 800 BCE. From this point on, the future of the two small nations of Israel and Judah was determined by the foreign policies of the emerging superpowers in Egypt and Mesopotamia. Assyria became the supreme power in Mesopotamia during the course of the century after 900 BCE. From their capital at Nineveh on the Tigris River, the Assyrian kings first gained control of the rest of Mesopotamia and then expanded westward toward the sea. Assyrian expansion eventually brought both Israel and Judah, as well as all of the other small nation states in Syro-Palestine and Transjordan, into **vassal** status. All of the economic and political decisions made by the kings of these small states were influenced either directly or indirectly by the political chess game played between Egypt and Assyria for the two hundred years following 800 BCE.

Our discussion of the period of the divided monarchy will touch on these historical events, but since our primary aim is to present what the biblical writers have to say about the period, we will devote most of our attention to the interaction between Israel's prophets and kings. The monarchs struggled with internal affairs as well as with the growing demands and threats of the international superpowers. The prophets were concerned that Israel and Judah maintain their covenantal obligations to Yahweh. Although they were not unaware of the political events of their time, they often demanded that a king take a course of action that made little political or practical sense (e.g., Isaiah's call for Ahaz to "be quiet" and leave the invaders of Judah to be dealt with by the Divine Warrior; see Isa 7).

Once the fates of Israel and Judah were sealed, the task of the prophets was to help rationalize why these events were necessary. They engaged in **theodicy,** an attempt to provide a religious explanation for why things happen the way they do (i.e., why God allows bad things to happen to the people). They tried to reassure the people while at the same time letting them know that it was Yahweh who brought about these destructive events. If the people were to continue to worship Yahweh, they had to be convinced that Yahweh was not defeated when their nation was defeated and that Yahweh would ultimately restore a **righteous remnant.** It is the combination of the exilic experience and the message of the prophets that transformed Judaism into a true monotheistic faith and created a people who could survive without a nation.

STUDY QUESTIONS

1. Describe "Jeroboam's sin."

2. Explain the political situation that so drastically affected Israel's future starting in 800 BCE.

3. Define: theodicy, righteous remnant, hegemony.

CHARACTERISTICS OF PROPHETS

In approaching the subject of the Hebrew prophets, it must be understood that these individuals were more than simple religious practitioners. Some of them were members of the priestly community, but they took a stance outside of it. Their role was to challenge the establishment and the social order, to remind the leadership and the people of their obligation to the covenant with Yahweh, and to provide the warning of punishment that accompanied a violation of the covenantal agreement.

The list of the characteristics of prophets that is provided in this chapter is designed to provide an overview. Not every prophet will exhibit each characteristic. But the student should be familiar with these characteristics and should be able to recognize them when they appear in the biblical text or in extrabiblical materials.

Call Narrative and Its Description The call narrative is the distinctive event marking the occasion when a person becomes a prophet. Some call narratives, like that of Moses, are quite elaborate. When a biblical writer includes a detailed description of a call narrative it is usually designed to enhance the importance of the prophet and the prophet's message.

The call narratives of Isaiah, Jeremiah, and Ezekiel were recounted by Israelites who had witnessed the coronation of monarchs. The literary pattern in these stories includes a divine encounter or **theophany** (Isa 6:1–2), an introductory word or greeting (Isa 6:3–5), an objection or demur (Isa 6:4–5), a commission (Isa 6:9–10), and a sign or talisman (Isa 6:11–13). The intention of the stories is to describe how God conferred authority on the prophet, not to provide an autobiography.

The call narrative has an important transformational element to it. A person who usually has been relatively undistinguished to this point in his or her life is transformed into a dynamic spokesperson for God. The new prophet is invested with special powers, a message, and a mission.

In addition to the simple calling of a person, the call narrative also highlights the majesty of God. Mountains shake, clouds or fog obscure human vision, earthquakes rumble, and divine beings (including angels) appear in theophanic manifestation. The reaction of the human to all this power is fear, hiding one's face, and amazement.

An identification sequence then takes place, with God providing both a name (although not always "*the* name," i.e., Yahweh) and a reason for appearing at this time and place. Identification is necessary because the Israelites lived their entire existence within a polytheistic milieu. All the other nations had many gods and it would have been only natural to wonder which god was speaking (note Moses' question to this effect in Exod 3:13).

The theophany provides the basis for the prophet's mission. Yahweh has identified a problem, and one of the people must be sent to provide a warning (e.g., Amos). The warning is necessary because, by definition, Yahweh is a righteous God. The wicked may be destroyed, but righteous humans must be given a warning that will allow them to rectify the problem and thereby save their own lives.

Perhaps because it is only natural or perhaps because it has been developed into a formal literary motif as part of the framework for these narratives, the human who has been singled out by God now attempts to demur. Excuses are given for why the person chosen is unworthy or incapable of doing the job. For example, Jeremiah claims that he is too young and does not know how to speak in public (Jer 1:6). Such excuses are swept aside by God with assurances of support, dissolved through the provision of special powers, or (in the case of Moses) nullified by incontrovertible signs.

Among the methods of dealing with the demur is an empowering event. This occurs in the call of Isaiah. Isaiah claims that he is not worthy to accept God's call or to speak God's words because he has "unclean lips." This means that his mortal lips could never be spiritually "clean" enough to speak holy words. The solution is for an angel to take a hot coal from the sacrificial brazier near the altar and to cauterize Isaiah's lips. This is not a physical burning but a spiritual purification that occurs in a vision, not in reality.

Once the excuses have been dealt with, a statement of mission is provided that charges the person called with a sense of what must be done. Sometimes a tone is created, such as in the charge given to Jeremiah, which speaks only of approaching punishment. But the primary purpose of the statement of mission is to identify the prophet with the call to mission and the message to be delivered.

Compulsion   A special compulsion is associated with being called as a prophet. A prophet's calling can be denied for a time (e.g., Jonah tries to flee from the Lord in Jonah 1:3–17). But ultimately the divine call must be answered. Prophetic compulsion includes the desire or ability to speak.

Many of the call narratives include a reassurance that God will give the prophet the words to be spoken (Exod 4:12; Jer 1:7-9). But prophets may be reluctant to speak harsh words or to condemn their own people. In these cases the prophet experiences a compulsion to speak that cannot be resisted (Jer 20:9).

At least in the case of Ezekiel, the prophet's speech is shown to be under the complete control of God. He was restrained early in his prophetic career from speaking any words of comfort or hope (Ezek 3:25-27). This restriction was then lifted after the fall of Jerusalem to Nebuchadnezzar's army in 587 BCE. He could then speak a more reassuring message that promised an eventual end to the exile and a restoration of the covenant between Yahweh and Israel.

Message   No prophet speaks his or her own message. It is always spoken in the name of God. One will never find an example of a prophet saying "Thus says Amos" or "Thus says Isaiah." The messenger formula is always "Thus says the LORD (Yahweh)" (see Mic 2:3; Jer 5:14).

The message is thus the most important aspect of the prophet, not the prophet himself or herself. This may be why they seldom mention specific names or dates that could draw the people away from the core of the message. Certainly, there are some prophets like Balaam (Num 22:4-6) and Elijah (1 Kgs 18:17) who acquire a reputation, but this is based on their message or their ability to speak for God.

Some prophets do stand out as individuals. Isaiah paraded through the streets naked. Jeremiah cried out his frustration from his prison cell and the public stocks. Ezekiel performed acts that were undignified and out of character for a priest. But no matter how oddly they may act or how flamboyant they may appear, the issue is ensuring that the people receive the message of God. Any outrageous acts were designed to attract the people's attention to that message.

Truth   For a prophet to gain credibility with the people, the message must come true. The Deuteronomic tradition cautions against prophets who call on the people to "follow other gods" (Deut 13:1-4). It also warns that a true prophet speaks in Yahweh's name alone, and that a true prophet's words come true (Deut 18:18-22). This is one reason why prophets note that they speak a message that comes from God. By doing this, they separate themselves from the words and thus cannot be charged with treason, sedition, or doomsaying themselves. It is also why some prophets speak an ambiguous message that can be interpreted in more than one way.

The greatest measure of trust and authority, however, comes to the prophet who takes the dangerous path of speaking about the present or the near future. In cases in which the prophet interprets present circumstances as signs of Yahweh's punishment or warns of impending judgment from an angry God, the prophet may arouse the hostility of the people who experience the punishment expressed in the prophetic message. A prophet may also face a trial by ordeal or a period of incarceration. The duration of the incarceration may correspond to the period from the presentation of the message until the moment when it is or is not fulfilled (e.g., 1 Kgs 22:26–28).

The audience that evaluates the truthfulness of a prophet must determine whether it will obey a true prophet's instructions, disobey them, or risk the possibility that the prophet is not a legitimate spokesperson for God. The urgency of determining the truthfulness of a prophet is heightened when two prophets speak contradictory messages. **Cognitive dissonance** results when both of the contradictory prophetic messages appear to be true and can be tested only by actual events (see Jer 28).

Vocabulary   It is only natural that prophets speak in the language of the people being addressed and use familiar images and vocabulary. This explains why there are so many pastoral and agricultural illustrations in the prophetic material. But prophets did not all speak to the same audience. The biblical prophets operated over a long period of time (ca. six hundred years). Their society and the political situation which they faced changed drastically during this period.

Nevertheless, one way that a prophet identified himself or herself as a prophet was by using the images or language of a previous prophet. It is not uncommon for one prophet to make statements similar to those of earlier prophets. Some portion of a prophet's career (often the call narrative) may have a parallel in the career of a past prophet. The career of Moses frequently played a paradigmatic role in the lives of later prophets (Deut 18:15). For example, Isaiah's call narrative (Isa 6:1–4) contains a visual image of the ark of the covenant, the earthquake, and the smoke found in Moses' Sinai theophany.

One example of the use of similar phrases or terms by various prophets is the phrase "all flesh." It appears most often in the latter chapters of Isaiah (Isa 40:5, 6; 49:26; 66:16, 23, 24; cf. Gen 6–9), which date to the end of the exile (ca. 538 BCE) and later. But it is also found in the writings of the exilic prophets Jeremiah (Jer 25:31; 32:27; 45:5) and Ezekiel (Ezek 20:48; 21:4, 5), as well as in the writings of the postexilic prophets Zechariah (Zech 2:13) and Daniel (Dan 4:12). This indicates that the phrase "all flesh" has become standard prophetic language in the period after 600 BCE.

What singles out a prophet from other prophets is most often the historical context of their message. Elijah spoke to Ahab, not to some future monarch of Israel. Isaiah's prophecy concerning the Syro-Ephraimitic war in Isa 7 was directed to a specific historical situation and referred to future events directly related to that situation. Haggai's pronouncement on the need to reconstruct the temple in Jerusalem fit only into the immediate postexilic period and to the rule of the governor Zerubbabel.

To be sure, the prophets alluded to the activities of previous prophets, but usually not by name (Amos 2:11; Zech 1:3-4). The prophets established a tradition of continuity in the message that they brought from Yahweh. This tradition linked the later prophets to the prophets known from the earliest stages in the history of the Israelite people.

Enacted Prophecies   Prophets were masters of the arts. They used not only words but also symbolic actions, or pantomimes. Prophets used three kinds of pantomimes: single dramatic gestures (e.g., Jeremiah buries his clothes in the river bank; Jer 13:1-11); austere practices or asceticism (e.g., Jeremiah refuses to marry, attend funerals, or celebrations; Jer 16:1-13); and interpretation of the silent actions of another (e.g., Jeremiah, like a teacher, draws the attention of his audience to the potter working at his wheel; Jer 18:2-4).

Pantomime emerged from the ancient and universal art of gesturing during social interaction. Anthropologists, sociologists, and dramatists continue to identify a wide variety of pantomimes first celebrated in the cave paintings of the Stone Age and still practiced in the magic practices, rituals, and dances of traditional societies. Technically, pantomime is theater without script. Performers in masks sometimes use words and music to accompany their gestures, but pantomime is primarily a visual art form whose medium is movement. Pantomime grew from a conviction in traditional cultures that only gestures, acrobatics, and dance can appropriately address human realities.

For the prophets, pantomime was not solely representational art describing coming events. It was a series of actions that were designed to bring changes that would alter the course of future events. Pantomime was a catalyst of social change that highlighted and sometimes ridiculed the faults of the establishment.

Both Male and Female Prophets   Both men and women functioned as prophets, and there does not seem to have been any distinction drawn between them as to authority or authenticity (e.g., see Huldah in 2 Kgs 22:14-20).

This is in harmony with the appearance of both male and female prophets elsewhere in the ancient Near East. Since these persons are "chosen" by a god to serve as a mouthpiece, their individual characteristics, including gender, have no bearing on the message. This is further evidence of the fact that prophets are not chosen for their self-importance, status, or personal abilities.

Manner of Prophetic Utterance

Prophetic speech is elicited in a variety of ways and uttered in several different styles. It is sometimes the result of a physical trance state (Ezek 8:1; 11:1-5). Occasionally prophecy is induced by music or dancing that creates a state of ecstasy (1 Sam 10:5, 10; 2 Kgs 3:15). Most often, however, prophecy is simply spoken as a report of a vision (e.g., 1 Kgs 22:19-22) or of the words of God as spoken to the prophet.

Prophetic words borrowed genres from a variety of social institutions. The woe or lament oracle portrayed the prophet as a mourner (Ezek 24:9-10). The parable and the proverb cast the prophet as a teacher (Isa 5:1-10). The miracle story and the call story drew upon features found in narratives about monarchs (2 Kgs 4:1-7; Jer 1:14-19). The covenant lawsuit and the oracle implied that the prophet was an emissary or a member of the divine assembly (1 Kgs 22:10-17; Hos 4:1-4). Oracles against nations placed the prophet in the role of a chief (Jer 48:46).

The miracle stories of Elijah and Elisha were told in villages from which monarchs taxed food and recruited warriors (1 Sam 8:11-17; 1 Kgs 21:1-29). The miracles of these prophets are not so much authorizations of the power of the prophets as they are indictments of the misuse of power by the monarchs. Virtually all the miracles focus on some aspect of feeding and protecting. Miracles demonstrated the effortlessness with which Yahweh could feed and protect the people in contrast to the costly efforts of the monarchs to feed and protect them through covenants with other nations. For example, monarchs took widows' sons for the army, thus putting them to death, whereas Elijah raised the son of the widow of Zarephath to life (1 Kgs 17:17-24). Monarchs taxed widows to death, but Elijah gave the widow an endless supply of oil (2 Kgs 4:1-7). When a borrowed ax necessary to clear the land is lost, Elisha returned it so that the lender would not foreclose on the land to pay for the ax (2 Kgs 6:1-7).

Social Role

As the loyal opposition to the priestly community and the monarchy, prophets expressed an egalitarian ideal of a society in which every person is equal under the law. Sometimes the prophets are mentioned as part of the cult community (e.g., Isaiah and Ezekiel) or as court prophets (e.g., Nathan). But they always seem to stand apart from these institutions in order to criticize them and to point out where they have broken the covenant with God. These prophets also created followings of disciples or schools of thought that spread the message of each prophet. The disciples and schools of various prophets ultimately organized the prophecies of their respective founding prophets into written, coherent documents.

Occasionally, a prophet (such as Elijah or Elisha) may appear to be a totally separate entity, peripheral to the mainstream of society. Prophets of this kind are not as isolated as they appear to be. They have a support group that functions as a sort of underground network, providing meals, offering a place to stay, and performing other tasks (2 Kgs 9:1–10).

In the political realm, the prophets served as the conscience of the kings. It was their job to remind the monarch that he was not above the law and could be punished like any other Israelite for an infraction of the covenant code. Prophets also participated in political acts. For example, Elisha has one of his "sons" (i.e., disciples) anoint Jehu as king (2 Kgs 9:1–13). Jeremiah counsels King Zedekiah to surrender the besieged city of Jerusalem to the Babylonians (Jer 21:1–10 and 38:17–18).

Prophetic   Since the prophets are viewed as the messengers of God, they
Immunity   are not held liable for the message they speak, and cannot be
killed because of that message. However, if for any reason suspicion is raised that the person may not be a true prophet, then the message is to be scrutinized to see whether or not it does come true (Jer 28:8–9). Should the message prove false, then the "false" prophet is subject to execution, either by the people or God (see Jeremiah's trial in Jer 26:12–19 and the contrasting fate of Hananiah in Jer 28:16–17).

Just because a prophet is spared from death, however, does not mean that he or she may not face public ridicule and physical punishment at the hands of dissenters. For instance, Amos is publicly denounced by Amaziah, the high priest at Bethel, for speaking without license in the "king's sanctuary" (Amos 7:12–13). Both Elijah and Jeremiah faced public censure (1 Kgs 18:17; Jer 36:21–26). Jeremiah was imprisoned (Jer 38:4–6) and placed in the stocks (Jer 20:2).

Audience   Prophets were concerned about the present and near future
because their job was to draw the people and the establishment back to the proper covenantal relationship with Yahweh. Sometimes their work was conducted prior to God's punishment. But many times their words explained why God had punished the people. The attempt to explain past or present

events as the result of divine punishment is known as a **theodicy.** Theodicy provides a rationalization for why evil or destruction has occurred to God's people.

The major exception to the emphasis on the contemporary context in prophetic speech is **apocalyptic** prophecies. Apocalyptic utterance is concerned with end times (**eschatology**). Apolcalyptic prophecy contains elements of tradition and history that are hidden in symbolic language. Zechariah and Daniel are the best examples of apocalyptic prophets in the Bible, but other portions contain apocalyptic literature. In general this material is dated from the exilic period to the mid-first century BCE. Apocalyptic literature employs many of the ideas and themes of earlier prophets, but speaks to a future time when the problems of the present are solved and God reigns over a restored nation.

Prophetic speech has often been quoted and reinterpreted in later texts. This was done first by other biblical writers (see the reuse of Micah's prophecy against Jerusalem [Mic 3:12] in Jeremiah's trial, Jer 26:17–19). The prophetic materials were later used by the writers of the New Testament (see Matt 1:23 for reuse of Isa 7:14) and later Christian theologians as the basis for their pronouncements and doctrines. These later commentaries on the prophetic works have their own intrinsic value in certain academic and religious contexts, but it should not be assumed that the original intent of a particular prophet in the Hebrew Bible was to foretell the establishment of Christianity.

Remnant Theme   All of the prophets use a remnant theme in their message. This springs out of the concept that a righteous God cannot utterly destroy righteous persons without providing them with a chance to survive. The story of Noah and the flood is one example of this theme. God speaks directly to Noah rather than employing a prophet, but in later Israelite history prophets serve as the bearer of a message of retribution by God for the failure of the people to obey the covenant. The prophets state that the punishment of the people is certain, but a few (a remnant) may survive the coming destruction and rebuild the nation from the ashes. Ezekiel's vision of the "marking of the innocents" (Ezek 9) is one of the best examples of this message. In this case, those persons who demonstrate a true repentance and sorrow over the sins of Jerusalem are marked by divine messengers and spared while the rest of the population is executed and the city is destroyed.

Having outlined and explained these basic characteristics of Israelite prophets, we will now turn to an examination of the message of each of them. The student should make an effort to identify the characteristics of prophets as they occur in their reading of the assigned texts.

Summary of Characteristics of Prophets

- **Call Narrative**: This is the event when a person is called to serve as a prophet. Some are quite spectacular, including a theophany, a demur by the person called, an empowering event, and a charge for mission. Others simply include the remark that a call has taken place—without any details.

- **Compulsion**: In whatever manner a person is called to be a prophet, it is unavoidable, and, once made, must be obeyed. The person cannot hold back or speak some other message.

- **Message**: The message of the prophets is from God and thus the prophets will speak "in the name of Yahweh," not in their own name. Certainly, prophets, such as Balaam, will acquire a reputation, but even so they must admit that when they speak as prophets it is God's word they are speaking.

- **Truth**: The question arises, When a person speaks in the name of God does that make him or her a true prophet? The answer is yes only if that message comes true. This also applies when two prophets present equally believable, but opposite, messages (**cognitive dissonance**).

- **Vocabulary**: Prophets will be "wordsmiths," that is, persons who use words or words plus gestures to get the point across. It is only natural that the prophets spoke in the language of the people being addressed, and used familiar images and vocabulary.

- **Enacted Prophecies**: These are generally easy to understand actions, but ones that require an explanation because they are so out of character for the person performing them. Like all pantomime, they require abstract thinking on the part of the audience.

- **Gender**: The prophetic office is not tied to a specific gender. Both men and women function as prophets and there does not seem to be any distinction drawn between them as to authority or authenticity.

- **Manner of Prophetic Utterance**: There are various means of receiving and then transmitting prophecies. It is sometimes the result of a physical trance state, occasionally induced by music or dancing (ecstatic prophecy), but most often the prophecy is spoken as a report of a dream experience or simply of what God has told the prophet to speak.

- **Role in Society**: Primarily, the prophet serves as the "loyal opposition" to the priestly community and the monarchy. They express an egalitarian ideal of a society in which every person is equal under the law. Sometimes the prophets are mentioned as part of the cult and as court prophets. However, they seem to always be able to stand apart from these institutions to criticize them and to point out where they have broken the covenant with God. Occasionally, the prophet will be a totally separate entity, peripheral to the mainstream of society. These prophets may have a support group, which functions as a sort of underground network, providing meals, a place to stay, and other aid.

- **Prophetic Immunity:** Despite the fact that prophets tell the people what they do not want to hear, they cannot be killed with impunity when it is certified that the words they are speaking are God's. This does not prevent imprisonment or physical punishment, but at least the messenger is not to be killed for an unpopular message.
- **Audience:** Nearly all of the non-apocalyptic material is directed to the prophets' own time. They were concerned about the present and the near future because their job was to draw the people and the establishment back to the proper covenantal relationship with Yahweh.
- **Remnant Theme:** This springs out of the concept that a righteous God cannot utterly destroy righteous persons without providing a chance for them to survive. Thus the prophet is sent to warn the nation, but with the expectation that it will be only the righteous who will heed that warning, do something about the problem, and therefore be allowed to survive and ultimately rebuild the nation.

STUDY QUESTIONS

1. Define "prophet" and discuss the significance of the call narrative.
2. Discuss the role of the prophet in relation to the king.
3. Discuss the use of enacted prophecies.
4. Define: theophany, messenger formula, cognitive dissonance, theodicy, apocalyptic, eschatology.

ELIJAH AND ELISHA

The Figure of Elijah   In the period immediately after the division of the kingdom, no strong prophetic figure emerges. A prophet named Ahijah does condemn Jeroboam, and an unnamed prophet publicly confronts Jeroboam during a sacrifice at Bethel (1 Kgs 13:1–10). But these are isolated incidents, not a systematic message of reform. It was not until the ninth century that the prophets Elijah and Elisha arose to challenge the king and the religious establishment in the northern kingdom.

The villains (Ahab and his Phoenician wife Jezebel) and the heroes (Elijah and Elisha) are bigger than life in the narrative of this period of Israelite history, and the text magnifies their actions. The drama begins with the marriage of Ahab and Jezebel. While this represents a logical political alliance between Israel and Phoenicia, the biblical writers present it as an invasion by the forces of Baal, a main deity in the pantheon of the Phoenician religion. Jezebel, whose name becomes synonymous with wickedness and infidelity, is portrayed as a fanatic. She hunts down the prophets and worshipers of Yahweh, killing all she can find. In the meantime, Ahab does nothing to stop her. This situation is ripe for a hero figure to set things right, just as in the Judges period.

Storm god astride a bull, lightning bolts in his hands.
From Arslan Task, eighth century.

Elijah, without a formal call narrative or even an introduction in the text, bursts on the scene and immediately confronts the powers of state and temple. He predicts a drought that lasts for three years and that brings famine throughout the land of Israel (1 Kgs 17:1). The significance of this prophecy is that Jezebel's god Baal is a god of storms and fertility. Thus the theme of this prophet and all others is firmly set forth: "Which god is really God?"

For Elijah, the three-year period is spent east of the Jordan and then in Phoenicia at Zarephath (1 Kgs 17:2–24). During this time, he demonstrates the power of his God, whose covenant promise was to provide land and children, by performing life-giving miracles. First Elijah miraculously feeds a starving widow and her son. Then he revives the son after he has apparently died. This stands in stark contrast to Ahab and Jezebel, who take away life with their purge of Yahweh worshipers and cause the famine in the land.

Bronze bull, dating around the twelfth century BCE.
Photo courtesy of Zev Radovan.

When the initial testing period is over, Elijah is instructed to return to Israel and challenge Ahab to a public contest. This staged test offers a dramatic demonstration of Yahweh's power and Baal's impotence (1 Kgs 18). Not since Moses' time (a fact emphasized here by the writers) has such a direct, public confrontation taken place between a political leader and a prophet.

The place of trial was Mount Carmel. This was a mountain-top shrine, a high place. Why did Elijah perform his religious trial in a place forbidden and condemned? One answer might be that he chose to take the fight to the enemy on their own ground. But the more likely reason is that high places were only condemned in the southern kingdom but were accepted as appropriate sacred sites in the north. It should be noted, however, that the altar to Yahweh on Mount Carmel had to be repaired before it could be used, which suggests that it had not been used recently.

The contest was quite simple. The four hundred prophets of Baal and Elijah constructed an altar and then in turn called upon their god to accept the sacrificial bull and bring rain to end the drought. The suspense, as well as the cosmic nature of this story, is heightened when Elijah lets the opposition go first. Their day-long pleading with Baal to appear goes unanswered despite their "limping" dance and ritual blood-letting (1 Kgs 18:26–28). Elijah takes the opportunity to taunt the failed performance and ridicule their nonresponsive god:

> Cry aloud! Surely he is a god; either he is meditating or he has wandered away, or he is on a journey, or perhaps he is asleep and must be awakened (1 Kgs 18:27).

When he took his turn, Elijah performed a series of symbolic acts designed to restore Yahweh as the God of Israel (1 Kgs 18:30–40). He gathered the people around him and publicly rebuilt the platform of a ruined altar that had previously been dedicated to Yahweh (cf. Gideon's actions in Judg 6:28–32). He then took twelve stones representing the twelve tribes of Israel and constructed the altar in Yahweh's name (cf. Joshua's monument of twelve stones in Josh 4:1–9). Finally, he had a trench dug around the altar and had water poured over the sacrificed bull and wood three times, filling the trench and saturating the fuel for the sacrifice. This last step symbolized the bounty of rain to come and also served as a means of demonstrating that no chance spark has lit his altar (much like magicians who announce to the audience that they "have nothing up their sleeve").

Then at a time specifically set aside during the day for sacrifices and oblations, Elijah called upon Yahweh to demonstrate that the "God of Abraham, Isaac, and Israel" is the "God in Israel" and that Elijah is his prophetic servant. The divine response was immediate: The sacrifice, the altar, and the water were all consumed by fire from heaven. Such a powerful act elicited two powerful emotions. The first is fear, which evokes an awed statement of submission by the people, "The Lord indeed is God!" (1 Kgs 18:39). The second is anger, which leads to a massacre of the prophets of Baal (1 Kgs 18:40). All that remained was for the rain to come, which it did after a sevenfold ritual by Elijah and his servant (1 Kgs 18:41–46). But Elijah and Yahweh had only won the battle, not the war. Jezebel remained an enemy to contend with, and when she threatened to kill Elijah, he ran away for fear of his life (1 Kgs 19:2).

One of the curious aspects of Elijah's career is his outsider status. He came from Gilead, a Transjordanian region, not specifically part of the kingdom of Israel. He had no ties to any group or person other than a servant. He relied solely on God to feed him or to direct him to persons to care for his needs. In his flight from Mount Carmel, Elijah became the ultimate loner in a society that defined itself in terms of familial, economic, and political relationships.

Elijah survived his journey to Mount Horeb (Mount Sinai) only because an angel provided bread and water (1 Kgs 19:4–8). This journey afforded an opportunity for the text to link Elijah to Moses and furnished the setting for the call narrative that is absent in the narrative of Elijah's first appearance.

Elijah's call on Mount Horeb is staged much like previous encounters with fugitives (cf. Adam and Eve in Gen 3:8–13 and Hagar in Gen 16:7–12). He is addressed with a rhetorical question, "What are you doing here, Elijah?" This sort of question generally produces an excuse or a justification by the person addressed.

Elijah explains that he has been working "zealously" for Yahweh but that he has now taken flight so that there will be at least one voice left to defend God.

What follows is a mystifying theophany in which the usual signs of power are discounted as not containing the Spirit of God. Elijah experiences strong winds, earthquake, and fire. But the prophet can only perceive the presence of Yahweh in the silence that follows all these manifestations (1 Kgs 19:11–13). This may be because Baal is a storm god and Yahweh is attempting to create a clear difference between them. It is also possible that this is an addition by a later writer whose theology has moved beyond simple natural events as signs for God and now wishes to show that Yahweh's presence is both universal and internal.

Whatever the case, the theophany is followed by a repeat of the question of why Elijah has come and a charge to the prophet to perform three acts that will transform Israel religiously and politically (1 Kgs 19:15–16). First, he is to anoint Hazael as king of Aram (Syria). Second, he is to anoint Jehu as king over Israel. Third, he is to anoint Elisha as his prophetic successor.

As it turns out, Elijah only performs one of these tasks and leaves the other two for his successor. He designates Elisha as his successor by **casting his mantle** (a length of cloth that serves as a cloak) over Elisha's shoulders. The newly appointed prophet asked and was granted permission to tell his parents goodbye (contrast Jesus' response to the man called in Luke 9:61–62). Elisha then disappears from the narrative until 2 Kgs 1.

The Elijah cycle of stories resumes in 1 Kgs 21 with the story of Naboth's vineyard. This is a classic example of the motif of **the king's call to justice.** It begins with Ahab's desire to own a fine vineyard that adjoined his property. The owner, Naboth, refuses because ownership and inheritance to the land was tied to Yahweh's covenantal promise. Jezebel then demonstrates once again the difference between Phoenician and Israelite royalty by obtaining the land for her husband through deceit and force. She hires two false witnesses, has Naboth charged with treason and blasphemy, and has him executed (along with his family; 2 Kgs 9:26). With the land left without an heir, Ahab claims it.

At this point the motif of the "king's call to justice" becomes the dominant element in the narrative. As Ahab is stepping off his new property, Elijah confronts him with his sin and condemns Ahab's family to a terrible fate (1 Kgs 21:17–24). The king, terrified by Elijah's curse, performs an act of contrition so complete that even Yahweh remarks on it: "Have you seen how Ahab has humbled himself before me?" The result is that the punishment is to be deferred to Ahab's successors.

The editors of this material apparently found themselves confronted with two endings to Ahab's story. First Kings 22 tells the story of Ahab's death. This story contains all of the chilling aspects of Elijah's curse (e.g., dogs licking up his blood). This seems to contradict what has just been resolved in chapter 21. It is probably only reflective of a common solution employed by the editors in other similar situations. They simply chose to include both stories rather than dispense with a narrative that explained how the wicked Ahab received his justly deserved end.

The episode in 1 Kgs 22 substitutes Micaiah for Elijah as the prophet "who never prophesies anything favorable about" Ahab. The prophet Micaiah must face ridicule, contradict the demonstrations staged by the four hundred court prophets of Ahab, and confront two kings (Ahab and Jehoshaphat) enthroned before the gate of Samaria (1 Kgs 22:10–11). In this version of Ahab's fate, Micaiah tells a tale of a "lying spirit" sent by Yahweh to "entice Ahab" to go to his death (1 Kgs 22:19–23). Ahab tries to tip the odds in his favor by imprisoning Micaiah and then disguising himself as a common soldier. This strategy fails. Ahab is killed and his blood is lapped up by dogs as it drips from the floor of his chariot (1 Kgs 22:29–38).

The cycle of Elijah stories continues with a short episode in which Elijah continues to condemn Ahab's family for trusting in every god except Yahweh (2 Kgs 1:3–16). The Elijah cycle finishes with the story of his being carried up to heaven (2 Kgs 2:1–14). This latter narrative includes Elisha's transformation into Elijah's successor and Elisha's receipt of Elijah's power. Elisha's new status as Elijah's successor is symbolized by Elisha's use of Elijah's mantle to cross the Jordan on dry land (cf. Joshua's crossing of the Jordan after he became the successor of Moses). Elijah departs as mysteriously as he had arrived. The traditions that surround him have made him unique, especially the fact that he is only one of two persons (Enoch in Gen 5:24) in the OT/HB who do not die. In early Judaism he becomes the precursor of the coming Messiah. An empty chair and a glass of wine are always left for him at the Passover celebration.

The Elisha Cycle   Elisha immediately takes up Elijah's mantle and assumes his responsibilities as the champion of Yahweh and as the chief critic of Israel's monarchy. The stories about Elisha give more attention to popular society than the stories involving Elijah. Much of what is told about Elisha includes episodes in which he helps members of Israelite society or his own support group, the **sons of the prophets** (prophetic apprentices) or their dependents. In that sense, there is less real narrative flow in the Elisha cycle than in the Elijah material. Elisha seems to move from one situation in which he performs a miracle to another (see inset). He spends only part of his time directly confronting the kings or priests and instead is frequently portrayed helping or encouraging the people of the land. This is extremely unusual in what is otherwise a royal annal and perhaps points up once again how important the **egalitarian** ideal was to the Israelites. Certainly, Elisha's concern for rewarding or protecting the members of his support group (especially in 2 Kgs 4) can be seen as a conscious attempt by the storyteller to demonstrate that the faithful will be cared for by Yahweh and his prophets.

Elisha's Miracles

*Crosses Jordan on dry land (2 Kgs 2:13–14)

Purifies Jericho's water (2 Kgs 2:19–22)

Curses boys at Bethel (2 Kgs 2:23–24)

*Multiplies oil in a jar (2 Kgs 4:1–7)

*Revives Shunammite's son (2 Kgs 4:18–37)

Purifies pot of stew (2 Kgs 4:38–41)

Feeds one hundred men (2 Kgs 4:42–44)

Makes iron ax head float (2 Kgs 6:1–7)

Revives dead man (2 Kgs 13:20–21)

Parallels a miracle of Elijah

In the cases in which Elisha deals with political matters and political leaders, his role is less condemning than Elijah's. Elisha appears to serve as a catalyst for events that Yahweh has previously predicted (see the charges given to Elijah in 1 Kgs 19:15–18). Thus he travels to Syria and anoints Hazael, a Syrian general, as the new king of that country (2 Kgs 8:7–15). Later Elisha sends one of the "sons of the prophets" to Jehu, an Israelite general, and anoints him as Yahweh's chosen king (2 Kgs 9:1–10). The result of these actions is war and murder. The prophet has set in motion the assassination of reigning kings in both countries (2 Kgs 8:15). His actions result in a civil war in Israel that ended in a general purge of Ahab's family, highlighted by Jezebel's being thrown from a window as Jehu rides triumphantly into the capital city of Samaria (2 Kgs 9:30–37). Subsequently, the supporters of Ahab's family and the worshipers of Baal are massacred (2 Kgs 9:14–10:27).

Only in the story of the campaign against Moab does Elisha assume the role of condemning prophet (2 Kgs 3). Here he travels with the combined armies of Jehoram, the son of Ahab, and Jehoshaphat. When their ill-conceived line of march through the wilderness of Edom takes the army into dry country that cannot support them, the prophet is called on to save them. Elisha is reluctant to act, but because the "righteous" king Jehoshaphat is present, he calls for a musician and subsequently enters a trance state. He then predicts life-giving water in the dry wadi bed (which eventually does come as a result of rain upstream) and promises ultimate success for the expedition (2 Kgs 3:13–20).

This episode is paralleled in the **Stele of Mesha,** written for the king of Moab who is mentioned in 2 Kgs 3:4. However, it is composed from the Moabite viewpoint, and it describes complete victory for Moab. Neither the prophet Elisha nor the desperate sacrifice of Mesha's son (2 Kgs 3:26–27) are mentioned in this document.

> **Stele of Mesha**
>
> I am Mesha, King of Moab. . . . Omri, the King of Israel, controlled Moab for many years because Chemosh, our chief god, was angry at his people. . . . In my time, however, I have triumphed over Omri's son causing Israel to be forced out of our land forever! . . . Chemosh dwells supreme (*OTPar*, p. 113).

One additional theme found in the Elisha cycle of stories is **universalism**. Both Elijah and Elisha demonstrate that Yahweh truly is a powerful God. In 2 Kgs 5, it is left to a Syrian general to make a statement of absolute faith in the total supremacy of Yahweh above all gods. Naaman is a high-ranking military commander afflicted with leprosy. When all other avenues fail to provide a cure, Naaman takes the advice of his wife's Israelite slave girl and seeks an opportunity to consult Elisha. Some difficult political maneuvering is necessary to gain him safe passage into what is otherwise enemy territory, but eventually he comes to Elisha's house (2 Kgs 5:5–9). Ironically, he never sees the prophet face to face. Instead the prophet's servant, Gehazi, relays instructions to the general. This is neither proper etiquette nor an impressive prophetic encounter, and the Syrian nearly storms off in anger. But he is convinced by his servants to try the cure suggested by the prophet: to dip himself seven times in the Jordan River. Miraculously, he is cured of his leprosy and he rushes back to reward Elisha. In his enthusiasm, Naaman states: "Now I know there is no God in all the earth except in Israel" (2 Kgs 5:15).

Elisha refuses any payment and the general asks him for a future consideration. It seems that Naaman is required to participate in an annual religious ritual honoring the Syrian god Rimmon as part of his job as adviser to the Syrian king. Naaman assures the prophet this will in no way conflict with his new devotion to Yahweh. He proves this by taking two loads of Israelite soil with him back to Syria (2 Kgs 5:17). Naaman's action was based on the belief that gods are localized within the lands in which they are worshiped. By taking Israelite soil back to Syria, Naaman believes he is physically taking the presence of Yahweh back to his country and, therefore, the ability to worship God there.

Although he dies, Elisha's narrative concludes with a story nearly as mysterious as in the Elijah cycle. Apparently, the site of Elisha's burial was forgotten.

Later the tomb was reopened and a new corpse was lowered into place. The burial party was interrupted by a band of raiders and they abandoned the body in their escape. When the body fell among Elisha's bones, the dead man revived, jumped from the tomb, and ran after his friends (2 Kgs 13:20–21). Just as Elijah's mantle had been left behind and functioned as an object of power, so too did Elisha's bones.

STUDY QUESTIONS

1. Describe and discuss the significance of the Mount Carmel contest.

2. Describe and discuss the significance of the story of Naboth's vineyard.

3. Discuss the responsibility of the prophet to the "sons of the prophet" in 2 Kings 4.

4. Discuss the use of the universalism theme in the story of Naaman.

5. Define: casting his mantle, calling the king to justice, cognitive dissonance, sons of the prophet, egalitarianism, Stele of Mesha.

THE LATE MONARCHIES

The divided monarchy contributed to a general lack of stability in Syro-Palestine. Although Judah had a stable system of hereditary rule, its natural resources and population were too limited to allow it to have a significant effect on the region as a whole. In the north, the monarchy was continually disrupted by coups and assassinations, leaving the government and the people without any stability. This played into the hands of the reemerging superpower nations of Egypt and Assyria. While Israel and Judah exhausted themselves in petty wars with Syria and the nations of the transjordanian region (1 Kgs 20, 22 and 2 Kgs 3, 6–7), the superpowers consolidated their power at home and prepared to expand into Syro-Palestine. The last period of relative independence for Israel and Judah came in the reigns of Israel's king Jeroboam II (786–746) and Judah's king Uzziah (782–742).

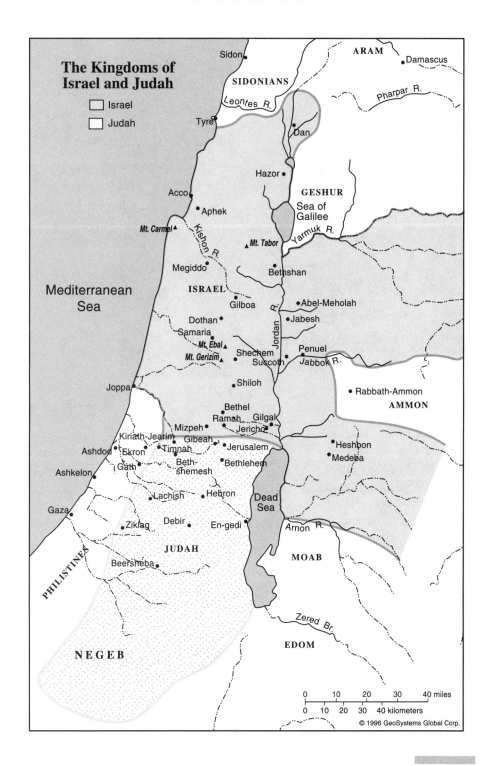

The Kingdoms of Israel and Judah

Israel

Judah

Sidon

SIDONIANS

ARAM

Damascus

Pharpar R.

Leontes R.

Tyre

Dan

Hazor

GESHUR

Acco

Sea of Galilee

Aphek

Mt. Carmel

Kishon R.

Yarmuk R.

Mt. Tabor

Mediterranean Sea

Megiddo

Bethshan

ISRAEL

Gilboa

Abel-Meholah

Dothan

Jabesh

Samaria

Jordan R.

Mt. Ebal

Penuel

Mt. Gerizim

Shechem

Succoth

Jabbok R.

Shiloh

Joppa

Bethel

Rabbath-Ammon

Ramah

Gilgal

AMMON

Mizpeh

Jericho

Kiriath-Jearim

Gibeah

Ashdod

Ekron

Timnah

Jerusalem

Heshbon

Ashkelon

Gath

Beth-shemesh

Bethlehem

Medeba

Lachish

Hebron

Dead Sea

Gaza

Ziklag

Debir

En-gedi

Arnon R.

JUDAH

MOAB

Beersheba

PHILISTINES

NEGEB

Zered Br.

EDOM

0   10   20   30   40 miles

0   10   20   30   40 kilometers

© 1996 GeoSystems Global Corp.

The Black Obelisk of Shalmaneser III records Jehu's payment of tribute to the Assyrians.
Courtesy of the British Museum.

Black Obelisk of Shalmaneser III

Hazael, king of Aram, ran for his life leaving 1,121 chariots, 470 horses, and a supply convoy on the battlefield.

Jehu, king of Israel, ransomed his life with silver, gold, lead, and hardwood (*OTPar*, p. 124).

The policies of Israel and Judah with regard to other nations proved to be shortsighted. After 740 BCE, the military might of the Assyrian king Tiglath-Pileser III (biblical Pul, 2 Kgs 15:19) transformed the political character of the entire region. The Assyrian war machine had first entered the area in 853 BCE. On that occasion their king Shalmaneser III was defeated at the battle of Qarqar by a coalition of Phoenician and Palestinian kings, including Ahab. After defeating the Syrians in 841, however, Jehu, king of Israel, was forced to pay tribute to the Assyrians (as recorded in the Black Obelisk inscription of Shalmaneser). From that time on the Assyrians repeatedly raided Syro-Palestine, devastating large areas and massacring entire city populations. Situated on the major trade routes, Syria, Israel, and the Philistine city-states were soon absorbed into the growing Assyrian empire.

These new vassal states were restive under foreign rule. With the encouragement of Egypt they repeatedly revolted. In 736 BCE, Israel and Syria precipitated the Syro-Ephraimitic war. This conflict was designed to drive King Ahaz of Judah from his throne because he had refused to join their revolt against the Assyrians. Ahaz subsequently allied himself with the Assyrians (against the advice of the prophet Isaiah, Isa 7:1–9), and this led to the defeat of the rebels. However, the price Ahaz paid for Assyrian help was full submission to the stronger nation. He even introduced Assyrian worship practices into the temple in Jerusalem (2 Kgs 16:1–18). His **syncretistic** practices (using borrowed cultural ideas) are first indicted under the general charge that he followed the practices of the kings of Israel rather than his ancestor David (2 Kgs 16:2–4). But he also constructed an Assyrian-type altar, adopted Assyrian sacrificial rituals, and removed cult objects previously used in the worship of Yahweh from the temple in Jerusalem. The explanation given in the text for these actions is quite simple: "He did this because of the king of Assyria" (2 Kgs 16:18b).

Syncretistic Practices

Ahaz was twenty years old when he began to reign; he reigned sixteen years in Jerusalem. He did not do what was right in the sight of the LORD his God, as his ancestor David had done, but he walked in the way of the kings of Israel. He even made his son pass through fire, according to the abominable practices of the nations who the LORD drove out before the people of Israel. He sacrificed and made offerings on the high places, on the hills, and under every green tree (2 Kgs 16:2–4).

A subsequent revolt by Israel's King Hoshea in 722 BCE caused the Assyrians to take the drastic measure of destroying Israel's capital at Samaria and deporting a large portion of the population to some other part of the Assyrian empire, never to return (2 Kgs 17:1–6).

The kingdom of Judah had more effective leadership during the reign of Hezekiah (727–698 BCE). Shortly after the death of Sargon II (705 BCE), Hezekiah moved to free Judah from Assyrian control (2 Chron 32:3–6, 28–29). He briefly ignited a political and religious reform movement that was designed to strengthen Jerusalem's role as the seat of power. Among his preparations he reinforced Jerusalem's defenses by constructing the Siloam tunnel (2 Kgs 20:20). He also attempted to establish alliances with surrounding states in an effort to create a united front against the Assyrians. The tenuous nature of these alliances, however, can be seen in

Hezekiah's refusal to join the Ashdod revolt in 711 BCE (perhaps at the urging of the prophet Isaiah; see Isa 20).

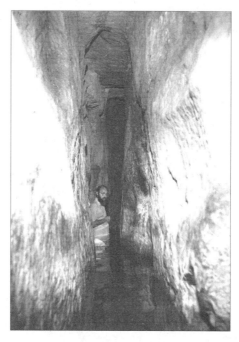

Hezekiah's tunnel connected the city of Jerusalem with water wells, thus enabling the city to have water during any military siege without exposure. Built ca. end of eighth century BCE. Photo courtesy of Zev Radovan.

But Hezekiah's alliances could not be overlooked by the Assyrians. The Assyrians repeatedly invaded Judah and caused the destruction of many cities, including the major fortress city of Lachish. The Assyrian king Sennacherib recorded the extent of this devastation in his royal annals. He proudly boasts that during the year 701 BCE he captured forty-six cities, and enslaved over 200,000 people (probably an inflated number). The biblical account of the siege of Jerusalem credits the miraculous survival of the city to divine intervention (2 Kgs 19:32–37; Isa 37:36–38). But the ransom paid by Hezekiah, internal politics of the Assyrian empire, and the appearance of an Egyptian army may have also contributed to the lifting of the siege. Second Kings 19:37 implies the degree of intrigue that existed at court when it states that Sennacherib was murdered by his sons upon his return to Nineveh (688 BCE).

As a result of the destruction of the northern kingdom in 722 BCE and the devastating Assyrian invasions of Judah that followed, Judah entered into a state of quiet vassalage to the Assyrians after Hezekiah's death. No prophetic voice was heard during the reign of King Manasseh (697–642). Only after the Assyrian empire began to crumble under assaults from the Babylonians and Medes was Judah once again able to assert a measure of independence. This came in the reign of Josiah (640–609 BC), who inaugurated a religious and political reform similar to that of Hezekiah. Josiah's reform was designed to purge the people of foreign gods and Canaanite worship practices. Like Hezekiah, Josiah made a concerted attempt to centralize all power and authority in the city of Jerusalem (2 Kgs 23).

Josiah's Reform

There are two accounts of Josiah's reform, 2 Chron 34:1–35:27 and 2 Kgs 22:1–23:30. The Chronicles account describes the reform as having three stages (2 Chron 34:1–8). The Kings account describes the reform with only one stage (2 Kgs 22:1–3).

Chronicles Account

Stage 1: In the eighth year of Josiah's reign (632 BCE), when Josiah was sixteen years old, he began to seek the God of David (2 Chron 34:3).

Stage 2: In the twelfth year of Josiah's reign (628 BCE), when Josiah was twenty years old, he purged Judah and Jerusalem of the high places, Asherim (cult objects symbolizing the pagan goddess Asherah), altars of the Baals, and other elements of the worship of foreign gods (2 Chron 34:3).

Stage 3: In the eighteenth year of Josiah's reign (622 BCE), when Josiah was twenty-six years old, he completed the purge of pagan worship and ordered the renovation of the temple; a biblical-like scroll was found, a covenant was made, and the Passover was celebrated (2 Chron 34:8ff).

According to the account in 2 Kgs, Josiah's reform was begun in his eighteenth year (622 BCE) and carried out by a group of priests from the city of Anathoth, including Hilkiah, Shaphan, and Ahikam (2 Kgs 22:3–13; 2 Chron 34:20). Their intent and that of the king was to restore the powers of the monarchy and of the Jerusalem priesthood with themselves as its leaders. To do this they instituted a legal code similar to that found in Deut 12–26, a code that set Jerusalem apart as the only true place of sacrifice and worship for the people (hence, it is sometimes called Josiah's Deuteronomic reform). But all vestiges of Canaanite and Assyrian worship in the land had to be eliminated first. To ensure that this became a national effort, the high places and local altars were destroyed, the seasonal religious festivals were localized in the capital, and the service of the levitical priesthood was restricted to the precincts of the temple in Jerusalem (2 Kgs 23:4–20).

Such a radical reform could not be put into effect overnight. Long years of polytheistic religious activity by the people must have made it difficult to enforce the reforms. Even with the backing of the prophet Huldah (2 Kgs 22:14–20), opposition existed within Judah as well as in the areas of Samaria where Josiah had extended his influence (such as Bethel; 2 Kgs 23:15–20). Archaeological evidence from this period points to a few successes. Altars that were dismantled and incorporated into the walls of buildings have been found. Few deposits of sacrificial remains at cultic sites derive from this period. But Josiah's reform was only enforced for the thirteen years preceding his death in battle against Pharaoh Neco II at Megiddo in 609 BCE (2 Kgs 23:29–30).

Josiah's death spelled the end for most of his reforms and inaugurated a new era of submission to the superpowers. First, Egypt claimed Palestine after the defeat of the Assyrians at the battle of Carchemish in 605 BCE. This meant a new master and a puppet king for Judah. Josiah's son and immediate successor, Jehoahaz, was taken hostage back to Egypt and his brother Eliakim was put on the throne. His status as a servant of the Egyptians was graphically portrayed when his name was changed to Jehoiakim by the pharaoh (2 Kgs 23:34).

What followed were the last days of Judah's monarchy. A series of political mistakes and revolts led the superpowers to crush the nation. The sequence of events began with a change of masters. In 604 BCE, the Babylonian king Nebuchadnezzar wrested Palestine from the Egyptians and Jehoiakim suddenly found himself a Babylonian vassal (2 Kgs 24:1). Perhaps because of Egyptian promises of aid, Jehohiakim revolted three years later and temporarily resumed his role under the Egyptian hegemony. This ended in 598 BCE when Nebuchadnezzar once again invaded Judah. He laid siege to Jerusalem and captured it in 597 BCE. This was the first time the city had fallen to a siege since David's time.

During this period the prophet Jeremiah condemned Jehoiakim's policies (Jer 36). Jeremiah also denounced the reliance of the people of Jerusalem on the temple of Yahweh as a guarantee of salvation from any threat (Jer 7 and 26). After Nebuchadnezzar's successful siege of the city, he took Jehoiachin, the son of Jehoiakim, back to Babylon as a hostage along with a group of Judah's leaders and priests (2 Kgs 24:10–17). The Babylonian king then installed as his puppet king the last of Josiah's sons, Mattaniah, and changed his name to Zedekiah (2 Kgs 24:17).

Again there was a period of relative quiet as Jerusalem licked its wounds. However, in the ninth year of his reign, Zedekiah revolted (probably again under the urging of Egypt; Jer 37:7). Realizing that this source of continual irritation and rebellion on his borders had to be silenced, Nebuchadnezzar chose to totally destroy Jerusalem. While Jeremiah urged the people to surrender to the Babylonians (Jer 38:17–18), Zedekiah continued to hold out until the city fell to Nebuchadnezzar's army in 587 BCE. The last reigning king of Judah was forced to watch the execution of his sons and then his eyes were gouged out (Jer 39:6–7). The only remaining member of the royal house, Jehoiachin, died in Babylon without an heir.

The fall of Jerusalem and the Babylonian exile spelled the end of the Davidic monarchy and the beginning of a community ruled by foreign officials and an increasingly powerful priesthood. The exile period transformed Judaism and created a sense of Jewish identity that helped the people survive as a nation.

STUDY QUESTIONS

1. Discuss the effect on Judah of the destruction of the nation of Israel.

2. Discuss the "Deuteronomic reform" of King Josiah.

3. Define syncretistic.

PROPHETS IN THE LATE MONARCHIES

The Book   Amos is the first of the eighth-century prophets. He has the
of Amos   peculiar distinction of being from a village (Tekoa) in the
                    southern kingdom of Judah who is instructed to serve as a
prophet in the northern kingdom of Israel. The only other individual among the classical prophets who was required to go to another country to carry out his mission was Jonah (Ezekiel was already in Mesopotamia when he was called; Elisha did take a trip to Syria to name Hazael the new king of Syria [2 Kgs 8:7–15], but this was not a major part of his mission as a prophet). Amos's status as an outsider set the tone for his message and attitude. Amos is an angry prophet, condemning the people of Israel for their social injustices and their unorthodox worship practices. He shows little compassion and appears relieved that he can deliver his message and then return home.

When a foreigner comes and speaks in a condemning manner, both the message and the messenger are often dismissed by the audience. Thus Amos wisely begins (1:3–2:8) with a rhetorical strategy that is designed to draw a crowd, not drive the people away. After all, he wants them to hear what he has to say. He cleverly announces the coming of divine judgment on each of Israel's enemy neighbors, using a repetitive opening phrase: "For three transgressions of _____, and for four, I will not revoke the punishment." The blank is filled in geographically, starting in the northeast with Damascus, and then moving in turn to Gaza (Philistia), Tyre (Phoenicia), Edom, Ammon, Moab, and even Judah. After each recitation it can be expected that the growing crowd would have cheered and urged Amos to continue—at least until he reached his intended climax, the condemnation of Israel.

Social Injustice Theme. The list of charges, starting in Amos 2, centers on violations of the egalitarian ideal that was so often championed by the prophets. Amos prophesied when Israel was ruled by Jeroboam II (786–746 BCE) and was experiencing a period of peace and prosperity. The capture of Damascus by the Assyrian king Adad-nirari III in 802 BCE had eliminated Israel's chief economic and military rival, giving Israelite merchants a period of freedom to trade in previously restricted areas. This increased the fortunes of the merchants, but the new wealth was not shared with the general populace.

An Example of Emendation

The word *harmon* in Amos 4:3 is untranslatable. It does not appear in any other biblical text or any non-biblical text. This is called a *hapax legomenon*. Scholars sometimes deal with this problem by employing an emendation, a suggested alternative reading of the text that fits the context. In this case the suggestion is to change one letter and transform *harmon* into *hadmon*, which means dung-heap, the place where the bodies of criminals were left unburied. The text would now read "you shall be flung out into the dung heap."

Amos spends much of his time condemning social injustices such as the bribery of judges (2:6a), the sale of persons into debt-servitude for default on small loans (2:6b), and the cheating of customers with false balances and contaminated bags of grain (8:5–6). He also levels charges at the greedy merchants who cannot wait for the Sabbath or other religious holidays to end so that they can resume business (8:5a).

Amos pulls no punches, even describing the wives of these greedy merchants as sleek "cows of Bashan," who fatten themselves indulgently on other people's grain and call for more. Their "Marie Antoinette" attitude is to be rewarded when the city of Samaria falls, their impaled bodies will be dragged through the breaches in the walls and flung unburied into a dung heap (4:1–3; see inset).

Hypocrisy Theme. The second major theme in Amos is hypocrisy. The worship practices of the Israelites are described as useless because they perform them without true faith and often mix them with Canaanite practices. Amos sets a tone here that will be followed in style and vocabulary by Isaiah and Jeremiah when they condemn similar practices as hollow worship.

Hollow Worship Condemned

²¹I hate, I despise your festivals,
 and I take no delight in your solemn assemblies.
²²Even though you offer me your burnt offerings
  and grain offerings,
 I will not accept them;
and the offerings of well-being of your fatted animals
 I will not look upon.
²³Take away from me the noise of your songs;
 I will not listen to the melody of your harps.
²⁴But let justice roll down like waters,
 and righteousness like an everflowing stream (Amos 5:21–24).

¹²When you come to appear before me,
 who asked this from your hand?
 Trample my courts no more;
¹³bringing offerings is futile;
 incense is an abomination to me.
New moon and sabbath and calling of convocation—
 I cannot endure solemn assemblies with iniquity.
¹⁴Your new moons and your appointed festivals
 my soul hates;
they have become a burden to me,
 I am weary of bearing them (Isa 1:12–14).

²⁰Of what use to me is frankincense that comes from Sheba,
 or sweet cane from a distant land?
Your burnt offerings are not acceptable,
 nor are your sacrifices pleasing to me (Jer 6:20).

Amos primarily centers on the rival temple at Bethel, which had been established as a high place by Jeroboam I when the kingdoms divided. At one point, Amos uses extremely sarcastic speech, "encouraging" the people to come to Bethel, to make their offerings and tithes there, and then to have the amounts published for all to hear about (Amos 4:4–5). The prophet speaks of Yahweh's complete rejection of Israel's worship as unacceptable and a "noise" to God's ears (5:21–24).

When confronted by Amaziah, the high priest of Bethel, Amos rejects the priest's charge that he has no right to speak in the "king's sanctuary" (7:10–12). Amos denies he has any "establishment" credentials, saying: "I am no prophet, nor a prophet's son" (7:14). Instead he cites the simple call that came to him from Yahweh to leave his fields and come to Israel to speak his message (7:15). In this way he reasserts the position that prophets are free agents, working directly for Yahweh and not requiring any certification other than the truth of their message.

Amos prefers to use the pastoral images of his country background, describing the people as "summer fruit" (8:2)—sweet and full of initial promise, but quick to decay and to become worthless. Amos leaves little hope for the nation of Israel in his statements but does make brief use of the remnant theme in chapter 5. Here he simply tells the people to "seek God and live" so that Yahweh will have an excuse to relent and lessen their punishment (5:4, 6). But it seems that this brief glimmer of hope is all he will hold out to them (the section in Amos 9:11–15 describing the restoration of the Davidic kingdom is probably a later addition to the book).

STUDY QUESTIONS

1. Discuss Amos's social injustice theme.

2. Discuss official reaction to Amos's message.

3. Discuss Amos's condemnation of hypocrisy and hollow worship.

The Book of Hosea   Unlike his eighth-century contemporary Amos, the prophet Hosea speaks to his own people. While harsh, Hosea offers more hope than Amos that a reconciliation with Yahweh is still possible. Hosea speaks at the end of an era. The reign of Jeroboam II is about to end and his successors are weaklings who fight among themselves. Assyria, under Tiglath-Pileser III (744–727 BCE), now emerges as a real international force and Israel first becomes a client-state, then a bound vassal, and finally is destroyed in 722 BCE because of a series of revolts. In this desperate period, Hosea almost ignores the Assyrian threat and instead concentrates on what he perceives as the root causes of Israel's problems: idolatry and the abuse of the land's resources.

Idolatry Theme.   Hosea traces his principal themes first in a tightly woven, enacted prophecy involving his marriage to a woman named Gomer. Scholars cannot agree whether Gomer is a prostitute prior to the marriage or simply becomes an unfaithful wife afterwards. It would be unheard of for a priest to marry a prostitute. This is one reason why Hosea's marriage has most often been interpreted as a metaphor for Israel's infidelity to Yahweh. The marriage metaphor identifies Gomer's promiscuity as a symbol of Israel's blatant idolatry. Hosea, in turn, represents literally and metaphorically the long-suffering husband (God), who laments his wife's (Israel's) actions and determines to dissolve the covenant between them. Gomer's chasing after other "lovers" becomes a metaphor for Israel's worship of the Baals and the Israelites' misuse of the land given to them by Yahweh as part of the covenant.

Tiglath-Pileser III, from Nimrud, ca. eighth century BCE.
Courtesy of the British Museum.

While this metaphorical understanding is the most common interpretation of this passage, it should be noted that some have wrongly concluded that Hosea abused his wife and his children (Hos 2:4–5) and have seen this as justification for similar action in modern relationships as well. This is a perversion. Hosea 1–3 is not a story about the submission of wives to their husbands, nor is it a story giving license to husbands to brutalize their wives for real or imagined transgressions.

In the story, the marriage between Hosea and Gomer produces three children, each of whom is given a symbolic name. **Jezreel:** This name derives from the place where Jehu's dynasty defeated Ahab's dynasty and took the throne of Israel (2 Kgs 9:15–26). It signifies to the reigning king of Jehu's house that he received his power from Yahweh's intervention, and he could just as easily have it taken away. In addition, the Jezreel Valley is the most fertile area of Israel. The threats by Yahweh to "take back my grain . . . and my wine in its season" (Hos 2:9) suggest both famine and political unrest.

Lo-ruhamah ("Not pitied"): This name speaks to the level of the current social injustice in which the plight of the poor and the weak was not pitied. In the same way Yahweh warned that God would not pity Israel when its punishment came.

Lo-ammi ("Not my people"): This name signifies a terrible rejection of Israel, which had prided itself on being God's chosen people. The covenant had assured them that Yahweh would provide them with land and children (the gifts of grain, wine, and oil in Hos 2:8–9). Their unfaithfulness in maintaining their allegiance to Yahweh, expressed in ascribing their abundant harvests to Baal, had destroyed this agreement (Hos 2:13). The name "Not my people" also suggested that Hosea suspected the child was not actually his.

In the face of Gomer's unfaithfulness, Hosea punishes her severely, first secluding her and eventually driving her from his home and divorcing her (Hos 2:3–12). However, paralleling Yahweh's desire to forgive unfaithful Israel, Hosea agrees to take Gomer back if she agrees to renounce her other lovers forever and acknowledge him solely as her lord (just as Israel must renounce the Baals and acknowledge Yahweh alone as her lord; Hos 2:14–20). Gomer's return leads Hosea to acknowledge that their children are his heirs. The names of their children are changed to symbolize the reversal of Israel's fortunes as fertility is returned to the land and a new covenantal agreement is put in place (Hos 2:21–23).

Hosea's allusion to the Valley of Achor emphasizes God's willingness to carry out the divine promise of forgiveness and restoration (Hos 2:15). This was the place where Achan and his family had been stoned to death for violating the **kherem** when he stole from the loot captured at Jericho (Josh 7:22–26). Israel's sin, like Gomer's, could be put aside if she truly became faithful to her husband.

Knowledge Theme.   A second element developed in the book of Hosea is the knowledge theme. The prophet casts the blame for Israel's failure to keep the covenant squarely at the doorstep of the monarchy and the priesthood (Hos 4:4–6; 5:1). They have made political alliances that have brought ruin on the nation and corrupted the people's worship with false idols (Hos 4:12–19). Hosea was a Levite. But in the northern kingdom he was not allowed to function as a priest because Jeroboam I had created his own non-Levitical priesthood when the kingdoms divided (1 Kgs 12:32). Hosea was prejudiced against these non-Levitical priests and angry at the monarchy that installed them. Hosea condemns both of these leadership groups for failing to provide the people with the knowledge they need to obey the covenant.

The Knowledge Theme in Hosea

[6]My people are destroyed for lack of knowledge;
   because you have rejected knowledge,
   I reject you from being a priest to me.
And since you have forgotten the law of your God,
   I also will forget your children (Hos 4:6).

Hosea's anti-monarchic attitude is found in a prophecy in which he alludes to the fact that the people "make kings, but not through me; they set up princes but without my knowledge" (Hos 8:4a). This speaks to the practice of succession by assassination, which had become the standard method in the northern kingdom for ending one ruling dynasty and beginning another. He also condemns the practice of foreign alliances and warns that these relationships will bring the destruction of the nation. "Though they bargain with the nations, I will now gather them up. They shall soon writhe under the burden of kings and princes" (Hos 8:10). "They sow the wind, and they reap the whirlwind" (Hos 8:7) with these alliances. In both cases, the people and their leaders have failed to keep the covenantal agreement that placed their safety and prosperity in Yahweh's hands.

The false or improper cultic practices of Israel's shrines and priesthood are chronicled in Hosea's condemnation of the rampant idolatry of Israel: "With their silver and gold they made idols for their own destruction" (Hos 8:4b). Their sacrifices, made to Yahweh as well as other gods, will be rejected by Yahweh, who demands their worship exclusively: "Though they offer choice sacrifices, though they eat flesh, the Lord does not accept them" (Hos 8:13). Their efforts are unacceptable because they do not understand what is truly expected of them: "For I desire steadfast love and not sacrifice, the knowledge of God rather than burnt offerings" (Hos 6:6).

Khesed as Treaty Language

Khesed is used in the context of a request by Abraham's servant that God adhere to a treaty obligation (Gen 24:12, 14, 27).

Khesed is used in Yahweh's promise to keep the covenant in the context of the Ten Commandments (Exod 20:6).

Khesed is used in a slave's contractual declaration of perpetual servitude (Exod 21:5).

Khesed is used in a definition of the faithful, "who love me and keep my commandments" (Deut 5:10).

Khesed is used in treaty language following the conquest: "to love the Lord your God, to walk in his way, to keep his commandments" (Josh 22:5).

Khesed is used in Solomon's citation of God's covenant with David's "house" (i.e., dynasty; 1 Kgs 3:6).

Khesed is used in Yahweh's assurance of compliance: "I act with steadfast love, justice, and righteousness" (Jer 9:24).

The term that Hosea uses in parallelism with knowledge in Hos 6:6 is "steadfast love." In Hebrew, the word is **khesed**, which is variously translated as love, abiding love, steadfast love, and mercy. This is a technical term found most often in the language of treaties and covenants (see inset).

Hosea 6:6 is also reminiscent of Samuel's condemnation of Saul for failing to keep God's commandments ("to obey is better than sacrifice" [1 Sam 15:22]). The difference, however, is that the people lack the knowledge they need to be able to obey. Their kings will be defeated by Assyria and their idols and temple treasures will be taken away as spoil (Hos 10:3–8).

Hosea cannot leave his own people to be destroyed without warning them of the coming destruction and assuring them that though they are to be punished as a parent punishes a wayward child (Hos 11:1–7), Yahweh will redeem them if they return to him (Hos 14:4–7). They can be healed and restored, but first they must regain their lost knowledge of Yahweh's power and the covenant.

STUDY QUESTIONS

1. Discuss the significance of Hosea's marriage to Gomer. Should it be understood literally or figuratively?

2. What are the names of Hosea's and Gomer's three children and what does each name symbolize?

3. Discuss Hosea's use of the "knowledge theme."

4. Discuss the role of the prophet in the last days of his country's existence.

5. Define: *kherem, khesed.*

The Book of Isaiah (Isa 1–39)   Isaiah is one of the longest and most structurally complex of the prophetic books. It reflects at least three separate time periods, with its traditionally accepted breaks being chapters 1–39; 40–55; and 56–66. The prophet is mentioned by name only sixteen times throughout the book. This suggests a deliberate effort to depersonalize the text, giving the message of Yahweh more prominence than the prophet who delivers it. In this segment we will discuss First Isaiah or the Isaiah of Jerusalem, who dates to the period of the late eighth and early seventh centuries BCE. He differs significantly from either of his contemporaries Amos or Hosea in that he speaks primarily to kings and high-ranking officials and is apparently a member of the religious establishment in the temple in Jerusalem. His message reflects a high education and a commitment to the Davidic monarchy, the temple, and Jerusalem. Nevertheless, as a prophet it was his task to condemn individual Davidic kings, the temple community, and the inhabitants of Judah and Jerusalem for their failure to keep the covenant with Yahweh.

Call Narrative. Isaiah's call narrative appears in chapter 6. It contains language that is familiar to many people today because it was used as a source for some of the lines of Handel's *Messiah*. The elements of the call help us to date it (the year King Uzziah died, 742 BCE) and determine its site (the temple in Jerusalem). The mention of seraphim or angels is based on the image of the ark of the covenant, which had crossed wings on the lid representing how angels uphold the throne of God (Exod 25:17–22).

> **Isaiah's Call Narrative**
>
> [1]In the year that King Uzziah died, I saw the Lord sitting on a throne, high and lofty; and the hem of his robe filled the temple. [2]Seraphs were in attendance above him; each had six wings . . . . [3]And one called to another and said:
>   "Holy, holy, holy is the LORD of Hosts;
>   the whole earth is full of his glory."
> [4]The pivots on the thresholds shook at the voices of those who called, and the house filled with smoke. [5]And I said: "Woe is me! I am lost; for I am a man of unclean lips, and I live among a people of unclean lips; yet my eyes have seen the King, the LORD of hosts!" (Isa 6:1–5).

The manifestations of power include: (1) an angelic acclamation of Yahweh's glory, (2) the earthquake, and (3) the smoke that fills the temple. All of these manifestations appear in previous **theophanies** (e.g., Exod 19:9–23). Also typical is Isaiah's reluctance. He makes the excuse that his mortal lips are "unclean" (ritually impure) and thus cannot speak the holy words of Yahweh.

As is the case in every detailed call narrative, no excuse is ever accepted by God. In this episode, an angel takes a burning coal from the altar fire and cauterizes Isaiah's lips with a holy fire, which then empowers him to speak the words God gives him to speak. This is most likely a vision, otherwise Isaiah's mouth would have been permanently damaged. Once the impediment has been removed, the call is made, "Who will go for me?" Isaiah's only response can now be "Here am I; send me" (Isa 6:8).

The commission that Isaiah receives from Yahweh is not an easy one. He is to speak, but the people will neither hear nor understand. The nation has rejected previous warnings and it is now Yahweh's intention to allow their cities to be destroyed and their people killed. Despite this inevitable punishment, Yahweh promises that a **remnant** will survive and serve as a "holy seed" to restore the nation (Isa 6:13).

One additional aspect of this call narrative that should be noted is the use of the term **holy**. Isaiah uses it as the opposite of human. However, human behavior could become holy, modeling itself after the "Holy One of Israel" whose covenant and laws provided direction for ethical behavior. Isaiah's emphasis on social justice, the obligation to aid rather than oppress the weak, and the requirement to worship only Yahweh, are keys to seeking to be holy. This is not unique to Isaiah. Injunctions against profaning Yahweh's holy name are found throughout the prophets (Jer 34:16; Amos 2:7; Ezek 36:22–32).

Terraced field. Terraces and vineyards were popular metaphors among the prophets and re-flect the agriculture-based society of ancient Israel. Photo L. DeVries.

Oracles of Warning.   Two examples of Isaiah's message will be presented here to illustrate his use of (1) condemnation, (2) judgment, and (3) choice. The first is found in Isa 1:10–23, where the prophet plays upon both the familiar tradition of the destruction of Sodom and Gomorrah (Gen 19) and the past experience of the people. This passage also has a close parallel with the message in Amos 5:21–24. In both Isa 1:10–23 and Amos 5:21–24, hollow worship is condemned as empty ritual. Yahweh refuses to accept false worship and instead calls for a resumption of the covenant stipulations that demand a just society. Isaiah offers the people of Judah a choice. He states that if they are willing to cleanse themselves of the innocent blood that they have shed in oppressing the weak, then redemption is possible (Isa 1:16–17). Yahweh once again promises land and descendants if they will obey. But if they choose to disobey, the threat of war and destruction remains, "for the mouth of the Lord has spoken" (Isa 1:20).

Oracles of Warning

Isa 1:13–15	Amos 5:21–24
[13]bringing offerings is futile; incense is an abomination to me. New moon and sabbath and calling of convocation— I cannot endure solemn assemblies with iniquity. [14]Your new moons and your appointed festivals my soul hates; they become a burden to me, I am weary of bearing them. [15]When you stretch out your hands, I will hide my eyes from you; even though you make many prayers, I will not listen; your hands are full of blood.	[21]I hate, I despise your festivals, and I take no delight in your solemn assemblies. [22]Even though you offer me your burnt offerings and grain offerings, I will not accept them; and the offerings of well-being of your fatted animals I will not look upon. [23]Take away from me the noise of your songs; I will not listen to the melody of your harps. [24]But let justice roll down like waters, and righteousness like an ever-flowing stream.

The other example of an oracle of warning is found in Isa 5. Here the prophet plays upon a familiar scene, a vineyard planted on a terraced hillside. The use of agricultural images is common among the prophets (Isa 28:24–28; Joel 1:11–12; 2:23–24; Amos 8:1). These images reflect the importance of agriculture in their society and demonstrate the effort that the prophets put forth to make their message relevant to the people.

In Isa 5, Isaiah describes the farmer's work of carving out a terrace from a hillside, building a wall, and filling the terrace with fertile soil. The steps of planting, cultivating of the vines, guarding its produce, and processing the fruit are also included. But a sour note is struck when the grapes prove to be bitter. The crop is worthless (Isa 5:2).

Now the vineyard owner (Yahweh) proclaims a lawsuit against his vines. Testimony is given to prove that he has done all that was needed to ensure a good crop. Yahweh's disappointment in the results of his labor is evident (Isa 5:3–4). Judgment is then pronounced. The sentence is that the vineyard is to be pulled up by its roots and its terrace thrown down. Even the clouds are commanded not to rain on it (Isa 5:5–6).

Finally, the meaning of the metaphor in the "Song of the Vineyard" (Isa 5) is revealed. Israel and Judah are identified as the corrupt vines. Their injustices include depriving the poor of their lands by creating huge estates (Isa 5:8), drunkenness and self-indulgent living (Isa 5:11–12), public deception by the leaders (Isa 5:18–21), and bribery (Isa 5:23). The punishment is to be a ruined land, just as the vineyard was laid waste. The nation will be left open to the assaults of other people (Isa 5:26–30) and the "chosen" who "are wise in [their] own eyes" will go into exile because of their lack of knowledge (Isa 5:13; compare Hos 4:1, 2 for the knowledge theme).

Political Message. Many of the major pronouncements of Isaiah are tied to historical events. The nation was in the throes of Assyrian expansion. Isaiah witnessed the destruction of Israel, the northern kingdom, and saw its people taken into exile (721 BCE). He saw Judah, the southern kingdom, devastated by invading Assyrian armies and Jerusalem besieged on two occasions (701 and 688 BCE). These were desperate times and the message that Isaiah brought provided little solace to Israel's leaders, despite his repeated use of the phrase "do not fear" (Isa 7:4; 10:24; 37:6).

In the 730s the small vassal states of Syro-Palestine were encouraged by the Egyptians to revolt against Assyria. This was a typical ploy of rival superpowers, using smaller states in border areas to weaken their opponent with the goal of absorbing these smaller states into their own empire. Israel and Syria, along with most of the rest of the Assyrian vassal states in Syro-Palestine formed an alliance. This had been successful in the past when Ahab had joined with other states back in the ninth century to prevent the Assyrians from controlling their region. However, the Assyrians were much stronger now and their ruthless use of psychological warfare techniques (spreading news of how they massacred whole cities and mutilated prisoners) gave them a decided edge in any conflict.

Because he did not see any advantage in assisting the rebellious states, Ahaz of Judah refuses to join the alliance. The result is what is known as the Syro-Ephraimitic War. Israel and Syria ally themselves against Judah and initiate hostilities. The crisis that Ahaz and his advisors faced was complex. On the one hand, as an Assyrian colony, Judah had a legal responsibility to use military force to put down any rebellion against Assyria. On the other hand, as an ally of Israel, Judah had a legal obligation to support Israel's struggle for freedom. Regardless of whether Judah decided to support Assyria or Israel, it faced dire consequences. If Judah did not join their struggle against Assyria, Israel and Syria would invade. If Judah did join in their struggle, Assyria would invade Judah!

Ahaz's advisers are unable to reach a decision. They shake "as the trees of the forest shake before the wind" (Isa 7:2). The king recesses the meeting ostensibly to inspect Jerusalem's defenses. Regardless of Judah's decision, there will be an invasion and Jerusalem must prepare for siege. But the strategy of a recess is primarily to offer the deadlocked participants time to negotiate.

Ahaz takes an inspection tour outside the city away from most of his advisers. This gives Isaiah the chance to lobby the king in virtual privacy. Isaiah proposes that Judah remain nonaligned in this conflict. A key assumption in Isaiah's argument is the tradition that considers the city of Jerusalem and Zion its citadel to be impregnable. If Jerusalem is impregnable, then Syria and Israel pose no real threat to Judah (Isa 7:1–9).

Another important component of Isaiah's argument is the premonarchic tradition that Judah has only one treaty, its treaty with Yahweh. This covenant with Yahweh recognizes Yahweh alone as king of Judah. It is Yahweh's responsibility as divine king, not the responsibility of Ahaz, to provide for and to protect the nation.

The Heart of Ahaz

The terms "heart of Ahaz" and "the heart of his people" may be more technical than poetic. The process in which these terms were used was certainly political. In a frantic effort to protect Judah against an invasion by Israel and Syria, Ahaz convenes a meeting. The "heart of Ahaz" and "the heart of his people" may identify the two groups that the king summoned.

The social structure of Judah provided for a wide range of decision-making and advisory groups. For example, municipal affairs were in the hands of the "bearded" elders, who made up the village assembly (1 Sam 30:26–31). Monarchs appointed some elders to be royal officials (Gen 12:15; Jer 25:19; 38:17; Esth 1:3; 2:18). They could be military officials (1 Sam 8:12) or civilians (1 Kgs 4:2; 20:14; 22:26; 2 Kgs 23:8; Jer 24:8; 26:10; 34:19, 21). Officials were especially numerous in the capital cities (Jer 38:24–25; 2 Kgs 21:23).

"Heart" is an important anthropological term in the Hebrew Bible, referring almost exclusively to the human heart (814 times). It is also used of "the heart of God," (26 times) and "the heart of the sea" (11 times). None of the references has been regularly identified with any advisory or government body. Mesopotamian literature uses "heart" in reference to royal officials, where the phrase "to devote the heart entirely" identifies the monarch's eunuchs, closest advisers, and vassals. In Isa 7:2, "the heart of Ahaz" could quite easily refer not just to his own human heart, but to those officials totally dedicated to him as well.

Thus "heart" becomes an easy metaphor for advisors who function in the same way for the government as the "heart" does for the individual. A "fat" heart is out of touch with the real needs of the country (Isa 6:10; 11:8; 13:10; 16:12; 18:12). A "stone" heart is unapproachable (Ezek 11:19; 36:26) or unswerving (Job 41:16). A "trembling" heart is indecisive (Deut 28:65; 1 Sam 28:5). In Hos 11:8, Yahweh saying "my heart turns over within me" is parallel to "the heart of the king and the heart of the people trembled" (Isa 7:2). When Solomon prays for a "hearing heart" (1 Kgs 3:9–12), he is praying for a cooperative council.

Finally, Isaiah announces the verdict of the divine assembly against Israel and Syria in an effort to convince Ahaz to remain nonaligned. The divine assembly indicts Syria and Israel for attempting to liberate themselves (Isa 7:8–9). Yahweh alone is the liberator of the Israelites and only Yahweh can set them free. Assyria is a mighty power, but certainly no mightier than Egypt, from whom Yahweh had previously delivered Israel.

When Ahaz refuses to ask for a sign that Yahweh will carry out this verdict against Judah's opponents, Isaiah proclaims a sign anyway. This is the prediction of the birth of a child whose name will be Immanuel. On the face of it, this is just another example of an **annunciation**, a birth announcement by a divine representative (cf. Gen 16:11–12; Judg 13:3–5). However, this is also a time-specific prophecy. Isaiah predicts that by the time the child is old enough to know the difference between right and wrong (between 5 and 13 years) Israel and Syria will have been destroyed and Judah will be impoverished (Isa 7:13–25; left to eat only curds and wild honey). The child's name, Immanuel, meaning "the Lord is with us," is a sign that the power behind these destructive forces (embodied in Assyria) is actually Yahweh. They should therefore fear the coming of the Lord. Isaiah matches this prediction with a second annunciation, this time predicting the birth and naming of his own son, who will see the destruction of Samaria and Syria before he can say the words "my father" and "my mother" (Isa 8:1–4).

The outcome of these events is that Ahaz requests aid from Assyria, and the Assyrians use the opportunity to intervene before the rebellious states have had sufficient time to organize their resistance. Their hopes of freedom from Assyrian rule are dashed and they are placed under even more restrictive treaty obligations. But Judah had to pay for Assyria's help. Their local autonomy was weakened and they had to pay additional tribute. Isaiah's prediction of destruction and impoverishment had come true.

The End of the Northern Kingdom. The Syro-Ephraimitic war (730s BCE) was symptomatic of the discontent within the Assyrian empire. More revolts occurred and the Assyrian emperor Shalmaneser V and his successor Sargon II decided to make an example of some of the rebels. Israel, once again a leader among the small states, was targeted and in 722 BCE was invaded. A year later the capital city of Samaria was captured and the nation of Israel ceased to exist. Though many escaped to Judah, the majority of the survivors were deported by the victorious Assyrians and the legend of the "ten lost tribes of Israel" was born (2 Kgs 18:9–12). Their ultimate fate was assimilation into the peoples of the empire. Israel's population was culturally absorbed, thereby losing their identity as a distinct people.

Judah's trauma is reflected in the prophets, who point to Israel's fate and warn Judah and Jerusalem of their possible future. Some people, including the writer of 2 Kings, took this as vindication of the Davidic monarchy and its covenant with Yahweh. Israel, which had broken away and had perpetuated the sin of Jeroboam, had finally been punished (2 Kgs 17:2–18, 21–23). But with the Assyrians still a threat to their own existence, most of the people of Judah felt shock, fear, and apprehension about the future.

It is into this atmosphere that Hezekiah succeeds his father Ahaz as ruler of Judah. His assessment of the political situation is similar to his father's, but he is more open to the message of Isaiah. The chronicle in the book of Kings that describes Hezekiah's reign indicates that unlike his father, "he did what was right in the sight of the LORD" (2 Kgs 18:3). Among his accomplishments is his attempt to purify the temple in Jerusalem (2 Kgs 18:4–6), removing images of other gods (including the Nehushtan, the bronze serpent that Moses had made). He also added a portion of the Philistine's territory to his holdings. These actions were in fact a political move defying the Assyrians who had imposed set boundaries, their religion, and their culture upon Judah.

The Assyrian Invasion in 701 BCE

Annals of Sennacherib

As for Hezekiah of Judah, he did not submit to my yoke, and I laid siege to 46 of his strong cities, walled forts, and to the countless villages . . . . I drove out of these places 200,150 people . . . . I made Hezekiah a prisoner in Jerusalem, like a bird in a cage . . . . and forced [him] to send me 30 talents of gold, 800 talents of silver . . . (*OTPar*, pp. 139–40).

2 Kgs 18:13–15

[13]In the fourteenth year of King Hezekiah, King Sennacherib of Assyria came up against all the fortified cities of Judah and captured them . . . . [14]The king of Assyria demanded of King Hezekiah of Judah three hundred talents of silver and thirty talents of gold. [15]Hezekiah gave him all the silver that was found in the house of the LORD and in the treasuries of the king's house.

Hezekiah was able to survive these initial moves of defiance because the Assyrians were distracted by more active rebellions within the empire. For example, in 711 BCE the Philistine city-state of Ashdod organized a revolt at the instigation of the Egyptians. Hezekiah was invited to join the alliance, but he remained neutral.

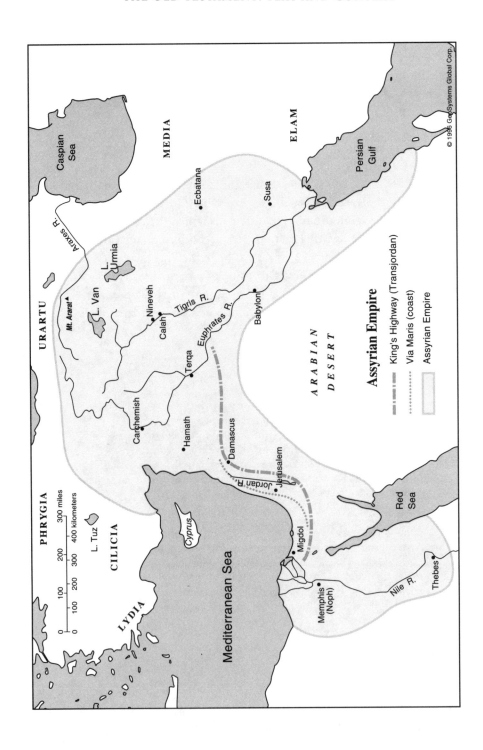

© 1996 GeoSystems Global Corp.

Assyrian Empire

- — King's Highway (Transjordan)
- ⋯ Via Maris (coast)
- ☐ Assyrian Empire

Isaiah may have influenced this decision by performing an unusual **enacted prophecy**. He paraded around the city naked for three years to demonstrate the fate of those who rebel against the Assyrians (Isa 20:3), who were identified as "the rod [of Yahweh's] anger" (Isa 10:5). His actions graphically portrayed the condition of war prisoners and undoubtedly had an effect on the decision not to support Ashdod and Egypt (Isa 20).

Hezekiah's attempt to gain a greater measure of independence soon brought his small kingdom to the attention of the Assyrians. On two occasions (701 and 688 BCE), Sennacherib invaded Judah, ravaging the countryside. His own chronicle, despite its boasting style, closely resembles the account found in 2 Kgs 18:13–15 (see inset). The destruction of many of Judah's cities, including the border fortress of Lachish (2 Kgs 18:14), forced Hezekiah into a situation in which his only means of saving the kingdom was to pay a huge ransom. This saved the city of Jerusalem from destruction, but that was little solace to the villagers outside its walls (cf. below on the prophet Micah).

Sargon and high official. The Assyrian king Sargon II
captured Samaria ca. 721 BCE. Photo courtesy of the British Museum.

These events are also described in Isa 36–37. In these chapters the emphasis is placed on two detailed speeches. The first of these is the taunting speech of the Assyrian diplomat named the Rabshakeh ("chief cupbearer"). Under a truce he stands outside the walls of Jerusalem and negotiates with Hezekiah's officials. The people, who have retreated inside the walls for safety, are straining to hear the negotiations despite the protests of Hezekiah's advisers. The Rabshakeh makes sure they can hear in their own Hebrew language (Isa 36:11–12). He sarcastically describes their alliance with Egypt, their king who has torn down Yahweh's altars in the shrines and villages outside Jerusalem, their lack of soldiers, and their inability to furnish a calvary even if Assyria gave them horses to ride. He tells them that the Assyrian army is besieging Jerusalem at the behest of Yahweh: "Is it without the LORD that I have come up against this land to destroy it? The LORD said to me, Go up against this land, and destroy it" (Isa 36:10).

This use of **theodicy** by a diplomat is a powerful, but not unusual, tactic. Isaiah himself had described Assyria as Yahweh's tool to punish the nation (Isa 10:5–11). Claims to divine sanction for the actions of a non-Israelite ruler can be seen elsewhere, both in the Bible (Jer 21:4–10) and in other ancient Near Eastern documents (see the inset on the Cyrus Cylinder, p. 207).

Isaiah's version of the second siege event in Isa 37 is a little difficult to separate from the first one in chapter 36 (2 Kgs 18:13–16 contains additional information that separates the two events). But the episode in chapter 37 more directly involves Yahweh's assurances that the city of Jerusalem shall be saved: "For I will defend this city to save it, for my own sake, and for the sake of my servant David." What is contained here is another example of an **apology** narrative (a literary style used to defend a character). The text promotes Hezekiah as a "faithful (Davidic) ruler." Hezekiah prays for Yahweh's assistance and the response is an angel who brings a plague, killing 185,000 Assyrians overnight (Isa 37:36). Mention is also made of political problems for Sennacherib back in Nineveh and the assassination of the emperor after his return (Isa 37:37–38). Plague in overcrowded army camps was certainly well known in the ancient world, and the evidence is clear that Sennacherib was assassinated. Isaiah's explanation for the survival of Jerusalem perpetuates the idea of the inviolability of the city and the temple (Isa 37:35). One hundred years later, Jeremiah would almost be killed for prophesying the destruction of the city and the temple (Jer 7 and 26) because of this myth of inviolability. In due course, the Babylonian king Nebuchadnezzar besieges the city and destroys both the city and the temple, demonstrating that the hopes of the people of Jerusalem had no substance.

Remnant Theme. While Isaiah describes the punishment of the people on several occasions, he matches nearly every prediction of destruction with a promise of restoration by a faithful remnant of the people (see Isa 10:20–23; 37:30–32).

Coupled with this is his assurance that the remnant will be led by a representative of the Davidic ruling house. Thus in Isa 11:1–2, "a shoot from the stump of Jesse" (David's father) will spring from the vestige of the nation that remains after many of its people have been cut off by invading armies. This future Davidic ruler will have Yahweh's wise counsel and will be the model for a people who must have the knowledge and fear of Yahweh to survive. Similarly, the familiar prediction of the "child born for us" in Isa 9:6–7 refers to an idealized Davidic king who, unlike Ahaz, can lead the people while still adhering to the covenant.

Additional attention will be given to the other two sections of Isaiah later in this book. Isaiah of Jerusalem apparently ended his activities with the end of the Hezekiah's reign (see Isa 38–39) in 687 BCE. His message was passed on to a school of his disciples, perhaps those who assisted him and are mentioned in Isa 8:16. They kept his themes, vocabulary, and style alive and revived it after the exile.

STUDY QUESTIONS

1. How is Isaiah's call similar to and different from the calls of other prophets (e.g., Jeremiah or Ezekiel)?

2. What emphasis in Isaiah is similar to that of Amos?

3. How is Isaiah's message similar to and different from his contemporaries Amos, Micah, and Hosea?

4. Define: theophany, remnant, annunciation, "heart of Ahaz," enacted prophecy, theodicy, apology.

The Book of Micah   A contemporary of Isaiah of Jerusalem, the prophet Micah has a distinctively different perspective on the events during the last three decades of the eighth century BCE and the beginning of the seventh century BCE (the reigns of Jotham, Ahaz, and Hezekiah; Mic 1:1). He represents the feelings and concerns of the rural farmers and villagers who bore the brunt of Assyrian pillaging. While the people of Jerusalem were under siege by Sennacherib's army, the rest of Judah's population was subject to rape, violent death, and enslavement as the Assyrian troops foraged in the countryside. As a result, Micah was highly critical of Jerusalem, the monarchy, and the temple community. His message is a simple one, with emphasis on the Mosaic covenant rather than the everlasting covenant given to the Davidic dynasty.

Lawsuit against the Nation. Micah frames his denunciation of Jerusalem, Samaria, and their leadership in the form of a divine lawsuit. Isaiah had also used a lawsuit form in his "Song of the Vineyard" (Isa 5:1–7). Micah points specifically to the urban centers as the cause of the despair and destruction of the people. The idolatry of the cities and foreign alliances had incurred both God's wrath and the heavy hand of the conqueror (Mic 1:15). Micah warns that just as the countryside has been trampled by the invaders, it will be the fate of the cities to be devastated and depopulated. The city of Samaria will become "a heap in the open country, a place for planting vineyards" (Mic 1:6). Jerusalem is specifically singled out by Micah for destruction. In Mic 3:12, he states that Jerusalem will "become a heap of ruins" and adds that Zion (the temple mount) "shall be plowed as a field." This harsh message is quoted again in Jer 26:18 as a part of Jeremiah's trial, demonstrating the transmission of prophetic speech over a period of a century.

> **Charges Filed Against Israel and Judah**
>
> [5]All this is for the transgression of Jacob
>   and for the sins of the house of Israel.
> What is the transgression of Jacob?
>   Is it not Samaria?
> And what is the high place of Judah?
>   Is it not Jerusalem? (Mic 1:5)

The failure of Israel's leaders to provide justice, as was their responsibility, is a common charge of the prophets (see Amos 2:6–8; 5:10–12; Hos 4:6–10). There is a sense of the world turned upside down in Micah's remarks which are similar to those found in Egyptian literature during the First Intermediate Period (2258–2050 BCE), when the social and economic structures of that country were crumbling. In the Egyptian story of the "Farmer and the Courts," an eloquent peasant pleads for justice when a corrupt official's greed has cost the man his donkey. So too, Amos and Micah, both prophets from the rural area of Judah, champion the weak and proclaim that God will have no mercy on their oppressors: "They will cry to the Lord, but he will not answer them" (Mic 3:4).

Covenant Relationship. Micah's solution to what he perceives as the nation's ills is to return to the Sinai covenant and its simple injunctions. Like Samuel and Hosea, he places ritual and ceremony second to obedience to the law. God will not tolerate those who for their own gain adulterate what is designed to serve the people's needs (Mic 6:10–15).

A World without Justice

The Distributer puts more grain in his own pile. The Giver of Full Measure shorts his people. The Lawmaker approves of robbery. Who is left to punish the wrongdoer? The Inspector condones corruption. One is publicly criminal, the other tolerates injustice ("Farmer and the Courts," *OTPar,* p. 216).

[10]They hate the one who reproves in the gate,
    and they abhor the one who speaks the truth (Amos 5:10).

[9]Hear this, you rulers of the house of Jacob
    and chiefs of the house of Israel,
who abhor justice
    and pervert equity,
[10]who build Zion with blood
    and Jerusalem with wrong!
[11]Its rulers give judgment for a bribe,
    its priests teach for a price,
    its prophets give oracles for money;
yet they lean upon the LORD and say,
    "Surely the LORD is with us!" (Mic 3:9–11).

Restoration. Although there is some concern that the passages in Micah that deal with restoration of the nation and the monarchy have been inserted by later editors, it is not out of character for a prophet in the seventh century BCE to use these themes. One of Micah's most important statements concerns the rise of a new Davidic ruler from Bethlehem (Mic 5:2). Having the future leader come from this insignificant village serves two purposes. First, it takes the monarchy back to its roots, since this is also David's birthplace. Second, it removes the taint of "career politician" or "insider" from the position of king. This new king will be obedient to Yahweh's voice, "feeding the flock" (compare Ezek 34:23–24) and providing the people with security and peace (Mic 5:4–5).

The restoration also includes a cleansing of the nation, i.e., a removal of idols and other signs of foreign worship (Mic 5:12–14). When Yahweh has removed the evildoers from the land and justice is restored, then the shame that was upon the nation will be removed. The nations of Assyria and Egypt will become desolate and will "stand in fear" of Yahweh (Mic 7:8–20). Like many prophets, Micah becomes a voice of both condemnation in the present and of hope for a better future.

Better to Obey than Sacrifice

6"With what shall I come before the LORD,
and bow myself before God on high?
Shall I come before him with burnt offerings,
with calves a year old?
7Will the LORD be pleased with thousands of rams,
with ten thousand rivers of oil?
Shall I give my firstborn for my transgression,
the fruit of my body for the sin of my soul?"
8He has told you, O mortal, what is good;
and what does the LORD require of you
but to do justice, and to love kindness,
and to walk humbly with your God? (Mic 6:6–8).

6For I desire steadfast love and not sacrifice,
the knowledge of God rather than burnt offerings (Hos 6:6).

22Has the LORD as great delight in
burnt offerings and sacrifices,
as in obeying the voice of the LORD?
Surely, to obey is better than sacrifice . . . (1 Sam 15:22).

STUDY QUESTIONS

1. Contrast the message of Micah to that of Isaiah with respect to the importance of the city of Jerusalem.

2. Discuss Micah's use of the theme that "it is better to obey than sacrifice," which is also found in Hosea and in 2 Sam 15.

3. Describe the restoration depicted by Micah.

PROPHETIC VOICES OF THE LATE SEVENTH CENTURY

There are no surviving prophetic voices from the period of Manasseh's reign (697–642 BCE). What little is known of this period is recorded in 2 Kgs 21:1–18, which is basically a litany of the king's crimes and religious apostasies (esp. vv. 2–9). In constrast, the Chronicler's account portrays Manasseh as a repentant sovereign and reformer (2 Chron 33:1–9), who could not be blamed for Jerusalem's fall to the Babylonians (as 2 Kgs 21:10–15 does). This may be a response to the length of his reign (fifty-five years) or the Chronicler's lack of real knowledge of the period.

In any case, there are several decades between the pronouncements made by Isaiah and Micah and the restoration of prophetic activity during the reign of Josiah (640–609 BCE). The four short books written by Nahum, Zephaniah, Habbakuk, and Obadiah serve as a bridge to the works of Jeremiah and Ezekiel.

The Book
of Nahum

Nothing is known about the author of the book of Nahum. This short book cannot be dated with certainty, although its optimism suggests a date prior to the end of Josiah's reign (609 BCE). It is a very unusual work in the sense that it so single-mindedly cheers the defeat of an enemy city.

Since no nation or tyrant remains in power forever, the prophet Nahum can be allowed his brief moment of glory in celebrating the destruction of Nineveh in 612 BCE to a combined army of Chaldeans/Babylonians and Medes. The hated Assyrians had at last received the justice they deserved. The use of a **theodicy** in which Yahweh is the force behind Nabopolassar's Babylonian army is typical of Israelite prophecy. It demonstrates a God who is both "jealous and avenging" (Nah 1:2) as well as "slow to anger" (Nah 1:3). Nahum's interpretation of Nineveh's fall would have been welcomed by Israelites who believed that a just God "never leaves the guilty unpunished." The graphic descriptions of shields dripping with blood and war chariots careening through the streets (Nah 2:3–4) must have been satisfying to the people of Judah who had suffered great devastation themselves at the hands of Assyrian armies.

The Annal of Nabopolassar's Fourteenth Year: The Fall of Nineveh

[Fourteenth year] The king of Akkad called up his army and Cyaxares, the king of the Manda-hordes (Medes) . . . pitched camp against Nineveh . . . From the month Simanu till the month Abu, three battles were fought, then they made a great attack against the city. In the month Abu . . . the city was seized and a great defeat he inflicted upon the entire population. . . . many prisoners of the city, beyond counting, they carried away. The city they turned into ruin-hills and heaps of debris (*ANET*, pp. 304–5, with modifications).

However, the nation of Judah was only able to revel in Nineveh's destruction for a few years. They were quickly swept up in the empire-building aims of Egypt and Babylonia. King Josiah was killed by the Egyptians at Megiddo in 609 BCE and the nation fell under the **hegemony** of rulers just as demanding as the Assyrians.

The Book of Zephaniah   Written during the period of Josiah's reign (640–609 BCE), the book of Zephaniah concerns itself primarily with oracles against idolatry and judgment of both Judah's sins and those of her neighbors. The most pervasive image used is the "day of the Lord" (Zeph 1:8, 14, 18; 2:2) and the judgment of God associated with it (Zeph 1:14–15). It is possible that the prophecies were uttered prior to the institution of the Deuteronomic reform (pre-621 BCE) because of Zephaniah's fierce condemnation of Judah's syncretized religious practices, but this could also be an argument used for the cleansing of Judah's religion during the midst of the reform movement.

The prophet's vision is one of total annihilation of all of creation:

²I will utterly sweep away everything
   from the face of the earth, says the LORD.
³I will sweep away humans and animals;
   I will sweep away the birds of the air
   and the fish of the sea.
I will make the wicked stumble.
   I will cut off humanity
   from the face of the earth, says the LORD (Zeph 1:2–3).

The Remnant Theme

¹⁴Seek good and not evil,
   that you may live;
and so the LORD, the God of hosts,
    will be with you,
   just as you have said.
¹⁵Hate evil and love good,
   and establish justice in the gate;
it may be that the LORD, the God of hosts,
   will be gracious to the remnant of Joseph (Amos 5:14–15).

³Seek the LORD, all you humble of the land,
   who do his commands;
seek righteousness, seek humility;
   perhaps you may be hidden
   on the day of the LORD's wrath (Zeph 2:3).

Such massive destruction recalls the Noah flood story (Gen 6–9). It may also be influenced by the vision of devastation described in Isaiah's call narrative: "Until cities lie waste without inhabitant, and houses without people, and the land is utterly desolate" (Isa 6:11).

The image of Yahweh searching Jerusalem with a lamp for "those who say in their hearts, 'The LORD will not do good, nor will he do harm'" (Zeph 1:12), is a reversal of Jeremiah's search for "the one person who acts justly and seeks truth" (Jer 5:1) and Ezekiel's vision of the marking of the innocents prior to Jerusalem's destruction (Ezek 9). As in Amos 5:14–15, Zephaniah offers little hint of mercy and leaves only a simple path for survival of a remnant.

The oracles against the nations are even more graphic in their descriptions of Yahweh's wrath:

> 9Moab shall become like Sodom
>   and the Ammonites like Gomorrah,
> a land possessed by nettles and salt pits,
>   and a waste forever. . . .
> 10The LORD will be terrible against them;
>   he will shrivel all the gods of the earth . . . .
> 13And he will stretch out his hand against the north,
>   and destroy Assyria;
> and he will make Nineveh a desolation,
>   a dry waste like the desert (Zeph 2:9, 11, 13).

The ultimate human boast of the Assyrians, "I am and there is no one else" (Zeph 2:15a) will not be left unchallenged, but will be the basis for total desolation and loathing: "Everyone who passes by it hisses and shakes the fist" (Zeph 2:15b).

The woe to Jerusalem in chapter 3 may be based on the failure of the people to continue the Deuteronomic reform after the death of Josiah in 609 BCE or may be the result of their rejection of the prophet (cf. Jeremiah's personal laments in Jer 20:7–18). Chapter 3 also contains a gracious promise of a remnant, which speaks of a transformation of the people's speech to "pure speech" (Zeph 3:9), perhaps in the same manner as Isaiah's purified lips (Isa 6:5–7). The nation also will have been purified of the "proudly exultant ones," leaving the humble and lowly, who "will pasture and lie down" as Yahweh's flock (Zeph 3:12–13).

The final segment of the book (Zeph 3:14–20) contains a proclamation of salvation for the people and the restoration of Jerusalem. It is out of character with the rest of the book, containing elements of postexilic apocalyptic literature, and is probably a late addition to the text.

THE OLD TESTAMENT: TEXT AND CONTEXT

The Book of Habbakuk

The book of Habbakuk contains three distinct parts that suggest that its contents were edited and put in final form by the prophet in the period after Josiah's death (608–598 BCE). The first segment (Hab 1:2–2:5) is a **theodicy** in the form of a dialogued litany of the world's ills and the seeming victory of evil: "The wicked surround the righteous—therefore judgment comes forth perverted" (Hab 1:4b). Faced with the oppression of Babylonian rule and the misrule of their own king, Jehoiakim, Habbakuk raises the question of how long the people must wait for God to intervene (Hab 1:2). This is followed by five statements of reassurance and of judgment or "woes" on the people and/or nations who temporarily prosper through illegal and violent means (Hab 2:6–20).

> [6]Shall not everyone taunt such people
> and, with mocking riddles say about them,
> "Alas for you who heap up what
>   is not your own!
> How long will you load yourselves with goods
>   taken in pledge?" (Hab 2:6).

The Wisdom of the Patient Person

[5]The plans of the diligent lead surely to abundance,
    but everyone who is hasty comes only to want (Prov 21:5).

[5]Thorns and snares are in the way of the perverse;
    the cautious will keep far from them (Prov 22:5).

The fool who talks publicly in the temple, . . . is like a tree planted indoors. A tree indoors blooms, but then withers, . . . it is thrown into the ditch, . . . it floats far from home, . . . it is burned as trash ("Teachings of Amen-em-ope," *OTPar*, pp. 191–92).

The wise who is reserved, is like a tree planted in a garden. A garden tree flourishes, Doubles its yield, . . . its fruit is sweet . . . its shade is pleasant, . . . it will flourish in the garden forever. If you do not seek the will of The Gods, what hope is there for success? Those who submit to the yoke of The Gods never hunger, . . . eat when food is scarce. Seek the soothing wind of The Gods, And a year's losses will be restored in a moment ("The Sufferer and the Soul," *OTPar*, pp. 221–22).

[4]Look at the proud!
    Their spirit is not right in them,
    but the righteous live by their faith (Hab 2:4).

The book contains elements of wisdom literature more fully developed in the book of Job. These elements place value on the person who can hope in the eventual triumph of Yahweh and the people of Judah over their enemies: "If it seems to tarry, wait for it; it will surely come, it will not delay" (Hab 2:3b). Taking such a patient view over the rash demand for action is found in many wisdom pieces from the ancient Near East. The emphasis placed by the prophet on "living by faith" (Hab 2:4) had a great impact on Martin Luther and the leaders of the Protestant Reformation.

The third section of Habbakuk (chapter 3) is a psalm, structured much like those in the book of Psalms. It contains a **superscription** (compare Ps 7) and is the only place outside the Psalms in which the **Selah rubric** is found (on this see the section on Psalms). The poem contains the marching forth of a transcendant creator using the elements of nature to manifest divine power and save the people: "In fury you trod the earth, in anger you trampled nations. . . . You trampled the sea with your horses, churning the mighty waters" (Hab 3:12, 15). This poem's liturgical character suggests that it was used in a priestly procession or dramatic ritual.

Procession of musicians. Music played a role in the religious, political, and social life of ancient peoples. Photo courtesy of the British Museum.

The Book of Obadiah

This brief prophetic book (just twenty-one verses) dates to the period after the Babylonian invasions and conquest of Judah (post-587 BCE). Nothing is known of its author. It consists primarily of oracles condemning Edom and other nations that exploited Judah's weakness by raiding and pillaging defenseless cities and towns. Edom's occupation of southern Judah and the hatred of the Herods (who were Idumeans/Edomites) generated an animosity toward Edom that continued into the rabbinic period, when Edom was equated with Rome in rabbinic denunciations of foreign oppressors. The theme fits into a collection of anti-Edomite literature from this period (see Ps 137:7; Joel 3:19; Jer 49:17–22; Ezek 25:12–16) and may relate back to the struggle between Jacob and Esau in Gen 27:41–45.

Lex Talionis

As you have done, it shall be done to you;
>   your deeds shall return on your own head (Obad 15).

[19]Anyone who maims another shall suffer the same injury in return (Lev 24:19).

If one citizen breaks a bone of another, then the sentence is the breaking of a bone (*CH* 197; *OTPar*, p. 66).

If a man without grounds accuses another man of a matter of which he has no knowledge, and that man does not prove it, he shall bear the penalty of the matter for which he made the accusation (from the Lipit Ishtar Code; quote in M. Roth, *Law Collections from Mesopotamia and Asia Minor* [SBL Writings from the Ancient World Series 6; Atlanta: Scholars Press, 1995], p. 29).

The principle upon which Obadiah justifies his call for revenge and destruction of Judah's enemies is based on the law of reciprocity. All nations, not just Judah, must observe the maxim that a people who are not at war should not do violence to their neighbors or gloat over their misery (Obad 12). This is especially the case for those who are already in distress because of natural or human-related catastrophe. Thus he confidently states: "As you have done, so shall it be done to you" (Obad 15). This statement provides a corollary to the legal principle of *lex talionis* found elsewhere in biblical law (Exod 21:23–25; Lev 24:19–20) and in the law codes of the ancient Near East.

Obadiah's oracle of restoration contains the familiar image of Yahweh triumphant on Mount Zion (cf. Isa 30:19–26; 31:4–9; Zeph 3:14–20). The "day of the Lord" will bring justice to the plunderers and the occupation of Edomite, Phoenician, and Philistine territories by the people of Judah (Obad 19–20). This political reversal of fortunes is matched by the restoration of Yahweh's name as Lord of all nations: "Those who have been saved shall go up to Mount Zion to rule Mount Esau; and the kingdom shall be the LORD's" (Obad 21; cf. Ps 22:28).

STUDY QUESTIONS

1. Discuss the effect that the incursions of the Mesopotamian superpowers had on the messages of Nahum, Zephaniah, and Obadiah.

2. Discuss and contrast the three sections of the book of Habbakuk.

3. Define: hegemony, oracles, superscription, rubric.

The Book of Jeremiah   The book of Jeremiah contains a poignant portrayal of the final years of Judah's monarchy and of the city of Jerusalem. It appears to be a combined effort of the prophet Jeremiah, Baruch (a professional scribe and friend of Jeremiah), and an unknown editor(s). The portions of the book that are written in the first person are powerful demonstrations of the emotions of anger, frustration, and great personal loss. In many ways, Jeremiah's distress is a mirror of Judah's disintegration as a nation. While the third person accounts are more dispassionate, they allow the reader to step away from the anguish, analyze why it has come upon the people of Judah, and understand the **theodicy** of a righteous God who punishes the nation but expects eventually to restore them as the chosen people.

Call Narrative.   The actual date of Jeremiah's call as a prophet is still debated. His statement that he is "only a boy" (Jer 1:7) suggests that he is a young adult (perhaps 16–18 years old) at this time. The question of dating his call depends on his age when he confronts the people before the temple (Jer 7 and 26). Certainly, his confidence level is quite high in that narrative and it is known to have occurred in the early reign of Jehoiakim (ca. 609 BCE). It seems likely therefore that Jeremiah received his call sometime during the reign of Josiah (640–609 BCE), experienced Josiah's Deuteronomic reform (632–609 BCE), and then became an accomplished spokesman and prophet during the turbulent years following Josiah's death, when Judah was subjugated by both Egypt (609–605, 601–598 BCE) and Babylon (604–601, 597–538 BCE).

As with others, Jeremiah's call narrative describes a change of status, accomplished through a ceremonial transformation of his person. This was similar to initiation rituals into a fraternal order, installation as a priest, or coronation as a king or queen. Each involved a programmed set of actions designed to apply a new label to the person and provide him or her with the symbols of membership peculiar to this new status. These symbols transform the individuals in the eyes of the public, at that instant, into what we say they now are. They may then use the new labels to further their aims or increase their authority.

The commissioning or "ordination ritual" of the prophet Jeremiah (Jer 1:4–18) contains stages reminiscent of previous commissionings, especially that of Moses in Exod 3:2–4:23 and that of Gideon in Judg 6:11–24. There is: (1) a theophanic appearance; (2) a statement by the deity of intention and relationship; (3) an objection by the candidate and a negative label applied by the candidate to himself; (4) a transforming action; (5) an injunction and a legal empowerment; (6) a sign given by the deity to reassure and strengthen the chosen one.

Yahweh appears to Jeremiah (no particular location is cited) and announces that a divinely-ordained plan has existed for him as a prophet even "before I formed you in the womb," (Jer 1:5; also found in Isa 49:1). The concept of a designation "from the womb" is well known in ancient Near Eastern literature, although it is usually reserved for kings (see inset).

Called from the Womb

A king am I; from the womb I have become a hero (*Hymn of Shulgi*, Ur III king [ca. 2050 BCE; *ANET*, p. 585]).

Amun says: It was in the belly of your mother that I said concerning you that you were to be ruler of Egypt; it was as seed and while you were in the egg, that I knew you, that (I knew) you were to be Lord (*Stele of Pianchi* [Twenty-fifth Dynasty Egypt, 751–730 BCE]; M. Gilula, "An Egyptian Parallel to Jeremia I 4–5," *VT* 17 [1967] 114).

Jeremiah pleads that he is powerless to fulfill the task that Yahweh has set before him because he is "only a boy" (Jer 1:6). He is reassured by Yahweh that this is no impediment and is empowered to speak by the touch of God's hand on his lips (paralleling events in Deut 18:18 for Moses, in Judg 6:15 for Gideon, and in Isa 6:6–7 for Isaiah).

At this point, a legal formula similar to the one used at royal coronations is employed (Ps 2:7–9; 89:19–37). The prophet, by means of the powerful words he is about to speak, wields the power usually reserved for kings or gods and elevates himself above kings in authority (Jer 18:7; 31:28). A similar formula is used by the divine assembly in the *Enuma Elish* when they inaugurate the reign of the Babylonian god Marduk (see inset). This ceremony transforms Jeremiah by giving him the title of prophet, a term that carries with it the power of the God for whom he speaks and acts.

> **The Power to Command**
>
> From this day unchangeable shall be thy pronouncement. To raise or bring low—these shall be (in) thy hand. Thy utterance shall be true, thy command shall be unimpeachable (*Enuma Elish* 4.7–9; *ANET*, p. 66).
>
> [10]See, today I appoint you over nations and over kingdoms,
>   to pluck up and to pull down,
>   to destroy and to overthrow,
>   to build and to plant (Jer 1:10).

The final step in the transformation process is the giving of a sign by Yahweh or the divine messenger that will provide some sense of the prophet's mission as well as serve as a reassurance that the prophet will not be alone. In Jeremiah's case, this involves a pair of visions and their interpretations that reassure him of divine protection (Jer 1:11–16; visions of an almond branch and a boiling pot). Yahweh also gives Jeremiah a final charge and imposes the additional symbolic labels of "a fortified city, an iron pillar, and a bronze wall" to denote his invincibility (Jer 1:18).

The structure of the narrative of Jeremiah's commissioning differs from the structures used in describing the commissioning of Moses and Gideon, but the differences are minor in comparison to the obvious parallels in each narrative. The variations are probably a result of Jeremiah's intentional use of a traditional tale recast to meet his own experience. If this is the case, then Jeremiah identifies himself through these parallels with earlier leaders. He did this to enhance his authority and legitimize his role as prophet.

Jeremiah's Temple Sermon. The first major event in Jeremiah's career as a prophet is his temple sermon. This occurs at the beginning of the reign of Jehoiakim (Jer 26:1) and reflects Yahweh's concern over influences brought by Egyptian control of Judah (ca. 609 BCE). Jeremiah is aware of the political realities of the time, but he focuses on covenant and proper worship practices. Accounts of this event are found in Jer 7 and 26. Chapter 7 is in the first person and it highlights the sermon given by the prophet. Chapter 26 is written in third person (possibly by Baruch). It only provides an abbreviated version of the sermon while concentrating on the public reaction to Jeremiah's indictment.

Location is always an important ingredient in giving speeches. Visibility and spatial symbolism are combined when God directs Jeremiah to stage his confrontation with the powers of Jerusalem in the entrance to the temple. This is the physical conduit between secular and sacred space. It marks the boundary between contact with the world and contact with Yahweh. By standing at this place, blocking free movement back and forth, Jeremiah is assured of a crowd. He comes here on a major feast day (possibly the Feast of Booths, implying a date in either September or October). Because of this he can expect not only the people of Jerusalem, but also persons and officials from all over the kingdom.

The sermon focuses on two crucial themes: (1) the temple does not ensure that Jerusalem will not be destroyed, and (2) obedience to the covenant and the stipulations of the Ten Commandments is necessary to prevent Yahweh's destruction of Judah and Jerusalem. Jeremiah uses a framework for his message based on repetition of the phrase "Amend your ways and your doings" (Jer 7:3, 5) and a mocking of the popular chant "the temple of the LORD" (Jer 7:4). The phrase "the temple of the LORD" was apparently both a ritual utterance used when entering the temple and a slogan reassuring the people of Yahweh's protection.

Covenantal Obligations

Jer 7:22–23

[22]For in the day that I brought your ancestors out of the land of Egypt, I did not speak to them or command them concerning burnt offerings and sacrifices. [23]But this command I gave them, "Obey my voice, and I will be your God, and you shall be my people; and walk only in the way that I command you, so that it may be well with you."

Mic 6:6–8

[6]"With what shall I come before
    the LORD,
    and bow myself before God
        on high?
Shall I come before him with
        burnt offerings,
    with calves a year old?
[7]Will the LORD be pleased with
        thousands of rams,
    with ten thousands of rivers
        of oil?
Shall I give my firstborn for my
        transgression,
    the fruit of my body for the sin
        of my soul?"
[8]He has told you, O mortal, what
        is good;
    and what does the LORD require
        of you
but to do justice, and to love
        kindness,
    and to walk humbly with
        your God?

Jeremiah uses the shrine at Shiloh (about twenty miles north of Jerusalem) as his example of destruction. Although this place had once served as the seat of Yahweh worship (1 Sam 1–4), it had been destroyed by the Philistines because of the unfaithfulness of Eli's sons (1 Sam 2:12–17). No amount of staged ritual behavior or sacrifice could save Eli's sons or the place of worship at Shiloh (1 Sam 3:11–14) because without due respect for Yahweh's covenant, sacrificial ritual was merely hollow worship.

Like Micah in the previous century, Jeremiah decries rote ritual behavior that does not contain the desire to obey Yahweh's covenant (Jer 7:23; cf. Mic 6:6–8). This is the familiar theme that sacrifice without the love (*khesed*) of Yahweh and the covenant has no worth. We have already seen this theme in Samuel's confrontation with Saul (1 Sam 15) and in the words of Hosea, "For I desire steadfast love (*khesed*) and not sacrifice, the knowledge of God rather than burnt offerings" (Hos 6:6).

Thus the people of Jerusalem could not expect the temple to save them, despite previous occasions in which the city had been spared (Isa 37). They could not freely violate every law and then blithely call on Yahweh's name, expecting forgiveness (see inset for lists of both righteous and unrighteous behavior in Jeremiah and Ezekiel). Yahweh is not blind to their actions (Jer 7:11b) and will abandon them just as the people of the northern kingdom were left to their fate (Jer 7:15).

Two Kinds of Behavior

Righteous Behavior

[6]if you do not oppress the alien, the orphan, and the widow, or shed innocent blood in this place, and if you do not go after other gods to your own hurt, . . . (Jer 7:6).

[6]if he does not eat upon the mountains or lift up his eyes to the idols of the house of Israel, does not defile his neighbor's wife or approach a woman during her menstrual period, [7]does not oppress anyone, but restores to the debtor his pledge, commits no robbery, gives his bread to the hungry and covers the naked with a garment, [8]does not take advance or accrued interest, withholds his hand from iniquity, executes true justice between contending parties, [9]follows my statutes, and is careful to observe my ordinances, acting faithfully—such a one is righteous . . . (Ezek 18:6–9a).

Unrighteous Behavior

[9]Will you steal, murder, commit adultery, swear falsely, make offerings to Baal, and go after other gods that you have not known . . . ? (Jer 7:9).

[11]. . . [He] who eats upon the mountains, defiles his neighbor's wife, [12]oppresses the poor and needy, commits robbery, does not restore the pledge, lifts up his eyes to the idols, commits abomination, [13]takes advance or accrued interest . . . (Ezek 18:11b–13a).

Such an attack on the foundations of their belief system and upon the icon that they had come to consider their safety net could not go unanswered. Baruch's version of the scene describes an immediate outcry against Jeremiah. A trial was organized on the spot, with the religious establishment serving as his accusers and prosecutors, the king's advisers serving as judges, and "all the people" (a collective phrase meaning the citizens present at the time) serving as a jury (Jer 26:7–11).

Once the charges of blasphemy and false prophecy have been levied against Jeremiah, he stands up to speak in his defense. Jeremiah freely admits that he has "prophesied against this house (the temple) and this city" (Jer 26:12–13). But he insists that his prophecy is Yahweh's words, not his own. If the people of Judah choose to kill him, they will be shedding "innocent blood," which is one of the worst crimes an Israelite can commit (Exod 23:7; Deut 19:10–11).

The decision of the officials and the people is to release Jeremiah, based on the injunction that a prophet cannot be killed for speaking Yahweh's words (Jer 26:16). Their decision is further strengthened when "elders of the land" (regional officials probably in Jerusalem for the feast day) cite the case of Micah, who had also spoken out against the city of Jerusalem in Hezekiah's day (715–687 BCE) and had not been punished (Mic 3:12). Jeremiah is somewhat vindicated by this verdict. However, he is quickly removed from the scene by one of the king's officials, Ahikam the son of Shaphan, in order to prevent any further disturbance.

Baruch's Mission to the Temple.   Apparently, Jeremiah's temple sermon created enough of an uproar that the prophet was forced into hiding. During the fourth year of Jehoiakim's reign (605 BCE) he uses Baruch to deliver another scathing denunciation of Jerusalem and its leaders (Jer 36). Jeremiah dictates his message to Baruch (Jer 36:4). The scribe then carries the scroll containing Jeremiah's words to the temple on a "fast day" when a large audience will be present, including the leaders from the temple and the palace (Jer 36:5–8).

The words of the prophet indict Jehoiakim for choosing to be faithful to one foreign monarch (Neco II of Egypt) and then to another (Nebuchadnezzar of Babylon). Micaiah, the grandson of Shaphan, is the first royal official to hear Baruch's performance in the chamber of Gemariah, a place open only to officials like Baruch (Jer 36:11). He discusses it with other royal officials who become alarmed (Jer 36:16). They order Baruch to retell parts of the story for them before deciding to "report all these words to the king" (Jer 36:12–18). They also quite apprehensively ask him: "Tell us now, how did you write all these words? Was it at his dictation" (Jer 36:17). The question certifies that both the scroll and Jeremiah the prophet are authentic. After due deliberation, they report the substance of his story to the king (Jer 36:20). Jehoiakim decides to get a second adviser, Jehudi, to reread and perhaps reinterpret the message for him (Jer 36:21).

Publicly, in the presence of the Babylonian messengers, Jehoiakim haughtily denies Jeremiah's indictment. Using a nearby charcoal brazier, Jehoiakim burns the scroll piece by piece as it is read, thereby disputing its contents as being the word of the Lord (Jer 36:22–23). Jehoiakim's gesture is as convincing to the messengers from Babylon, who are present in Jehoiakim's throne room, as it is scandalous to the people of Judah who are loyal to their covenant with Yahweh. The king does not want to provide the Babylonian messengers with any evidence of his disloyalty to Nebuchadnezzar.

Publicly Judah will remain faithful to its covenant with Nebuchadnezzar and abrogate its treaty with Yahweh. For his crime, Jeremiah sentences Jehoiakim to a shameful death (Jer 36:32). Privately, however, the political overtures of Egypt, Jeremiah's indictment, and the stories of Baruch and Jehudi do move Jehoiakim to declare Judah's independence from Babylon. By 600 BCE, Judah is free. Soon, however, the Babylonians lay siege to Jerusalem, and Jehoiakim meets his end as the monarch of an independent, but embattled state.

Enacted Prophecies. Jeremiah made effective use of physical acts, symbolic gestures, and street theater in presenting his prophecies to the people of Jerusalem. Chapters 16–19 contain several of these **enacted prophecies.** Each demonstrates a sense of urgency on the part of the prophet as well as a graphic demonstration of the events to come.

In Jer 16, the prophet's personal life and his normal emotional reactions are restricted. He is forbidden to marry and raise a family (Jer 16:2–4). This celibacy symbolizes the fast-approaching doom of the city and its people. Celebrations at this time would be inappropriate and it would be cruel to bring children into a world in which they could only experience destruction and pain.

Jeremiah is further restricted in Jer 16:5–9 from participating in mourning, even for his parents. He may not gash himself nor shave his head, nor could he attend funeral rites where the dead are memorialized and the mourners comforted. These actions for an individual death could only serve as a mockery of the approaching death of the whole nation. There will be so many dead that their bodies will lie unburied and unmourned by the few survivors.

Another sort of warning occurs in Jeremiah 18. In this chapter, Jeremiah is instructed to go to the potters' district of the city and to watch a potter work with the clay. While he watched, the prophet noted that the potter was dissatisfied with his creation. The potter reworked the clay and once again began shaping it on his wheel (Jer 18:3–4). The explanation that Jeremiah received of this scene was that the clay was the nation of Judah and Yahweh was the potter. Like the initial pot formed on the wheel, the nation had not shaped itself according to the desires of its maker. As a result, Yahweh would remold the clay and begin again, using the essence of the pot to shape a new vessel.

This is an excellent example of the **remnant theme**. Although the prophet must warn the people of inevitable punishment because of their failure to obey the stipulations of the covenant, total destruction would not occur. Just as the clay was saved to be used in the creation of a new pot, so too would a remnant of the people be spared in order to restore the nation.

Egyptian Execration Text

All men, all people, all folk, all males, all eunuchs, all women, and all officials, who may rebel, who may plot, who may fight, who may talk of fighting, or who may talk of rebelling, and every rebel who talks of rebelling—in this entire land . . . shall die (*ANET*, p. 329).

A third example of Jeremiah's use of **enacted prophecies** is found in his **execration ritual** in Jer 19. This public denunciation, similar to the curses found on Egyptian incantation bowls denouncing their enemies, provided an opportunity for the prophet to challenge the temple establishment and make the point that Yahweh had condemned the temple and the city of Jerusalem. He purchases a pottery vessel and then marches in an informal procession to the Potsherd Gate, picking up witnesses and supporters along the way. When he reaches his destination he lists a bill of particulars of the people's sins: idolatry, the shedding of innocent blood, and the sacrifice of children. Jeremiah then describes the utter devastation of the city and its population: "Everyone who passes by it will be horrified and will hiss because of all its disasters" (Jer 19:8; Zeph 2:15).

Then, to enact the curse, he smashes the pot within the gate and makes the statement that Yahweh will "break this people and this city, as one breaks a potter's vessel, so that it can never be mended" (Jer 19:11). The curse was horrible enough, but to smash the pot in a gate, a place of law and judgment, made this act a living reality for the people who witnessed it.

Such a challenge could not be left unanswered. Pashur, one of the chief officials of the temple, arrested Jeremiah and placed him in the stocks (Jer 20:2). This was an attempt to silence Jeremiah by humiliating him. The comic posture of someone in the stocks was an easy thing to ridicule. Pashur hoped that Jeremiah's credibility and that of his prophecies would be damaged along with his pride.

> **Why Do the Wicked Prosper?**
>
> Why does the way of the guilty prosper?
>   Why do all who are treacherous thrive?
> ²You plant them, and they take root;
>   they grow and bring forth fruit;
> you are near in their mouths
>   yet far from their hearts (Jer 12:1b–2).

Certainly this angered Jeremiah. He called on Yahweh to take revenge on his enemies (Jer 20:12), as he had done when his own Anathoth neighbors had plotted against him (Jer 11:18–12:6). He questions why the wicked are allowed to prosper and to mislead the people. Jeremiah also questions himself, cursing his own birth and the task that has brought him to this fate (Jer 20:14). But he also acknowledges that even if he wished to keep silent, and thereby stop his persecutors, he cannot. He feels an inner compulsion to speak that cannot be denied:

> ⁹If I say, "I will not mention him,
>   or speak in his name,"
> then within me there is something like a burning fire
>   shut up in my bones;
> I am weary with holding it in,
>   and I cannot (Jer 20:9).

Cognitive Dissonance and Opposition to Jeremiah's Message. In the period between 597 and 587 BCE, Jeremiah and the people, both in Judah and in the exile, had to cope with conflicting prophetic voices. While Jeremiah continued to warn of the ultimate destruction of Jerusalem, other prophets and officials were speaking of a quick end to the exile; a return of Jehoiachin, the people, and the sacred objects taken from the temple; and divine retribution against the Babylonians (Jer 28:3–4). The optimistic message of these prophets was much more pleasing to the people than Jeremiah's words of doom. As a result Jeremiah faced both overt hostility and open opposition.

The most dangerous of these opponents was Hananiah, a prophet from Gibeon. Confronting Jeremiah in the temple in the presence of the priests, Hananiah predicts that within two years the exiles would return and Babylon's power would be broken (Jer 28:1–4). A message so diametrically opposed to Jeremiah's position demanded a response from Jeremiah. He first affirms the hope that this message would come true, but he then argues that peace had never been a part of prophetic speech: "The prophets who preceded you and me from ancient times prophesied war, famine, and pestilence against many countries and great kingdoms" (Jer 28:8).

In this way Jeremiah explains the role of the prophet as he might explain it to a child. Prophets were to alert the people and their leaders of deviation from the covenant. They were to warn of the righteous anger of Yahweh and present the proper course that would bring the people back into compliance with their obligations to their God. Peace, however, was not part of the usual prophetic message because it implied two things: (1) an end to current troubles, and (2) that the people deserved to have Yahweh intervene to end these troubles. Jeremiah concludes with a reminder of the adage that the "true prophet" is the one whose words come true:

> [9]As for the prophet who prophesies peace, when the word of that prophet comes true, then it will be known that the LORD has truly sent the prophet (Jer 28:9).

Faced with a classic example of **cognitive dissonance** (that is, a situation where two conflicting statements are both credible), Hananiah performs a physical act to gain the advantage. He breaks a wooden yoke off of Jeremiah's neck (Jer 28:10). Jeremiah had been wearing this as a symbolic prop to remind the people that they must submit to the "yoke of Babylon" and thus to Yahweh's will (Jer 27:2-8). By breaking the yoke, Hananiah can symbolically negate Jeremiah's message and reaffirm his message that Yahweh intended to "break the yoke of King Nebuchadnezzar" within two years (Jer 28:11).

Temporarily defeated, Jeremiah leaves. When he later receives a new revelation from Yahweh, he returns to confront Hananiah with a new symbol of submission—an iron yoke. The wooden yoke may have been broken, but Yahweh has forged an even stronger restraint to hold his people in submission to Babylon (Jer 28:12-14). Jeremiah also announces that Yahweh would discredit the false message and bring an end to the dissonance. Jeremiah predicts the death of the false messenger. The text notes that Hananiah dies that same year (Jer 28:16-17).

> [4]Thus says the LORD of Hosts, the God of Israel, to all the exiles whom I have sent into exile from Jerusalem to Babylon: [5]Build houses and live in them; plant gardens and eat what they produce. [6]Take wives and have sons and daughters; take wives for your sons, and give your daughters in marriage, that they may bear sons and daughters; multiply there, and do not decrease. [7]But seek the welfare of the city where I have sent you into exile, and pray to the LORD on its behalf, for in its welfare you will find your welfare (Jer 29:4–7).

Apparently there were also voices of dissension among the exiles as well (Jer 29:8). Jeremiah attempts to deal with these voices of false hope by writing a letter to the exilic community (Jer 29:4-7). First he discounts any idea that the exile will be over soon. Yahweh's "plan" provides for a seventy-year period during which the people must seek the Lord "with all their hearts" before they can be returned to their land (Jer 29:10–14).

Jeremiah also removes the limits on worship that had been placed on the people by the reforms of Hezekiah and Josiah. They no longer have to be in Judah or Jerusalem to worship or to be assured that God will hear their prayers. Yahweh is not just a local God. The people may worship Yahweh in exile—even without the temple priesthood to direct them. This new opportunity set the stage for the development of **diaspora Judaism** in the next two centuries. It was also the first sign of the divergence that took place after the exile between the Judaism of the exile and the Judaism of the return.

Jerusalem's Final Days. In 589 BCE, after nearly ten years of relative peace, Zedekiah was lured by Egypt into revolting against the Babylonians. Nebuchadnezzar resolved to eliminate the troublesome kingdom of Judah, and in 588 BCE he again besieged Jerusalem. In the midst of the siege, Zedekiah sent messengers to Jeremiah to see if Yahweh would once again intervene to save the city (Jer 21:1–2). The prophet could offer them no consolation. He warned that Yahweh, the Divine Warrior, would fight on the Babylonian side against the city. Its people would be slaughtered without mercy (Jer 21:4–7).

Jeremiah stated that there was only one way to save their lives: surrender to Babylon. "Those who stay in this city shall die . . . but those who go out and surrender to the Chaldeans . . . shall have their lives as a prize of war" (Jer 21:9). Such a message must have shocked the king and his advisers. It is no wonder that they imprisoned Jeremiah in a dry cistern to prevent him from totally demoralizing the city's defenders (Jer 38:4–6).

Eventually Zedekiah released Jeremiah and in a private interview asked him again for some ray of hope. Jeremiah elicited an oath from the king that the king would not kill him for speaking disturbing words. Then he repeated his message that surrender to the Babylonians was the only chance for survival (Jer 38:16–23). The king placed Jeremiah under house arrest and there he remained until the fall of the city (Jer 38:28).

With the fall of the city only days away, Jeremiah engages in one last symbolic act. He receives a message that one of his relatives has died and it is his kinship right to purchase the man's fields and thus keep them within the family (Jer 32:6–8). Real estate at this point is totally worthless because the people are about to be taken into exile. In spite of this Jeremiah goes on with the process of weighing out the money and signing and sealing a deed before witnesses (Jer 32:9–10). We have seen the symbolic importance of this kind of action in the way Abraham had established his stake in the promised land by purchasing the cave of Machpelah (Gen 23). Now

Jeremiah preserves for future generations a title to the land. He gives the copies of the documents to Baruch in front of witnesses and charges him to "put them in an earthenware jar, in order that they may last for a long time" (Jer 32:11–14). This assured the people that when Yahweh's plan was fulfilled they would be returned from exile, and this deed to the promised land would serve as their legal claim to its ownership.

Jeremiah also delivers oracles of restoration and return just before the fall of the city. In chapter 31, he describes a future end to the exile and a reversal of the current destruction (Jer 31:27–28). He also addresses the issue of individual responsibility and the casting of blame for the exile in much the same terms as Ezek 18 (Jer 31:29–30). The exiles must recognize that they are not paying for the sins of their ancestors, but for their own. He also envisions a new covenant that has an internal nature to it.

> I will put my law within them, and I will write it on their hearts; and I will be their God, and they will be my people. No longer shall they teach one another, or say to each other, "Know the LORD," for they shall all know me, from the least to the greatest (Jer 31:33b–34; compare Ezek 11:19).

When the city of Jerusalem falls to the Babylonian forces, the royal court is dissolved. Zedekiah is forced to watch the execution of his children and then is blinded before being taken into exile (2 Kgs 25:7). The monarchy of Judah has effectively ended, although Jehoiachin lives on as a king in exile (2 Kgs 25:27–30). The Babylonians appoint a non-Davidic official, Gedaliah, as governor, but he is assassinated after only a short time in office (2 Kgs 25:22–26). His assassins flee to Egypt, taking Jeremiah with them. Thus ended the ministry of a prophet whose career spanned the period from the glorious expectations of Josiah's nationalist movement to the dregs of despair as Judah met its fate at the hands of Nebuchadnezzar.

STUDY QUESTIONS

1. Compare and contrast the call narratives of Isaiah and Jeremiah.

2. Discuss Jeremiah's trial after he delivers his "temple sermon."

3. Describe Jeremiah's execration ritual and the reaction to it.

4. Discuss the conflict between Jeremiah and Hananiah.

5. Define: enacted prophecy, remnant theme, diaspora Judaism.

WISDOM LITERATURE

Introduction   We have left our historical progression with the prophet Jeremiah, a figure who begins in the seventh century during the reforms of King Josiah, and who ends his career in the early sixth century when Babylon destroys Jerusalem and exiles significant numbers of its population. Before we turn our attention to the exile itself and its prophetic voices, we will take a detour and discuss the wisdom literature of ancient Israel. To a great extent this is an arbitrary location for this discussion, since the wisdom traditions span the length of Israel's history.

Every culture produces its own store of wisdom. Wisdom may be expressed in the form of oral pronouncements or stories, or it may blossom into major philosophical works that carefully explore the questions that have troubled humanity since the cave. In this section, we will examine the types of wisdom literature produced by the ancient Israelites. We will make a distinction between passages that contain the **wisdom** theme and traditional works of **wisdom literature**. We will also compare these works with ancient Near Eastern wisdom texts and reference will be made to "wisdom sayings" outside the traditional "wisdom books." As a genre separate in theme and style from other biblical writing, wisdom literature has the following major characteristics: (1) little concern with history, chronology, genealogy, or even place; (2) strong emphasis on an established moral or social code of conduct; (3) concern with the question of good and evil in the world; (4) a glorification of God as creator and source of all true knowledge.

Wisdom Is   The wisdom theme runs throughout the biblical text. It is
Where You   woven into nearly every narrative and literally springs from the
Find It   tongues of characters in scenes as varied as historical annals and private discussions. Here are a few examples. (1) Eve's dialogue with the serpent in Gen 3:1-6 is a typical wisdom piece, examining a truism and testing its validity. (2) Jacob employs "native wisdom" by placing peeled rods in front of his flocks to ensure that they produce the proper types of offspring (Gen 30:37-43). (3) Joseph's answer to Potiphar's wife references "right behavior" in terms of obedience to his master and to God (Gen 39:8-9). (4) Jethro provides good advice on administration of the people in telling Moses to appoint judges instead of hearing all the cases himself (Exod 18:19-26). (5) The wise and the fool are graphically displayed in the story of Nabal (whose name in Hebrew means "fool") and Abigail, the wise wife, in their dealings with David (1 Sam 25:2-38).

(6) In attempting to protect her honor, Tamar urges her brother Amnon not to rape her and act "as one of the scoundrels in Israel" (2 Sam 13:12–13). (7) Solomon earns his reputation as a "wise king" by discerning the truth in the case brought to him by two prostitutes (1 Kgs 3:16–28).

The wisdom theme is especially common in the sayings of the prophets and in books traditionally known as "wisdom literature." (1) The prophets quote well-known proverbs to make a point in their message. Ezekiel 18:2–4 and Jer 31:29–30 both quote the proverb, "The parents have eaten sour grapes and the children's teeth are set on edge." (2) The knowledge of God and right behavior are often paired. Samuel chides Saul for failing to be obedient, "Surely, to obey is better than sacrifice" (1 Sam 15:22–23). Hosea points to the people's distress when he says, "My people are destroyed for lack of knowledge" (Hos 4:6). (3) The path to wisdom is found throughout the books of Psalms and Proverbs in statements like "The fear of the LORD is the beginning of wisdom" (Ps 111:10; Prov 1:7; 9:10). There are also "wisdom psalms" like Ps 1, which points to the proper way and the dangers of association with the foolish:

> [1]Happy are those
>   who do not follow the advice of the wicked,
> or take the path that sinners tread,
>   or sit in the seat of the scoffers;
> [2]but their delight is in the law of the LORD,
>   and on his law they meditate day and night (Ps 1:1–2).

The Book of Proverbs

The book of Proverbs is a collection of traditional wisdom sayings from many periods of Israelite history. These sayings are generally short, although some, like Prov 31:10–31, may run to considerable length on a single topic. Their purpose is to summarize the basic values of Israelite society in a form that can easily be remembered. These sayings are not unique to Israel because much of their wisdom is borrowed or recycled from older Near Eastern cultures. This is not a criticism by any means. Wisdom, by its very nature, is universal and timeless. While its vocabulary or details may occasionally need to be updated, the basic kernel of truth within the statements remains valid as it travels from one nation to another. Like law, wisdom is borrowed and refitted to new cultures.

Parallels Within a Common Wisdom Heritage

Prov 6:25–29: Do not desire her beauty in your heart, | and do not let her capture you with her eyelashes; | for a prostitute's fee is only a loaf of bread, | but the wife of another stalks a man's very life. | Can fire be carried in the bosom without burning one's clothes? | Or can one walk on hot coals without scorching the feet? | So is he who sleeps with his neighbor's wife; | no one who touches her will go unpunished.

'Onchsheshonqy Col. 23:6–7: Do not make love to a married woman. He who makes love to a married woman is killed on her doorstep. Col. 8:12: Do not marry a wife whose husband is alive, lest you make for yourself an enemy (S.R.K. Glanville, *The Instructions of 'Onchsheshonqy* [British Museum Papyrus 10508; London: British Museum, 1955] pp. 23, 54).

Prov 23:9: Do not speak in the hearing of a fool, | who will only despise the wisdom of your words.

Sirach 21:14: The mind of a fool is like a broken jar; | it can hold no knowledge.

Sirach 22:9: Whoever teaches a fool is like one who glues potsherds together, | or who rouses a sleeper from deep slumber.

'Onchsheshonqy Col. 7:4–5: Do not instruct a fool, lest he hate you. Do not instruct him who will not listen to you. Col. 10:6: "It irks me what they do," says the fool, when he is instructed (Glanville, pp. 21, 27).

Prov 26:17: Like somebody who takes a passing dog by the ears | is one who meddles in the affairs of another.

'Onchsheshonqy Col. 19:11–12: When two brothers quarrel, do not come between them. The man who comes between two brothers when they quarrel is apt to be placed between them when they are at peace (Glanville, p. 45).

Prov 29:19: By mere words a servant is not disciplined, | for though he understands, he will not give heed.

'Onchsheshonqy Col. 7:18: A servant who is not beaten is full of scorn (Glanville, p. 21).

Prov 16:1: The plans of the mind belong to mortals, | but the answer of the tongue is from the LORD.

Prov 16:9 The human mind plans the way, | but the LORD directs the steps.

'Onchsheshonqy Col. 26:14: The plans of the god are one thing, the thoughts of men are another (Glanville, p. 59).

Prov 2:3: If you cry out for insight, | and raise your voice for understanding, | if you seek it like silver, | and search for it as for hidden treasures— | then you will understand the fear of the LORD | and find the knowledge of God.

Prov 19:20: Listen to advice and accept instruction, | that you may gain wisdom for the future.

> Ptah-Hotep 54–56: Seek advice from the simple, as well as from the wise. No one ever reaches their full potential, there is always more to learn. Wisdom hides like emeralds, but it can always be uncovered—in a poor man, in a young woman grinding grain (*OTPar,* p. 185).
>
> Prov 15:16–17: Better is a little with the fear of the LORD | than great treasure and trouble with it. | Better is a dinner of vegetables where love is | than a fatted ox and hatred with it.
>
> Amenemope 8:19–20; 9:6–9: Better a single bushel from God than 5,000 stolen bushels. Better is poverty from the hand of God, than wealth from a granary full of stolen grain. Better is a single loaf and a happy heart, than all the riches in the world and sorrow (*OTPar,* pp. 192–93).

Wisdom literature in the ancient Near East reflects a broad ranging cultural milieu, not isolated cultural pockets. Connections exist between the wisdom literature produced in ancient Egypt, Mesopotamia, and Israel. These connections do not indicate the total dependence of Israel upon its neighbors. Rather, the wealth of available material was utilized and reworked to reflect regional, ethical, and chronological differences. Thus Prov 22:20 can speak of "thirty" admonitions, perhaps in direct reference to the Egyptian "Instructions of Amenemope," but that does not mean that all subsequent wisdom writers had to employ this strict literary framework.

A turn of phrase, a particular situation, or even direct borrowing of entire sayings therefore can be seen as acceptance of the validity of wisdom literature in general, wherever it may have originated. The most commonly shared concepts in wisdom include (1) the need for children (embodied in the image of clients, slaves, apprentices, and offspring) to listen to and obey the commands of parents (embodied in the image of employers, masters, and biological parents); (2) that a man needs to exercise discretion in dealing with women outside his immediate family; and (3) that honesty is the best policy. Plagiarism of these principles was the highest form of cultural flattery.

Of course, some biblical proverbs reflect distinctive Israelite culture and thought. These sayings express both the character of Yahweh and the Israelite concept of justice.

> [19]The LORD by wisdom founded the earth;
>   by understanding he established the heavens;
> [20]by his knowledge the deeps broke open,
>   and the clouds drop down the dew (Prov 3:19–20).

> [4]The LORD has made everything for its purpose,
>   even the wicked for the day of trouble.

⁵All those who are arrogant are an abomination to the L<small>ORD</small>;
   be assured they will not go unpunished (Prov 16:4–5).

¹⁰The name of the L<small>ORD</small> is a strong tower;
   the righteous run into it and are safe (Prov 18:10).

These and other sayings reinforce the concept of the divine origin of wisdom. Proverbs 8:22–31 celebrates wisdom as the first product of Yahweh's action in creation. This establishes the authority of wisdom and identifies it as female. The origin of this gender designation is most likely the fact that the woman is the first teacher of her children. It is her first responsibility to instill within them the principles of Israelite culture and religion.

The Book of Ecclesiastes   Like Proverbs and Song of Songs, the book of Ecclesiastes (also called Qoheleth) has been traditionally ascribed to Solomon. This is based, at least in part, on Solomon's prayer for wisdom in 1 Kgs 3:3–15 (2 Chron 1:7–12). But like all wisdom literature, it is impossible to determine the authorship conclusively or even be certain of when the material was composed. It is probably best to think of this work as simply an extended monologue discussing wisdom issues without trying to tie it to any particular person or time.

> **Gilgamesh's Consolation**
>
> Go up, Urshanabi, walk on the ramparts of Uruk. Inspect the base terrace, examine its brickwork, whether its brickwork is not of burnt brick, and if the Seven Wise Ones laid not its foundation! (*ANET*, p. 97).

The primary theme of this book is the seeming uselessness of human endeavor. Nothing that a person accomplishes in this life has any lasting value. It is therefore useless to strive for power, knowledge, or property since we all come to the same end. Unlike Gilgamesh, the hero of ancient Mesopotamian legend, the author of Ecclesiastes can draw no consolation from his city's walls, apparently built to last forever.

Such a negative view of life is difficult for modern readers to deal with. It seems to allow for no joy of accomplishment. It inspires few emotions whatsoever, except perhaps frustration and depression. As in most ancient wisdom literature, the author takes a very realistic view of life and its uncertainties. The Israelites, like the Mesopotamians, did not believe in a resurrection or afterlife. Death was both the great equalizer as well as the destroyer of all hopes and desires.

The author of Ecclesiastes draws upon this view of death to demolish the case that promotes human pride and foolishness. Once that is done, then the wisdom writer can lead the reader to recognize that it is contemplation of Yahweh's power and acceptance of God's purpose for the world and humankind that is of most value in life.

Death as the Destroyer

[20]All go to one place; all are from the dust, and all turn to dust again (Eccl 3:20).

[9]Remember that you fashioned me like clay;
and will you turn me to dust again? (Job 10:9).

Baal and Anat 5.1:20–21: The dust of the grave devours its prey.
. . . [It] eats whatever it wants with both hands (*OTPar*, p. 165).

The author does not turn away from life or reject normal existence on earth. Instead, he promotes balance, temperance of thought and word, and a more reasoned understanding of humanity's place within the scheme of creation.

STUDY QUESTIONS

1. Discuss how wisdom literature is a reflection of the society that produces it.

2. Compare and contrast the proverbial statements in the Bible and those from the ancient Near East.

3. Compare and contrast Proverbs and Ecclesiastes.

4. Discuss the purpose behind including Ecclesiastes in the canon.

The Book of Job   A definite date for the book of Job cannot be determined. The message, as is the case with most wisdom literature, is a timeless story. Arguments can be made for a date of composition as early as the ancestral period of Abraham, Isaac, and Jacob. But it is also possible to argue that this book should be dated as late as the exilic or postexile period. The date is simply uncertain. The author is also impossible to identify. All that can be said is that the author is one of the world's greatest psychological dramatists.

Literary Analysis. The book can certainly be examined as a whole. But the prologue (Job 1–2) and the epilogue (42:7–17) are written in narrative style while the remainder of the book (3:1–42:6) in poetry. This suggests that at least two separate stories have been joined together by the biblical editors. The character of Job in the two segments is also quite different. In the narrative sections, Job is long-suffering and totally faithful. He accepts his fate and never questions the justice of God. His attitude is quite different, however, in the poetic chapters. Here he cries out against the day he was born, demands that God appear to him to explain what appears to be a clear case of injustice, and refutes all of the charges of sin made by his three "friends." There is an artificial character to the "dialogues" between Job and his friends. Each man makes his case for why Job has been afflicted. Job then answers the charges made, sometimes indirectly, and then speaks to God about the injustice of the situation. The dialogues contain three "rounds" in which a great deal of repetition is found, but this is fairly common in wisdom material. The sequence is broken in chapters 29–31, where Job leaves his friends and speaks directly to God. In these speeches he details his former condition, his current affliction, and his plea of innocence (through an oath of clearance). One other person, Elihu, also comes forward to sum up the arguments of the friends and to reiterate Job's need to repent (chs. 32–37). The final segment of the poetic section then contains the **theophany** in which Yahweh appears to Job, not to answer his questions, but to demonstrate the gulf between human understanding and divine majesty.

Story Summary. In the prologue of the book we learn that there is a man named Job who lived in the land of Uz, which some have identified with the area of Edom. This man was blameless and upright, one who feared God and turned away from evil. And we are told that Job had many children and was quite wealthy.

After these initial statements, the scene shifts to the divine realm where one day the heavenly beings came to present themselves before the Lord (Job 1:6). These angels or heavenly beings are part of the divine assembly, which forms a royal court for God (cf. the use of "us" in the first Genesis creation story; Gen 1:26). A similar gathering is mentioned in 1 Kgs 22 in the story of the prophet Micaiah. The angels come to God and with them is a being whose Hebrew title, *hasatan,* means "the adversary."

Our modern conception of Satan or the devil is influenced by writings and art created after the OT/HB; such images can cloud our understanding of this character in Job. To think of the devil or Satan with horns and a tail and in some of the ways medieval people thought of him or drew him, or even in the sense of the New Testament, is to miss the role and concept of this adversary. The reason why we prefer to identify this being as "the adversary" rather than Satan is that the Hebrew definitely implies that the term is not a proper name.

The adversary was among the heavenly beings who came to the council. The Lord said to the adversary, "Where have you come from?" The adversary answered the Lord, "From going to and fro on the earth and from walking up and down on it" (Job 1:7). This means he had been traveling all over the world. The Lord said to the adversary, "Have you considered my servant Job?" (Job 1:8). Job has been described as blameless, a righteous and good man. He prayed for his children and strictly obeyed all of the religious statutes. Now God says, "There is no one like him on the earth, a blameless and upright man, who fears God and turns away from evil."

Such an assertion in wisdom literature requires a test, and thus the adversary answers the Lord,

> Does Job fear God for nothing? Have you not put a fence around him and his house and all that he has on every side? . . . But stretch out your hand now, and touch all he has, and he will curse you to your face (Job 1:9–11).

The Lord said to the adversary, "Very well, all that Job has is in your power; only do not stretch out your hand against him!" (Job 1:12). That is, don't touch his body. The adversary then departs. What we need to know as readers is what Job does not know. Job does not know that he is the object of a contest going on in heaven, a contest between God and the adversary.

Now the adversary, under the direction of Yahweh, takes away everything Job has. First his children are killed. Then his ranches, his barns, and his houses are ruined in one kind of catastrophe after another. But after all this Job rises, tears his robe, shaves his head, falls on the ground, and worships. He says,

> Naked I came from my mother's womb, naked shall I return there, the LORD gave, the LORD has taken away, blessed be the name of the LORD (Job 1:20–21).

After Job passes this first test, a second dialogue occurs between Yahweh and the adversary. Once again Yahweh extols Job's virtues, but the adversary says, Well, he's still got his health, let me take away his health and then see if he still worships you. So God says, All right, you can take away his health, but you can't kill him. The adversary then inflicts loathsome sores on Job from the sole of his foot to the crown of his head (Job 2:7). Job is in such distress that he takes a potsherd to scrape himself and sits among the ashes. Then Job's wife says to him, "Do you still persist in your integrity? Curse God and die" (Job 2:9).

What is the implication from the ancient Israelite perspective of saying "curse God and die"? What happens to somebody who curses God? Remember the story of Naboth's vineyard in 1 Kgs 21? Cursing God or the king is a capital offense. What Job's wife is saying to him is to commit suicide, for if one curses God one would be killed. Job said to her, "You speak as any foolish woman would speak. Shall we receive the good at the hand of God and not receive the bad?" (Job 2:10). In all of this, Job did not sin with his lips.

Now come three so-called friends, often referred to as "Job's comforters." When Job's three friends heard of all of the troubles that had come upon him, each of them sets out from his home. Eliphaz the Temanite, Bildad the Shuhite, and Zophar the Naamathite met together to go and console and comfort Job. When they saw him from a great distance they did not recognize him. They raised their voices and wept aloud. They tore their robes and threw dust in the air upon their heads. These are typical ancient expressions of grief (see the inset on "Ancient Israelite Grief Rituals" in the section on Lamentations). They sat with Job on the ground seven days and seven nights and no one spoke a word to him because they saw that his suffering was great (Job 2:11–13).

In his anguish, Job curses the day of his birth (Job 3:1) and complains to God about the unfairness of his affliction. After Job completes his lament, each friend speaks in turn in an effort to convince Job that he has committed some sin, perhaps a secret or forgotten one, that explains his condition. They argue in this fashion for over thirty chapters. Their arguments present the standard moral and legal viewpoints that were present in ancient Israel about suffering and punishment. (1) No mortal is perfect and therefore all persons must expect that God will punish them for their transgressions. This is the doctrine of individual retribution. (2) The evidence of history proves that God is just. God does not reject the upright or take up the cause of the evildoer. (3) Self-righteousness is self-delusion. God's wisdom is beyond the understanding of any human. To deny the justice of affliction is to demonstrate a lack of desire to learn from the experience.

The Egyptian Book of the Dead

I have not committed evil against men.

I have not mistreated cattle.

I have not committed sin in the place of truth.

I have not blasphemed a god.

I have not done violence to a poor man.

I have not made (anyone) sick.

I have not made (anyone) weep.

I have not killed.

I have given no order to a killer.

I have not caused anyone suffering.

I have not had sexual relations with a boy.

I have not defiled myself.

I am pure! (*ANET,* pp. 34–35).

Job interrupts the statements of his three friends in chapter 29 with a series of **soliloquies,** private statements made to the audience, in which he speaks directly to God. He details the happy condition in which he and his family once lived. He attributes this previous happiness to his piety and devotion to Yahweh. In chapter 30 he graphically describes his current pitiful state. Then, to complete his courtroom-like performance, Job takes an oath of clearance (Job 31) similar to that found in the Egyptian Book of the Dead. He lists a series of sins that might explain his afflictions and then denies that he has committed them.

At the conclusion of the argumentation section, the story says that the Lord answered Job out of the whirlwind (Job 38:1), "Who is this that darkens counsel by words without knowledge? Gird up your loins like a man, I will question you and you shall declare to me." This opening challenge is followed by question after unanswerable question.

> [4]"Where were you when I laid the foundation of the earth?
>   Tell me if you have understanding.
> [5]Who determined measurements—surely you know!
>   Or who stretched the line upon it?
> [6]On what were its bases sunk,
>   or who laid its cornerstone
> [7]when the morning stars sang together
>   and all the heavenly beings shouted for joy?" (Job 38:4–7).

What is Job's response to these sixty to eighty rhetorical questions extending over a series of chapters? In 40:4–5, Job answers the Lord,

> [4]"See I am of small account, what shall I answer you?
>   I lay my hand on my mouth.
> [5]I have spoken once, and I will not answer;
>   twice, but will proceed no further."

Then Job gets a second final exam, filled with more rhetorical questions, including: "Do you control the thunder, tornadoes, or the rain?" Of course Job doesn't answer directly. Beaten down by the volume of God's questioning, Job at last says,

> [2]"I know that you can do all things,
>   and that no purpose of yours can be thwarted.
> [3]. . . Therefore I have uttered what I did not understand,
>   things too wonderful for me, which I did not know" (Job 42:2–3).

Job is now admitting that he had spoken about things he really didn't understand and that God is far beyond what he ever envisioned: "I heard of you by the hearing of the ear, but now my eye sees you" (Job 42:5). I have had a new experience, Job says, "therefore, I despise myself and repent in dust and ashes" (Job 42:6). In other words,

Job had developed a new understanding of God and he sees his own puniness and inadequacy in the face of God's awesomeness, sovereignty, power, and omniscience.

Wisdom Themes in Job.   There are obviously several possible purposes for this book. One is to provide a **theodicy** that answers the question, "How can God be a righteous God and allow righteous people to suffer?" Traditional wisdom had failed to address this question. For example, the book of Proverbs emphasizes that the righteous shall be rewarded and the wicked will be punished. But the cosmic justice described in Proverbs does not always appear to operate in daily life. We have all seen good people who suffer in our world. Job may have been written to explain this phenomenon. It suggests that righteous persons like Job suffer in order to gain a new understanding of God, particularly of God's power and greatness.

Second, the book may be emphasizing that theological arguments about the relation between sin and suffering are useless. Persons in many ancient cultures believed that if people sinned they would be punished. All sickness and misfortune were the result of sin. The same belief is expressed in the Deuteronomic history as well as in the book of Proverbs. Psalm 1 reiterates the belief frequently enunciated in Proverbs: the wicked will be punished and the righteous will be rewarded. The books of Job and Ecclesiastes challenge the traditional forms of expressing this belief.

Third, the book of Job suggests that readers should not complain and demand answers for these troubling issues. In this respect Job expresses a much older theme in traditional wisdom. Wisdom literature often addresses fundamental problems of life with which we all wrestle and offers a variety of solutions. Even in Genesis there is some indication that life is not perfect and that the righteous are not always rewarded. Jacob has twelve sons and one of them apparently is killed by an animal. The other sons pretend that they found his coat with blood on it and Jacob obviously mourns and has the normal grief experience of a father who has lost a son. He does not say that there must be some sin in his life and that this is the result. Wisdom material takes this issue up and tries to address it in a new way. In the book of Job the ultimate resolution of the fundamental problem that it raises is unclear. This lack of clarity may be the means by which the author encourages the reader to leave the resolution of such problems in the hands of God.

The fourth possible purpose of the book of Job is to argue that faith should not depend on material rewards. But if we take that approach, which is certainly the approach of the first couple of chapters in the argument between God and the adversary, then what about the end of the book of Job? There we learn the following: God says his wrath is kindled against Eliphaz and his two friends for they had not spoken correctly. They are instructed to take seven bulls and seven rams to Job for him to offer up for their sakes as burnt offerings. God says that Job is to pray for them so that God will not deal harshly with them, "For you have not spoken right of me." God condemns the three comforters or friends for the explanation that they gave, namely, that Job had sin in his life. In Job 42:10, the Lord restores the fortunes of Job when he prays for his friends and gives Job twice as much as he had before. He dies old and full of years. The blessing that Job receives because of his righteousness seems to contradict the rest of the book.

If a single author actually wrote this book, including the ending, then it is only logical to say that faith should depend on material rewards. Job persevered and therefore he was rewarded with twice as much in the end. Therefore, some scholars have argued that Job 42:10–17 is a later ending added to reform the book into an orthodox statement similar to the Deuteronomistic statements about the God who punishes wickedness and rewards righteousness.

STUDY QUESTIONS

Create a chart sketching the arguments of each speaker: God, the adversary, Job, Job's wife, Eliphaz, Bildad, Zophar, and Elihu. What are the major questions asked and what are the most significant issues raised?

1. Discuss the role of the satan (adversary) in the prologue to the book of Job. Is this character independent of God?

2. Discuss the use of the knowledge theme in Job. Note how knowledge is used as the basis for Job's test, as his defense, and as the basis for his repentance.

3. Compare and contrast the story of Job with the garden of Eden story. How are the themes of knowledge and death developed in both of these books?

4. Describe the role of Job's three "friends." What are their individual arguments? Note the pattern of argument and response that ties their statements together.

5. Discuss Job's use of the oath of clearance in chapters 29–31 and compare it to the Egyptian Book of the Dead.

6. Compare the theophany in chapters 38–42 with other theophanies in the biblical text.

7. Job repents in chapter 42. Why does he do so? What is his sin?

8. Are the three "friends" right and Job wrong? Explain.

9. Why does God reward Job with riches, a new family, and a long life in the epilogue to this book?

10. Define: soliloquies, theodicy.

The Book of
Psalms

The book of Psalms is a collection compiled over a long period of time. The psalms reflect nearly every period of Israelite history and some are fairly easy to date simply because they describe a specific historical event. Like any songbook associated with worship practices, some of the psalms can be identified with particular cultic events: coronation of a king (Pss 2, 20, 45), covenant renewal (Pss 78, 105), celebrations of creation (Ps 104), sacrificial offerings (Ps 100), the Sabbath (Ps 92), or pilgrimages (Pss 120–134). Most of the psalms can simply be categorized as either songs of general thanksgiving or laments.

Technical Aspects. Because these songs were designed to be used in both individual and corporate worship, many of them were given **rubrics** (instructions) for orchestration, instrumentation, and tempo at some point after they were composed. The majority of these rubrics appear in the **superscriptions**, which appear at the beginning of about two-thirds of the psalms. Some are quite simple: "A psalm of David." Others commemorate a specific event in David's career (Pss 51, 52, 56), though we should remember that such superscriptions may be traditional but not necessarily historically accurate. Still others describe instruments and the tune to be used (Ps 22), or mention persons who were apparently choirmasters (Pss 73, 77, 78 [Asaph]; 84, 85, 88 [Korah]; see 1 Chron 25:1–8 for their appointment). What is clear from these rubrics is that there were trained musicians and organized choirs within the temple community whose responsibility was to perform the musical accompaniment to cultic events (cf. Ps 84). Perhaps particular choirs had their own repertoire that became traditional and exclusive to them.

Superscriptions of Psalms

To the leader: According to "The Deer of the Dawn." A psalm of David (Ps 22).

To the leader: "Do Not Destroy." Of David. A *miktam,* when he fled from Saul, in the cave (Ps 56).

To the leader. Of David, for the memorial offering (Ps 70).

A song. A psalm of the Korahites. To the leader: According to "*Mahalath Leannoth.*" A *maskil* of Heman the Ezrahite (Ps 88).

A song of ascents. Of Solomon (Ps 127).

One aspect of the rubrics that prevents a total understanding of the musical performance of the psalms is that many of them contain words that only appear in Psalms. These words are technical terms similar to those we use today (e.g., andante, allegretto), but they are now untranslatable. Some may refer to tone, tempo, or volume, but we simply do not know. One that appears in the body of some of the psalms is the word *selah* (Pss 54, 55, 57; also in Hab 3). It may be a signal to repeat a phrase, sing a chorus, or just to take a breath. Perhaps these words eventually will be found in texts outside the Bible so that we may discover more about what they mean.

Authorship.   In the superscription of seventy-three (almost half) of the psalms, there appears the Hebrew expression *l dvd*. The Hebrew word *l* is a preposition that indicates direction or relationship. In the superscription of a psalm, it may signify that the psalm is a psalm of David, a psalm from David, a psalm from David's time period, or a psalm from David's hand. It can also mean a psalm to David in the sense of one honoring David. All of these translations are possible. The expression does not necessarily mean authorship by David. In religious circles, we often say that David wrote the book of Psalms. This is really a popularization, both modern and ancient (see, e.g., 2 Sam 23:1; Amos 6:5; 4 Macc 18:15; Luke 20:42; and a note attached to a psalms scroll found at Qumran, 11QPsª col. 27, lines 2–11). David could have written some of the psalms, but probably they were composed by scribes during the monarchic period who wished to celebrate or commemorate David.

Another point regarding authorship is that the names of many persons are mentioned in the superscriptions (Asaph, Korah, Ethan, Heman, Solomon). One psalm is even attributed to Moses (Ps 90). But many psalms are anonymous. The same is true of a church hymnal. In some cases the hymnal may identify the author of a hymn and in other cases it may simply state that the writer is unknown.

Content and Classification of the Psalms.   Why is Psalms the most popular book in the OT/HB? One reason is that people find it much easier to relate to Psalms than to Genesis or Leviticus. The psalms describe human feelings, sources of discouragement, frustrations, and the worship of God. They are the closest thing we have to individual expression in the biblical text.

The psalms were designed to be used for worship. They formed Israel's ancient hymnal because they were probably sung. We do not have the music, but we do have the words. Modern Judaism uses cantors in worship, who read the psalms with a kind of musical intonation based on an ancient pattern. Attempts to recreate the music of the ancient Near East have been made, and it is possible that these ancient sounds may one day be heard again.

One of the most important contributors to modern Psalms studies is Herman Gunkel. Gunkel was the first to group the Psalms by class or type. He based his classification system on the use of the psalms in worship or on their setting in life (*Sitz im Leben*). Gunkel outlined five major types or classifications.

(1) *Hymns.* Psalm 8 is an example of a hymn. The first verse and the last verse of this psalm are exactly the same. A literary bracket formed in this way is called an **inclusio.** This device occurs typically in music, but seldom characterizes speech except in dramatic contexts.

(2) *Royal psalms.* A royal psalm appears in Ps 2. This psalm speaks about the role of the king as Yahweh's political agent. It may have been used at coronation ceremonies or on the anniversary of a king's coronation.

(3) *Communal laments.* Examples of communal lament are Pss 74 and 80. Since they deal with the fall of Jerusalem and the destruction of the temple, these psalms probably were written sometime after 587 BCE. In Ps 74 one can feel the frustration of the psalmist who asks God why he does not use his hand to save his people. The text goes on to mention the deliverance of God in the past and asks God to deliver his people in the present. Human experience is filled with periods of frustration. In composing laments the psalmist provides a means of expressing feelings of anger and despair.

(4) *Individual laments.* One example in this category is Ps 51. The writer of this psalm asks God to purify and cleanse him. In exploring the nature of sin, the psalm resolutely relies on God's ability to forgive the penitent. It also refers to the preferability of right behavior to sacrifice (Ps 51:16–17; see 1 Sam 15:22).

Psalm 104 and the Hymn to the Aton

[12]By the streams the birds of the air have their habitation;
   they sing among the branches (Ps 104:12).

Birds fly to their nests, they spread their wings to praise your Ka (Aton).

[27]These all look to you
   to give them their food in due season;
when you give to them, they gather it up;
   when you open your hand they are filled
      with good things (Ps 104:27).

You assign each a place. You allot to each both needs and food, you count out to each the days of life (Aton).

[29]When you hide your face, they are dismayed;
   when you take away their breath, they die
      and return to their dust.
[30]When you send forth your spirit, they are created;
   and you renew the face of the ground (Ps 104:29–30).

When you rise, the Earth lives. When you set, the Earth dies.
You are life itself, all live through you (Aton; *OTPar,* pp. 154–56).

---

(5) *Communal songs of thanksgiving and individual songs of thanksgiving.* Psalm 116 includes the words that the people uttered when they were making their sacrifices in the temple. This chant lists the blessings that Yahweh has given the people and justifies the giving of sacrifices in acknowledgement of the covenant.

Songs, like legal pronouncements and wisdom sayings, were part of the store of literature common to the entire ancient Near East. Literary borrowing was quite common. The text of a song was often reshaped to fit individual cultures or religions while the theme remained the same. The Egyptian Hymn to the Aton, composed in the reign of Akenaton (1365–1348 BCE) contains many themes and phrases resembling those in Ps 104. Both are creation hymns, celebrating the creative and life-giving power of the deity. The Egyptian song glorifies the Aton, the sun disc, while Ps 104 praises Yahweh. The author of Ps 104 probably drew on existing material, choosing to use statements that could extol Yahweh without regard to the original context of another culture's religious literature. It is also possible that the intent of the writer was to add the power of other gods to that of Yahweh. It was a common belief that when a god became a supreme power within a **pantheon** that lesser gods gave their names and attributes to the "chief" of the gods. This is certainly the case in the Babylonian story of creation, the *Enuma Elish,* when the gods meet in Assembly and "proclaim his fifty names" (*ANET,* p. 69). As Israel began to see their God as the one true power in the universe, it would have been natural for them to devalue other gods by using their literature and words of praise for Yahweh.

STUDY QUESTIONS

1. Discuss the authorship of the Psalms.

2. Discuss the different types of psalms and their intended audience.

3. Discuss the use of the superscriptions.

4. Discuss the cultic purposes evident for many psalms.

5. Define: *selah,* pantheon, rubric.

The Song of Solomon (Canticles)	Examples of romantic love are rare in the biblical text. They do occur, as in the case of Jacob's love for Rachel (Gen 29:20) and Michal's love for David (1 Sam 18:20). The emotion expressed

is more often lust or infatuation, such as Samson's desire for Delilah (Judg 16:4) and Amnon's lovesickness for his half-sister Tamar (2 Sam 13:1–4). Examples of romantic love are only infrequently mentioned in the Bible because marriages were arranged between families. Personal relationship generally took second place to the honor and advancement of the household. This makes the Song of Solomon (also known as Canticles and Song of Songs) a unique set of romantic songs that clearly expresses the love of two people for each other.

It is probably best to refer to these songs as a collection rather than a unified composition. They are similar only in their common theme and some repetition of language, which may be standard to this literary type (compare Song Sol 2:6–7 with 8:3–4). The authorship is uncertain. Tradition ascribing it to Solomon is doubtful and is based primarily on the references to Solomon in Song Sol 3:9, 11 and 8:11–12.

Basic to the dialogues found in this book is the passion that the lovers express for each other and the graphic descriptions of each other's physical charms (see Song Sol 4:1–7). The use of the term "sister" is synonymous with "bride" (see Song Sol 5:1) and reflects both endearment and equal status with her husband.

Direct comparison can be made between the erotic phrasing of these poems (Song Sol 5:3–5) and those of Egyptian love songs from the eighteenth to the twentieth dynasties (1570–1197 BCE). Literary borrowing is possible, since the Egyptian songs were originally composed orally and traveled with merchants and soldiers from one region to another.

The Song of Solomon and Egyptian Love Songs

My cup is still not full from making love with you—my little wolf, you intoxicate me. I will not stop drinking your love, even if they batter me with sticks into the marsh (Egyptian Love Songs, *OTPar*, p. 229).

How sweet is your love, my sister, my bride!
  How much better is your love than wine,
  and the fragrance of your oils than any spice! (Song Sol 4:10).

I come to my garden, my sister, my bride;
  I gather my myrrh with my spice,
  I eat my honeycomb with my honey,
  I drink my wine with my milk (Song Sol 5:1).

Her hair is the bait in the trap . . . to ensnare me (*OTPar*, p. 228).

Your head crowns you like Carmel,
  and your flowing locks are like purple;
  a king is held captive in the tresses (Song Sol 7:5).

In addition to being seen as an example of romantic poetry, the Song of Solomon has often been understood as symbolic of Yahweh's love for Israel. This would place it in the same metaphoric genre as Hosea's marriage to Gomer (Hos 1–3) and the marriage between Yahweh and the foundling girl (Ezek 16:3–14). The emphasis on fidelity and personal devotion in Song of Solomon (e.g., "My beloved is mine and I am his"; Song Sol 2:16) made them useful to the religious establishment and to society in general.

Another interpretation of the Song of Solomon is as an allegory on the search for wisdom. Wisdom is described as a woman who offers an ordered existence and maturity of thought in the book of Proverbs (Prov 8:1–9:6). This is comparable to the desire expressed in Song of Solomon for food and drink. This and other allegorical interpretations should not obscure what is most likely the original intent of the authors of these poems. They serve as examples of romantic feeling (perhaps to be sung during wedding celebrations). They expressed emotions that were common even in a society of arranged marriages.

The Desire for Wisdom

I come to my garden, my sister, my bride;
    I gather my myrrh with my spice,
    I eat my honeycomb with my honey,
    I drink my wine with my milk.

Eat friends, drink,
    and be drunk with love (Song Sol 5:1).

STUDY QUESTIONS

1. Compare and contrast the love poetry in Song of Solomon and that in Egyptian love songs.

2. Discuss possible interpretations of the Song of Solomon.

4

THE EXILE AND THE PERSIAN PERIOD

EXILIC PROPHECY

The Book of
Ezekiel

Social context is a key to understanding the message of the prophet Ezekiel. Carried off with the first group of exiles in 597BCE (including Jehoiachin, the royal family, and many of the chief priests), Ezekiel has a dual perspective. He has a definite tie to Jerusalem and its temple priesthood, but he also is a member of the exilic community and must deal with their fears and concerns. Like many other prophets, Ezekiel's message is divided into two parts: judgment and restoration.

The force with which God imposed these two elements of the message upon Ezekiel is demonstrated by his inability to speak anything but words of judgment, doom, and destruction until the second fall of Jerusalem in 587 BCE. Any other ideas are immediately suppressed by God. After the destruction of Judah's capital, Ezekiel is released from his selective silence and can begin assuring the exiles of the merciful intentions of Yahweh. Once the people have been purged they will be returned to their homeland, purified and restored as God's covenantal nation (Ezek 36:24–25).

The principal theme in the book is the "presence of Yahweh." It is the departure of God's presence and "glory" from the temple in chapter 10 that marks the doom of the nation. Likewise, Yahweh's return to the throne in the temple in Jerusalem in chapters 40–48 is the crowning vision of restoration.

Call Narrative. Although Ezekiel's call narrative is similar to those of Moses, Isaiah, and Jeremiah, it has its own distinctive character. Perhaps most important is its sense of mystery. There is little that is anthropomorphic in this theophany. Whenever the prophet has to speak of God's appearance, he uses a qualifying phrase (such as "in the likeness of" or "something like") so that he does not have to actually describe Yahweh in human terms. This creates a majesty similar to Isaiah's "temple filled with smoke" (Isa 6:4). The clear distinction that this vision draws between the human and the divine is emphasized by the phrase used by Yahweh when addressing the prophet. Yahweh calls Ezekiel "son of man," i.e., "mortal."

The sense of Yahweh's "glory" as a separate, roving aspect of the deity can be observed in this scene. Instead of being a fixed entity (like the seated figure in Isa 6:1), God is a being of ever changing motion ("wherever the spirit would go"; Ezek 1:12) in Ezekiel's vision. This may imply the immediacy of action that is about to occur. It would certainly make it more difficult to determine the extent of Yahweh's "glory" or the degree of power that is behind all of this movement (see especially Ezek 1:12–28).

As is the case in other call narratives, Ezekiel is confronted with a vision of God and is called to serve as a spokesperson. His task is not an easy one, but unlike Isaiah and Jeremiah, Ezekiel does not voice his reluctance. Instead he expresses a sense of fear and respect for divine power (Ezek 1:28). He makes no excuses for why he cannot serve but obediently consumes the scroll presented to him (Ezek 2:9–3:3). This gesture is similar to the purification of Isaiah's lips and the touching of Jeremiah's mouth as a means of empowering them to speak God's word. But a period of seven days of muteness delays Ezekiel in taking up his task. For this amount of time he sits "stunned" among the exiles (Ezek 3:15). This in itself suggests the magnitude of Ezekiel's message and perhaps his reluctance to take on the prophetic mantle.

This narrative also contains an image of prophetic responsibility. Ezekiel is portrayed as a "guard" or "sentry" whose task is to cry out an alarm when an army approaches (Ezek 3:17–21). Failure to do this will result in the condemning of the sentry for failing to warn the people. Just as in Isaiah's time, the imminent danger faced by the people is the anger of Yahweh and God's use of a foreign power to punish Judah (see Isa 10). Ezekiel makes his announcement of Yahweh's judgment and then shuts himself up in his house to await the inevitable events. Ezekiel differs from other prophets who made their statements of doom but also offered a hope that God would relent (see this hope expressed by the people in Jer 26:19). The hope of being spared ultimate destruction does not appear in Ezekiel.

As noted earlier (see **Stele of Mesha** inset above), the belief that a god is in control of historical events is not limited to Israel. This belief provides two important keys to the purpose of Israelite prophecy. The role of the prophet is to call the people back into compliance with the covenant and to warn them of Yahweh's judgment and punishment when they do not respond as they should. The failure of the people to respond to the prophet's message can then be used as the basis of the **theodicy** explaining why Yahweh has allowed his people to be oppressed and defeated by foreign nations. It also serves as the basis for the belief in the essential righteousness of a God who is willing to provide a warning even though this warning may only be heard by a core group of righteous persons within the nation. But it has always been for the benefit of the righteous that Yahweh has chosen to act in history. Without this set of beliefs in place, there would be no reason for the Israelites to continue to worship a God who had failed to protect them.

Enacted Prophecies. During the period prior to the final fall of Jerusalem in 587 BCE, Ezekiel used a series of enacted prophecies to present his message. He performed symbolic and outrageous acts that draw attention to himself and make an indelible impression on his audience. In chapter 4, the prophet employs a simple strategy to portray Jerusalem's fate. He is instructed to take a clay brick (an item used in the construction of all the buildings in Mesopotamia) and inscribe an outline of the city of Jerusalem on it. Then this priest dispensed with his personal dignity, and played like a child with toy soldiers, besieging his brick/city and showing how it would be destroyed. For a grown man to do this must have caused talk and perhaps raised apprehensions of impending doom for Jerusalem.

A second action taken by Ezekiel was lying on his side for an extended period, 390 days on his right side and forty days on his left side. He explained that this symbolized the number of years that the people of the northern and southern kingdoms respectively would remain in exile (Ezek 4:4–6). The number forty is particularly significant here because it is the number of years the people were condemned to wander in the wilderness following the exodus (Num 14:33). Thus the current exile came to symbolize a new period of winnowing and transformation like the period in the wilderness. The use of the wilderness motif once again demonstrates a cyclical understanding of history.

During the time that Ezekiel was undergoing this difficult ordeal, he was required to prepare sparse meals to demonstrate the starvation faced by the exiles and by those who were besieged in Jerusalem (Ezek 4:9–13). At first God commanded him to cook these meals on an "unclean" fire (with human dung), but at this point Ezekiel finally protests. As a priest he had dedicated his life to maintaining a "clean" (ritually pure) existence. He asks God's indulgence not to have to contaminate himself in this way and God relents, allowing him to use conventional fuel (animal dung) instead (Ezek 4:14–15).

A third graphically portrayed prophecy appears in chapter 5. To set the stage for what could be described as a form of street theater, the prophet is told to shave his head and beard. Shaving the head or beard is normally an act of persons in mourning or a sign of those who have been humiliated (cf. 2 Sam 10:4). Ezekiel divides his hair into three piles and then chops up one pile with a sword, scatters another in the wind, and throws a third pile into the fire. Only a few hairs, a **remnant**, are left to survive. These are bound up in the edges of the prophet's robes (Ezek 5:3). This set of actions is so visually oriented that it would be most impressive in the open air where the wind could play its part and the fire and sword could be used effectively.

Explanations of Judgment.   All of this condemnation and prediction of doom has to be justified. The visions of Ezekiel provide more than adequate explanation for Yahweh's anger. The most devastating image of disobedience appears in the vision of the abominations in the temple in chapter 8. The structure of this vision confirms that Ezekiel is a priest who is both intimately familiar with the temple and highly concerned with issues of ritual purity. He makes an inspection tour that takes him from the outer court to the inner court. The tour provides vivid evidence that the temple has been corrupted, from one end to the other.

The vision begins when Ezekiel is cast into a trance while he sits with the elders in exile. He is lifted by the hair through the air back to Jerusalem and returned to earth in front of the temple. He is unable to enter by the gate because his way is blocked by an abhorrent "image of jealousy" (probably an idol; cf. "jealous God" in Exod 20:4–5). He is instructed to go to a wall where a hole appears and tunnel his way into the building. He emerges in a chamber whose walls are covered with pictures of other gods and their symbols. Even worse is the presence of the **seventy Elders**, who have previously appeared in positive contexts and represented the people's acceptance of the covenant (Exod 24:9–10). Ezekiel saw them burning incense and worshiping other gods (Ezek 8:10–12). Their presence and actions represent the entire nation's idolatry, which has reached such a level of audacity that it is carried out even within Yahweh's temple.

Ezekiel continues his tour of the temple precincts and finds one example after another of idolatry. He witnesses a scene in the outer court in which a group of women are "weeping for Tammuz" (Ezek 8:14). Tammuz was the Babylonian god of new growth and fertility who dies each year during the dry season and will only be released by the gods of the underworld in response to the tears of his worshipers. Worship of Tammuz represented a rejection of Yahweh as the provider of land (including its produce) and children (i.e., fertility).

Next Ezekiel moves to the inner court, between the porch and the altar. There he sees twenty-five men prostrating themselves as they worship the sun. This forces them to bow with their backs to the altar and the Holy of Holies (Ezek 8:16), which is a sign of disrespect for Yahweh.

These abominations form the basis for Yahweh's decision in chapter 10 to abandon the temple in Jerusalem. Once again the image of Yahweh's "glory" appears, again in motion, but this time departing the sacred precinct. The "glory" fills the temple one last time (Ezek 10:4; cf. Isa 6:1) and then is carried away amidst clouds and fire in a chariot drawn by cherubim (Ezek 10:6-19).

Ezekiel does provide one other very powerful explanation for Yahweh's decision to abandon the temple and the nation; it is found in chapter 16. This oracle contains a parenting image of a kind often associated with the Exodus event (cf. Hos 11:1-7). Ezekiel portrays Jerusalem as a foundling female child. Unwanted, the infant has been left to die (Ezek 16:6a). This image was especially poignant because infanticide of female infants was fairly common in times of famine or among impoverished families. It is Yahweh who takes pity on the infant Jerusalem and serves as her surrogate parent (Ezek 16:6b-7). All of her needs are met and when she grows up God marries her, providing her with rich robes and jewelry (Ezek 16:8-14). But just like a new bride who is not satisfied and seeks out the favor of other lovers, Jerusalem becomes unfaithful to Yahweh and seeks after other gods (Ezek 16:15).

All that had been given to her, including her children, are dedicated to other gods as sacrifices (Ezek 16:17-22). She constructs "high places" (cf. Hos 4:13) and makes alliances with Egypt instead of trusting Yahweh (Ezek 16:24-26; Isa 30:1-7). She is a peculiar harlot who pays her lovers instead of receiving payment from them (Ezek 16:33-34). For these crimes, Jerusalem will be given into the hands of her enemies. The "older sister," Samaria, the capital of the northern kingdom, and other disobedient "sisters" (like Sodom) sinned and were destroyed (Ezek 16:46-50). Now the "younger sister," whose sins have made her older siblings appear righteous, must face the same judge. This judge condemns but also promises to forgive (Ezek 16:60-62).

The opportunity for the survival of a remnant of the people of Judah appears in a vision of seven men (six executioners and a scribe) in Ezek 9. In what is clearly a parallel with the Passover (Exod 12), the men are instructed to pass through the city of Jerusalem. Wherever they find a person mourning the sins of the people, that person is to have a dot placed on his or her forehead. Then during a second circuit of the city, they are commanded to slay everyone who does not have the mark of innocence. In this way, the righteous are set aside for survival. These few will form the core of the future, rebuilding the temple and the city of Jerusalem. Ezekiel's warning as a "sentinel" proves true, and the unity between his word and the action mark an end of one period and the beginning of a new one.

Visions of Restoration. Prior to the fall of Jerusalem, Ezekiel lays the groundwork for the proposition that the evil that had come upon the people of Jerusalem was caused by their own sins. He also emphasizes that the current punishment will not extend into later generations if they prove to be faithful to Yahweh. To do this Ezekiel makes two related statements in chapters 14 and 18. In the first case, he gives a list of three righteous wise men of the past: Noah, Daniel, and Job. All survived trials because they were righteous and all were probably non-Israelites. Noah, chronicled in the primordial era, had survived the flood. Daniel (not Ezekiel's contemporary) was a wise king in ancient Ugarit (see Tale of Aqhat), who judged his people fairly and was rewarded with a son and heir. Job of Uz survived a legendary test of afflictions only to rise from the dust heap and regain God's favor. Always before (Gen 18:17–21; Jer 5:1), tradition had held that the righteous could help spare a city from destruction. Now, however, Ezekiel assures the people that even if these three exemplary characters were all assembled they could only save themselves.

Cause and Effect of the Exile

[23]And the nations shall know that the house of Israel went into captivity for their iniquity, because they dealt treacherously with me. So I hid my face from them and gave them into the hand of their adversaries, and they all fell by the sword (Ezek 39:23).

[25]. . . Now I will restore the fortunes of Jacob, and have mercy on the whole house of Israel; and I will be jealous for my holy name. [26]They shall forget their shame, and all the treachery they have practiced against me, when they live securely in their land with no one to make them afraid, [27]when I have brought them back from the peoples and gathered them from their enemies' lands, and through them have displayed my holiness in the sight of many nations (Ezek 39:25–27).

Ezekiel further develops this thought in chapter 18 where he quotes an old proverb, "The parents have eaten the sour grapes, and the children's teeth are set on edge" (Ezek 18:2). This proverb expresses the legal principle of corporate identity, under which the children are viewed as participants in the sins of the father. Thus Achan, who had stolen from the goods under the *kherem* at Jericho (Josh 7:16–27), was condemned along with his entire family to be stoned to death in order to purify the nation of his sin. In the new world of the exile, however, Ezekiel assures the people that they will not have to pay for the sins of their fathers. Only "the person who sins . . . shall die" (Ezek 18:3). This is not an argument for individual responsibility. It applies to the entire exilic community and is an exhortation for them to recognize the exile as a period of purification and rededication. Individualism is a western concept. It is a concept that was simply unfathomable for the communally-oriented people of the ancient Near East.

Once the city of Jerusalem had fallen to Nebuchadnezzar's army in 587 BCE, God no longer compelled Ezekiel to speak only words of judgment. His new task was to explain what was ahead for the exiles in relation to their God. They were to understand that the exile was a direct result of their iniquity and Yahweh's decision to leave them unprotected. It was analogous to the time in Egypt, when they had lived "among the nations." They would be tested and purged, as in the wilderness period, and then those who measured up to the stipulations of the covenant would once again be brought forth to the land of Israel (Ezek 20:33–38). In addition, the name of God would be restored as the nations and exiles recognized Yahweh's power to return them when the period of "instruction" was complete (Ezek 39:25–29). Whatever tarnish may have been attached to Yahweh's apparent failure to protect the people in 587 BCE would thereby be vindicated (cf. the oracles against Tyre and Egypt in Ezek 28–29 and against Gog in Ezek 39:1–16).

A new world was envisioned by the prophet in which old injustices, poor leadership by kings and priests, and the very idea of a desire to violate the law and covenant would not exist. In his use of the "good shepherd" image in chapter 34, Ezekiel describes how Yahweh, the owner of the flock, will take it away from the shepherds (kings and priests) who serve only themselves and neglect the sheep. Yahweh is the perfect shepherd, who takes them to good pasture during the day, brings them to a safe haven at night, cares for the sick, and seeks out the strays. Once order has been reestablished, a new shepherd (of the line of David) would be appointed, one who would follow Yahweh's example and properly care for the sheep.

What makes this possible is the exilic experience. It puts a truer understanding of Yahweh's power and wisdom into the people's consciousness. As the prophet says, Yahweh will place a "new heart" and a "new spirit" of obedience within them (Ezek 36:26–32). These new sources of obedience will make the experience of the exile worthwhile. The example of a God who allowed the nation to be taken away and who then brought them home again will demonstrate to all nations the power of Yahweh (Ezek 36:22–24; 39:27–28; cf. Isa 40:5–26).

Ezekiel made it clear that the exile was not the end of all things in his vision of the "valley of dry bones" (Ezek 37:1–14). In this oracle the prophet uses an ancient battlefield to serve as the symbol of Israel's covenantal relationship with Yahweh. The Spirit of the Lord takes Ezekiel to a battlefield and asks him whether the dry bones of the long dead warriors could rise and live again. Realizing that this is a question that only Yahweh can answer (as in the sequence of questions in Job 38–39), Ezekiel simply says "O Lord GOD, you know" (Ezek 37:3). At that point he is commanded to speak the word of God to the bones and it is the creative power of this word, as in the first creation story in Genesis (Gen 1:1–2:4a), that causes the bodies to rearticulate and take on flesh again. A second action is needed to animate the bodies. The breath of God is called upon to fill them. Because "breath" and "spirit" are the same word in Hebrew, the reference to the "breath" is another allusion to the creation story. The first sign of order and life within the primordial earth's watery void was the Spirit of God passing over the waters. Ezekiel's description of the "breath" also recalls the second story of creation, in which Yahweh "breathed . . . the breath of life" into the body of the first human (Gen 2:7).

Ezekiel's vision describing the reanimation of dead bodies is not the basis for a belief in a general resurrection of the dead in Judaism. It relates to the covenant and how the people's disobedience had killed their relationship with Yahweh. Now when God takes the initiative a new creation is possible with the word and the breath reviving a dead nation. Resurrection as a theological concept did not enter Jewish thought until the Hellenistic period (fourth–second centuries BCE) and only appears in the OT/HB in Dan 12:1–2, which dates to the time of Persian and Greek influence on Judaism.

The crowning vision of restoration for Ezekiel is found in his final section, chapters 40–48. Here the prophet, in great detail, describes the reconstruction of the Jerusalem temple. In this vision its grand scale and monumental construction are designed to match the power and majesty of Yahweh's restorative act. Within this narrative, the key point is the reestablishment of the throne of Yahweh by means of the return of God's presence to the temple (Ezek 43:7–12). God's presence is equated with the receipt of God's blessings. Full restoration of the land and the people could not be possible without this divine return. When it occurred the covenantal promise of land and progeny would once again be in effect (Ezek 47:1–12).

The reality did not match the vision. When a new temple was built after the exile in 515 BCE, it was only a fraction of the size of Solomon's temple and not as beautifully decorated. It was not even constructed immediately after the return of the exiles (Hag 1). The discrepancy between the vision and the reality is the basis for concerns in the priestly history (1 and 2 Chron) and for the reforms of Ezra and Nehemiah in the Persian period. The people had to wait until the time of Herod the Great (30 BCE) for a truly magnificent temple to appear once again in Jerusalem. Herod's edifice reflected the political connections that he had with the Romans, not Ezekiel's vision.

STUDY QUESTIONS

1. Discuss Ezekiel's use of enacted prophecies in chapters 4–5.

2. Discuss Ezekiel's theme of "individual responsibility" as it appears in chapters 14, 18, and 36.

3. Discuss the fall of Jerusalem as a watershed in ancient Israel's history.

4. Compare the judgment image in Ezekiel 16 with the theme of restoration found in Ezekiel 37.

5. Define: theodicy, Stele of Mesha, remnant, *kherem*.

The Book of Lamentations   The book of Lamentations represents a distinct category of ancient Near Eastern literature known as a "lament." Short laments are found in a number of the Psalms (Pss 12, 22, 44, 69, 137). In the case of Lamentations, the lament is specifically for the fall of the city of Jerusalem in 587 BCE and the deportation of its people. There are close parallels between this work and the "Lament for the Destruction of Ur" from ancient Mesopotamia. Traditionally, Jeremiah is thought to be the author of several laments from this period (2 Chron 35:25; Jer 9:1), but it is unlikely, because of a dissimilarity of style and vocabulary, that he is the author of Lamentations (compare Lam 4:17 with Jer 2:18; 37:5–10).

Lamentations and the Lament for Ur

[3]Even the jackals offer the breast
    and nurse their young,
but my people has become cruel,
    like the ostriches in the wilderness.
[4]The tongue of the infant sticks
    to the roof of its mouth for thirst;
the children beg for food,
    but no one gives them anything.
[5]Those who feasted on delicacies
    perish in the streets;
those who were brought up in purple
    cling to ash heaps.
[6]For the chastisement of my people has been greater
    than the punishment of Sodom,
which was overthrown in a moment,
    though no hand was laid on it (Lam 4:3–6).

Where crowds once celebrated festivals, bodies lay in every street, corpses piled on every road. . . . The wise of Ur were scattered, the people mourn. Mothers abandoned their daughters, the people mourn. Women and children were abandoned, their property looted ("The Lament for Ur," *OTPar*, pp. 173–74).

In form, the book consists of alphabetic **acrostics** in the first four chapters. In these chapters each line or stanza begins with a consecutive letter of the Hebrew alphabet. The fifth chapter contains the same number of verses as there are letters in the Hebrew alphabet. Such a programmed piece of literature, using a 3:2 meter, suggests close adherence to a set style of writing designed for public recitation on days commemorating the fall of Jerusalem. It also served as a memory aid and symbolically expressed the notion of the end of an era or completeness (symbolized in the inclusiveness implied in using all the letters of the alphabet, as in English A to Z). The central theme is the agony caused by the abandonment of the city by Yahweh:

> [8]The LORD determined to lay in ruins
>   the wall of the daughter Zion;
> he stretched the line;
>   he did not withhold his hand from destroying;
> he caused rampart and wall to lament;
>   they languish together.
> [9]Her gates have sunk into the ground;
>   he has ruined and broken her bars;
> her king and princes are among the nations;
>   guidance is no more,
> and her prophets obtain
>   no vision from the LORD (Lam 2:8–9).

Even in the face of such massive destruction there also exists an expressed hope that God will eventually return to rule a humbled nation once again:

> [40]Let us test and examine our ways,
>   and return to the LORD.
> [41]Let us lift up our hearts as well as our hands
>   to God in heaven (Lam 3:40–41).

The book includes typical Israelite grief rituals, in which the physical destruction of the city and its people are recounted and a **catharsis** is made possible through these expressions of grief (e.g., Lam 5:1–18). The people also show repentance in their attempt to demonstrate to Yahweh that they deserve another chance under the covenant (Lam 2:10; 3:48–57). Like the Babylonian lament that concludes with the prayer, "It is enough . . . . May he rebuild Ur" (*OTPar*, p. 175), the author of Lamentations exhorts Yahweh to be the people's enemy no longer (Lam 2:5). He pleads, "Restore us to yourself, O LORD" (Lam 5:21).

Ancient Israelite Grief Rituals

- Weeping, wailing, or lamenting
    Amos 5:16–17
    Jer 9:18
- Tearing clothes
    2 Sam 1:11
    2 Sam 13:31
    Job 1:20
- Wearing sackcloth (coarse material)
    Gen 37:34
    2 Sam 3:31
- Cutting hair or shaving head
    Jer 7:29
    Mic 1:16
- Putting hands on (or over) head
    2 Sam 13:19
    Jer 2:37
- Putting dust or ashes on one's head and rolling on the ground
    Ezek 27:30
    Mic 1:10
- Fasting
    2 Sam 1:12

Other examples of mourning

- Wives mourn in separate groups
    Zech 12:12–14
- Professional mourners (usually women) are hired
    Eccl 12:5
    Amos 5:16

STUDY QUESTIONS

1. Compare the use of the lament in Lamentations to that in Babylonian literature.

2. Discuss how this literature serves as a catharsis for the people of Judah after the destruction of Jerusalem.

3. Describe ancient Israelite grief rituals. How did they help the griever?

**Isaiah of
the Exile
(Isa 40–55)**

Second Isaiah and His Historical Context. Starting in chapter 40, a second voice of Isaiah begins to speak. This Isaiah (called Second Isaiah or Deutero-Isaiah) comes from the time of the exile, not from the eighth–seventh centuries BCE (the historical context of Isaiah of Jerusalem, or First Isaiah). The section begins with a call to speak words of "comfort" to God's people, a message that clearly was not in the style of the First Isaiah. The prophet speaks when the exile is about to end and the people must begin thinking about the return to Judah and Jerusalem. The most spectacular aspect of this change in fortunes is that it will be accomplished by a god whose people have been vanquished and exiled. Previously, this would have been taken as proof that the God of Israel was a failure, no longer worthy of the people's worship. By freeing them from their second period of captivity (the prophet compares the exile to the Egyptian experience), Yahweh now proves to the Israelites and to "all flesh" that there is no God but Yahweh. This "new thing" never accomplished by any other god marks Yahweh as supreme and becomes the basis for the formation of the monotheistic belief of the Jews.

Second Isaiah says that the physical instrument of liberation for the exiles will be the Persian king Cyrus. This monarch began his career in 550 BCE by consolidating control over Persia and Media in the area east of the Tigris River. Over the next ten years, he systematically conquered and pacified the northern and western portions of the Chaldean empire, leaving only Babylon and its immediate area for last. By the year 542, Cyrus prepared to take on this final bastion of Babylonian power. He was aided in this by the dissatisfaction of the priests of Marduk in Babylon. Nabonidus, Nebuchadnezzar's successor, had deemphasized Marduk's worship in the capital city, refused to participate in the new year festival staged by the Marduk priests, and elevated his own patron deity, the moon god Sin, to a position of supremacy. In addition, Nabonidus spent a great deal of his time and efforts in the areas south of Babylon, especially around what is now the Saudi Arabian city of Teima. This provided ample cause for complaint and unrest within the capital, a condition that was not controlled effectively by Belshazzar, the son and co-regent of Nabonidus.

It is not surprising then that as the Persian army approached Babylon, discontented leaders and captive peoples such as the Israelites welcomed Cyrus. Second Isaiah hailed Cyrus as a savior in chapter 45, where he takes the extraordinary step of applying the title "anointed one" (Heb. *meshiakh*, which is the source of the English word "messiah") to this Persian king. No other non-Israelite was ever given this title, but as Yahweh's tool of liberation, he was truly a savior in the eyes of Second Isaiah and the people.

Cyrus Cylinder. This political propaganda justified the Persian king Cyrus's conquering of Babylon. Photo courtesy of the British Museum.

The Cyrus Cylinder and Isaiah 45

He [Marduk] spoke the name of Cyrus, King of Anshan, declaring him Ruler of All the World. . . . Marduk ordered Cyrus to march against his city of Babylon. He marched with Cyrus as a friend while the army strolled along without fear of attack. Marduk allowed Cyrus to enter Babylon without a battle . . . and delivered Nabonidus, the king who did not worship him, into Cyrus' hands (The Cyrus Cylinder, *OTPar,* p. 148).

[1]Thus says the LORD to his anointed, to Cyrus,
     whose right hand I have grasped
to subdue nations before him
     and strip kings of their robes,
to open doors before him—
     and the gates shall not be closed:
[2]I will go before you
     and level the mountains,
I will break in pieces the doors of bronze
     and cut through the bars of iron,
[3]I will give you the treasures of darkness
     and riches hidden in secret places,
so that you may know that it is I, the LORD,
     the God of Israel, who call you by your name.
[4]For the sake of my servant Jacob,
     and Israel my chosen,
I call you by your name,
     I surname you, though you do not know me (Isa 45:1–4).

Second Isaiah's statements about Cyrus are closely paralleled in a document prepared by Cyrus' administration justifying their capture of Babylon and the deposing of Nabonidus. This victory decree is a piece of political propaganda and thus must be read carefully. It refers to Nabonidus's crimes against the god Marduk and Marduk's eventual decision to seek out a champion to liberate his people. Cyrus's army is allowed to travel unmolested through the countryside and when they reach Babylon the priests of Marduk open the city's gates so that Cyrus can take the Chaldean capital with a minimum of fighting.

Cyrus had used Marduk and his priesthood to gain the support of the Babylonian people. This was not an unusual tactic in the ancient Near East. The statues of gods were often held as hostages along with their conquered people. Cyrus understood the political value to be gained in the manipulation of such religious objects. Thus his decree included the command that these divine prisoners be released along with their people.

It may be that Second Isaiah wrote after Cyrus had taken the city and issued his victory decree. This would have been typical of persons or groups who were attempting to gain favor with the new ruler and his administration. The prophet's familiarity with the details of the decree suggest at least an adaptation of its text. His use of the term "anointed" and his recital of Cyrus's easy victory would have pleased the Persians. But Second Isaiah's insistence that Yahweh had chosen Cyrus, even though the king did not know Yahweh, stands in contrast with the statement that Marduk had sought out a ruler who would keep Marduk's religious festivals and honor him as the chief god of Babylon.

Second Isaiah claims that Yahweh alone is responsible for Cyrus's victory. No other god helped Yahweh, the creator of the earth and humankind (Isa 45:12), for this God is the only divine being: "there is no god besides him" (Isa 45:14). The idols that Cyrus so magnanimously liberated are simply objects. It is the God of Israel who has taken steps to save the people (Isa 45:16–17).

Servant Songs (Isa 42:1–4; 49:1–6; 50:4–9; 52:13–53:12). The other major theme in the second voice of Isaiah is his use of four "servant songs" to provide a **theodicy** of the exile. If the people are to resume their allegiance to Yahweh and return to their devastated homeland, they must recognize some value in the dislocation and pain caused by the exile. Thus it is not surprising that the prophet closely parallels the exile with the exodus event. Just as the people were purified in the wilderness prior to the conquest of the land, the exiles were purified in Mesopotamia. Now that "she [Jerusalem] has served her term" (Isa 40:2), the way to freedom is open for their return to Zion.

This did not negate the historical fact that some were taken into exile, some were killed in the destruction of Jerusalem, and some remained behind. What sense could God or the prophet make of this division? Why did any of the people have to suffer at all? The answer comes in a classic **theodicy.** The exile was necessary because of the sin of the people who violated their covenant with Yahweh. The pain and suffering associated with their period of exile was a demonstration of Yahweh's justice. The suffering of Israel, God's servant (Isa 49:3), expiates Israel's sin.

With the end of the exile comes a new purpose for the servant. Suffering for the sins of the nation (Isa 53:3–6) is now at an end and the servant, despite his "marred appearance" will triumph and astonish kings and nations by returning to the promised land (Isa 52:14–15). The prophet assures the people that as Yahweh's servant their faith will be vindicated and they shall not be put to shame for their belief in their God (Isa 50:7–11).

In the midst of their rejoicing over the triumph of Yahweh, the servant is given a new mission. It is not enough that Yahweh's power is demonstrated by the return of the people from exile. They must now become "a light to the nations" to spread the news of Yahweh's power and require the obeisance of kings and rulers (Isa 49:6–7). While this may be an indication of **universalism** and a further strengthening of the emerging concept of monotheism, Judaism did not become a proselytizing religion. Conversion has never been one of its principal tenets. It is unlikely that the prophet encouraged his hearers to engage in a mission to the surrounding nations. More likely, he sought to demonstrate Yahweh's power, not to convert the world's peoples.

The identification of the "servant" has been a problem for scholars. In some passages, such as Isa 49:3, Israel is clearly identified as the servant. In other cases, the servant appears to be an individual, or perhaps the prophet. The indeterminate nature of this person or group known as the servant allows for multiple interpretations of these passages.

Predictive Prophecy. One of the difficult issues in dealing with Second Isaiah and other prophets is whether their prophecies were intended to predict future events, including events in the New Testament. Some of the writers of the New Testament and many other Christians, in reading the "servant song" in Isa 52:13–53:12, see a description of Jesus' suffering and his role as redemptive savior. But like many prophecies this one is imprecise. While similarities can be observed, neither an actual naming of names nor indications of date occur in Isa 52:13–53:12.

Another proof that is often cited as an example of predictive prophecy is the passage in Hos 11:1, "Out of Egypt I called my son." A careful study of the context here shows that the writer was retelling the story of early Israel and its apostasy. Yet, it is cited by the gospel writer in Matt 2:14–15 as a fulfillment of prophecy with regard to Jesus' birth and sojourn in Egypt. Such use of OT/HB prophetic speech by the New Testament writers must be recognized as an argument made to "insiders." It was designed to reinforce the faith of the early Jewish-Christian community and followed the pattern of discourse common to that time in which ancient texts were cited to demonstrate the validity of a group's interpretation of current events. The people of ancient Israel and early Judaism believed that past events could fore-shadow future events, and that interpretations could focus on key terms and phrases, even if taken out of context. Thus Hosea could speak of Israel's origins in the exodus event while at the same time later interpreters could legitimately use the prophet's words to bolster their claims about Jesus.

These "insider" arguments are quite satisfactory proof for members of the insider group. But it is too much to expect that outsiders would find them convincing. Outsiders would interpret the words of Hosea and Isaiah in context and not see them as a basis for their own belief. Just as Cyrus shaped historical events in his victory decree to suit his view of what happened, so too the New Testament writers used the body of prophetic materials from the OT/HB to make a case for their newly established religion. Neither is invalid, but they must be seen for what they are. If insiders try to understand the positions of outsiders, they should be able to develop an appreciation of other positions while continuing to hold to their own conclusions. Ultimately, this mutual respect of both sides for each other is the basis for peace and harmony in a pluralistic society (i.e., one made up of many different groups).

Response to the Call to Return.   Despite Second Isaiah's rallying cry to return to Zion, the question that stuck in the minds of most of the exiles was: Why should we leave all that we have created in Babylonia to go back to Judah? Throughout the roughly sixty years of the exile they had started businesses, purchased land, and established their families. If they returned to their homeland they could expect to have to start over in a land that had lain uncultivated for generations. It would have taken persons of real conviction to decide to go back. The majority chose not to leave. In a series of waves over a period of nearly a hundred years, perhaps fifteen percent of the exiled community returned to Judah. So, who were the people that made the difficult decision to return to Jerusalem to rebuild the nation?

(1) One group consisted of political appointees of the Persian government whose job it was to rebuild this area into a tax-paying province.

(2) A second group had a vested interest in the temple and the status associated with the cult community. Priests and their families expected to play a major role in the revitalized nation, especially since there would be no restoration of the monarchy.

(3) A third group likely to make the trek were speculators and opportunists who saw this as a type of "land rush" in which they could claim large tracks of land and make a fortune. Among these were younger sons who could not inherit their

families' property in Mesopotamia and thus saw this as their chance for economic independence.

(4) Finally, there were those who saw the return as their religious duty to Yahweh and the covenant. Like Isaiah, they envisioned a glorious procession, proclaiming the glory of God from the heights of Zion.

> **The Cyrus Cylinder Decree**
>
> I returned the images of their gods to their sanctuaries which had been in ruins for a long period of time. I now established for them permanent sanctuaries. I also gathered all the former inhabitants of these places and returned them to their homes (*OTPar*, pp. 149–50).

What these people discovered when they arrived must have shocked them. The city of Jerusalem was not only in ruins from Nebuchadnezzar's systematic destruction, but it was overgrown after fifty years of neglect. The few inhabitants had allowed most of the cultivated fields to lie fallow, and the terraced hillsides had crumbled and eroded. The Samaritans, the inhabitants of the former northern kingdom of Israel who had not been taken into exile by the Babylonians, claimed political control over the entire area of Palestine. They were not pleased to see these returnees with their claims to land and their political independence from the rule of the Samaritan governor.

All of these factors resulted in attention to the immediate needs of the returned community: building housing, the back-breaking task of restoring and planting the fields and terraces, and the management of water resources. This not only occupied their time but it also exhausted the funds that the Persian government had provided to rebuild the temple. During the first twenty years after the return of the exiles only the foundation of the temple was completed.

STUDY QUESTIONS

1. Compare and contrast Isaiah 45 and the Cyrus Cylinder.

2. Discuss the identity of "the Servant" in the Servant Songs.

3. Discuss the reasons why some exiles chose to return to Palestine and some chose to remain where they were.

4. Define: messiah, theodicy, universalism.

THE JEWISH IDENTITY MOVEMENT

The experience of exile produced in Judaism a religion that was able to maintain its identity in the midst of cultural diversity and the pressures of assimilation. This new commitment to maintain a distinct identity may be the result of the shock associated with the destruction of Jerusalem, the demolition of Solomon's temple, and the demise of the monarchy as an institution. Another factor may have been the condition of the people of Judah as exiles for a period of roughly sixty years. An

---

A Song of Lament

[1]By the rivers of Babylon—
        there we sat down and there we wept
        when we remembered Zion.
[2]On the willows there
        we hung up our harps.
[3]For there our captors
        asked us for songs,
and our tormentors asked for mirth, saying,
        "Sing us one of the songs of Zion!"

[4]How could we sing the Lord's song
        in a foreign land?
[5]If I forget you, O Jerusalem,
        let my right hand wither!
[6]Let my tongue cling to the roof of my mouth,
        if I do not remember you,
if I do not set Jerusalem
        above my highest joy.
[7]Remember, O LORD, against the Edomites
        the day of Jerusalem's fall,
how they said, "Tear it down! Tear it down!
        Down to its foundations!"
[8]O daughter Babylon, you devastator!
        Happy shall they be who pay you back
        what you have done to us!
[9]Happy shall they be who take your little ones
        and dash them against the rock! (Ps 137).

---

intensification of devotion to Israelite institutions is peculiar because such disasters would have surely driven many Israelites to abandon their "failed" god and to seek the gods and the culture that now dominated their lives. But for those who listened to Jeremiah and Ezekiel and agreed with the premise of the theodicy that Yahweh was triumphant rather than defeated in these events, closer ties to their religion made perfect sense. In fact, to think otherwise would be to discount their entire cultural heritage. Perhaps the grief, the hope, and the anger expressed in Ps 137 (see inset) are clues to what was forming in their minds.

The basic elements of what came to be the Jewish identity movement include: (1) The earliest development of *Scripture:* Previous documents, including royal annals, primordial stories, ancestral narratives, and legal documents were compiled, edited, and arranged. It seems likely that a formal attempt was made at this point to give these compiled written and oral materials a definite slant that sustained the understanding that (a) Yahweh is the sole, transcendent, creator God; (b) Israel is the chosen people; (c) special legal obligations have been placed upon them; and (d) ultimately they would regain their special status and their country.

(2) The use of *Hebrew* as a liturgical language: There is a comparable example of this practice in Mesopotamia, where Sumerian remained in use in cultic contexts for thousands of years after it ceased to be a spoken language. For many centuries Latin was also used this way.

The Bitterness of Exile

[3]Judah has gone into exile with suffering
    and hard servitude;
she lives now among the nations,
    and finds no resting place;
her pursuers have all overtaken her
    in the midst of her distress.
[4]The roads to Zion mourn,
    for no one comes to the festivals;
all her gates are desolate,
    her priests groan;
her young girls grieve,
    and her lot is bitter (Lam 1:3–4).

---

(3) Emphasis on *Sabbath* worship: This was a direct result of the destruction of the Jerusalem temple and the sorrow this destruction created (see inset). Private family celebration of the Sabbath accomplished several things. It commemorated Yahweh's creative act. It also affirmed Yahweh as the sole creative force and therefore was a weekly argument for monotheism. The simplicity and repetition of the Sabbath as a teaching device made it helpful in explaining theology to children. When the temple was rebuilt in Jerusalem the priesthood once again sought to justify its existence by laying additional requirements upon the worshipers. In the

face of this attempt, Third Isaiah opposed the priesthood with the claim that all that was necessary to be a faithful Jew was Sabbath worship (Isa 58:13–14). After the destruction of Herod's temple in 70 CE, Sabbath worship became the center of rabbinic Judaism.

(4) A renewed emphasis on *circumcision* as a necessary ritual act of initiation for Jewish males: While a precedent for circumcision is found in Gen 17, the origin of circumcision is unknown. The emphasis it receives in the royal annals where the Philistines are labelled as the "uncircumcised" may suggest a possible date, but it may be a practice borrowed from the Egyptians during the monarchic period or even earlier.

(5) An intensification and democratization of interest in *ritual purity*: Ritual purity takes several forms, including ritual bathing and strict dietary laws. It is unknown when these laws were first instituted, although there is evidence of the practice of ritual purity in Hittite texts (1500–1400 BCE). Endorsement of purity laws in the Daniel stories, which date to the Hellenistic period (300–100 BCE), suggests a formal acceptance by the Jews at least by the time of the postexilic period.

(6) Insistence upon *endogamy*: Marriage within a group makes sense if the group is trying to protect its culture from outside influence. The mother is always the child's first teacher. If the mother comes from a non-Jewish household she will present mixed signals that could draw the child away from Judaism. The only other time in which the biblical tradition emphasized endogamy is in the ancestral narratives. As in the postexilic period, the ancestral narratives emphasize endogamy for the purpose of cultural survival. Otherwise, endogamy makes little economic or political sense. Thus it was not an issue during the monarchic period and it had to be enforced on the descendants of the returned exiles by the more stringent Diaspora Jews Ezra and Nehemiah.

The exile did not produce a single, monolithic Judaism. In fact, several branches existed, including the "normative," which required strict adherence to the dictates of the law, the "wisdom" group, which advocated a life of moderation and rational thought, the more extreme **apocalyptic** movement, which advocated an eschatological vision of battles and last judgment, and the "universalism" movement, which took its cue from Isaiah's "light to the nations" image and saw the sharing of the law and Yahweh as the true mission of the Jews. This latter group is most likely responsible for the stories of Ruth and Jonah and their clearly universalistic motifs.

What seems curious is that the writings of all of these groups have found their way into the canon. Each has been allowed to voice its vision of Judaism despite the fact that "normative" Judaism ultimately came to dominate.

PERSIAN RULE

A number of factors contributed to significant changes in Jewish culture during the Persian period. First, the Jews of Palestine enjoyed a period of nearly two hundred years of relative peace under the rule of the Persians. This allowed them to rebuild their destroyed cities and reestablish economic stability within their province. Agricultural lands were cultivated again and business activity resumed after being dormant during the Babylonian exile.

Second, a greater emphasis on urbanization also began in the Persian period. Jerusalem, with its walls rebuilt (Neh 2–4), and the temple once again functioning as a center of religious activity (Ezra 6:13–15), provided a focal point for life and a model of urbanism for the other cities and towns of Judah. The strength of Persian authority throughout the empire also assured a continuous stream of foreign businessmen into Palestine and the creation of a more cosmopolitan culture. A greater acceptance of the outside world made the transition to Hellenistic domination easier for many Jews.

The third major factor influencing the formation of Jewish culture during the period of Persian rule was the elimination of the civil office of the king of Judah. One direct result of this policy was the enhancement of the position of the high priest in Jerusalem. He became the titular religious and civic head of the Jewish community, bowing only to the authority of the Persian king and his governor. The high priest's position was confirmed by the Persian government (Ezra 7:11–26) and further solidified by his control of the sacrificial cult in Jerusalem.

According to tradition, the office was to be held by a member of the Zadokite priestly family (Ezra 7:1–6). The connection that this family had to temple worship during the preexilic period provided legitimacy for the position of high priest. It also reassured the people that, at least in matters of religion, nothing had changed. The power wielded by this office led to a gradual process of increasing secularization of the high priesthood. In the later period of Hasmonean rule (165–63 BCE), the office of high priest and the privilege of choosing who would hold that post were transformed into coveted political prizes.

A fourth important development during the Persian period was the initiation of the canonization process. Canonization was related to the growth in importance of the priestly community. Among the concerns of the priesthood was that the oral as well as written traditions of the people of Israel be compiled. After the traumatic experience of the exile, the priests wanted to ensure that sacrifice and other cultic acts were performed regularly and correctly. They hoped to gain God's continued good will by a strict conformity to the law. This required that the law be written down and canonized into an authoritative document, the Torah, which could be consulted to prevent future mistakes or misunderstandings of what was expected of the people.

Once this was done, the entire body of traditional writings was edited again into what eventually became the "Hebrew **canon**" of scriptures. This compilation and editing process, which took several centuries to complete, also sparked increased study of the text and the development of a group known as scribes or rabbis (teachers). They became authorities on the law and its interpretation and were consulted on these matters by the religious community.

A final development that can be ascribed to the Persian period is the separation between the Jews of Judah and the Samaritans. This break has its roots in political conflicts and religious differences between the Persian provinces of Yehud (Judah) and Samaria. The returning exiles excluded the Samaritans from participation in the rebuilding of the Jerusalem temple (Ezra 4:1–3). Later, Nehemiah also stood up to Samaritan pressure, raised by their governor Sanballat, against the rebuilding of the city's walls. Nehemiah literally threw their representatives out of the temple precincts (Neh 13:4–9). With the Jews denying them participation in the cult in Jerusalem and calling them unfit because of their mixed cultural heritage, it is no wonder that the Samaritans rejected Jerusalem as the true temple site and place of God's presence. Instead they declared Mount Gerizim near Shechem as their place of worship. In 325 BCE the Samaritans took advantage of Alexander's political good will to construct an alternative temple there (Josephus, *Jewish Antiquities* 11.346–347).

STUDY QUESTIONS

1. Discuss the various elements of the Jewish identity movement and how they reflect either earlier traditions or a new understanding of the covenant and God.

2. Discuss possible Babylonian and Persian influences on Judaism.

3. Define: apocalyptic.

POSTEXILIC PROPHECY

The Books of Haggai and Zechariah (chs. 1–8)   In the second year of the reign of the Persian king Darius (518 BCE) the prophets Haggai and Zechariah (chapters 1–8 only) begin to provoke the people to rebuild the temple in Jerusalem. Haggai uses a negative approach, pointing to crop failures and other natural disasters as evidence of Yahweh's displeasure at the delinquency of the people in completing this task (Hag 1:9–11). In doing this, he followed a pattern set by previous prophets who also proclaimed that famine, war, and natural disaster were signs of God's wrath (compare Hos 2:8–9 and Amos 4:6–11).

Zechariah describes a series of eight "night visions," each with the pattern: vision, question, answer. He employs a hopeful tone, in which Yahweh promises a return to prosperity and a restoration of comfort for Zion when the temple is rebuilt (Zech 1:16–17). Full restoration of the nation's fortunes and of the covenantal relationship with Yahweh are promised, as God once again dwells in the midst of the chosen people in the "holy land" (Zech 2:12 [2:16 in Hebrew]; this is the only reference in the Hebrew canon to Judah as the "holy land").

> ### Zechariah's Image of the Branch
>
> [8]Now listen, Joshua, high priest, you and your colleagues who sit before you! . . . I am going to bring my servant the Branch. [9]For on the stone that I have set before Joshua, on a single stone with seven facets, I will engrave its inscription, says the LORD of hosts, and I will remove the guilt of the land in a single day (Zech 3:8–9).
>
> [12] . . . Here is a man whose name is Branch; for he shall branch out in his place, and he shall build the temple of the LORD. [13]It is he that shall build the temple of the LORD; he shall bear royal honor, and shall sit and rule on his throne. There shall be a priest by his throne, with peaceful understanding between the two of them (Zech 6:12–13).

Both prophets pressure the leadership in Jerusalem to move forward with the construction of the temple. Haggai calls on Zerubbabel, the Persian-appointed governor and possibly a grandson of the last king, Jehoiachin, to take on the mantle of Davidic kingship. The prophet uses the title "the signet ring" for Zerubbabel, indicating the legitimacy of the governor's Davidic origins and his right to exercise the power of the office, which included using the signet ring to stamp and certify official documents (Hag 2:23). Haggai encourages him to trust in Yahweh's support and aid the people in their work.

Perhaps because Haggai's efforts bore no fruit, Zechariah directs his efforts toward influencing the high priest Joshua. In his fourth vision, Zechariah describes Joshua "standing before the angel of the LORD, and the *satan* (God's prosecuting attorney) standing at his right hand to accuse him" (Zech 3:1). Joshua's priestly robes are filthy, a representation of the sins of the people and the priesthood. Yahweh orders that Joshua be given a new, clean set of clothes and a fresh turban

(Zech 3:3–5). This is followed by the reassurance that obedience to the covenant will ensure Joshua's place as high priest and the priestly community's role in administering the temple and the courts (Zech 3:6–7).

At this point, Zechariah uses the image of the "Branch" as a messianic figure who will restore the temple and the nation under Yahweh's guidance (Zech 3:8). This figure could be compared to "the branch of the LORD" in Isa 4:2 and 11:1 as an ideal Davidic ruler. He will usher in an era of restoration and justice which will also include the return of Yahweh to Zion (Zech 8:2–3) and an ingathering of people from all nations "to seek the LORD of hosts" (Zech 8:21).

Zerubbabel, fearing possible political repercussions from the Persian government, did not accept the royal messianic titles assigned by Haggai and Zechariah. This would explain the change of referent in Zechariah's second use of "the Branch" in 6:9–15. It appears that this passage, once referring to Zerubbabel, has been changed and that the title was bestowed on Joshua (Zech 6:11).

Despite the urging of these prophets, Zerubbabel did not continue the rebuilding of the temple in Jerusalem until additional funds and a political confirmation were received from Darius' court. Opposition from the "people of the land" (persons who had not been taken into exile) and from the Samaritan leaders had complicated the political situation (Ezra 4:1–6; 5:1–17). Once these impediments had been resolved through bureaucratic and diplomatic means, Darius gave the order and construction resumed. The temple was completed in 515 BCE (Ezra 6). This temple, while in no way as grand as the one envisioned in Ezek 40–48, allowed the resumption of priestly offices and animal sacrifices. It also provided a religious focal point for the returned community in Judah.

STUDY QUESTIONS

1. Discuss why Haggai and Zechariah were so adamant that the temple be rebuilt in Jerusalem. Why were the Samaritans so opposed to it?

2. Discuss the use of royal images to urge Zerubbabel to rebuild the temple.

3. Compare Zechariah's use of "the satan" with that figure in Job.

4. Define: apocalyptic.

Isaiah of the Return (Isa 56–66)   The restoration of the temple in Jerusalem was a source of pride for the people of the province of Judah. The temple quickly became one means of defining Jewish religious identity. The restoration of the priestly community brought restrictions on the use of the temple and its facilities. These restrictions required the creation of detailed criteria to determine who was a Jew and what privileges one could enjoy based on kinship, gender, or physical infirmity.

Emphasis on Sabbath Worship

All who keep the Sabbath, and do not profane it,
   and hold fast my covenant—
[7]these I will bring to my holy mountain,
   and make them joyful in my house of prayer;
their burnt offerings and their sacrifices
   will be accepted on my altar;
for my house shall be called a house of prayer
   for all peoples (Isa 56:6b–7).

In this exclusive and restrictive atmosphere another voice of Isaiah is raised; generally called Third Isaiah, and identified in chapters 56–66. This prophetic voice challenges restrictions placed on eunuchs and **proselytes** (converts) who wanted to enter the temple to offer sacrifices. The sole criterion established by Third Isaiah, other than obedience to the covenant, is the celebration of the Sabbath.

This prophetic figure also warned the people about form without faith. They had resumed ritual practices such as fasting, but these practices had become a source of contention rather than a means of worship and humbling themselves (Isa 58:2–5). The often-voiced statement (see Mic 6:6–8; Jas 1:27) that God's interest in ritual is based on proper motivation is once again used here:

[6]Is not this the fast I choose:
   to loose the bonds of injustice,
   to undo the thongs of the yoke,
to let the oppressed go free
   and to break every yoke?
[7]Is it not to share your bread with the hungry,
   and bring the homeless poor into your house;
when you see the naked to cover them,
   and not to hide yourself from your own kin? (Isa 58:6–7).

The period after the return from exile was one of readjustment and striving for normalcy. The prophets who called for the restoration of the temple did so as a way of refocusing the attention of the people on the former modes of living in Jerusalem and the covenant that they had made with Yahweh. But simply constructing a new temple did not eliminate the abuses of power and excesses of exclusivism that are a part of any institution and its leadership. Third Isaiah's prophetic voice was raised to remind the nation of the simplicity of its covenant agreement.

The Book of   The final chapters of the book of Zechariah continue the theme
Zechariah   of the establishment of a messianic era, which was first de-
(chs. 9–14)   scribed in Zech 6–8. However, this last section appears to have
                       been written by an unknown author and attached to Zechariah
by editors during the middle Persian period (ca. 500–425 BCE). It consists of two oracles that contain many familiar prophetic elements: indictment of foreign nations (Zech 9:1-8), the use of the image of "on that day" (Zech 12:4, 6, 8), and condemnation of false prophets (Zech 13:3-6). It also contains elements of apocalyptic style, similar to that found in Daniel 7-12, including the vision of the final victory of Yahweh over the earth (Zech 14:9).

The first oracle (Zech 9-11), written in poetry, is concerned with a call for the exiled people to return to Jerusalem (Zech 9:12; 10:6, 10-12). It includes a very militant tone in which the people are transformed into Yahweh's bow (Zech 9:13-14). The prophecy then concludes with a description of a "wicked shepherd," who oppresses the people and may represent the officials ruling in Judah after the exile.

> ### Zechariah's Vision of Peace
>
> [6] On that day there shall not be either cold or frost. [7] And there shall be continuous day (it is known to the LORD), not day and not night, for at evening time there shall be light.
> [8] On that day living waters shall flow out from Jerusalem, half of them to the eastern sea and half of them to the western sea; it shall continue in summer as in winter.
> [9] And the LORD will become king over all the earth; on that day the LORD will be one and his name one (Zech 14:6–9).

The second oracle (Zech 12-14) is written in prose style and includes a series of statements that begin with the phrase "on that day." This provides a greater sense of future action by God rather than the more immediate acts of aiding the returning exiles that are found in the first oracle. There is a mixture in these chapters of military action and lamentation over the losses incurred in the fighting (Zech 12:7-11). Of particular interest here is the restructuring of the cosmos after a long and devastating struggle in which Jerusalem (as well as the nations) suffer greatly. In the final scene, peace will at last come to Jerusalem and the survivors of the war are required to come there to worship Yahweh at the Feast of Booths, celebrating Yahweh's rule and the restored covenant (Zech 14:16–19).

The Book of Malachi

Although the book of Malachi stands as the final volume in the prophetic corpus, it probably dates to the period between 500–450 BCE and reflects the activities of the priestly community immediately after the reconstruction of the temple. It consists of six oracles, the last five of which concern themselves with the failures of Judah and the priests to obey the covenant. The first, a condemnation of Edom (Mal 1:2–5), is out of character. But this may indicate that the author has simply adopted the traditional theme of enmity between Edom and the Jews (cf. Ps 137:7; Obad 6–14, 18–21). The authorship of Malachi is uncertain because Malachi is not a personal name. It simply means "my messenger," a reference, perhaps, to the promised messenger of God in chapter 3.

> ### Charges Against the Priesthood
>
> [7]For the lips of a priest should guard knowledge, and people should seek instruction from his mouth, for he is the messenger of the LORD of hosts. [8]But you have turned aside from the way; you have caused many to stumble by your instruction; you have corrupted the covenant of Levi, says the LORD of hosts (Mal 2:7–8).
>
> [4] . . . with you is my contention, O priest.
> [6]My people are destroyed for lack of knowledge;
>   because you have rejected knowledge,
>   I reject you from being a priest to me.
> And since you have forgotten the law of your God,
>   I also will forget your children (Hos 4:4, 6).
>
> [13] . . . from prophet to priest,
>   everyone deals falsely.
> [14]They have treated the wound of my people carelessly,
>   saying, "Peace, peace,"
>   when there is no peace (Jer 6:13–14).

The charges made against the priests are similar to those made by Hosea and Jeremiah. They speak of a lack of knowledge, false teachings, and improper attention to their sacrificial duties: "You bring what has been taken by violence or is lame or sick, and this you bring as your offering!" (Mal 1:13). The law is very explicit that sacrificial animals were to be healthy and without blemish (Lev 22:17–25; Deut 15:21), yet these priests think they can cheat God. They are cursed for "robbing God" of the required tithes and offerings (Mal 3:8–9). Those who do bring their tithes into the temple storehouse can be assured that Yahweh will reward their faithfulness by giving them abundant harvests and protecting their crops from locust plagues and other natural calamities (Mal 3:10–12).

Weary of such unfaithful servants, Yahweh resolves to send a messenger to "prepare the way" for the coming of the Lord to the temple and for the reestablishment of the covenant (Mal 3:1). An appendix to the book identifies the messenger as the prophet Elijah (Mal 4:5–6 [3:23–24 in Hebrew]). This mysterious figure, who did not die like other mortals (2 Kgs 2:11–12), is an appropriate harbinger of change. The New Testament writers, seeing the coming of a new age, applied Malachi's prophecy to John the Baptist in Luke 1:17.

Another theme developed in Malachi is a condemnation of divorce. This theme stands in contrast to the demands of Ezra and Nehemiah that mixed marriages between Jews and non-Jews be dissolved (Ezra 9:1–10:5; Neh 13:23–30). Malachi asserts, "Have we not all one father? Has not one God created us all?" (Mal 2:10). This apparent example of **universalism** may be part of the minority voice within Judaism that argued for the extension of the covenant to all nations (see Isa 63:16; 64:8). The prophet's argument against divorce may also be an argument for converting spouses to Judaism so that they will not remain "the daughter of a foreign god" (Mal 2:11) and so that their families will produce "godly offspring" (Mal 2:15).

The conclusion of the book is a reference to a day of judgment when those "who revered the LORD" will be recorded in a "book of remembrance" (cf. Dan 12:1) and will be spared when God separates out the righteous from the wicked (Mal 3:16–4:3 [3:16–21 in Hebrew]). This is followed by two appendices: the first commands the reader to obey the law as given to Moses and the second identifies Elijah as the messenger whose coming will presage the "day of the LORD." These verses serve as a **colophon** to the entire set of prophetic books (see Hos 14:9 for another example of a wisdom colophon).

The Book of Joel   Written in the period after 400 BCE by an otherwise unknown author, the book of Joel reflects the uncertain existence of the Jewish community in Palestine. Their world is so fragile that a plague of locusts can create a famine and the specter of starvation. They can also be victimized by their neighbors and sold into slavery. Into this reality of want and misery, Joel injects a ray of hope for a "day of the LORD" that does not involve punishment of the nation, but rather a newly revived creation and vengeance on the enemies of God's people.

The lack of any mention of identifiable historical events in the text prevents an accurate dating of Joel. The author's intimate knowledge of the Jerusalem temple and its priesthood (see Joel 2:17) suggests a date after 500 BCE. The mention of Jews being sold as slaves to the Greeks (Joel 3:6; 4:6 in Hebrew) requires a date closer to 400 BCE, when, under cosmopolitan Persian rule, more frequent contacts were made with Greek merchants.

The principal theme in this short prophetic book is the "day of the LORD." The day of the Lord is first symbolized in a locust plague, which strips the land like an invading army (Joel 2:1–11). In the midst of the devastation, the prophet reminds the people again that it is better to repent than to perform rituals: "Rend your hearts and not your clothing" (Joel 2:13a; cf. 1 Sam 15:22 and Hos 6:6). Then Joel uses the day of the Lord as the moment of Judah's restoration, when plenty will replace want and the presence of God will be made manifest in the people's words and hearts (Joel 2:18–32). This pattern of a plea followed by a reassurance of hope and restoration identifies this portion of Joel as a cultic liturgy. It is a common pattern in Psalms (e.g., Ps 22).

Apocalyptic Vision

[28]Then afterward
    I will pour out my spirit on all flesh;
your sons and your daughters shall prophesy,
    your old men shall dream dreams,
    and your young men shall see visions.
[29]Even on the male and female slaves,
    in those days, I will pour out my spirit.

[30]I will show portents in the heavens and on the earth, blood and fire and columns of smoke. [31]The sun shall be turned to darkness, and the moon to blood, before the great and terrible day of the LORD comes (Joel 2:28–31 [3:1–4 in Hebrew]).

Joel also contains **apocalyptic** language and visions. Among them is a passage (Joel 2:28–32; 3:1–5 in Hebrew) that is quoted in the New Testament book of Acts (2:17–21) as an example of the last days and final judgment. However, Judaism in Joel's time had not incorporated the idea of resurrection of the dead or a specific afterlife following judgment. For the prophet, his words referred to a day when this world will be transformed and judgment will be made on the deeds of Judah's enemies (Joel 3:1–8; 4:1–8 in Hebrew). The emphasis that Joel placed upon the use of war as a means of righting injustice and gaining revenge is also found in Esth 9 and Nah 2. This attempt to justify war sounds cruel, but it spoke to the pain and suffering of an oppressed people who wished to strike out against Edom, Phoenicia, and the Philistines (cf. Ps 137:8–9).

Like other **minor prophets** ("minor" with reference to the length of the book), Joel provides only a few images, not fully developed sets of teachings like the ones that appear in Isaiah or Jeremiah. He draws on both his own experience of his world and on the views of the growing **apocalyptic** movement, which are more completely expressed in Daniel, the Qumran texts, and the writings of the New Testament.

STUDY QUESTIONS

1. Discuss the use of the universalism theme in Isaiah of the return's message—with particular attention to his emphasis on the Sabbath.

2. Discuss the concern over tithing in the book of Malachi.

3. Discuss the apocalyptic images of the "day of the Lord" in Joel.

POSTEXILIC NARRATIVE

The Books of
Chronicles

In the canon of the Christian Old Testament, Malachi is the final book. This prophetic book ends with a prediction of the return of Elijah as the precursor to God's return and the restoration of the people. Christian theologians have interpreted this to refer to John the Baptist's role as the proclaimer of Jesus' messiahship (see Matt 11:11–14). But the order of the original Hebrew canon set by Jews in the Yavneh (Jamnia) conference (90–100 CE) ends with Chronicles (divided into two books, 1 and 2 Chron). The final words of Chronicles are from the decree of Cyrus allowing the exiles to return to Palestine. In both cases, the canon ends with a promise for the future and a hope for a restoration of relationship with God.

Chronicles is a "revisionist history," written in the period after the reconstruction of the Jerusalem temple by the returned exiles (after 500 BCE). Its purpose, in addition to retelling the story of Israel's history from Adam to the time of the exile, was to establish a link between the "ideal" worship community of David's reign and the community of the time when the book was written. This link helped to legitimize the author's community and its priesthood. The author created the impression that his own community was simply a continuation of that created by David and Solomon. He did this in order to encourage the people to hold fast to their identity.

The Chronicles Revision of the Narratives of David and Solomon

Chronicles reverses the narrative order of two events: the story of the transport of the ark of the covenant to Jerusalem (2 Sam 6:2–11; 1 Chron 13) and the episode in which David obtains materials and workmen from Hiram of Tyre to construct his palace (2 Sam 5:11–25; 1 Chron 14:1–17).

The Chronicler tries to clean up the picture of David presented in Samuel–Kings. The story of David's unclothed dance before the ark as it enters Jerusalem and his confrontation with Michal (2 Sam 6:14–23) are omitted in the parallel story in 1 Chron 16. The episodes involving David's adultery with Bathsheba, Absalom's rebellion, and David's flight are also omitted (2 Sam 11–16).

The Chronicler changes the title for David's sons from "priests" to "chief officials" (2 Sam 8:18; 1 Chron 18:17) in order to maintain the ideology that only descendants of Levi and Aaron could serve as priests.

Second Samuel 9, with its story of David's care for Jonathan's son Mephibosheth, is omitted by the Chronicler. First Chronicles 10:6 simply asserts that all of Saul's family was dead.

The political purge that began Solomon's reign is omitted and his first official act is to visit and sacrifice at the high place at Gibeon where the tent of meeting had been erected (2 Chron 1:2–6).

The story of the two prostitutes (1 Kgs 3:16–28) is omitted.

Hiram of Tyre's name is changed to Huram and Chronicles adds a letter from the Phoenician king that does not appear in 1 Kgs 5. The letter expands on the statement, "the LORD God of Israel, who made heaven and earth" (2 Chron 2:11–16).

The Chronicler omits vv. 27–37 from the description of the temple equipment in 1 Kgs 7:23–51 (2 Chron 4:1–22).

The story of the bringing of the ark into the temple (based on 1 Kgs 8:1–11) has an additional section on the priests and levitical singers (2 Chron 5:11b–13a).

Solomon's offering of incense (1 Kgs 9:25) is qualified in 2 Chron 8:12, where it explicitly notes that his altar was built "in front of the vestibule," thus reserving service within the temple for priests alone.

The sources used by the Chronicler (a modern designation for the author or authors of 1–2 Chron) include large portions of the Deuteronomic history (1 Sam 31–2 Kgs 25). A number of other lost sources are also cited, such as "the records of the seer Samuel, . . . the records of the prophet Nathan, and . . . the records of the seer Gad" (1 Chron 29:29). Since none of these documents currently exist, it is impossible to determine how extensively they were used or even whether they are real or fictitious. It has been suggested that Chronicles was originally part of a larger work that included the books of Ezra and Nehemiah, but this proposal is not accepted by all scholars and requires further linguistic and historical analysis before a final determination can be made.

What is unique about this version of Israel's history is its selective use of material. For example, the period from Adam to the death of Saul is told simply through the recitation of genealogies. This ensures that the reader will focus on what the author(s) viewed as the starting point for Israel's history, the reign of David and the designation of Jerusalem as the religious and political capital of the monarchy.

In addition, where the Chronicler deemed it appropriate, the Deuteronomic narrative of Samuel–Kings is rearranged or edited. Usually the goal of these modifications was to put greater emphasis on cultic rather than political motives and to cleanse from the text the scandalous behavior of David and his court.

David's role as the originator of cultic practice and the organizer of priestly groups who serve in various capacities is also described in great detail. For example, David commands the chiefs of the Levites to appoint long lists of persons who will serve as singers and musicians (1 Chron 15:16–24). As part of his final instructions to Solomon, David organizes the body of officials who will administer and serve in the temple (1 Chron 23:2–32). Chronicles also shows interest in the administration of the government and provides lists of officials. The information provided in Chronicles contains some differences from that in Samuel. The information about David's officials in Chronicles serves to magnify the importance of David's position (e.g., 1 Chron 27:1–15 gives the inflated figure of 288,000 for the size of David's bodyguard).

When the narrative moves to Solomon's reign, again it is evident that the emphasis is on cultic matters. Of particular importance, of course, was the construction of the temple in Jerusalem. The Chronicles' version tends to condense and revise the material found in 1 Kgs 6–7. Throughout the process Solomon is portrayed as simply carrying out the work that his more important father David would have done had he been permitted to do so by circumstances and by God's command (see 2 Chron 6:7–9, 14–17; 7:17–18).

As was the case with the chronicle of David's reign, no mention is made of Solomon's apostasy (1 Kgs 11:1–13) or any other unfavorable aspect of his administration (2 Chron 9:22–31). With the transition to the reign of Rehoboam and the division of the kingdom, it becomes clear that the Chronicler's interests are with the Davidic kings and this is the focus of every event. This is poignantly illustrated in the Chronicler's use of the term "Israel." In Chronicles "Israel" refers to "Judah," not the northern tribes (see 2 Chron 19:8).

The chapters narrating the history of Judah after the division of the kingdom (2 Chron 10–36) describe the misdeeds of kings and the basis upon which Yahweh became angry with the nation (see 2 Chron 20:33, 35–37). But the Chronicler, like the Deuteronomist (2 Kgs 8:18–19), makes a point of noting that evil individuals will not negate the covenant that Yahweh has made with David.

> Yet the LORD would not destroy the house of David because of the covenant that he had made with David, and since he had promised to give a lamp to him and to his descendants forever (2 Chron 21:7).

This assertion could then be used as the basis for the claim of a restored people after the exile.

The Chronicler often adds a short comment to the narrative to ensure that the reader understands the reason why certain acts are considered wicked. For example, in 2 Chron 21:8–10, the text describes the Edomite revolt in the time of King Jehoram. The Chronicles' story is based on the same story in 2 Kgs 8:20–22. But the Chronicler adds an explanation of the cause of this revolt (v. 11): "[Jehoram] made high places in the hill country of Judah, and led the inhabitants of Jerusalem into unfaithfulness, and made Judah go astray" (cf. 2 Chron 21:16–19). The rewriting of 2 Kgs 16 to magnify the portrayal of Ahaz' sins is typical of the Chronicler's commentary style of presentation (2 Chron 28).

Those kings who were righteous are singled out for special attention by the Chronicler and generally given longer treatment than in 1–2 Kgs. Jehoshaphat, Hezekiah, and Josiah all are pictured as reformers and faithful kings who ordered the people to return to proper worship. The Chronicler also takes the opportunity to note the repentance of evil kings and their subsequent restoration to favor (e.g., Manasseh in 2 Chron 33:10–17). The heightened role of Levites in these reforms is also typical of the Chronicler (see 2 Chron 29:12–19; 31:2–19).

Another example of the way that the material from the Kings' account has been revised to reflect the fifth-century attitudes of the Chronicler is the account of the siege of Jerusalem by Sennacherib (2 Chron 32). Even though the speech of the Rabshakeh is paraphrased and condensed, it contains most of the taunts made by the Assyrian official (cf. 2 Kgs 18:17–35; 19:1–37). But it fails to reflect the Assyrian's argumentative style and omits the Rabshakeh's argument that Yahweh had sent the Assyrians in response to Hezekiah's unfaithfulness (2 Kgs 18:22). In addition, the monotheistic theology of the Chronicler's time is injected in 2 Chron 32:19 with the comment, "They spoke of the God of Jerusalem as if he were like the gods of the peoples of the earth, which are the work of human hands."

Josiah is singled out as the best king since David. The narrative of his reign is rearranged, so that the Deuteronomic reform occurs prior to the discovery of the tablets of the law in the temple (2 Chron 34:3–7; contrast 2 Kgs 22–23). The Passover celebration is described in much greater detail in the Chronicles' version to give it the prominence that the priestly community associated with it (compare 2 Kgs 23:21–23 to 2 Chron 35:1–19). Even his death at Megiddo is given a more theological basis with a speech, not found in the 2 Kings' version, in which the Egyptian pharaoh Neco II commands Josiah to stand aside while the pharaoh obeys Yahweh's command to go to war (2 Chron 35:21).

The confusing years of Josiah's successor are given little attention and the fall of Jerusalem to the Babylonians is condensed into only a few verses. At the end of the Chronicles' account, the decree of Cyrus is highlighted:

> The LORD, the God of heaven, has given me all the kingdoms of the earth, and he has charged me to build him a house at Jerusalem, which is in Judah. Whoever is among you of all his people, may the LORD his God be with him! Let him go up (2 Chron 36:23).

This sets the stage for the postexilic community's restoration of the temple and priestly orders. In the present arrangement of the Jewish canon of the Hebrew Bible, this statement completes the canon on a note of hope.

STUDY QUESTIONS

1. Discuss the Chronicler's revision of official historical accounts to emphasize a later, theological understanding of events. How would this be helpful to readers living in postexilic times?

2. Compare the treatment of David and Solomon in the books of Samuel and Kings with that in Chronicles.

The Books of Ezra and Nehemiah   After the community of returned exiles had settled into an established pattern and a rebuilt temple, the concerns for the strength and security of that community were far from ended.

In response to such news from the province of Judah, some time during the period after 450 BCE, we hear of two Diaspora Jews who received permission to return to Jerusalem to help administer its affairs.

This is the subject of the books of Ezra and Nehemiah. These men may have been contemporaries. Certainly, the issues they deal with in Jerusalem are similar. In the former book, Ezra consistently appears as a priestly figure. His activities are almost exclusively concerned with the temple and with religious conformity. In contrast, Nehemiah is clearly a political figure who is interested in the efficient administration of the province and in what he considers necessary religious reforms, which he instituted to bring the people back into his vision of the covenant. Ezra and Nehemiah could have worked side-by-side, but if that were the case it seems likely there would have been many more direct contacts and references to each other in the text.

Judah and Jerusalem had been ignored by the Persian government for nearly sixty-five years after Darius had provided the funds to rebuild the temple in 515 BCE. No mention is made of affairs in Judah between 515 BCE and the reign of Artaxerxes I (465–424 BCE). This was due to the Persians' preoccupation with wars against the Greeks, which drained their resources during the period from 490 to 449. Only after the Peace of Callias (449 BCE) did the Persians once again turn their attention to the minor complaints of their outlying provinces.

Nehemiah's Administration. Jerusalem and the province of Judah once again reenter our historical records when a series of countercharges are made by Samaritans and Jews regarding the reconstruction of the walls of Jerusalem. As is so often the case in dealing with a large bureaucracy, many of these letters were not sent directly to the king. Instead, petty officials and persons who had the king's ear were consulted to see if they could intercede in the cause. Nehemiah, the cupbearer of Artaxerxes I, was one of these officials (Neh 2:1). Because one of the duties of the cupbearer was to test the king's food to see if it had been poisoned, the cupbearer was a trusted member of the court. Nehemiah's title indicates that he was a person of rank and influence.

Nehemiah was also a Jew. This implies that Persia appointed persons based on merit, not ethnic origin. Sympathizing with his fellow Jews, Nehemiah obtains a commission as governor of Judah and begins a career that will include two separate terms of office. His narrative is written in an apologetic memoir style. It includes a number of personal defenses of his policies (Neh 5:14–19) as well as a recitation of the actions of his enemies (Neh 6:1–14).

Upon arrival in Jerusalem, Nehemiah showed good judgment by making a surprise inspection of the wall system (Neh 2:11–16). This allowed him to see it with his own eyes, thereby assessing the difficulty of rebuilding the walls, its probable costs, and the dangers involved. The next day he entertained the arguments for and against the project and made the decision to push ahead with construction. Why was the reconstruction of the walls of Jerusalem such an important matter to the people of Judah? The answer to this question cannot be that they expected to use these rebuilt walls to declare their independence or to protect them from Persian armies. The real answer lies in the symbolic value of the walls. Jerusalem's defense system had lain in ruins since the time of Nebuchadnezzar. Now, as Judah attempted to restore itself as a province separate from Samaria within the Persian empire, its capital city had to be restored.

It was for exactly this same reason that Sanballat, the Samaritan governor, opposed rebuilding the walls. He had ambitions to oversee all of Israel and thus an independent Judah would be a threat to his plans. As a result, when Nehemiah agreed to begin the construction, Sanballat and his allies, Tobiah of Ammon and Geshem the Arab, threatened to intervene with the Persian government and to physically attack the workers (Neh 2:19; 4:1–3, 7–8, 11).

Nehemiah's Reforms

- Prohibition of charging interest on loans (Neh 5:7–13).
- Institution of a lottery requiring ten percent of the people to live in Jerusalem (Neh 11:1–2).
- Appointment of temple treasurers (Neh 12:44–47).
- Return of Levites and singers to temple service and institution of practices designed to ensure their upkeep (Neh 13:10–11).
- Closing gates and prohibiting commerce on the Sabbath (Neh 13:15–22).
- Dissolution of mixed marriages (Neh 13:23–27).

Despite these threats, Nehemiah kept the work force on the job with an armed escort and completed the project in fifty-two days (Neh 6:15). Such a short period of time raises questions about how much work really had to be done or how extensive the wall system was. Nehemiah probably rebuilt the walls around the citadel and temple mount, the most important political structures in the city. This answered the need for a symbolic wall and quieted the opponents, perhaps allowing later construction to be done on the rest of the city.

Once his position was firmly established, Nehemiah initiated a series of social reforms, some of which made him extremely unpopular. It seems clear that his intent was to put the province on a sound administrative and financial footing. He appointed temple treasurers to collect and distribute the produce of the land to the people and the temple community (Neh 12:44–47). He expelled Tobiah from his rooms in the temple complex (Neh 13:4–9). These and similar actions were components of a plan to establish Judah as a separate Persian province.

Locking the gates on the Sabbath (Neh 13:15–22) and prohibiting mixed marriages (Neh 13:23–27) served a dual purpose. First, these actions reflected the exclusivism that formed a part of the Jewish identity movement in the Diaspora. Nehemiah felt the people should maintain themselves as a separate nation by means of unique institutions such as the Sabbath and a refusal to marry individuals outside of the group. Nehemiah's control over commerce, inheritance through marriage, and charging interest on loans (Neh 5:7–13) strengthened his administration and centralized his authority within the province.

Nehemiah served two terms as governor of Judah. His strong-handed treatment of the people probably did not win him many friends, but in his memoir he seems quite satisfied with his accomplishments. He concludes his memoir with an administrator's epitaph: "Remember me, O God, for good" (Neh 13:36).

Ezra the Priest.   The initial portion of the book of Ezra is simply a continuation of the history found in the books of Chronicles. This is one of the factors that has led scholars to conclude that Ezra was Nehemiah's predecessor. But the actual chronology of Ezra and Nehemiah is still unclear and it is not possible to determine with certainty whether they were contemporaries or whether one came before the other. Both mention Artaxerxes as king, but there were two kings by that name: Artaxerxes I (465–424) and Artaxerxes II (404–358). If Ezra came to Jerusalem in the reign of Artaxerxes II, then he would have been active in the generation after Nehemiah's terms of office.

A Decree of Artaxerxes

[21] "I, King Artaxerxes, decree to all the treasurers in the province Beyond the River: Whatever the priest Ezra, the scribe of the law of the God of heaven, requires of you, let it be done with all diligence, [22]up to one hundred talents of silver, one hundred cors of wheat, one hundred baths of wine, one hundred baths of oil, and unlimited salt. [23]Whatever is commanded by the God of heaven, let it be done with zeal for the house of the God of heaven, or wrath will come upon the realm of the king and his heirs. [24]We also notify you that it shall not be lawful to impose tribute, custom, or toll on any of the priests, the Levites, the singers, the doorkeepers, the temple servants, or other servants of this house of God.
[25] "And you, Ezra, according to the God-given wisdom you possess, appoint magistrates and judges who may judge all the people in the province Beyond the River who know the laws of your God; and you shall teach those who do not know them. [26]All who will not obey the law of your God and the law of the king, let judgment be strictly executed on them, whether for death or for banishment or for confiscation of their goods or for imprisonment" (Ezra 7:21–26).

This would explain why Ezra's company traveled without an armed escort (Ezra 8:22), and the recurrence of mixed marriages (a practice Nehemiah had strictly forbidden; Neh 13:23–27). Whatever the actual chronology may be, Ezra functions in a much different capacity than Nehemiah, despite the fact that he is given a letter in Aramaic from the Persian king empowering him to serve as chief administrator of the province (Ezra 7:12–20; see a slightly different version in Josephus, *Jewish Antiquities* 11.121–130). This decree, however, may have been intended to ensure the cooperation of the temple community when Ezra arrived. Its chief attributes are (1) tax-exempt status for all members of the temple community; (2) a grant of authority to appoint magistrates and judges who will administer the "law of the God of heaven"; (3) a grant of authority to educate the people in this law; and (4) an empowerment clause that gives Ezra powers of life, death, and confiscation. Ezra's powers were probably granted to keep order and were granted to administrators as part of any royal decree (see reference to the letter given to Nehemiah in Neh 2:7–9).

Ezra's purpose for returning to Jerusalem is not explained in any detail in his narrative. It simply states that he is to "make inquiries about Judah and Jerusalem according to the law of your God" (Ezra 7:14). Gold and silver are also to be transported to purchase sacrificial grain and animals for dedication in the temple (Ezra 7:15–20).

It appears that this new attempt to entice people to return to Jerusalem was not initially successful. Ezra had to make a special effort to recruit Levites (Ezra 8:15–20) and he could not ask for a group of soldiers to accompany them, despite the treasures they were transporting (Ezra 8:22). Clearly he envisioned this as a procession much like the one that Moses led out of Egypt or the one that journeyed into Palestine to conquer it in Joshua's time.

As the book of Ezra describes it, the principal matter facing Ezra upon his arrival is the issue of mixed marriages (Ezra 9:1–2). This seems like a small thing considering all of the administrative matters that might have been brought to his attention. However, by focusing on this one issue, the writer can bring the crisis to a climax and present Ezra as the stern enforcer of the law of Moses. After assembling the heads of households and forcing them to stand in a driving rain while he chastised them (Ezra 10:9), a committee is formed to investigate individual cases and to demand divorces (Ezra 10:14–16).

It is now necessary to switch from the narrative in Ezra to the one in Neh 8–9 to complete the story. In these chapters, Ezra staged a **covenant renewal ceremony** (cf. earlier examples in Exod 24, Josh 24, and 2 Kgs 23:1–3). He assembles the people, reads them the law, and then asks them to pledge obedience to it (Neh 8:1–12). Once they have made this affirmation, a period of celebration and sacrifice is observed, the Feast of Booths (Neh 8:13–18).

One curious aspect of this scene is the appearance of men in the crowd who "helped the people to understand the law" (Neh 8:7-8). This is probably because the law was written in Hebrew and by this time Aramaic had become the common language of the people. It also provides a precedent for rabbis to explain the law, which in later periods became the heart of interpretative Judaism.

The final step in Ezra's attempt to rejuvenate the worship of Yahweh and the proper behavior of the people is the recitation of the covenant history (Neh 9:6-37). This is probably a part of every covenant renewal ceremony in the period after the establishment of the monarchy. Psalm 78, for example, is designed to be recited during such a ceremony. After Ezra reads the law, the leaders and the people pledge not to intermarry or to violate the Sabbath (Neh 10:28-31). These two principles appear to be the basis of Diaspora Judaism as it was imposed on the Jerusalem community by Ezra and Nehemiah.

The End of an Era.   The tradition is that prophecy came to an end with Ezra. Thereafter the canon was closed and no further revelation was expected or needed. The law had been given to the people and it was now their task, in the centuries ahead, to obey it. The reality is of course that a great deal of additional material was written after 400 BCE (including Jonah, Ruth, Esther, Daniel and the Apocrypha/Deuterocanonical books). Judaism had begun to institutionalize itself, but its greatest test, Hellenism, was yet to come.

STUDY QUESTIONS

1. Compare the reform measures of Nehemiah to the elements of the Jewish identity movement. Is he doing anything new here?

2. Discuss why the people of Jerusalem wanted to rebuild the city's walls and why the Samaritans opposed the project.

3. Compare Ezra's covenant renewal ceremony (Neh 8) with those performed by Moses (Exod 24), Joshua (Josh 24), and Josiah (2 Kgs 23).

4. Define: covenant renewal ceremony.

The Book of Ruth   While this short story is set in the period of the judges, its theme and its use of legal structures from the Deuteronomic code suggest a date of composition in the postexilic period. In the Hebrew

Bible Ruth follows Proverbs and precedes the Song of Solomon (Canticles). Its placement in the modern Christian Bible immediately after Judges is therefore based more on tradition and similarity of story type than on the social institutions found in the tale. It may be useful, however, to compare the story in Ruth with the stories in Judges to demonstrate that a tale set in the Judges period does not have to contain violence.

The book of Ruth contains three major elements: (1) the theme of levirate obligation; (2) a segment of the Davidic genealogy; and (3) an assimilation ritual, allowing foreigners to become a part of the Israelite community. These elements are all interrelated within the story, which suggests a careful editing of an original tale. The primary agenda of the writer(s) is to argue against the increasing emphasis on **endogamy**, which was being forced on the Jerusalem community during the time of Ezra and Nehemiah (Ezra 9–10; Neh 13:23–27). In doing this, the book forms the basis for a more universal understanding of the covenant and of Yahweh's concern for all the peoples of the earth.

Initial Premises. The story begins with an Israelite family from Bethlehem, who immigrate to Moab in order to escape a famine in their own area (Ruth 1:1). Similar migrations are described in the ancestral narratives (Gen 12:10; 26:1). While they lived in Moab, the family's sons married Moabite women. The turning point came for them when a plague struck down all of the men in the family. Naomi, the mother, decides to return to Bethlehem to spend the remainder of her life (Ruth 1:3–7). Realizing it would be difficult for her sons' widows to find a life for themselves in Israel, Naomi offers them the opportunity to return to their families in Moab without further obligation to her. Orpah chooses to return, but Ruth pledges to remain with her mother-in-law and adopt Israelite ways:

> [16] . . . Where you go, I will go;
> where you lodge, I will lodge;
> your people shall be my people,
> and your God my God.
> [17] Where you die, I will die—
> there will I be buried.
> May the LORD do thus and so to me,
> and more as well,
> if even death parts me from you! (Ruth 1:16–17).

Ruth's statement is a classic example of an **assimilation ritual**, a ceremony that requires a person to renounce his or her former condition or status. In what is clearly treaty language, including a curse on those who break the oath, Ruth transforms herself from a Moabite into an Israelite. Her vow is similar in form to that taken by a slave who chooses to remain in his master's household after his six years of debt-servitude are completed (Exod 21:2–6; Deut 15:16–17).

The Conversion Ritual for a Slave

[5]But if the slave declares, "I love my master, my wife, and my children; I will not go out a free person," [6]then his master shall bring him before God. He shall be brought to the door or the doorpost; and his master shall pierce his ear with an awl; and he shall serve him for life (Exod 21:5–6).

Legal Obligations. Fortunately for the two widows, they arrived in Bethlehem at the beginning of the barley harvest and could survive by gleaning in the fields (Ruth 1:22–2:3). Naomi had the right to do so as a poor widow, and Ruth, the Moabitess, could exercise this right as a resident alien.

Gleaning Rights

[9] When you reap the harvest of your land, you shall not reap to the very edges of your field, or gather the gleanings of your harvest. [10]You shall not strip your vineyard bare, or gather the fallen grapes of your vineyard; you shall leave them for the poor and the alien: I am the LORD your God (Lev 19:9–10).

Ruth's diligence, obedience, willingness to work hard, and her concern for Naomi are continually emphasized in the narrative (Ruth 2:6–7, 11–12, 17–18, 22–23; 3:5, 10). In this way a sympathetic case is made for a foreigner, who might otherwise be distrusted or treated badly (Ruth 2:22).

Naomi then devises a strategy to meet the needs of both herself and Ruth, and to provide an heir for her deceased husband's property in Bethlehem. Since she no longer has either husband or sons, the law of **levirate obligation** comes into play. By this law, the nearest male kin is required to impregnate and take legal responsibility for the widow. This is designed to provide an heir for the dead man and to provide for the needs of the widow until her son is old enough to take legal responsibility (see Gen 38:7–11). Thus Naomi, who is beyond childbearing age, sends Ruth to Boaz to ask him to serve as their **levir**, guardian (Ruth 3:1–5).

Ruth's plea was made on the threshing floor where the harvesters, including Boaz, sleep to protect their grain. The threshing floor in village culture was the equivalent of the gate in walled towns and cities. It served as a place of business transactions and of legal decisions (see Judg 6:36–40; 2 Sam 24:18–25). The main function of the threshing floor was to provide a place in which seed could be separated from the harvested grain. During the harvest and at other times, the threshing floor commanded the attention of the entire community. The seed would also be distributed here to the field owners and presumably any disputes that might arise over distribution or some other related matter would also be handled here on the spot.

The Use of a Threshing Floor for Legal and Judicial Purposes

- In the Laws of Eshnunna 19 a man who has made a farm loan "shall make (the debtor) pay on the threshing floor" (*ANET*, p. 162).

- In the Ugaritic epic of Aqhat, King Danil is portrayed as "sitting before the gate, under a mighty tree on the threshing floor, judging the case of the widow" (*ANET*, p. 153).

Based on the same legal tradition, Ruth's meeting with Boaz at the threshing floor in Ruth 3:10–14 concerned both the redemption of her father-in-law's fields and the establishment of an intimate contact with the person she would eventually marry. Her request, "spread your cloak over your servant, for you are next of kin" (Ruth 3:9), is a legal formula obligating Boaz to take action. His response is a blessing that recognizes Ruth's legitimate claim, and he congratulates her for serving her mother-in-law and not just her own desires (Ruth 3:10–11).

Legal Resolution. Boaz reveals that he is not Naomi's closest kin. He can be their advocate, but it is up to another man to decide whether he will carry out the levirate obligation (Ruth 3:12–13). Boaz's gift of six measures of barley may therefore serve as either a bride price, if the levir refuses his duty, or as a kinsmen's gift to Naomi, the poor widow (Ruth 3:15–18).

In the formal "courtroom" scene that follows, Boaz follows strict legal protocol by going to the gate and asking the "next of kin" to join him in determining in accordance with the law, what should be done with Ruth and Naomi (Ruth 4:1). Ten elders (a legal quorum) are asked to sit in judgment, and Boaz puts two questions to the levir: (1) Since you are the nearest male kin and thus have the first right of refusal on the purchase of Naomi's field, do you wish to buy it (Ruth 4:3–4; compare Jer 32:6–15)? He is happy to say yes to this. (2) When you purchase the field, are you willing also to take Ruth, "to maintain the dead man's name on his inheritance"? This the levir refuses to do since it would mean he could not pass the field to his own heirs (Ruth 4:5–6).

At that point, the narrative breaks and a legal **gloss** (addition) is inserted which refers to the custom of removing the sandal of the levir who refuses his duty.

This gloss assumes a practice based on the law in Deut 25:7–10, although the characters do not follow that law exactly. The gloss demonstrates that the date for this version of the story of Ruth must come after the compiling of the Deuteronomic code (after 600 BCE).

Boaz then claims possession of the property of Naomi's husband and asserts his right to take Ruth as his wife in front of the elders who are witnesses.

> [9] . . . "Today you are witnesses that I have acquired from the hand of Naomi all that belonged to Elimelech and all that belonged to Chilion and Mahlon. [10]I have also acquired Ruth the Moabite, the wife of Mahlon, to be my wife, to maintain the dead man's name on his inheritance, in order that the name of the dead may not be cut off from his kindred and from the gate of his native place; today you are witnesses" (Ruth 4:9–10).

Concluding Issues. The response of the elders is to echo Boaz's claim and bless the marriage. The blessing, like the subsequent genealogy of Boaz's family, is political. The witnesses refer to Perez in Ruth 4:12 and then the genealogy of Perez is found in Ruth 4:18–22. Boaz is listed as a descendant of Perez and as the ancestor, with Ruth, of King David. In this way, these two stories of levirate obligation (Gen 38 and Ruth) are tied together and the line of David is allied with the concepts of concern for the law and the freedom to marry outside the Israelite tribes. The presence of a foreigner in the lineage of David, the king of Israel's golden age, would have been a particularly effective argument against any insistence upon endogamy in the postexilic period.

Finally, the song of blessing sung by the women to Naomi (Ruth 4:14–15) celebrates Yahweh's role as the covenantal provider of land and children. Like so many barren women before her, Naomi can now rejoice in children. When she places the child on her breast and gives him a name, Naomi claims Obed as her son, born in a surrogate fashion through Ruth. This son is now the legal heir of Naomi's husband Elimelech (Ruth 4:16–17). The legal complication that motivated the story is thus resolved at the same time that the author makes the final point in his argument for legitimizing mixed marriages and the rights of converts to Judaism (see Isa 56:3–8).

STUDY QUESTIONS

1. Compare the administration of levirate obligation in Ruth to that found in Gen 38 and Deut 25.

2. Why are there no villains in this book?

3. Discuss the implications of Ruth's Moabite origins and her status as an
    ancestress of David in the light of Ezra and Nehemiah's insistence on endogamy.

4. Define: assimilation ritual, gloss.

***The Book
of Jonah***
This book is set in the period of Assyrian control over much of
the ancient Near East (850–605 BCE). But it was most probably
written during the postexilic period (after 500 BCE). This date is
based on Jonah's strong emphasis on the universalism theme and the inability to
trace the events in this book to any established historical sources.

Purpose of the Book. The purpose of the book of Jonah is to provide a
showcase for the principle that Yahweh has the power to control the fate of all
peoples, even the sworn enemies of Israel. There is a good deal of comic irony in this
story of a reluctant prophet. Jonah may have thought he was protecting his own
people by refusing to save the Assyrians from destruction at the hands of Yahweh. It
is certainly understandable that he would not have wanted to aid the people who
had destroyed the northern kingdom of Israel and devastated the towns and villages
of Judah. Instead, he would have liked to shout like the seventh-century prophet
Nahum "Celebrate!" (Nah 1:15). The Assyrians are no more!

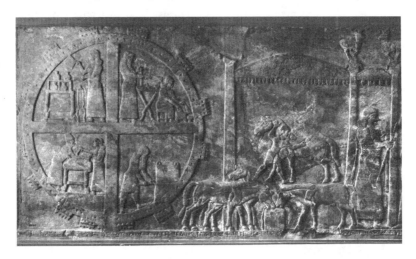

Assyrian encampment. The Assyrians were well organized, well equipped, and usually
conquered their enemies easily. Photo courtesy of the British Museum.

Jonah's task, however, is to go to Nineveh, the Assyrian capital and "cry out
against it" (Jonah 1:2). Knowing that through Jonah's message, Yahweh intended to

give the Assyrians an opportunity for repentance (cf. the angels' mission to Sodom in Gen 19:13), the prophet flees in the opposite direction. He takes a ship from the port of Joppa in hope of traveling to the end of the world, Tarshish in Spain, and thus escaping "the presence of the Lord" (Jonah 1:3). What he discovers is that there is no place to hide from Yahweh.

Assyrian Atrocities

I tore out the tongues of those whose slanderous mouths had uttered blasphemies against my god Ashur and had plotted against me, his god-fearing prince. . . . The others, I smashed alive with the very same statues of protective deities with which they had smashed my own grandfather Sennacherib— now (finally) as a (belated) burial sacrifice for his soul. I fed their corpses, cut into small pieces, to dogs, pigs, *zîbu* birds, vultures, the birds of the sky and (also) to the fish of the ocean (*ANET*, p. 288; the annals of Ashurbanipal [668–633 BCE]).

Universalism Theme. Throughout much of the narrative, Jonah appears to be stubbornly avoiding or even resisting God. This stands in stark contrast to the keen awareness of Yahweh's power by all of the non-Israelites he deals with in the story. For example, during the storm that tosses his ship about, the sailors fervently pray for deliverance while Jonah sleeps unaware of the danger (Jonah 1:4–6). These men, all non-Israelites, are aware of God's anger and acknowledge tacitly God's power over nature as attested by the storm. Jonah merely advises them that they should throw him overboard to appease Yahweh. There is no emotion here at all from Jonah! The sailors very reluctantly carry this out.

Similarly, it took Jonah three days to react to his incarceration in "the belly of the fish" before he prays for release (Jonah 2:2–9). His prayer may not have even been part of the original narrative. It may have been added later to give Jonah a bit more of a human character. The idea of imprisonment inside a fish, while a bit unusual, merely follows the theme of Yahweh's control of the forces and creatures of nature.

The Decree of the King of Nineveh

7 ". . . No human being or animal, no herd or flock, shall taste anything. They shall not feed, nor shall they drink water. [8]Human beings and animals shall be covered with sackcloth, and they shall cry mightily to God. All shall turn from their evil ways and from the violence that is in their hands" (Jonah 3:7–8).

The resolution of the drama comes when Jonah enters Nineveh and reluctantly begins to proclaim the message, "Forty days more, and Nineveh shall be overthrown!" (Jonah 3:4b). Even in carrying out this task, he once again shows his stubborn and rebellious nature. He walks a full day into the city before saying anything, perhaps hoping to find some corner where no one will hear him (Jonah 3:4a). The curious thing about this is that the people of this "great city," which took a person three days to walk from one end to the other, immediately believed Yahweh's prophet: "They proclaimed a fast, and everyone, great and small, put on sackcloth" (Jonah 3:5). Unlike Sodom, which had shown that all of its citizens were evil (Gen 19:4), Nineveh's entire population, including the king, demonstrate their contrition and willingness to repent. Their change is based on the hope that Yahweh may relent and spare the city. There is a close parallel between the statement in Jonah 3:9—"Who knows? God may relent and change his mind; he may turn from his fierce anger, so that we do not perish"—and the explanation given at the end of Jeremiah's trial for his acquittal and release—"Did he (Hezekiah) not fear the LORD and entreat the favor of the LORD, and did not the LORD change his mind about the disaster that he had pronounced against them?" (Jer 26:19b). Obviously these people recognized the possibility of "changing God's mind," and they were willing to go to extremes to do it.

Jonah's reaction to his success was that he was displeased and angry (Jonah 4:1). The universalism theme, which had made it possible for God to even be concerned about the most bloodthirsty people in the ancient world, allows for the righteous to be spared. Jonah, who knew Yahweh, can only be angry with God for relenting. The key to his stubborn nature is found in Jonah 4:2. In this verse Jonah reveals his reason for not going when he was first called as a prophet. He can proclaim Yahweh's loving and forgiving nature, but Jonah cannot forgive the Assyrians and thus does not want God to do so either.

Jonah's Complaint

[2] . . . "Oh LORD! Is not this what I said while I was still in my own country? That is why I fled to Tarshish at the beginning; for I knew that you are a gracious God and merciful, slow to anger, and abounding in steadfast love, and ready to relent from punishing" (Jonah 4:2).

The final expression of the universalism theme comes when Jonah constructs a booth outside of the city and God causes a bush to grow and give him shade (Jonah 4:5–6). The comfortable prophet is stripped of his pleasant vantage point when God sends a worm to destroy the bush and a hot wind to parch his throat and make him faint from the heat (Jonah 4:7–8). Just as when Nineveh was spared, Jonah's response here is anger at the unfairness of life. He would just as soon depart: "It is better for me to die than to live."

Jonah's self-centered philosophy is then condemned by God, who teaches him to be concerned for all of creation. The prophet's anger had been based not on the death of the plant, but the end of its comfort-giving shade. His concern over this petty matter is then compared in a typical wisdom statement (cf. the questioning of Job in Job 38–41):

> [10] . . . "You are concerned about the bush, for which you did not labor and which you did not grow; it came into being in a night and perished in a night. [11]And should I not be concerned about Nineveh, that great city, in which there are more than a hundred and twenty thousand persons who do not know their right hand from their left, and also many animals?" (Jonah 4:10–11).

The book ends with a question and leaves the reader to ponder Jonah's rigid nationalism.

Connection with Postexilic Period. Those who decided to remain loyal to Yahweh during the exile (and in the subsequent postexilic period) generally identified their God with themselves and their own country. Some, like Isaiah of the exile (Isa 40–55), attempted to broaden the scope of Judaism and portray God as universal. This was a pleasant task when it allowed the prophetic writers to show Yahweh crushing their oppressors and demonstrating through their return from exile that the God of Israel was supreme over all other nations and gods.

What is not so pleasant is when Yahweh helps their enemies to repent and be delivered from justified destruction. This message would have been difficult to accept in the period of Assyrian control of the Near East. At that point, the people's hopes were kept alive by prophecies of the impending annihilation of Nineveh and its rulers. The book of Jonah, however, comes from the postexilic period when some voices within the Jewish community argued that if Yahweh is truly the only God, then all peoples, even the seemingly unredeemable Assyrians, deserve a chance to accept a message of repentance.

STUDY QUESTIONS

1. Discuss why Jonah is such a reluctant prophet.

2. Discuss the use of the universalism theme in this book.

3. Suggest several purposes behind the writing of the book of Jonah.

*The Book
of Esther*

Summary. Two books in the OT/HB are named for women, Esther and Ruth. The book of Esther begins with the story of the Persian king Ahasuerus (Xerxes) and his queen, Vashti. In the midst of a party, the king orders his queen to come out and show off her beauty for his friends. Not wishing to exhibit herself, the proud queen refuses. As a result, the king demotes her, and he begins the search for a new queen. A beauty contest is conducted to select Vashti's replacement. Esther wins the beauty contest and becomes the queen (Esth 2:2–18). Unknown to the king, however, Esther is a Jew. This factor and a plot to exterminate the Jewish people then become the basis for the remainder of the story. Esther was raised by her cousin (or uncle in some translations) Mordecai. At one point, he was able to warn the king of an assassination attempt (Esth 2:21–23). Initially, the king is grateful, but he does not reward Mordecai until later in the story when a comic element is added to foretell the downfall of the villain (Esth 6:1–13).

Making Tough Decisions

Consider these crises that required a tough decision:

- Eve chooses to eat the forbidden fruit (Gen 3:1–7).
- Abram (Abraham) chooses to leave his homeland at God's command (Gen 12:1–4).
- Abraham chooses to sacrifice his son Isaac (Gen 22:1–12).
- Ruth chooses to leave Moab and accompany Naomi to Bethlehem (Ruth 1:15–17).
- Jonathan chooses to aid his rival David (1 Sam 20).
- Jeremiah chooses to speak God's message in the face of persecution (Jer 20:7–12).

This villain is named Haman the Aggagite, and he plots to take revenge on Mordecai and all of the Jews because Mordecai refused to bow his head when this official entered the palace gate. Haman's inherent hatred of the Jews is communicated to the reader by his name. Agag was a king of the Amalekites (1 Sam 15:32), the long-time enemies of the Jewish people. Now a descendant of Agag will attempt to wreck vengeance on their ancient enemies and exterminate all of the Jews in the Persian empire.

Mordecai's refusal to bow to Haman (Esth 3:2) publicly humiliates this very vain man and sets the evil plot in motion. Haman is able to convince the king that the Jews are a dangerous element in the Persian empire and must be exterminated (Esth 3:8–13). Mordecai learns of the plot and goes to Queen Esther. He tells her that she must take the side of Jews now because they are going to be killed by order of the king (Esth 4:13–16). Esther is forced to choose a difficult path and fearfully decides that she has to go to the king, reveal that she is a Jew, and explain to him that his decree will lead to her execution as well.

She invites Haman and her husband to a banquet in her chambers. Of course Haman thinks this is a great privilege and a sign of favor to be invited to a private banquet with the king and his wife. He believes his influence and power are on the rise. The story is about to reach its climax.

The night before Haman and the king return to Esther's rooms for another banquet the king is troubled by a nagging memory. He orders his archivists to search the records for any official omission and they find that the king has failed to reward Mordecai for saving his life (Esth 6:1–3). Haman, as the "officer of the day," is summoned and instructed to parade Mordecai about the city wearing royal robes and a crown while Haman proclaims that Mordecai is honored at the king's command (Esth 6:4–10). This was not what Haman had planned for his enemy, but he cannot disobey the king's orders.

In chapter 7:1–4, the king and Haman go to feast with Queen Esther for a second time. As they are drinking wine, the king offers to grant any request Esther wishes to make. Now, at last ready to make her appeal, Queen Esther answers.

> [3] . . . "If I have won your favor, O king, and if it pleases the king, let my life be given me—that is my petition—and the lives of my people—that is my request. [4]For we have been sold, I and my people, to be destroyed, to be killed, and to be annihilated. If we have been sold merely as slaves, men and women, I would have held my peace; but no enemy can compensate for this damage to the king" (Esth 7:3–4).

Esther then tells the angry king that Haman is actually his enemy. Haman is terrified and falls prone before Esther. When the king sees this he exclaims that Haman is trying to seduce his wife and has him arrested (Esth 7:8). Haman is hanged from the gallows he had built to execute Mordecai (Esth 7:9–10) and the Jews are saved. The Persian king gives them the right to defend themselves and the Jews kill many thousands of their enemies (Esth 8:9–9:16). This event is subsequently commemorated in a festival named Purim (Esth 9:17–32).

Purpose of the Book. The book of Esther, while set in the Persian period (538–332 BCE), contains a narrative that is directed at the Jews of the Hellenistic empire, established by the conquests of Alexander of Macedon. Its primary purpose is to provide an example of courage to the Jews who were living in the lands of the **Diaspora** (cf. the stories in the first six chapters of Daniel). The story maintains that by using their wits and holding to their traditions and identity as a people, the Jews would eventually overcome their enemies. Much of the tale of Esther has an unreal character to it. Many of the principal characters are little more than stereotypes: the foolish king, the proud queen, the wise Jew, the unscrupulous villain, and the clever woman. They play their parts exactly according to the script and the only truly realistic aspect of the story comes with Esther's decision to reveal her true identity in an attempt to save her people. Such martyrdom, while also subject to becoming idealized, has a personal element with which the reader can easily identify.

This story has apparently gone through a number of different versions. One sign of this is the additions to the book found in the Apocrypha/Deuterocanonical books. However, it is not among the scrolls discovered at Qumran and thus may not have appealed to all Jewish sects. Opposition to the story may be based on its ties to the festival of Purim (Hebrew *pur* means "lot"). If this was originally a Babylonian or Persian festival, which was later adopted by the Jews, it might well have been a source of contention among various Jewish groups in the Diaspora and in Palestine.

Date of the Book. The author of Esther is unknown and the date of its composition is uncertain. The actual reign of King Ahasuerus (Xerxes I) was from 486–465 BCE. This suggests a fifth-century date for the book, and most scholars would say it is no later than the second century BCE.

One argument for a late date is the earliest reference to the festival of Purim. The earliest mention of Purim outside the book of Esther is in 2 Maccabees 15:36, which dates to the first century BCE.

A second argument for a late date is the fact that we have thirty-eight of the thirty-nine books of the OT/HB in the Dead Sea Scrolls corpus. Only Esther is not found there.

Third is the lack of any mention of Mordecai or Esther in the list of heroes of the faith found in the book of Ecclesiasticus (Wisdom of Jesus Ben Sira or Sirach; ca. 180 BCE), an apocryphal wisdom book very much like Ecclesiastes or Proverbs. Citing the absence of a reference to Esther in Ecclesiasticus is an argument from silence and must be used cautiously. On the one hand, it may mean that Esther was not known in 180 BCE. On the other hand, the writer of Ecclesiasticus may have excluded Esther because he did not have a high regard for women.

One final argument for a second-century date is the mention of the dispersion or Diaspora of the Jews found in Esth 3:8. This passage states that the Jews are scattered all over the Persian empire. Haman's charge includes a warning that these people strongly adhere to their own law code and traditions. This warning indicates the maturing of the Jewish identity movement. None of these arguments are entirely convincing in themselves. But collectively they suggest a late date for the book of Esther.

Canonical Analysis. Why is Esther not found in the Dead Sea Scroll corpus? Was this book considered unworthy of inclusion in the canon at the time that the

Dead Sea Scrolls were produced (ca. 100 BCE–70 CE)? Why then, was it present in the Hebrew canon at the **Jamnia** conference in 90–100 CE? One possible reason may be that the book shows the workings of God behind the scenes. Despite the fact that this book never explicitly mentions the name of God, there is a sense within the story of the Jews' identity as "God's people." Another reason for the omission of God's name may be suggested by the use of the phrase "the kingdom of heaven" in the Gospel of Matthew. Other New Testament books use "the kingdom of God." Matthew's Gospel, written for the early Jewish-Christian community, considered the name of God too sacred to mention and therefore used "kingdom of heaven" instead of "kingdom of God." Similarly, the book of Esther does not exclude God, it simply excludes the name of God.

An example of this is found in the passage in which Mordecai and Esther are talking about Esther going to the king and telling him about Haman's decree (Esth 4:5–17). The discussion includes the statement that "Perhaps you have come to royal dignity for just such a time as this" (Esth 4:14). This statement is an oblique reference to God and a divine plan for human actions. The statement is quoted to emphasize how Jews have survived persecution when they take the initiative to deal with danger.

Among the other purposes for this book are that it describes the origin of the festival of Purim, and it entertains with an interesting story. It has everything: two beautiful queens, love, romance, suspense, violence, and the death of the villain.

Historical Analysis. The book of Esther raises a number of historical questions:

The fifth-century BCE Greek historian Herodotus states that the Persian king was required to marry only Persian women. In addition, no extrabiblical text mentions either Vashti or Esther as wives of the Persian king Xerxes (Ahasuerus).

The genealogy of Mordecai in Esth 2:5 ("Now there was a Jew in the citadel of Susa whose name was Mordecai, son of Jair son of Shimei son of Kish, a Benjaminite") raises some questions about Mordecai's age (over 118) if he was in fact taken into captivity in 597 BCE. This has been resolved by some scholars who want to preserve the historicity of the book. They say it was not Mordecai who was taken captive in 597 but one of his ancestors.

Would a Persian king encourage Jews to kill Persian subjects? Generally kings want peaceful stability in their kingdoms because the more turmoil, the more likely it is that they will be overthrown. Of course, we do not know with certainty what kings would do.

Although some details in the book are consistent with Persian customs and culture, the story or the message is more important than the historicity of the characters. As we noted when we discussed the flood narratives, it is possible to communicate truth through non-historical events.

STUDY QUESTIONS

1. Discuss why this book has been included in the biblical canon.

2. Discuss Esther's moral dilemma and provide other, similar biblical and non-biblical examples.

3. Discuss the literary characteristics of this book which suggest it may be a work of fiction.

4. Discuss the historical questions raised by the book of Esther.

5. Define: Diaspora, Purim, Jamnia conference.

5

THE HELLENISTIC PERIOD

HISTORICAL OVERVIEW

Alexander and the Diadochi

Alexander of Macedon (northern Greece) burned the Persian capital of Persepolis and broke Persia's control over the Near East in the years from 333 to 323 BCE. This set the stage for the introduction of an entirely new period in the region's history.

Alexander believed in the creation of a "world culture" based on Greek philosophy, law, and political administration. Hellenistic culture developed from a synthesis of Greek ideas with the customs and traditions of the areas into which those ideas were introduced.

One sign of Alexander's determination to create such a synthesis of cultures can be seen in his inclusion of Greek scholars and scientists in his army. They introduced Greek as the principal language in conquered regions. These scholars also studied local languages and customs, popularizing some of them among the Greeks and thereby speeding the process of cultural blending. An even more far-reaching contribution to the spread of Greek culture was the founding of many new cities, such as the Egyptian port city of Alexandria. The Greeks had organized their society around the *polis*, the political community of the city-state. New immigrants to the Near East expected their lives to continue to revolve around the *polis*. The *polis* thus became the major vehicle for the transmission of Greek culture to the rest of the ancient world.

The speed with which Alexander conquered the Near East reflected his own genius as a military commander as well as a general discontent with Persian rule, especially in Egypt and Syro-Palestine. Pacification of these conquered regions was made even easier by keeping the old administrative structure. To establish political stability, Alexander and his successors retained officials who proved loyal to the new regime. The local economy was then stimulated by the introduction of Greek marketing techniques and fresh operating capital.

Following Alexander's death in 323 BCE, his generals divided the empire among themselves. These successors, or **Diadochi**, completed the process of pacifying conquered regions and introducing Hellenistic culture. Two of these generals established themselves in the principal areas of the former Persian empire. Ptolemy ruled Egypt and Syro-Palestine while Seleucus gained control over the provinces of Asia (Mesopotamia and Persia) and Asia Minor. Their successors introduced elements of Greek culture: the gymnasium, the theater, and social associations for professional, cultural, and religious groups. At the same time, these foreign rulers and their Greek subjects acclimated themselves to the patterns and traditions of their new environment, forming the Hellenized culture that would dominate the area until the arrival of Islam.

Palestine under the Hellenistic Rulers During the early years of Greek rule, Palestine saw no drastic cultural changes. The Ptolemies introduced new coinage and exploited the economic resources of the region, but they did not attempt to impose Hellenistic ideas on the Jews. Temple worship continued unhindered and the office of high priest still exercised great authority in matters of religion.

For over a century after Alexander's conquest, Hellenization was a choice rather than a requirement. Greek culture was most popular among Jews of the new generation after the conquest and among Jews who had contact with Greeks outside of Palestine, such as those who lived in the large Jewish communities in Antioch, Alexandria, and Damascus. Jewish merchants and administrators were especially open to Hellenization because those who adopted Greek language and manners acquired financial and political advantages.

Competition between the Ptolemies and Seleucids for control of Syro-Palestine intensified during the mid-third century BCE. Both sides sought to create or maintain support for their rule. One of the most significant political conflicts occurred when the high priest Onias II took a pro-Seleucid position, refusing to pay tribute to the Ptolemaic government in 245. Even members of the high priest's family chose sides. His nephew Joseph, the son of Tobias, remained loyal to the Egyptians and obtained a post as chief tax collector of Syria and Palestine. Joseph's economic success persuaded the Tobiads to become

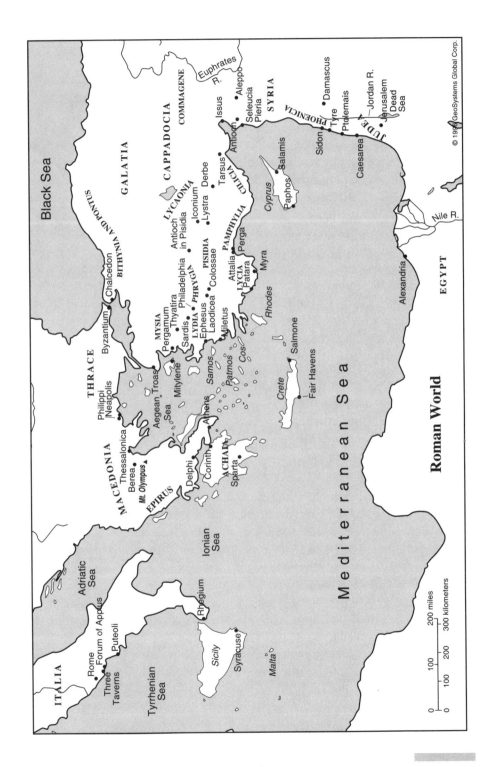

Roman World

major advocates of Hellenization and was heralded by Josephus (*Jewish Antiquities* 12.160–195).

The political loyalties of the Tobiads shifted after 200 BCE when Antiochus III won the battle of Panion in the Upper Galilee region and gained control over Palestine and Jerusalem. This battle changed the political balance, leaving the Ptolemies bottled up in Egypt. The new high priest, Simon II, quickly transferred his allegiance to Antiochus. Simon was the leader of a group that advocated strict adherence to Jewish tradition with as little Hellenization as possible. To obtain the support of this group, Antiochus made a series of concessions to the leaders in Jerusalem. His decree forbade Gentiles from entering the precincts of the Jewish temple. He also made grants of financial assistance to the Jerusalem temple and authorized an exemption from taxes for members of the priesthood and the council of elders, the Sanhedrin (Josephus, *Jewish Antiquities* 12.145–153).

These concessions and promises of religious freedom quickly evaporated as Antiochus became embroiled in the international disputes of the Romans. He helped the Carthaginian general Hannibal and tried to aid the embattled Greeks of Asia Minor. Roman territorial ambitions and military prowess were too much for both the Greeks and Antiochus. He was forced to sign a treaty in 188 BCE deeding his territories in Europe and Asia Minor to Rome. His nephew Demetrius was also sent to Rome as a hostage, an event that later destabilized the Seleucid monarchy. The loss of revenues from the areas taken by the Romans forced Antiochus to increase taxes and to seek additional revenues by plundering the temple of Bel in the Persian city of Susa. He was killed during this expedition in 187 BCE. A brief struggle then ensued for the throne. This struggle ended when Antiochus IV, who surnamed himself *Epiphanes* ("god appearing"), took power in 175 BCE by usurping the rights of Demetrius and other legitimate claimants.

The weakened position of the Seleucids sparked a new wave of political shifts. Onias III, Simon's successor, revived interest in a pro-Ptolemaic policy. The Tobiads, at least outwardly, continued to support Antiochus and responded to the Oniad party by taking advantage of Antiochus IV's desire for allies and additional revenues. The Tobiads purchased the office of high priest by offering to pay higher tribute to the Seleucid ruler. Antiochus then ousted Onias and replaced him with his pro-Seleucid brother Jason (2 Macc 4:7–10). Onias apparently fled to Transjordan, but his proximity to Jerusalem and his vocal opposition to the actions of the high priest led to his murder in 171 BCE (2 Macc 4:33–34).

As high priest Jason hoped to further his own political position with Antiochus IV by transforming Jerusalem and the rest of Palestine into a Hellenized state. His model for this was the capital of the Seleucid kingdom, Antioch. First Maccabees 1:11–15 describes Jason's role in carrying out Antiochus's policy of Hellenization. The text describes a group of "lawless men" (Hellenizers) who willingly violated the covenant in order to please the Greek king. Opposition became increasingly vocal to the construction of gymnasia and the neglect of sacrifices (2 Macc 4:10-15). Jason was deposed after three years when a fellow Tobiad ally, Menelaus, outbid him for the office of high priest by three hundred talents of silver (2 Macc 4:24).

As the new high priest, Menelaus only made matters worse. He embezzled funds and stole sacred vessels from the temple treasury to pay his debts to Antiochus (2 Macc 4:27-32). When Onias III denounced him for doing this, Menelaus ordered his murder (2 Macc 4:33-34). A struggle between Jason and Menelaus then ensued for control of the office of high priest. Jason captured the city of Jerusalem and drove out the Seleucid officials (2 Macc 5:5-7).

These chaotic conditions were interpreted by Antiochus IV as open rebellion. He sent in troops who subdued the province at the cost of tremendous loss of life (2 Macc 5:11-14). In 169 BCE, with Menelaus's aid, he defiled the temple, and looted its treasury (2 Macc 5:15-16). Antiochus then began an anti-Jewish campaign designed, according to 1 Macc 1:41-42, to make all of the people of the Seleucid realm "one people" and to force them to renounce their old traditions and religion. His anger may have been increased by continued pressure on his kingdom by the Romans. But the stipulations of his decree suggest that his plan was to completely Hellenize the Jews. Their shrines and altars were to be defiled and swine were to be sacrificed in the temple. Other ritual acts, like circumcision, were no longer to be performed (1 Macc 1:45-48).

Temporary Independence: The Hasmonean Kingdom

Antiochus's policies culminated in the construction of an altar to the Greek god Zeus Olympios in the Jerusalem temple (Dan 11:31; 1 Macc 1:54; Mark 13:14). This "abomination that makes desolate," combined with his other anti-Jewish measures, sparked a revolt led by the priest Mattathias of the house of Hasmon. The revolt, reflecting the more conservative attitudes of the rural areas of Palestine, began in the village of Modin, northwest of Jerusalem. Mattathias refused to obey the decree to sacrifice to idols and went so far as to kill the first Jew in Modin who attempted to obey this command. His justification for the killing was the precedent set by Aaron's grandson Phinehas, who killed an Israelite for marrying outside the congregation (Num 25:6-8). In both cases the principle involved obedience to the covenant and the purity of the nation.

Following his act of defiance, Mattathias led his five sons into the hill country where they began to wage a guerrilla war against the Seleucids and their supporters. The rebels, joined by the traditionalists called the **Hasidim** (holy ones), saw this war as both a national struggle and a cultural one. Their adherence to the law, however, led at least in one instance to a massacre when a group of one thousand Jews refused

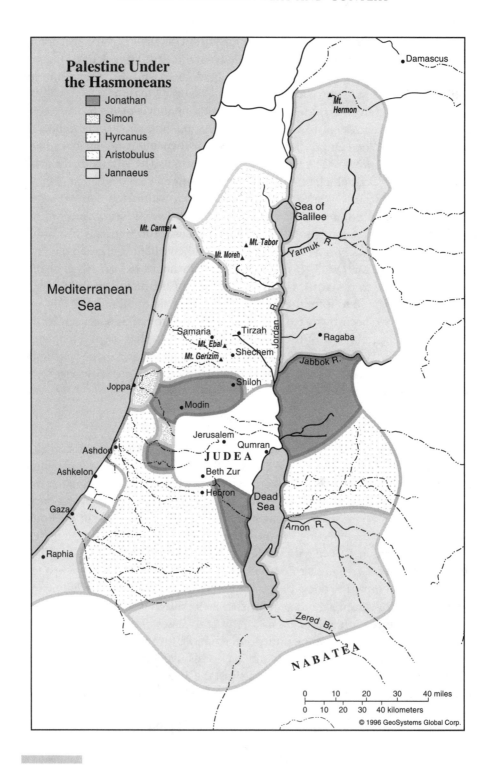

**Palestine Under
the Hasmoneans**

- Jonathan
- Simon
- Hyrcanus
- Aristobulus
- Jannaeus

Damascus

Mt.
Hermon

Sea of
Galilee

Mt. Carmel ▲

Mt. Tabor ▲

Mt. Moreh ▲

Yarmuk R.

Mediterranean
Sea

Samaria
Mt. Ebal ▲
Mt. Gerizim ▲

Tirzah

Shechem

Ragaba

Jabbok R.

Joppa

Shiloh

Modin

Jerusalem
Qumran
JUDEA
Beth Zur

Ashdod

Ashkelon

Hebron

Dead
Sea

Gaza

Arnon R.

Raphia

Zered Br.

N A B A T E A

0   10   20   30   40 miles

0   10   20   30   40 kilometers

© 1996 GeoSystems Global Corp.

to defend themselves when they were attacked on the Sabbath (1 Macc 2:29–38). This reluctance was eventually overcome as the idea of holy war made it possible to set aside legal restraints temporarily.

By 165 BCE, Judas, Mattathias's oldest son, had recaptured most of Jerusalem (1 Macc 3:1–9) and justified his title *Maccabaeus* (the hammer) by his exploits. This title is the source of the name for the revolt and is sometimes applied to the rest of Judas' family (i.e., Maccabees). After Judas recaptured the temple, it was rededicated and restrictions on the practice of Judaism were removed. The rededication of the temple is still celebrated today as the feast of **Hanukkah**.

Final victory was made possible by the disputes within the Seleucid royal house. Since the death of Antiochus IV in 164 BCE, rival claimants had attempted to outbid each other for the support of the provincial leaders. The Maccabees were also approached by some of these aspiring kings and received legitimization of their position as secular leaders. This process went a step further in 153 BCE when Judas's successor, Jonathan, was appointed high priest by the Seleucid Alexander Balas (1 Macc 10:20).

After Jonathan's death, the people proclaimed his brother Simon to be "their leader and high priest forever, until a trustworthy prophet should arise" (1 Macc 14:41; Josephus, *Jewish Antiquities* 13.213). This appointment was particularly important since Simon was not of the Zadokite line and thus was not, according to tradition, entitled to hold the office of high priest (see 1 Kgs 2:35). Josephus (*Jewish Antiquities* 16.163) describes John Hyrcanus, the successor of Simon, as the high priest of "God Most High." The implication is that the Maccabees were attempting to justify their position as priests and civil leaders through a comparison with the OT/HB figure of Melchizedek, who was described as a king of Salem and priest of "God Most High" (Gen 14:18).

Political developments and a shift in expectation by the people in favor of a return of prophetic direction had made Simon's appointment possible. The Hasmoneans, as they now called themselves, took full advantage of the situation. But a significant number of Jews disputed Maccabean claims to the high priesthood. Documents associated with the Essene community (*Rule of the Community* and the so-called *Damascus Document* from the Cairo Geniza) indicate that this was when the Essenes broke from the Hasmoneans and created their separatist group. The *Testament of Moses* (6:1), most likely a Pharisaic document dating to about 100 BCE, expresses discontent with the Hasmonean claims to both civil and religious authority.

Simon and his son John Hyrcanus continued to use the unsettled political situation in the Seleucid empire to their advantage. Simon obtained official recognition of his position from the Roman senate in 138 BCE to add a further dimension of support. The Seleucids attempted to reassert their power at the beginning of the reign of John Hyrcanus. However, according to Josephus (*Jewish Antiquities* 7.393), when Antiochus VII besieged Jerusalem, John succeeded in bribing him to leave after giving him spoil taken from David's tomb. John expanded his area of control throughout his long reign (135–104 BCE). Moving north, he conquered Samaria and destroyed the temple on Mount Gerizim. In the south, he forced the Idumeans, living in the area once known as Edom, to convert to Judaism and to be circumcised.

Cave 4 at Qumran, the site near the Dead Sea of a religious sect that separated
from the temple in Jerusalem. The Dead Sea Scrolls were found there.
Photo courtesy of L. DeVries.

Despite these accomplishments, John was not popular with all segments of his people. His Hellenized court and lifestyle were offensive to the stricter elements of Jewish society. One group, known as the Pharisees, demanded that he renounce the office of high priest and in one instance accused him of uncertain parentage, saying his mother had been a captive of Antiochus IV (Josephus, *Jewish Antiquities* 13.288–292). This did not prove to be a particularly damaging accusation, however, since John was able to rely on the support of the wealthier landowners and merchants. This group, known as the Sadducees, also controlled membership in the priesthood (Josephus, *Jewish Antiquities* 13.293–296). Both of these groups eventually emerged as important elements in the political and religious history of the nation.

John Hyrcanus's son, Aristobulus I, was the first to bear the title of king of Judea (Josephus, *Jewish Antiquities* 13.301). He continued his father's expansionist policies in the north, but was deposed after only one year in 103 BCE by his brother

Alexander Jannaeus. This particularly cruel and ambitious ruler used the support of the Sadducees and a company of mercenary troops to impose his rule on the people. The Pharisees, however, were ardently opposed to his position as high priest. They ridiculed him as he officiated at sacrifices (Josephus, *Jewish Antiquities* 13.372) and allied themselves with the Seleucid king Demetrius III in an effort to depose him. Alexander managed to gain his revenge after resisting the Seleucid invasion. He systematically exterminated the leading families of the Pharisees, crucifying eight hundred of them and killing their wives and children during a banquet for his supporters (Josephus, *Jewish Antiquities* 13.380).

The potential problems of continuing this dispute against his own people took their toll on Alexander. On his deathbed he advised his wife and successor Salome Alexandra (76–67 BCE) to make peace with the Pharisees. Alexander Jannaeus's older son Hyrcanus II was appointed high priest by his mother. His more energetic brother Aristobulus II was not satisfied with this arrangement, however. After their mother's death in 67 BCE he initiated a civil war to gain the throne.

During this period of political chaos, two new elements significantly influenced Judean politics. The first was Antipater of Idumea. Seizing the opportunity to gain influence in Judean affairs, he advised Hyrcanus to seek refuge with the Nabatean ruler Aretas in Petra while he sought help in his struggle against Aristobulus. The other new factor was the decisive element in the dispute between the brothers—the Mithridatic wars with Rome. A direct result of these wars was the arrival in Jerusalem of Pompey, the Roman general. Romans had made alliances with the leaders of Judah as far back as Jonathan and Simon. Their interests in the Near East had brought them into conflict with the Armenian king Mithridates. In 63 BCE, Pompey was sent to unseat him and protect the new Roman province of Syria. His success in this mission made Rome the emerging power in the area.

Thus when Pompey arrived in Damascus he was met by representatives of many of the small kingdoms of the Near East, including both Hyrcanus II and Aristobulus II of Judea. Pompey sided with Hyrcanus. Aristobulus was spared so that he could be taken as a captive to Rome as part of Pompey's triumphal procession (Josephus, *Jewish Antiquities* 14.69–79). As a result of Pompey's intervention, Judea was added to the Roman province of Syria and was administered by Pompey's chief lieutenant Gabinius. The country was divided into five districts, each centered on a major population center: Jerusalem, Jericho, Sepphoris in Galilee, Amathus (east of the Jordan River), and Gazara (Gezer). The Romans also claimed all the cities in the north and in Transjordan that had been ruled by the Hasmoneans, but that did not have large Jewish populations.

STUDY QUESTIONS

1. Discuss the changes Alexander and his immediate successors brought to the ancient Near East.

2. Describe the actions of Antiochus IV (Epiphanes) which led to the Maccabean revolt and the formation of the Hasmonean kingdom.

3. Define: polis, Diadochi.

THE BOOK OF DANIEL

We have chosen to place the book of Daniel at this point in the textbook because it is most likely a Hellenistic work. Although the first half of this prophetic narrative is set in the period of the exile (ca. 597–538 BCE), the many similarities between the trials of Daniel and his friends and the Maccabean revolt suggest a much later date. Some of the traditions about Daniel may certainly predate the Hellenistic period, but clearly the placing of Daniel in the "Writings" section of the canon, its historical problems, and the use of late Hebrew and Aramaic words by the writer, point to a date of composition in the second century BCE.

	The Chronological Framework for the Book of Daniel
626–539	(Neo-) Babylonians
605–562	Nebuchadnezzar
550–332	Persians and Medes
332–63	Hellenistic Age in Palestine
301–198	Ptolemies (Egypt)
198–63	Seleucids (Asia)
175–163	Antiochus IV (Epiphanes)
	—tried to Hellenize Jews
	—outlawed Judaism (167)
	—forced Jews to eat forbidden foods
	—forced Jews to sacrifice on pagan altars
	—set up altar to Zeus in temple and sacrificed pigs on it

Literary Analysis   The book of Daniel can be divided into two sections. Chapters 1–6 contain what could be called the "Tales of the Young Men," i.e., stories about Daniel and his three friends. Written in narrative form, these stories describe how they are brought to Babylon with the first group of exiles in 597 BCE. The tales concern their heroic championing of their Jewish identity by means of strict adherence to the dietary laws and monotheistic injunctions in the covenant. In every way they resist being transformed into Babylonians or accepting, even under threat of death, any changes in their religious practices. Daniel's ability to interpret dreams further reinforces the superiority of Yahweh over the gods of Mesopotamia and Persia.

Characteristics of Apocalyptic Literature

Primary Characteristics

1. Dualism (universe divided between two opposing forces of good and evil)

2. Eschatology (study of last things, last times, last events)

Secondary Characteristics

1. Visions

2. Animal Symbolism

3. Numerology (mystical significance of numbers)

4. Angelology and Demonology

The remaining chapters (7–12) are **apocalyptic** visions. Apocalyptic literature can be defined as a special type of literature that contains secrets of the future or knowledge possessed only by God and revealed to the elect. The revelation is usually marked by bizarre imagery, cryptic numbers, and angelic interpreters. In the apocalyptic chapters, Daniel or an angel describes the visions, which deal with the eventual triumph of Yahweh over the kings, gods, and angelic armies of the Babylonians and Persians. These visions are difficult for modern readers to interpret because they are based on Israelite traditions and the political agenda of the writer at the time they were composed.

There is no direct relation between the earlier chapters and the apocalyptic visions. The chronology of events and the order of the kings are both different. There are even linguistic differences that further complicate the authorship problem: Dan 1:1–2:4a and 8:1–12:13 are written in Hebrew, while Dan 2:4b–7:28 are composed in Aramaic. These differences probably reflect separate authorship and eventual joining of the sections based on the appearance of Daniel in each.

Differences Between an Apocalypticist and a Prophet

Apocalypticist	Prophet
Writer, uses literary conventions	Speaker
Uses a pseudonym	Uses own name
Theme: how to cope with this evil world	*Theme*: sins of prosperity
Goal: encourage people to hold on until the end	*Goal*: encourage people to repent
Deliverance in next world	Deliverance in this world

Because Daniel's visions are written in the form of apocalyptic literature, they have definite characteristics that differentiate them from other prophetic visions (see inset). Particularly important here is the fact that prophets wrote and spoke in their own names while apocalypticists used the authority attached to the name of an ancient hero or prophet as their pseudonym. In addition, the sense of time is different between these two groups. Prophets believed God worked within history while apocalypticists believed this world was evil and that God's deliverance would come outside of history with a new creation.

Tales of the Young Men

Following their capture by the Babylonian king Nebuchadnezzar, Daniel and his friends are given Babylonian names: Belteshazzar, Shadrach, Meshach, and Abednego. This is only the first step in **acculturizing** these young men in Babylonian customs, with the aim being to seduce them into the lifestyle of their captors, making them more loyal and sympathetic officials when they are sent back to Judah to serve as administrators. This was a policy used by many of the empires in the ancient Near East. The conquerors assumed that conquered peoples would be less likely to revolt if they were overseen by their own people. In order to ensure the loyalty of these officials, they were brought at an early age to the capital of the empire, educated, and acculturized. The problem in these stories, however, is that Daniel and his friends refuse to be "educated."

We will first describe the tests of courage faced by Daniel and his companions (chapters 1, 3, 6) and then discuss the chapters in which Daniel displays his ability to interpret visions and dreams (chapters 2, 4, 5).

Kosher Regulations (Dietary Laws)

- "Sinew of the thigh" forbidden (Gen 32:33).

- Passover regulations on paschal sacrifice and grain fermentation (leavened bread) (Exod 12:8–14).

- "Seething the kid in its mother's milk" forbidden (Exod 23:19; 34:26; Deut 14:21).

- Kosher animals (Lev 11).

Dietary Laws Upheld. The new "trainees" are privileged to eat from the king's table. However, since these foods were not prepared in a **kosher** manner according to the dietary laws of the Jews, and may have contained elements that were forbidden, Daniel and his friends refused to eat them. Instead they asked to be tested for ten days during which they would consume only water and vegetables while other persons ate from the king's table (Dan 1:8–14). At the conclusion of the test, Daniel and his companions were healthy and well-nourished, and they were rewarded by God with wisdom and insight (Dan 1:15–17). Here and in the other stories as well, Nebuchadnezzar rewards them with positions of importance (Dan 1:18–20; 2:48–49). The courage and intelligence shown by Daniel and his friends would have been an inspiring example for the people during the oppression of Antiochus IV and the Maccabean revolt.

Shadrach, Meshach, and Abednego refuse to obey Nebuchadnezzar's command to bow down and worship an idol (Dan 3:1–12; cf. 1 Macc 2:15–28). Their punishment was to be thrown into a furnace (possibly a brick kiln) to be consumed by the flames (Dan 3:13–23). They survive with the miraculous aid of an angelic being (Dan 3:25–26). Nebuchadnezzar's response to this miracle is a statement of faith in the "God of Shadrach, Meshach, and Abednego" that follows the pattern of other examples of the universalism theme found elsewhere in the OT/HB (Dan 3:28–30; cf. 2 Kgs 5:15–19 and Dan 2:46–47).

In an episode very similar to the harrowing escape in chapter 3, Daniel is placed in a den of hungry lions for disobeying the king's decree and praying to Yahweh (Dan 6:13–17). Once again divine intervention saves the life of the faithful person (Dan 6:19–22). A comic twist takes place when the king, who had been tricked into sentencing Daniel to death, orders his unfaithful advisers to be cast into the lions' den (Dan 6:24; cf. Haman's fate in Esth 7:5–10).

The stories of Daniel's ability to interpret dreams and signs are found in chapters 2, 4, and 5. Each story demonstrates the insight given to Daniel as a *khakam*, a wise man. Daniel's wisdom far exceeds that of the king or any of his advisers (cf. Joseph's ability in Gen 41:1–45). The first story involves the interpretation of Nebuchadnezzar's troubling dream of a mighty statue which was divided into four separate sections of different metals: gold, silver, bronze, and a mixture of iron and clay (Dan 2:31–35). Daniel's interpretation of the statue which is destroyed by a stone thrown from heaven is similar to the one that is given to the four monsters described in Dan 7. Each layer represents one of the successive kingdoms that have conquered and ruled Israel or Judah. The destruction of the statue marks Yahweh's intervention and heralds the establishment of an eternal kingdom (Dan 2:36–45). Nebuchadnezzar is greatly impressed by Daniel's wisdom, and he promotes Daniel and praises the power of Daniel's God (Dan 2:47–49).

Babylonian boundary stone. Babylon's powerful influence throughout the ancient world affected the telling of history years later, as the book of Daniel attests.
Photo courtesy of the British Museum.

Nebuchadnezzar's second troubling dream begins and ends much like the first. It involves a bounteous tree, which like the statue is to be destroyed by the "decree of the Most High" (Dan 4:10–17). The tree, which had brought great blessings to the creatures that inhabited its branches, is identified by Daniel as Nebuchadnezzar himself. Daniel states that the king is doomed to a period of insanity to humble him, after which he will acknowledge the power of Yahweh above all else (Dan 4:24–37).

The final example of Daniel's interpretative ability is found in the story of Belshazzar's feast. This man, the co-regent in Babylon with his father Nabonidus, arrogantly stages a feast using the sacred vessels from the Jerusalem temple to serve his guests. In response, a hand appears and writes a series of Aramaic words on the banquet hall's wall: "*Mene, Mene, Tekel, and Parsin*" (Dan 5:2–9). At his queen's urging, Belshazzar summons Daniel to interpret the meaning of these words and is confronted with a prediction of the destruction of a kingdom, whose days have been numbered *(mene)*, whose sins have been weighed on the scales *(tekel)*, and which will be "divided *(parsin)* and given to the Medes and Persians" (Dan 5:25–28). This story varies from the other two, since it does not result in a statement of praise for Yahweh nor in Daniel's personal advancement. However, Daniel's stature as a true seer is proven when the events he described occur (Dan 5:30).

Apocalyptic Visions

The apocalyptic visions in Daniel can be treated more as a whole than the earlier tales. They share the common **eschatological** theme that the present age is evil. All good things have been subverted and evil seems to be winning everywhere. The righteous are oppressed and need encouragement to continue in their faith. The climactic intervention of God is the last hope of the righteous in the face of such disaster because this age cannot be expected to survive. When God does take action, a new utopian age has to come before any significant change can be expected. Great persecution, turbulence, and warfare must precede the end. The more intense the conflict, the more evident it is to the righteous that the end is approaching. An ancient Egyptian text, the Vision of Neferti, describes the disintegration of Egyptian society prior to the breakup of the Old Kingdom (1991–1786 BCE) and contains the same gloomy appraisal of a world gone mad.

> **The Vision of Neferti**
>
> The land is in torment. What is happening should never happen. Take up arms, the land is in turmoil. Soldiers stockpile arrows: to eat blood, not bread; to laugh at the wounded. No one weeps for the dying, no one mourns and fasts, everyone looks after their own welfare. No one mourns for another, every heart goes astray (*OTPar*, p. 238, lines 38–48).

All of these beliefs, as well as the appearance of angels as leaders of Yahweh's forces, may have been influenced or at least reinforced by Zoroastrianism, the Persian religion during the Hellenistic period. The stories in Daniel express themes similar to some of the major tenets of this religion. Zoroastrianism may have been one factor in some of the substantial changes that Judaism experienced during the Persian and Hellenistic periods, including the concept of resurrection: "Many of those who sleep in the dust of the earth shall awake, some to everlasting life, and some to shame and everlasting contempt" (Dan 12:2).

Major Tenets of Zoroastrianism

Dualistic universe with forces of light (good) led by Ahura-Mazda and the forces of darkness (evil) led by Ahriman

Continual conflict between light and darkness, expressed in battles fought between rival angel armies and the human supporters of each side

Eventual victory for light in a final battle

Resurrection of the dead

Judgment of the forces of darkness and their punishment in a lake of fire

Eternal reward for the forces of light in blissful afterlife

Summary of the Visions   The visions found in the last six chapters of Daniel are filled with conflict and describe the eventual downfall of the kingdoms that had oppressed Israel. Chapter 7 contains a vision of deliverance illustrated by four fantastic beasts: a lion with eagle's wings, a bear with three ribs from its prey in its mouth, a leopard with four wings and four heads, and a terrible beast with iron teeth and ten horns (Dan 7:3–8). Like the multilayered statue in Dan 2, each of these beasts represent an oppressive kingdom and the various wings, heads, and horns are symbolic of the number of kings who reigned during the time they controlled Palestine. Various identifications have been made for these kingdoms in an attempt to establish a chronology for Daniel. The consensus today is that they run in this sequence: Babylon (Chaldean), Medes, Persians, Seleucids (with Antiochus IV being the small horn in the fourth beast who plucks out three other horns; Dan 7:8, 23–25).

The reign of these kingdoms ends with the decree of the enthroned "Ancient One," who appoints a messiah-like figure to have dominion over all peoples and nations forever (Dan 7:9–14). Daniel also receives an explanation of the judgment of God over the fourth beast, which was the last to oppress Israel (Dan 7:23–28).

The vision in chapter 8 has a similar explanation. Daniel sees a vision of a ram and a male goat, representing the Medes/Persians (the ram) and the successors of Alexander (the male goat). An angelic interpreter, Gabriel, is introduced to soften the terrifying experience for Daniel (Dan 8:15–17). Gabriel's interpretation of the vision reaffirms the promise given in Daniel's earlier visions: The destructive efforts of evil leaders will be extinguished by the "Prince of princes" (Dan 8:23–25).

The vision of the "seventy weeks," found in Dan 9, provides an explanation of the amount of time Israel will be oppressed. It is a lengthy interpretation of the meaning of Jeremiah's prophecy of a seventy-year exile (Jer 25:11–12; 29:10).

In chapters 10–12, the last days are described for Daniel by the angel Michael (Dan 10:13–14). This description includes a historical outline that begins at the end of the Persian period, progresses through the Seleucid period, and concludes with events that the writer believed would occur in the immediate future as viewed from his own point in time. This section contains a series of episodes, each prefaced with the statement, "in those times" or "at the time of the end" (Dan 11:7, 14, 20, 29, 40). These visions are filled with descriptions of the disorder caused by uprisings and the overthrow of Seleucid kings (Dan 11:2–45).

The culmination of these events is found in Dan 12. Here the visionary is assured that despite the long periods of conflict, evil, and disorder, those who remain faithful will ultimately be delivered by God:

> "At that time Michael, the great prince, the protector of your people shall arise. There shall be a time of anguish, such as has never occurred since nations first came into existence. But at that time your people shall be delivered, everyone who is found written in the book" (Dan 12:1).

> [12]"Happy are those who persevere and attain the one thousand three hundred thirty-five days. [13]But you, go your way, and rest; you shall rise for your reward at the end of the days" (Dan 12:12–13).

These statements encourage the Jews to remain faithful to their ancestral religion despite the oppression of society and the allure of Hellenistic culture. They demonstrate the superiority of Yahweh, who controls everything, including events of history and the gods of the other nations. This **theodicy** thus explains how the Jews can continue to face oppression without succumbing to cultural extinction.

STUDY QUESTIONS

1. Discuss the possible date for the book of Daniel in the light of your knowledge of the (Neo-) Babylonian and the Hellenistic periods.

2. Describe the characteristics of apocalyptic literature.

3. Discuss Daniel and his three friends as role models for the Jewish identity movement.

4. Discuss Daniel's use of apocalyptic images and the resurrection theme in chapter 12.

5. Define: acculturizing, kosher, eschatological, theodicy.

THE APOCRYPHA OR DEUTEROCANONICAL BOOKS

There is a gap in Jewish tradition and history between the OT/HB and the New Testament writings. This space is partly filled by the books of the **Apocrypha**, which are also called the Deuterocanonical books. Because they can be counted in various ways (as individual works or additions to previous books), the Apocrypha/Deuterocanonical books consist of seven to eighteen books. This collection includes history and literature of the period from 300–100 BCE (see the description of this period in the Historical Overview of the Hellenistic Period), continuations of books in the Hebrew canon (Daniel and Esther), and additional works of wisdom literature and prophecy. Although the Deuterocanonical books appear in both the Septuagint and the Vulgate, they were not included in the Hebrew canon which was compiled at the Jamnia (Yavneh) conference (90–100 CE), and they were not included in most of the Bible translations that followed the Protestant Reformation (16th–17th centuries CE). The result is that many Protestants have little or no awareness of these books.

The following section will describe and analyze the books of the Apocrypha in the context of their time and relate them to the rest of the canon. Many of these books were composed to entertain and encourage rather than report on actual events. They contain numerous historical errors and anachronisms that may confuse the casual reader. The theological perspective of the writers is that of the Hellenistic period, when Judaism was undergoing a transformation that affected its very roots. Jews were debating the nature of life after death, the existence and function of "guardian angels," and the role of the law in their lives.

Tobit   Set during the period immediately after the Northern Israelites were deported by the Assyrians (in 722 BCE), the book of Tobit is a **novella** (a literary form shorter than the novel, with a compact style and plot) similar in tone to the first six chapters of Daniel. Tobit was probably written sometime in the second century BCE. The book contains several literary genres in addition to the narrative: wisdom admonitions (Tob 4:5–19), laments (Tob 3:1–6,

11–15), and prayers of thanksgiving (Tob 11:14–15; 13:1–17). The story describes the trials of a devout Jew who suffers for upholding the traditions of his people but is eventually rewarded by God for his devotion.

The story begins with a description of Tobit's acts of charity, which include burying Jews who have been executed or murdered by the Assyrians (Tob 1:17–18). When the Assyrian authorities discover what he is doing they seize his property and leave him and his family destitute. Tobit's troubles are magnified when he becomes blind (Tob 2:9–10), forcing the family to be supported by his wife and his son, Tobias.

The only way that Tobit's family can survive is if Tobias can retrieve some money that his father had entrusted much earlier to a man in Ecbatana, the capital of Media in Persia (Tob 1:14–15; 4:1–4). His journey ultimately brings Tobias into contact with another grieving family. This family has a daughter named Sarah who has been plagued by a demon, Asmodeus. The demon killed seven of her bridegrooms on their wedding night (Tob 3:8). In her anguish, Sarah prays (Tob 3:11–15) in much the same way that Tobit had prayed for help from God (Tob 3:1–6).

Such devout behavior warranted God's attention. An angel, Raphael, is sent to help both Tobit and Sarah. Raphael brings Tobias and Sarah together, which fulfills the requirements of Tobit's advice to his son to "marry a woman from among the descendants of your ancestors" (Tob 4:12–13). The angel accompanies Tobias in the disguise of an old man named Azariah, providing him with the advice needed to win Sarah as his wife (Tob 6:16–7:14). Raphael also advises Tobias on how to defeat the demon, using the odor of liver and heart of a fish as a protective charm (Tob 8:1–3).

The angel also cures Tobit's blindness (Tob 11:7–15). Raphael explains that the prayers of Tobit and Sarah and Tobit's previous acts of charity had brought him to their aid (Tob 12:11–22). The positive outcome of the story encouraged the Jews of the Diaspora to hold to their traditions and trust God to intervene when they were in distress or danger.

Judith   The many examples of historical confusions (e.g., Nebuchadnezzar is said to be the ruler of the Assyrians) and the author's familiarity with Palestinian Jewish religious practice indicate that Judith was probably written toward the end of the second century BCE. This short story focuses on an event described with a combination of historical and non-historical details in order to highlight the heroic actions of Judith, a Jewish widow. She is described in glowing terms as pious and upright (Jdt 8:4–8). She is also quite capable of coolly beheading the enemy of her people in order to save them from destruction. Her story fits into the same genre as those of Esther, Susanna, and Jael (in the Song of Deborah in Judg 4–5).

The first section of the book details a military and political struggle within the "Assyrian" empire. The conflict begins in Persia and eventually spreads as far as the unknown Israelite town of Bethulia (Jdt 1:1–7:32). This section of the book contains a brief recitation of the history of the Israelites, as told by Achior, the leader of the Ammonites (Jdt 5:5–21). This speech provides the key to the book, citing the **Deuteronomic** maxim that "as long as they did not sin against their God they prospered, for the God who hates iniquity is with them" (Jdt 5:17). Thus the audience is forewarned of the Israelites' struggle to obey and trust God.

The Assyrian response to Achior's speech provides the occasion for enunciating the traditional question raised by opposing armies who claim to operate under the patronage of a different deity: "Who truly is God?" The besieged people of Bethulia are about to surrender and bow down to the divine-king Nebuchadnezzar when they are convinced by the elder Uzziah to give God five more days to save them (Jdt 7:23–31). At this point Judith is introduced. She cautions the people that they should not put God to the test, but should instead pray that God will give them the courage to continue to trust that the enemies of Israel would be defeated as in times past (Jdt 8:11–27).

Realizing that she must also take direct action, Judith prays for success with her plan (Jdt 9). She then transforms herself by removing her widow's garments (compare Tamar in Gen 38:14) and bathing and perfuming her body. The result is a startling beauty that enchants the Assyrian commander Holofernes and blinds him to any danger she may represent (Jdt 11; compare the Jael and Sisera episode in Judg 4:18–21).

After inviting her to his tent, where he hopes to seduce the beautiful widow, Holofernes overindulges and falls into a drunken stupor (Jdt 12:10–20). Judith takes advantage of the opportunity and she beheads the general (Jdt 13:6–10). She returns to Bethulia with the grisly trophy hidden in her food bag and exhorts the people to use it. The ensuing confusion caused by Holofernes' death leads to the defeat of the enemy (Jdt 14:1–4; 14:11–15:7).

For Jews during the Hellenistic period, perhaps the most significant event is the conversion to Yahweh worship of Achior the Ammonite, who had led the Assyrians to attack Israel (Jdt 14:5–10). This follows the pattern of the **universalism** theme as it appears elsewhere in the OT/HB by using a non-Israelite to highlight the power of Yahweh.

Judith functions as a **trickster** figure in this story, much as Jacob or Esther did in their times. She stands as a model of proper behavior, even though she lies and murders to save God's people. These themes and characters would have been very popular with Jews during the Hellenistic period.

Additions to Esther
The Greek version of Esther dates to the period of the second or first century BCE and is considerably longer than the Hebrew version. In most of the chapters one finds additions that clarify and elaborate upon the narrative details (including copies of the king's letters [13:1–7; 16:1–24] and a description of Mordecai's dream [11:2–11]). They may have been added to deal with theological concerns raised in the Hebrew version, such as the absence of any direct mention of God. A woman serving as the central figure in the story may have also bothered the Hellenistic Jewish community; thus Mordecai is given a much more significant role in the Greek version. The vengeance factor, so prominent in Esth 9:5, is also softened, and the number of enemies slain is drastically reduced (75,000 in Esth 9:16, compared to 15,000 in the Greek version; Add Esth 9:16).

Wisdom of Solomon
The Wisdom of Solomon was written between 30 BCE and 50 CE. This collection of wisdom sayings and admonitions was produced by the Jewish community in Alexandria, Egypt. It is written in a lyric Greek style, fiercely attacking pagan worship and the Egyptians (perhaps in response to anti-Jewish riots in 38 CE). Its late date is also indicated by the theme of the immortality of the soul, which only developed in Judaism after the Hellenistic period.

As is common in Greek and Hebrew wisdom literature (see Prov 8:22–31), the central figure in these sayings is "Woman Wisdom" (Greek *sophia*), the manifestation of God's power and glory:

> [25]For she is a breath of the power of God,
> and a pure emanation of the glory of the Almighty;
> therefore nothing defiled gains entrance into her.
> [26]For she is a reflection of eternal light,
> a spotless mirror of the working of God,
> and an image of his goodness (Wis 7:25–26).

Although other names are also used for wisdom (*logos;* Wis 18:15), the concept remains the same.

The author also uses the theme of "measure for measure" as the basis for wise judgment and divine action. Comparison is a device that is employed here, using seven separate antitheses to show how Egypt is punished and Israel rewarded (see Wis 11:1–14; 16:1–19:22). In each of these antitheses, the Egyptians are subjected to plagues (hunger, darkness, thunderstorms, etc.) while the Israelites are protected or provided for by God.

Throughout the book the author exhorts fellow Alexandrian Jews to take pride in their heritage and to hold to their faith despite the allure of Greek and Roman religions. The arguments for remaining in the faith are designed to offset anti-Jewish attacks and the fears of a minority people.

Sirach

Unlike most biblical books, Sirach (Ecclesiasticus) is signed by its author, Jesus Ben Sira (Joshua son of Sirach; Sir 50:27). Ben Sira was a teacher in Jerusalem during the period 200–180 BCE. His book was completed prior to the Maccabean revolt (168–142 BCE), during a turbulent time when the issue of Hellenization was tearing the Jews apart. The cultural conflict was compounded by the political ambitions of the priestly family to gain favor with the Ptolemaic and Seleucid rulers. Ben Sira's task was to uphold Jewish identity (defined as strict obedience to the law) and its traditional beliefs and practices.

Ben Sira did this by directing attention to the law and was based on "the fear of the Lord," which holds the believer to right action and right speech. The following are examples of this theme:

> [10]Do not glorify yourself by dishonoring your father,
>   for your father's dishonor is no glory to you.
> [11]The glory of one's father is one's own glory,
>   and it is a disgrace for children not to respect their mother (Sir 3:10–11).

> [29]With all your soul fear the Lord,
>   and revere his priests.
> [30]With all your might love your Maker,
>   and do not neglect his minister (Sir 7:29–30).

> [19]Whose offspring are worthy of honor?
>   Human offspring.
> Whose offspring are worthy of honor?
>   Those who fear the Lord.
> Whose offspring are unworthy of honor?
>   Human offspring.
> Whose offspring are unworthy of honor?
>   Those who break the commandments (Sir 10:19).

One important element in Ben Sira's work is the prologue, which includes a mention of "the Law and the Prophets and the other books of our ancestors." These three collections of books suggest the groupings of the **canon**. During the course of his admonitions, Ben Sira mentions every book of the Hebrew canon except Ezra, Daniel, Esther, and Ruth. This may be due to the fact that these books were not yet set in their final written form at the time that Ben Sira was active.

Because Ben Sira's aim is to model his work after other wisdom pieces, his statements have close parallels to statements in the book of Proverbs and in Egyptian wisdom literature. Like many of these works, Sirach has little patience for "the fool."

Hymn in Praise of Famous Men

Enoch pleased the Lord and was taken up. . . .

Abraham was the great father. . . .

Moses . . . [was] made . . . equal in glory to the holy ones. . . .

He exalted Aaron, . . . a holy man like [Moses]. . . .

Phineas . . . ranks third in glory. . . .

Joshua son of Nun was mighty in war. . . .

As the fat is set apart from the offering of well-being, so David was set apart from the Israelites. . . .

Solomon reigned in an age of peace. . . .

Elijah arose, a prophet like fire. . . .

Josiah is like blended incense (Sir 44:16, 19; 45:1–2, 6, 23; 46:1; 47:2, 13; 48:1; 49:1).

Since Ben Sira wishes to focus the people's attention on the guidance provided by the law, his central theme is the requirement to be honorable and to avoid shameful action. Much of his advice centers on "right speech" and thoughtful reflection before speaking (Sir 20:7; 21:11; 23:7–15). The one who acts in an honorable manner is careful to observe proper discretion while still speaking out when the law demands it (Sir 11:7–9).

The book employs several typical styles of wisdom literature (e.g., use of parallel lines) in much the same way they are used in the book of Proverbs. However, the structure of the book is too disjointed to allow for a coherent reading from beginning to end. Among its many notable features are the "psalm to Wisdom" in chapter 1 and the hymn honoring "famous men" in chapters 44–51 (including figures from Enoch to Nehemiah). The choice of people in this list is interesting, especially the obvious exclusion of important females. Ben Sira thus reflects a Jewish society that has placed greater restrictions on the roles of women.

Due to the varied nature of its contents, it is probably best to see this book as a reference work, with advice provided on individual items (e.g., physicians, death, women, and friends). Its rather rigid views on other cultures reflects the struggle with Hellenistic influences during this time period.

Baruch   Although authorship of this book is attributed to Baruch, the friend of Jeremiah, this is unlikely. The book of Jeremiah says that both Jeremiah and Baruch were taken to Egypt (Jer 43:1–7), not Babylon, following the destruction of Jerusalem in 587 BCE (contrast Bar 1:1). In addition, the writing style and the apparent dependence on Daniel resemble features of compositions of the second century BCE. This suggests that Baruch's name was chosen to add importance to this work.

Hebrew bulla, "To Brekhyahu son of Neriyahu the scribe." Baruch son of Neriah is mentioned in the Bible as the prophet Jeremiah's faithful friend and secretary (Jer 36:4, 8). Photo courtesy of Zev Radovan.

The book consists of three unconnected poems, using varied vocabulary (e.g., each respectively uses "Lord," "God," and "Everlasting" for God) tied together by a narrative introduction. These are a prose prayer (Bar 1:15–3:8), a wisdom poem (Bar 3:9–4:4), and a poem of consolation (Bar 4:5–5:9). There are a number of quotations taken from both Daniel and Jeremiah in the prose prayer (compare Bar 1:15–2:19 with Dan 9:4–19). The poem of consolation appears to be heavily influenced by the work of Second and Third Isaiah (Isa 40–66), especially in Baruch's use of the Zion theme: "Take courage, O Jerusalem, for the one who named you will comfort you" (Bar 4:40; see Isa 40:1–2).

The metaphorical use of clothing in Baruch has interesting parallels with a passage in the apostle Paul's letter to the Ephesians:

> [1]Take off the garment of your sorrow and affliction, O Jerusalem,
>   and put on forever the beauty of the glory from God.
> [2]Put on the robe of the righteousness that comes from God;
>   put on your head the diadem of the glory of the Everlasting;
> [3]for God will show your splendor everywhere under heaven (Bar 5:1–3).

> [14]Stand therefore, and fasten the belt of truth around your waist, and put on the breastplate of righteousness. [15]As shoes for your feet put on whatever will make you ready to proclaim the gospel of peace (Eph 6:14–15).

This suggests either a common theme throughout ancient literature or influences from the Apocrypha on the New Testament writers (see Isa 11:5; Hos 6:5; Wis 5:17–20; 2 Cor 6:7; 1 Thess 5:8).

The Letter of Jeremiah

Composed as a letter (included as chapter 6 in Baruch in the King James Version and the Vulgate), the Letter of Jeremiah is almost unique in the writings attributed to the OT/HB period. The letter form is quite common in the New Testament, however. This suggests a late date for the Letter of Jeremiah and perhaps an early influence on various New Testament works. The letter imitates the style of Jer 29:1–23 and purports to be addressed to the exiles in Babylon. Its primary purpose is to exhort the exiles not to worship foreign gods and images, and it uses several canonical texts to make its case (Deut 4:27–28; Isa 40:18–20; Jer 10:2–16). Biting satire is used to ridicule these idols as a way of challenging their divinity and arguing that Yahweh is the only true God. Since it draws on these earlier works, it is usually dated to the Hellenistic period, most probably the early second century BCE.

The Futility of Idols

They are bought without regard to cost, but there is no breath in them (Let Jer 1:25).

Goldsmiths are all put to shame by their idols;
for their images are false,
and there is no breath in them (Jer 10:14b).

The letter consists of ten warnings against idolatry. Statues of deities are denounced as mere human creations; they are not representations of the true God. The style and content of the Letter of Jeremiah are not particularly original. The author has remained content to use the arguments of earlier writers.

Additions to Daniel

The Prayer of Azariah and the Song of the Three Jews. The Prayer of Azariah and the Song of the Three Jews is an addition to the book of Daniel, which is generally found inserted between Dan 3:23 and 3:24 as part of the story of the survival of three Jewish heroes (Shadrach, Meshach, and Abednego) in a fiery furnace. The insertion provides additional information on this episode as well as unrelated theological reflection. For example, the Prayer of Azariah (vv. 1–22) is a "national lament" similar to those found in Pss 44 and 80. Since the three young men in Daniel's version are without sin when they are ordered into the furnace by Nebuchadnezzar, this prayer of confession and repentance does not fit the character of the story. But it did have value for the postexilic Jewish community.

The second portion of this insertion (vv. 23–27) provides a detailed description of the furnace and its fuel. The last section (vv. 28–68) is a song of thanksgiving by the three young men who have been miraculously saved from the flames. It is a litany, with the phrases "blessed are you" and "bless the Lord" at the beginning of each statement, followed by the antiphonal response "sing praise to him." The structure of the song could be compared to the structure found in Pss 146–149.

Susanna. Susanna is considered to be chapter 13 of the Greek version of the book of Daniel and probably dates to the late second century or early first century BCE. This fictional addition provides yet another example of the righteous person who is first persecuted and then is completely vindicated (compare Joseph in Gen 37–50, Esther, the three young men in Dan 3 and 6, and Tobit). One unique aspect of this story is its setting in a local court of law rather than in a royal court. It has a detective-story quality with the flavor of "courtroom drama" added to make the story even more suspenseful.

The principal theme of Susanna is false accusation. A beautiful married woman arouses the sexual desire of two of the elders who serve as judges in the exilic community in Babylon. They are overcome with lust and when they have the opportunity they propose that she give herself to them or they will denounce her as an adulteress (vv. 15–21; compare the seduction of Joseph by Potiphar's wife in Gen 39:7–18). Their argument is a strong one, because she is caught with them alone and there are no witnesses to refute the claims of the elders. Rather than commit the sin of which they threaten to accuse her, Susanna cries out (vv. 22–27). The accusations of the two elders force her to trial where she is condemned to death (vv. 34–41).

Susanna's prayers are heard by God, and at this point Daniel appears in the story as the inspired and fair judge. He separates the two elders and takes their testimony to prove that they are lying (vv. 47–59). Absolved of her guilt, Susanna and her husband rejoice in a God who raises up such men as Daniel to aid the people. In this way, the exilic community reinforces its faith in God and in the protection afforded by the law.

Bel and the Dragon. Another addition to the book of Daniel (chapter 14 in the Greek version), Bel and the Dragon includes two parts that denounce the worship of idols. Like Susanna, it was probably composed in the period between the third and first centuries BCE. It contains a slightly more fantastic version of the "lions' den" episode than the version found in Dan 6. But it is more true to historical and political fact than Dan 6 because Cyrus is the Persian ruler rather than Darius the Mede.

The story describes Daniel's conflict with the priests of Bel, who denounce him for not worshiping their god. Daniel is able to prove to the king that the sacrificial meals fed to the god Bel have actually been eaten by his priests and their families (vv. 19–20). He then kills the "great dragon" that they have been worshiping by feeding it a mixture of pitch, fat, and hair (v. 27). In this way Daniel proves that Bel is not a god.

Faced with public outcry over the destruction of the native cult, the king is forced to throw Daniel into the lions' den. The prophet Habakkuk is suddenly thrust into the story to provide an additional miraculous element. An angel transports him by his hair (compare Ezek 8:3) to Babylon to feed Daniel. This allows the hero to survive a week with the lions. The king acknowledges the power of Israel's God with the statement, "You are great, O Lord, the God of Daniel, and there is no other besides you!" This exclamation follows the pattern of similar statements made by Nebuchadnezzar in Dan 3:28 and 4:3 and the pattern found in other examples of the **universalism** theme (Rahab in Josh 2:11 and Naaman in 2 Kgs 5:15).

1 and
2 Maccabees
The usefulness of the books of the Maccabees for reconstructing the Hellenistic period can easily be seen in our survey of the history of the period (above). These books contain an enormous amount of data on the history of the period and of various developments within Judaism. But the material in these books, as with the books of Kings and Chronicles, must be used carefully in historical reconstruction because of the strong propagandistic slant of the writers.

> **The Decision of Mattathias**
>
> But Mattathias answered and said in a loud voice: "Even if all the nations that live under the rule of the king obey him, and have chosen to obey his commandments, everyone of them abandoning the religion of their ancestors, I and my sons, and my brothers will continue to live by the covenant of our ancestors" (1 Macc 2:19–20).

The book of 1 Maccabees was probably composed during the reign of John Hyrcanus (134–104 BCE). Its narrative traces the events from the conflicts leading up to the Maccabean revolt and concludes with John Hyrcanus's accession to the high priesthood in 134 BCE. Like other documents of its time, the poems, speeches, and letters quoted in the text may well be free compositions by the author(s) in their attempt to bolster the program and the rule of the Hasmonean kings (1 Macc 3:3–9; 14:4–15; cf. 2 Macc 8:18–20). The appearance of a number of quotations or paraphrases from the books of Samuel and Kings in 1 Maccabees indicates the availability of earlier biblical tradition and its use in later writings:

> [17]"The flesh of your faithful ones and their blood
>   they poured out all around Jerusalem,
>   and there was no one to bury them" (1 Macc 7:17; Ps 79:2–3).

> [21]"How is the mighty fallen,
>   the savior of Israel!" (1 Macc 9:21; 2 Sam 1:19).

1 Esdras (Latin Vulgate: 3 Esdras or Greek Ezra) First Esdras is made up of a selection of parallel passages from Chronicles, Ezra, and Nehemiah. But this Greek work from the second century BCE serves as a slightly different version of the older material. The return from exile (compare 1 Esd 2:1–15 with 2 Chron 36:22–23 and Ezra 1:1–3), the rebuilding of the temple and its community in Jerusalem (compare 1 Esd 5:47–55 to Ezra 3:1–7), and the expulsion of foreign wives by Ezra (compare 1 Esd 9:37–55 to Neh 7:73b–8:13) dominate the narrative of 1 Esd. Its emphasis on the roles of Ezra and Zerubbabel and its exclusion of Nehemiah suggests a group who saw Ezra and Zerubbabel as important figures in their version of history. Josephus, the Jewish historian of the first century CE, used 1 Esd in compiling his *Jewish Antiquities*. Thus it is likely that prior to the Jamnia conference, this version of events held equal weight with the Hebrew text and is therefore of interest to those who wish to compare the material.

Which Is the Strongest?

[5]"Let each of us state what one thing is strongest. . . ." [10]The first wrote, "Wine is strongest." [11]The second wrote, "The king is strongest." [12]The third wrote, "Women are strongest, but above all things truth is victor" (1 Esd 3:5, 10–12).

A unique portion of this book is the "debate of the three bodyguards" in chapters 3–4 over the relative strength of wine, kings, and women. The authors modified the original story by appending "truth" to the statement regarding the power of women (1 Esd 3:12) and by naming Zerubbabel as the third young man (1 Esd 4:13). Zerubbabel wins the debate and is rewarded by King Darius. For impressing the monarch and his court, Zerubbabel was able to ask the Persian king to fulfill Cyrus' vow to rebuild the temple in Jerusalem (1 Esd 4:42–62; compare Joseph in Gen 41:37–45 and Daniel in Dan 5:10–29).

2 Esdras (4, 5, 6 Ezra; Apocalypse of Ezra; Latin Vulgate: 4 Esdras)   Though the bulk of 2 Esd was probably written originally in Hebrew or Aramaic, the present form of the book derives from a Greek translation to which substantial additions have been made. Much of the Greek text of this book has survived only in later translations into Latin, Syriac, Coptic, Arabic, and Armenian.

Chapters 3–14 of 2 Esd were composed around 100 CE. This part of 2 Esd was a Jewish work that is usually called 4 Ezra in modern scholarship. Chapters 1–2 of 2 Esd are a later Christian addition that is often called 5 Ezra. Chapters 15–16 are an even later Christian addition now known as 6 Ezra. Our discussion will be limited to the original Jewish document (4 Ezra = 2 Esd 3–14).

The book of 4 Ezra is the only book of the Apocrypha that is an apocalypse (a book containing symbolic visions and revelations concerning the end of time). It is comparable in form to Isa 24–27, Dan 7–12, and Zech 9–14. As in the visions described in these books, 4 Ezra includes signs and premonitions:

> "Now concerning the signs: lo, the days are coming when those who inhabit the earth shall be seized with great terror, the way of truth shall be hidden, and the land shall be barren of faith" (2 Esd 5:1).

> "At that time Michael, the great prince, the protector of your people, shall arise. There shall be a time of anguish, such as has never occurred since nations first came into existence" (Dan 12:1).

> See, a day is coming for the LORD, when the plunder taken from you will be divided in your midst (Zech 14:1).

Like other apocalyptic literature, 4 Ezra speaks of both public and secret testimony. The latter should only be revealed "to the wise among your people. For in them is the spring of understanding, the fountain of wisdom, and the river of knowledge" (2 Esd 14:46–47). The author of 4 Ezra also attempts to establish a greater authority for the book by using a **pseudonym** (a fictitious name derived from some great figure of the past, in this case Ezra).

The book of 4 Ezra consists of seven revelations which are presented to the author by the angel Uriel (2 Esd 3:1–5:20; 5:21–6:34; 6:35–9:25; 9:38–10:59; 11:1–12:51; 13:1–58; 14:1–48). These revelations are primarily concerned with the wickedness of Rome (symbolically named Babylon just as in Rev 14:8) and how to deal with the problems and concerns voiced by the Jewish community as an oppressed people within the Roman empire. In particular, Uriel instructs the author on the issues of divine justice and the relative merits of human and divine knowledge (cf. Job 38:1–7; Wis 9:16).

> **Questions of a Seer**
>
> [28]"Then I said in my heart, Are the deeds of those who inhabit Babylon any better? Is that why it has gained dominion over Zion? [29]For when I came here I saw ungodly deeds without number, and my soul has seen many sinners during these thirty years. And my heart failed me, [30]because I have seen how you endure those who sin, and have spared those who act wickedly, and have destroyed your people, and protected your enemies, [31]and have not shown to anyone how your way may be comprehended. Are the deeds of Babylon better than those of Zion?" (4 Esd 3:28–31).
>
> [1]Then the angel that had been sent to me, whose name was Uriel, answered [2]. . . "Your understanding has utterly failed regarding this world, and do you think you can comprehend the way of the Most High?" [3]. . . "I have been sent to show you three ways, and to put before you three problems." [5]. . . "Go, weigh for me the weight of fire, or measure for me a blast of wind, or call back for me the day that is past" (2 Esd 4:1–3, 5).

Prayer of Manasseh
The Prayer of Manasseh was written in the first century BCE. It is a penitential prayer based on 2 Chron 33:10–17 that provides the occasion for Manasseh's restoration to the throne in Jerusalem. The narrative in 2 Kgs 21:10, unlike the Chronicles account, leaves Manasseh as the most evil king in Judah's history in order to contrast him with his righteous grandson Josiah. For the postexilic community, however, it was important for God to be both just and forgiving. Thus Manasseh's repentance, his prayer, and ultimately his restoration served as a model for the people. In this way, Yahweh retained the image of a God of justice while maintaining the ability to be merciful in the face of true repentance.

> [9]For the sins I have committed are more in number than the sand of the sea;
> my transgressions are multiplied, O Lord, they are multiplied!
> I am not worthy to look up and see the height of heaven
> because of the multitude of my iniquities (Pr Man 9).

This belief in the redemption of the worse offender can also be found in the story of Ahab's repentance in the face of Elijah's curse (1 Kgs 21:25–29). Clearly the

theodicy of the exile is explained in the portrayal of a just God who takes notice of the people's cleansing confession.

STUDY QUESTIONS

1. Define the Apocrypha or Deuterocanon and explain how these books differ from those in the Hebrew canon.

2. Discuss the ways in which the book of Tobit can be used to describe the exiles and the problems they faced.

3. Compare the book of Judith with the book of Susanna, the book of Esther, and the story of Jael in Judg 4–5. In what ways do these women exemplify the basic values of their community?

4. Point out examples of how the book of Sirach compares and contrasts with the book of Proverbs. What is particularly distinctive about Sirach's view of the world?

5. Discuss the possible reasons for the additions to the book of Daniel and to the book of Esther. Do they add substantially to the story, or are they designed to reflect a later understanding of the meaning of these books?

6. Compare the book of Maccabees with the stories of the young men in Dan 1–6. How do the events of the Maccabean revolt compare to the trials faced by Daniel and his friends?

7. Define: novella, universalism, trickster, canon, pseudonym, theodicy.

6

CONCLUDING REMARKS

EPILOGUE

Although the narrative of the OT/HB officially ends in the Persian period, the influence of these stories on the culture continued to live on in the works of the Apocrypha and in the New Testament writings. Since the people of the ancient world considered history to be a significant source of identity, it was only natural that they would continue to study and use their literary and religious heritage. This is not to say that no change was possible, for Judaism did not remain static. The immediate inheritors of the biblical tradition of law and story, the Jews of the rabbinic period (first century BCE through fourth century CE) and the early Christian community, created new and vibrant religious movements that built upon the foundation of the OT/HB and allowed for the changes made necessary by life within the Roman empire. They used their cultural heritage to shape dynamic and growing cultures that built upon the past and laid the foundation for the future of their religions.

Evidence for the use of the material in the OT/HB can be found in the Jewish commentaries of the Babylonian Talmud and subsequently in the comments and decisions laid down by the great medieval rabbis—Maimonides, Rashi, and Ibn Ezra. Mysticism and elaboration of law developed side by side during this period. The richness of the text allowed for multiple interpretations that created new religious communities and inspired a vast range of scholarly discussions on the relation between the Jewish people and God.

In Christian writings it is easy to find the use of the OT/HB in both thought and quotation. Nearly ten percent of the New Testament alludes to the OT/HB and about four-and-a-half percent is direct quotation. Although it became fashionable to discount the importance of the OT/HB and to emphasize the "gospel message" in the period after the Protestant Reformation, it is clear that the New Testament writers were steeped in the ancient traditions of the Israelites. They would not have abandoned their past, and for those who wish to study the development of Christian tradition it would be misguided to do this.

The other religious descendant of Judaism and the writings of the OT/HB is Islam. Mohammed pointed to Abraham and Ishmael as the founders of the Arab tribes and accepted both Judaism and Christianity as "religions of the book" and precursors to his own revelation. As a result, the third major western religion, Islam, shares a common background and monotheistic perspective with Judaism and Christianity.

The relevance of the biblical materials for our own world can be found in the value attributed to biblical traditions in the modern writings produced by members of these three vibrant religions. If we are to understand the cultural complexities of our own multinational community and of the world community at large, then we must start with the religious values that have shaped these communities. Conflict and compromise or war and peace may well hinge upon how well we do this.

OUTLINE OF ISRAELITE HISTORY

A. *Premonarchic periods portrayed in the biblical text*

1. *Primeval* period: Adam and Eve, Noah and the flood (date uncertain).

2. *Ancestral* period: Abraham and Sarah, Isaac and Rebekah, Jacob and Rachel and Leah (possible dates range from 2000 to 500 BCE, with a preference for 2000–1750 BCE by most scholars).

3. Movement of Jacob/Israel's family into Goshen, Egypt (perhaps dated to Hyksos Period, ca. 1750–1570).

4. *Exodus* from Egypt: Moses and Aaron (perhaps in the reign of Rameses II, ca. 1290–1226).I, ca. 1290–1226).

5. *Settlement* Period: Joshua, Merneptah Stele, incursions of the Sea Peoples, Philistines (ca. 1250–1150).

6. *Judges* period: Ehud, Deborah, Gideon, Jephthah, Samson (ca. 1200–1020).

B. Monarchy period

1. *Early Monarchy:* Samuel and Saul (ca. 1020–1000).

2. *United Kingdom:* David and Solomon (ca. 1000–922).

3. *Divided Monarchy:* Beginning with division under Rehoboam (ca. 922); Israel survives until 721 and Judah until 587.

Names to remember in *Israel.* Important rulers: Jeroboam (first king), Ahab and Jezebel. Important prophets: Elijah, Elisha, Amos, Hosea. Capital city: Samaria, conquered by Assyrian king Sargon II in 721, population deported.

Names to remember in *Judah.* Important rulers: Rehoboam (first king), Jehoshaphat, Hezekiah, Josiah. Important prophets: Isaiah, Micah, Jeremiah. Capital city: Jerusalem, conquered by Nebuchadnezzar of Babylon in 597, Ezekiel and others taken into exile. Final fall of Jerusalem in 587, second deportation.

C. Exile and Persian period

1. *Babylonian Exile* (597–538): Ezekiel, Isaiah of exile.

2. *Persian period* (538–332): Cyrus, Darius, Xerxes, Artaxerxes; temple rebuilt (515), Zerubbabel, Haggai; Jerusalem's walls rebuilt (ca. 445), Nehemiah; renewal of covenant by Ezra (ca. 400).

D. Hellenistic and Roman period

1. Conquests of Alexander of Macedonia (336–323) end Persian control over Judah. All of Palestine became a part of the Hellenistic empire. Palestine was ruled first by the Ptolemies and after 198 by the Seleucids. Maccabean revolt against Seleucid king Antiochus IV in 168 brought brief period of independence led by the Hasmoneans.

2. Roman general Pompey captures Jerusalem in 63 BCE. First unsuccessful revolt against Roman rule occurred in 66–73 CE (when Herod's temple was destroyed) and the Bar Kochba revolt occurred in 132–35 CE.

GLOSSARY OF TERMS AND CONCEPTS

acculturize: to cause a people to adopt the culture of another people through close contact.

acrostic: a literary device in which each line or stanza begins with a consecutive letter of the alphabet.

AD: see CE.

anachronism: a detail or word in a story that does not fit the time period of the story and that often reflects the time in which the story was written.

ancestral narratives: stories in Genesis about Abraham, Sarah, Isaac, Rebekah, Jacob, Rachel, and Joseph.

ANET: James B. Pritchard, *Ancient Near Eastern Texts Relating to the Old Testament* (3d edition with Supplement. Princeton, N.J.: Princeton University Press, 1969).

annunciation: a birth announcement.

anthropomorphism: giving a god human characteristics, specifically human physical form.

apocalyptic: a type of literature dealing with "end things," which is characterized by word or number symbols, monstrous visions, and predictions of final battles.

Apocrypha: see Deuterocanonical books.

apodictic: a type of legal statement that is in the form of a command given without supporting explanation.

apology: a literary defense of a character.

apostasy: any action that allows or condones false worship.

archaeology: the scientific examination of the ancient remains of human settlements and the artifacts produced by the people inhabiting them.

ark of the covenant: the golden covered box created to house the Ten Commandments. It was carried by the Levites and was kept in the Holy of Holies of the tabernacle during the wilderness period.

artifact: anything human beings have modified. In an archaeological excavation, artifacts are those objects found within each stratum or occupation layer that are used to clarify and date the site.

assimilation ritual: a set of ceremonial actions designed to transform an outsider into a member of a group.

autograph: the original copy of any manuscript. No autographs of any biblical text have survived. Only later hand copies have survived.

barren wife: the theme of childlessness principally found in the ancestral narratives. This theme was used to add dramatic tension to the search for the covenantal heir in each generation.

BC: see BCE.

BCE: "Before the Common Era." an abbreviation used in this book in place of BC, but with identical dates.

call narrative: the event in which a person is called to become a prophet.

canon: those books designated by a faith community as holy scripture and as the standard for faith and practice.

casting one's mantle: an action designed to designate someone as a person's successor.

casuistic: a form of law that is based on an "if . . . then" structure.

catharsis: any action taken to purge an individual or a group of painful emotions or high tensions.

CE: "Common Era." an abbreviation used in this book in place of AD, but the dates are the same.

circumcision: the religious ritual of removing the foreskin from the penis. This ritual was used to mark Israelite males as members of the Israelite community.

city-state: an ancient political unit comprising an urban center and its immediate environs and villages.

codex/ pl. codices: a book manuscript with individual pages. This innovation in book binding replaced scrolls.

cognitive dissonance: a mental state resulting from a situation in which two completely credible statements are made, both of which may appear true although one of them is false. The dissonance is caused in the decision making process.

colophon: a statement or phrase placed at the end of a document that may serve as a summary or simply an end marker.

concubine: a secondary wife, who may have come to the marriage without a dowry (often as a slave) and whose children may not inherit from their father unless he publicly declares them his heirs.

corporate identity: a legal principle that rewards or punishes an entire household for the righteousness or the sins of the head of the household.

cosmopolitan: having an attitude of cultural openness and sophistication.

covenant: a contractual agreement between Yahweh and the chosen people that promises land and progeny in exchange for exclusive worship and obedience.

covenant renewal ceremony: a ritual used several times by Israelite leaders to reenforce the importance of the covenant with Yahweh.

criticism: scholarly analysis of texts (e.g., textual criticism, the attempt to reconstruct the original words of a text).

culling process: the method of eliminating the unfaithful during the wilderness period.

cultic: anything having to do with religious activity.

cuneiform: the wedge-shaped script invented by the Sumerians and used by every subsequent civilization in Mesopotamia until the coming of the Greeks. It is a syllabic (e.g., la, ba, ku) script rather than an alphabetic script (e.g., a, b, c).

D-source: according to the documentary hypothesis, the layer of the editing of the biblical text dated to ca. 600 BCE and associated primarily with the book of Deuteronomy, specifically chs. 12–26. Also called Deuteronomic Code. See also Deuteronomist.

Dead Sea Scrolls: the scrolls discovered in the caves near Qumran on the northwestern shore of the Dead Sea beginning in 1947. These scrolls include the oldest copies of the OT/HB books that have been found to date. They date from the second century BCE to the first century CE.

Decalogue: the Ten Commandments.

demythologize: to use a myth from another culture without ascribing any powers to the gods in those stories.

Deuterocanonical books or **Apocrypha**: the seven to fifteen books (e.g., 1 and 2 Maccabees, Judith, and Baruch) written between 300 BCE and 100 CE that are contained in the Septuagint and the Vulgate and are accepted as authoritative by Roman Catholics, but not by Protestants and Jews.

Deuteronomic historian: see Deuteronomist.

Deuteronomist: the name given to the author(s) or editor(s) of the long and complex history found in Deuteronomy through 2 Kings, called the Deuteronomic History. It is characterized by a strict moralism and a view of Israelite history in which the people continually fail to obey the covenant and therefore deserve Yahweh's punishment.

Diadochi: the generals of Alexander the Great who succeeded him in ruling the territories they had conquered together.

Diaspora Judaism: the life and practice of Jews outside of Palestine. The major impetus for the development of the Diaspora was the Babylonian exile. Diaspora Judaism found continued vitality among Jews who remained in the lands of the exile or who emigrated from Palestine in the centuries following the exile.

disqualification stories: a set of stories designed to eliminate a person or a family from succession to the throne of Israel or from inheriting the covenantal promise.

dittography: a scribal error created when a scribe accidently writes the same word twice.

Divine Warrior: Yahweh in the role of a combatant in warfare.

Divine Assembly: the divine company that serves Yahweh in the form of messengers and that is portrayed surrounding the enthroned Yahweh.

documentary hypothesis: the literary theory voiced most cogently by Julius Wellhausen that identifies four strands of editing in the Pentateuch, signified respectively by the letters J, E, D, and P.

dowry: the property or goods provided by the bride's parents as a part of a marriage contract.

E-source: according to the documentary hypothesis, the layer of editing of the biblical text dated to ca. 850 BCE that reflects a northern or Israelite viewpoint from the period after the division of the kingdom.

egalitarian: a social system in which all persons have equal status.

Elohim: one of the names for the Israelite God in the Bible. Associated with the E-source, it is translated as "God" in English translations of the Bible.

enacted prophecy: a prophecy that includes an action by the prophet designed to attract attention and reinforce the message.

endogamy: the practice and policy of marrying only within one's own identifiable group.

eschatology: the study of "last things" or events just prior to the end of time.

etiology: a story that is designed to explain the origin of an event, the background of a place name, or the basis for a tradition.

execration ritual: a series of ceremonial actions that curse a person or place.

exodus: the event described in the book of Exodus in which the Israelites escaped Egypt after the occurrence of ten plagues and under the leadership of Yahweh and Moses.

framework story: a narrative that has an outline structure that can be applied whenever a similar set of events occur or that can be used as the basis for a drama.

genealogies: family histories.

genre: a category of literature (e.g., short story, poetry).

gerrymandering: a political policy designed to eliminate the possession of a majority by one's political opponents in a geographical area by redrawing political boundaries.

gloss: a scribal addition to the text.

HB: Hebrew Bible; see also OT.

Hanukkah: the festival that commemorates the rededication of the temple in 165 BCE after the initial victory of the Maccabees over the Seleucid Greeks during the Maccabean revolt.

haplography: a scribal error created when a scribe accidentally deletes a word or a phrase.

Hebrew canon: the set of thirty-nine books identified at the Jamnia conference (90–100 CE) as holy scripture. It does not include the Apocrypha (deuterocanonical books).

hegemony: a political situation in which a powerful nation or empire exercises extensive influence over the policies and actions of neighoring states.

henotheism: belief in the existence of many gods conjoined with the choice to worship only one of them.

inclusio: a literary device in which the same element occurs at the beginning and at the end (e.g., ABCDA).

infrastructure: the public works projects that aid communication, travel, and economic activity (e.g., roads, bridges, irrigation canals, and dams).

J-source: according to the documentary hypothesis, the first layer of editing of the biblical text, which may be dated to ca. 900–850 BCE, contains a narrative style, and reflects the political boundaries of David's kingdom.

Jeroboam's sin: the actions taken by King Jeroboam I to establish a separate identity for the northern kingdom. They were used by the biblical writers as the hallmark of the "evil king."

khabiru: (ʿabiru) a term used in Mesopotamian texts for stateless persons.

kherem: an element of "Holy War" in Israelite warfare that requires the complete destruction of all persons, animals, and property as a dedicatory sacrifice to Yahweh.

khesed: "everlasting love," a covenantal term that is used as the basis for Yahweh's willingness to make a covenant with the people of Israel and Judah.

kosher: a term used for "clean" (i.e., ritually pure) food.

lament: a form of writing found principally in the Psalms and the book of Lamentations and that recounts sorrow or suffering by an individual or a group.

Law: see Torah.

legend: a story that centers on human heroes or founders of nations and that includes superhuman feats or dealings with gods.

levir: the brother or nearest male relative who has the obligation to impregnate the childless widow of his deceased brother or relative and to provide for her needs.

levirate marriage: a marriage based on the obligation of the brother or nearest male relative to provide a deceased kinsman with an heir. The brother or relative is required to impregnate the widow and to provide for her needs. An actual marriage tie is not necessary, however.

lex talionis: the legal principle of retaliation in kind or measure, epitomized in the phrase "an eye for an eye."

liturgy: the outline, body of material recited or sung, and stages of a worship service.

Masoretes: Jewish scholars who ca. 500 CE added a vowel pointing system to the Hebrew text of the Bible in order to facilitate its pronunciation. They also developed checks on scribal errors.

Messiah: a derivative of the Hebrew word for "anointed" applied to those individuals chosen by Yahweh for leadership positions.

midwife: a person who assists with the birth of children and the instruction of mothers in child care.

minor prophets: a designation based on length not importance. This category includes twelve short prophetic books: Hosea, Joel, Amos, Obadiah, Jonah, Micah, Nahum, Habakkuk, Zephaniah, Haggai, Zechariah, and Malachi.

motif: a repeated story element in a narrative.

murmuring motif: a recurrent theme in the wilderness period consisting of complaints by the Israelites about their needs for food and water or rebellion against Moses' leadership and the resulting punishment by God. The murmuring motif is paired with a culling process designed to eliminate the unfaithful.

myth: a story that centers on the origin of events or things (see etiological) and usually involves the activities of gods.

Nazirite: a Jew (either male or female) who takes an oath to refrain from consuming any product of the grape, from coming in contact with the dead, and from cutting his or her hair.

nepotism: the hiring of one's relatives.

oracle: a prophetic speech.

OT: Old Testament; see also HB.

OTPar: V. Matthews and D. Benjamin, *Old Testament Parallels: Laws and Stories from the Ancient Near East* (Paulist, 1991).

P-source: according to the documentary hypothesis, the final layer of editing of the biblical text, dated to ca. 500 BCE, which reflects priestly concern for matters of religious ritual and purity after the exilic period.

pantheon: all of the gods in a religious system.

parallelism: a literary device, found in the Psalms and elsewhere, in which similar statements are made in succeeding lines in the text.

Pentateuch: the first five books of the Old Testament/Hebrew Bible, i.e., Genesis through Deuteronomy.

prophetic immunity: protection given to prophets when they speak in a god's name that prevents people from killing the messenger because of a negative message.

proselytes: converts to a faith community.

prostitute: a male or a female who engages in sexual activity for compensation.

remnant: the portion of the community who will, according to the prophets, survive God's wrath and rebuild the nation.

retribalization: the process of moving from an urban existence to a semi-nomadic existence, which requires the formation of tribal loyalties and a cautious attitude to strangers.

ritual purity: the steps taken to transform persons or objects into a "clean" or "pure" religious state.

rubric: an instruction that is usually placed in margins or as footnotes in a text.

Sabbath: the celebration of Yahweh as the creator God and the commemoration of the creation event by ceasing work one day each week.

sackcloth: a roughly woven garment worn as a sign of mourning or repentance.

Septuagint: the Greek translation of the Hebrew Bible by the Jews of Alexandria, Egypt, in the fourth through second centuries BCE, which contains the Apocrypha (Deuterocanonical books) and is abbreviated LXX.

seventy elders: that group of men selected to help administer the Israelites and who represented them at major events.

Shema: the statement of faith of the Israelites found in Deut 6:4.

Sheol: meaning "pit," a place identified with the underworld in Hebrew tradition, but not perceived as a part of punishment or reward for the dead.

sojourner: a person belonging to a specific legal category in Israelite tradition consisting of transients, visitors, and strangers. These persons were protected by law and were guaranteed food and other services.

soliloquy: a private statement made to the audience, such as the statements in Job 29–31.

sons of the prophets: apprentice prophets who served Elijah and Elisha as a support group and as messengers.

superscription: the rubrics of instruction found at the beginning of many of the psalms.

suzerain: a king or ruler.

syncretism: the mixing together of cultural ideas and traits borrowed from neighboring peoples.

tabernacle: the tent of meeting used by the Israelites during the wilderness and judges periods as a portable temple, which housed the ark of the covenant.

tell: an artificial hill that has been created by successive layers of settlements on a site.

theodicy: an explanation for God's actions most often found in the words of the prophets.

theophany: the appearance of God to a human being.

Torah: "Law," a term used for the first five books of the Old Testament/Hebrew Bible, which are also called the Pentateuch.

transcendent: characteristic of a deity who is separate from the creation and is not affected by the forces of nature.

treaty: an agreement between two nations or peoples.

trickster: a character who constantly struggles to outwit other characters and generally ends up being tricked.

universalism: a theme in biblical narrative that attempts to demonstrate that Yahweh is a universal god.

Vulgate: the Latin translation of the OT/HB and New Testament made by Jerome in the fourth century CE. It contains the Apocrypha (Deuterocanonical books).

wife/sister motif: a theme in the ancestral narratives that appears three times and in which the patriarch portrays his wife as his sister in order to deceive a local ruler.

wisdom (literature): a type of literature that concentrates on the basic values and common sense of a culture.

xenophobic: fearing the stranger or what is different.

Yahweh: one of the names for the Israelite God in the Bible that is sometimes anglicized into Jehovah. This name is associated with the J-source. In English translations of the Bible, Yahweh is usually translated as "LORD."

Index of Names and Subjects

tabernacle, 66
Tadmor, 53
Tamar, 105, 178, 193
Tammuz, 198
technology, 91, 100
Tekoa, 101, 105
Tell Beit Mirsim, 69
temple, 66, 91, 103, 107–10, 133, 145, 154,
    167–68, 198–99, 202, 212–13, 220, 225,
    229
teraphim, 99
text criticism, 8, 26
theodicy, 4, 82, 112, 120, 154, 159, 162,
    165, 187, 208–9, 212, 263, 277
theophany, 59, 95, 113–14, 116, 126, 145,
    166, 183, 196
threshing floor, 86–87, 108, 235–36
Tiamat, 46, 48
Tirzah, 110
tradition criticism, 30
transcendant, 43, 45, 50
Transjordan, 41, 66, 112, 125, 130
trickster, 55–56, 84, 100, 266
Tyre, 37, 108, 138, 225

Ugarit, 18, 20, 37, 69, 200
universalism, 3, 71–72, 129, 209, 222,
    239–40, 259, 266, 273

Ur, 33, 44, 51, 203
Uriah, 104–5
Uruk, 33
Utnapishtim, 49

Via Maris, 40
Vulgate, 23

wife/sister motif, 56
wisdom, 3–4, 108, 163, 177–82, 214, 264,
    267
wise woman, 101, 105, 107
withdrawal theory, 73

Yarmuk, 42

Zadok, 107–8, 215, 253
Zedekiah, 175–76
Zered, 42
Zerubbabel, 217–18, 274
Ziklag, 100
Zimri, 111
Zion, 108, 149, 156, 164–65, 204, 208,
    210–11, 218
Zoroastrianism, 261–62

INDEX OF ANCIENT SOURCES

APOCRYPHAL/ DEUTEROCANONICAL BOOKS

NEW TESTAMENT